# How to Think about Data Science

This book is a timely and critical introduction for those interested in what data science is (and isn't), and how it should be applied. The language is conversational and the content is accessible for readers without a quantitative or computational background; but, at the same time, it is also a practical overview of the field for the more technical readers. The overarching goal is to demystify the field and teach the reader how to develop an analytical mindset instead of following recipes. The book takes the scientist's approach of focusing on asking the right question at every step as this is the single most important factor contributing to the success of a data science project. Upon finishing this book, the reader should be asking more questions than I have answered. This book is, therefore, a practising scientist's approach to explaining data science through questions and examples.

# CHAPMAN & HALL/CRC DATA SCIENCE SERIES

Reflecting the interdisciplinary nature of the field, this book series brings together researchers, practitioners, and instructors from statistics, computer science, machine learning, and analytics. The series will publish cutting-edge research, industry applications, and textbooks in data science.

The inclusion of concrete examples, applications, and methods is highly encouraged. The scope of the series includes titles in the areas of machine learning, pattern recognition, predictive analytics, business analytics, Big Data, visualization, programming, software, learning analytics, data wrangling, interactive graphics, and reproducible research.

Published Titles

**Statistical Foundations of Data Science**
*Jianqing Fan, Runze Li, Cun-Hui Zhang, and Hui Zou*

**A Tour of Data Science: Learn R and Python in Parallel**
*Nailong Zhang*

**Explanatory Model Analysis**
Explore, Explain, and, Examine Predictive Models
*Przemyslaw Biecek, Tomasz Burzykowski*

**An Introduction to IoT Analytics**
*Harry G. Perros*

**Data Analytics**
A Small Data Approach
*Shuai Huang and Houtao Deng*

**Public Policy Analytics**
Code and Context for Data Science in Government
*Ken Steif*

**Supervised Machine Learning for Text Analysis in R**
*Emil Hvitfeldt and Julia Silge*

**How to Think about Data Science**
*Diego Miranda-Saavedra*

**Massive Graph Analytics**
*Edited by David Bader*

**Data Science**
An Introduction
*Tiffany-Anne Timbers, Trevor Campbell and Melissa Lee*

**Tree-Based Methods**
A Practical Introduction with Applications in R
*Brandon M. Greenwell*

**Urban Informatics**
Using Big Data to Understand and Serve Communities
*Daniel T. O'Brien*

For more information about this series, please visit: https://www.routledge.com/Chapman--HallCRC-Data-Science-Series/book-series/CHDSS

# How to Think about Data Science

Diego Miranda-Saavedra

Kellogg College
University of Oxford

CRC Press
Taylor & Francis Group
Boca Raton London New York

CRC Press is an imprint of the
Taylor & Francis Group, an **informa** business
A CHAPMAN & HALL BOOK

First edition published 2023
by CRC Press
6000 Broken Sound Parkway NW, Suite 300, Boca Raton, FL 33487-2742

and by CRC Press
4 Park Square, Milton Park, Abingdon, Oxon, OX14 4RN

© 2023 Diego Miranda-Saavedra

*CRC Press is an imprint of Taylor & Francis Group, LLC*

Reasonable efforts have been made to publish reliable data and information, but the author and publisher cannot assume responsibility for the validity of all materials or the consequences of their use. The authors and publishers have attempted to trace the copyright holders of all material reproduced in this publication and apologize to copyright holders if permission to publish in this form has not been obtained. If any copyright material has not been acknowledged please write and let us know so we may rectify in any future reprint.

Except as permitted under U.S. Copyright Law, no part of this book may be reprinted, reproduced, transmitted, or utilized in any form by any electronic, mechanical, or other means, now known or hereafter invented, including photocopying, microfilming, and recording, or in any information storage or retrieval system, without written permission from the publishers.

For permission to photocopy or use material electronically from this work, access www.copyright.com or contact the Copyright Clearance Center, Inc. (CCC), 222 Rosewood Drive, Danvers, MA 01923, 978-750-8400. For works that are not available on CCC please contact mpkbookspermissions@tandf.co.uk

*Trademark notice*: Product or corporate names may be trademarks or registered trademarks, and are used only for identification and explanation without intent to infringe.

| **Library of Congress Cataloging-in-Publication Data** |
| --- |
| Names: Miranda-Saavedra, Diego, author. |
| Title: How to think about data science / Diego Miranda-Saavedra. |
| Description: First edition. | Boca Raton : CRC Press, 2023. | Includes bibliographical references and index. |
| Identifiers: LCCN 2022024832 | ISBN 9781032375687 (hardback) | ISBN 9781032369631 (paperback) | ISBN 9781003340850 (ebook) |
| Subjects: LCSH: Statistics. | Information visualization. | Artificial intelligence. | Algorithms. |
| Classification: LCC QA276.12 .M57 2023 | DDC 001.4/22--dc23/eng20221123 |
| LC record available at https://lccn.loc.gov/2022024832 |

ISBN: 978-1-032-37568-7 (hbk)
ISBN: 978-1-032-36963-1 (pbk)
ISBN: 978-1-003-34085-0 (ebk)

DOI: 10.1201/b23197

Typeset in Nimbus
by KnowledgeWorks Global Ltd.

*Publisher's note*: This book has been prepared from camera-ready copy provided by the authors.

À Hugo, Victoria et Willemina qui, au milieu de l'hiver,
m'ont appris qu'il y avait en moi un été invincible.

# Contents

Foreword     xiii

Preface     xv

Acknowledgements     xvii

List of Figures     xix

List of Tables     xxiii

CHAPTER 1 ▪ A Bird's-Eye View and the Art of Asking Questions     1

| | | |
|---|---|---|
| 1.1 | WHO IS THIS BOOK FOR? | 1 |
| 1.2 | ASKING GOOD QUESTIONS IS THE ULTIMATE SUPERPOWER | 2 |
| | 1.2.1   The Data Scientific Method | 2 |
| | 1.2.2   What Makes a Good Question? | 3 |
| | 1.2.3   What Kinds of Questions Can Data Science Not Answer? | 5 |
| | 1.2.4   The Apollo 11 Mission: Raw Processing Power Is Not as Important as Asking the Right Questions | 7 |
| 1.3 | THE DATA LIFE CYCLE | 8 |
| 1.4 | DATA VOLUME AND PROCESSING REQUIREMENTS DETERMINE LARGE-SCALE COMPUTER ARCHITECTURES | 12 |
| | 1.4.1   The Evolution of Uber's Data Science Needs | 13 |
| 1.5 | FURTHER READING | 14 |
| 1.6 | CHAPTER REVIEW QUESTIONS | 19 |

CHAPTER 2 ▪ Descriptive Analytics     21

| | | |
|---|---|---|
| 2.1 | DESCRIPTIVE AND PREDICTIVE ANALYTICS: WHAT IS THE DIFFERENCE? | 21 |
| 2.2 | DESCRIPTIVE STATISTICS | 24 |
| 2.3 | WHY IS DATA VISUALISATION ESSENTIAL? | 26 |
| 2.4 | THE BOX PLOT: EXTENDING VISUALISATION OF KEY STATISTICS TO MULTIPLE SAMPLES | 26 |
| | 2.4.1   Outliers: Keep or Drop Them? | 29 |

| | | |
|---|---|---|
| 2.5 | FAMOUS HISTORICAL VISUALISATIONS | 30 |
| | 2.5.1 Florence Nightingale's Soldiers | 30 |
| | 2.5.2 John Snow and the Transmission of Cholera | 31 |
| | 2.5.3 Napoleon's Defeat or the Most Brutal Military Tactic in History | 32 |
| 2.6 | HOW CAN WE CHOOSE THE RIGHT VISUALISATION? | 34 |
| 2.7 | CLUSTER ANALYSIS: MOST DATA HAVE AN INTRINSIC STRUCTURE | 36 |
| | 2.7.1 Clustering in Practice: What's the Most Dangerous State in the USA? | 37 |
| | 2.7.2 Advantages and Limitations of $K$-Means Clustering | 41 |
| 2.8 | ASSOCIATION RULES | 42 |
| | 2.8.1 Quantifying the Relevance of Association Rules | 45 |
| | 2.8.2 Limitations of Association Rule Mining | 48 |
| | 2.8.3 Predictive Rule Learning | 48 |
| 2.9 | FURTHER READING | 49 |
| 2.10 | CHAPTER REVIEW QUESTIONS | 52 |

CHAPTER 3 ■ Predictive Analytics                                55

| | | |
|---|---|---|
| 3.1 | WHAT IS PREDICTIVE ANALYTICS? | 56 |
| 3.2 | THE THREE MAIN LEARNING PARADIGMS | 58 |
| | 3.2.1 Pseudolabelling | 61 |
| 3.3 | AN OVERVIEW OF MACHINE LEARNING ALGORITHMS | 63 |
| 3.4 | LINEAR REGRESSION | 65 |
| | 3.4.1 How Good Is Our Linear Model? | 66 |
| | 3.4.2 Assumptions of Linearity and Independence, Multiple Regression and Non-Linearity | 68 |
| | 3.4.3 Linear Thinking or How We Can Be Easily Fooled | 69 |
| | 3.4.4 And a Short Historical Note | 70 |
| 3.5 | LOGISTIC REGRESSION | 71 |
| | 3.5.1 Interpreting Simple Logistic Regression | 71 |
| | 3.5.2 Multiple Logistic Regression | 73 |
| 3.6 | NAÏVE BAYES CLASSIFICATION | 75 |
| | 3.6.1 The Assumption of Predictor Variable Independence | 77 |
| 3.7 | TREES | 78 |
| | 3.7.1 Tree Pruning | 81 |
| 3.8 | ENSEMBLE LEARNING: INDIVIDUAL MODELS ARE WEAK, FAMILIES ARE NOT | 82 |
| | 3.8.1 Bootstrap Aggregating (Bagging) | 82 |
| | 3.8.2 Random Forests or the Wisdom of the Crowd | 83 |
| | 3.8.3 Boosting Machines | 85 |

3.9    SUPPORT VECTOR MACHINES                                    85
    3.9.1   The Kernel Trick                                      87
    3.9.2   Multi-Category Separation by SVMs                     88
    3.9.3   Advantages and Disadvantages of SVMs                  88
3.10   ARTIFICIAL NEURAL NETWORKS                                 89
    3.10.1  The Perceptron                                        89
    3.10.2  Beyond the Perceptron                                 91
    3.10.3  How Do ANNs Learn?                                    91
    3.10.4  Advantages and Disadvantages of ANNs                 92
3.11   DEEP LEARNING                                              94
    3.11.1  AlexNet and the ImageNet Competition                 95
    3.11.2  Transfer Learning                                     97
3.12   WHY THERE ARE SO MANY DIFFERENT LEARNING ALGORITHMS
       AND HOW TO CHOOSE                                          98
    3.12.1  Why Making Assumptions Is Good and the No Free Lunch
            Theorem                                               98
    3.12.2  Some Families of Algorithms Are Better than Others   100
    3.12.3  How Can We Choose the Right Algorithm for Our Problem? 100
    3.12.4  Interpretability vs Explainability                   101
3.13   FEATURE SELECTION AND ENGINEERING IS WHERE A LOT OF
       MAGIC HAPPENS                                             102
    3.13.1  The Curse of Dimensionality                          103
    3.13.2  Feature Selection Methods                            103
    3.13.3  What Is the Best Feature Selection Method and How Many
            Features Are Enough?                                  106
    3.13.4  Dimensionality Reduction                             106
    3.13.5  Feature Engineering                                  108
3.14   HOW DOES AMAZON RECOMMEND BOOKS THAT YOU WILL
       ACTUALLY LIKE?                                            109
    3.14.1  Item-to-Item Collaborative Filtering Is Faster and More
            Scalable                                              111
    3.14.2  Are Recommender Systems Supervised or Unsupervised
            Learning?                                             111
    3.14.3  Democracy of Choice, the Real Potential of Recommender
            Systems                                               112
3.15   BUILDING A MOVIE RECOMMENDER SYSTEM MANUALLY              112
    3.15.1  Calculation of an Item-to-Item Similarity Matrix     113
    3.15.2  Prediction of the Ratings for Items That Have Not Yet Been
            Rated                                                 113
    3.15.3  Making Movie Recommendations                         114
3.16   THE NETFLIX GRAND PRIZE WAS WON BY AN ALGORITHM THAT
       WAS NEVER IMPLEMENTED                                     114

3.17  FURTHER READING                                                      115
3.18  CHAPTER REVIEW QUESTIONS                                             118

CHAPTER 4 ■ How Are Predictive Models Trained and Evaluated?              121

4.1  HOW DO PREDICTIVE METHODS LEARN?                                     121
4.2  UNDERFITTING AND OVERFITTING                                         123
4.3  OVERFITTING IN THE CONTEXT OF THE FUKUSHIMA NUCLEAR
     PLANT DISASTER                                                       125
4.4  EVALUATING MODEL PERFORMANCE BY CROSS-VALIDATION                     126
     4.4.1  Beyond the Test Set: The Validation and Final Testing Sets    127
4.5  WAYS TO DESCRIBE THE PERFORMANCE OF A CLASSIFIER                     129
4.6  ACCURACY, PRECISION AND RECALL IN PRACTICE                           131
     4.6.1  Image-Based Identification of Terrorists                      131
     4.6.2  The Precision-Recall Curve                                    132
     4.6.3  The $F_1$-Score                                               132
     4.6.4  The Receiver Operating Characteristic (ROC) Curve            133
4.7  CLASSIFICATION ERRORS OF CONTINUOUS DATA PREDICTIONS                 134
4.8  FURTHER READING                                                      136
4.9  CHAPTER REVIEW QUESTIONS                                             137

CHAPTER 5 ■ Are Our Algorithms Racist, Sexist and Discriminating?        139

5.1  HOW DO SMART ALGORITHMS MEDDLE IN OUR LIVES?                         139
     5.1.1  Outlook                                                       142
5.2  RELEASE ON PAROLE: NOT IF YOU ARE BLACK                             142
5.3  MEN ARE PROFESSIONALS, WOMEN ARE HOT                                143
5.4  'FUCK THE ALGORITHM'                                                 145
5.5  PREDICTIVE POLICING OR HOW TO REPRODUCE THE BIAS OF
     THE POLICE WITH AN ALGORITHM                                        146
5.6  WHOSE FAULT WAS IT? DIFFERENT TYPES OF BIAS                         148
     5.6.1  Bias on the Web                                               151
5.7  HOW CAN WE BUILD FAIRER ALGORITHMS?                                 152
     5.7.1  What Is Actually 'Fair'?                                      153
     5.7.2  Is Being Fair Enough?                                         155
     5.7.3  The Bias Impact Statement                                     157
     5.7.4  Fair Machine Learning                                         158
     5.7.5  The Key Is in the Design Team                                 159
5.8  THE FAILURE TO CONTROL THE COVID-19 PANDEMIC FROM
     BIASED DATA                                                          160
5.9  FURTHER READING                                                      162
5.10  CHAPTER REVIEW QUESTIONS                                            166

Chapter 6 ▪ Personal Data, Privacy and Cybersecurity 169

6.1 HOW MUCH IS YOUR DATA WORTH? 169
  6.1.1 The Cost of a Data Breach 170
6.2 WHY IS PRIVACY IMPORTANT? 172
6.3 ARE COMPANIES KEEPING OUR DATA PRIVATE? THE ADA HEALTH CASE STUDY 175
  6.3.1 Business Summary 175
    6.3.1.1 Application Details 175
    6.3.1.2 Technical 176
    6.3.1.3 Market and Legal 176
    6.3.1.4 Application Walk-Through 176
  6.3.2 Data Audit 177
    6.3.2.1 Description of Data Collected and Processed 177
    6.3.2.2 Storage of Personal Data 177
    6.3.2.3 Why Is This Data Held? 178
    6.3.2.4 Legal Basis for Holding the Data? 178
    6.3.2.5 How Long Is the User Data Kept For? 179
    6.3.2.6 Who Has Access to the Data? 179
    6.3.2.7 Security Controls in Place? 180
  6.3.3 Privacy by Design 180
  6.3.4 Experimental Privacy Analysis 182
  6.3.5 End-to-End Security 183
    6.3.5.1 Technical Controls 184
    6.3.5.2 Procedural and Administrative Controls 187
    6.3.5.3 Physical Security Controls 187
    6.3.5.4 Governance and Legal/Compliance Controls 188
6.4 A FEW SIMPLE RULES FOR OWNING YOUR PRIVACY 188
6.5 FURTHER READING 193
6.6 CHAPTER REVIEW QUESTIONS 197

Chapter 7 ▪ What Are the Limits of Artificial Intelligence? 199

7.1 MACHINES OUTPERFORM HUMANS BUT ONLY AT VERY SPECIFIC TASKS 200
  7.1.1 The Protein-Folding Problem 200
7.2 WHY 'TORONTO' AND OTHER EXAMPLES OF HOW MACHINES THINK DIFFERENTLY 202
  7.2.1 Adversarial Examples 202
  7.2.2 (Lack of) Common Sense 203

7.2.3    Catastrophic Forgetting and Continual Learning    204

7.2.4    Mathematical Reasoning    205

7.3    HOW CAN WE TELL IF A MACHINE IS BEHAVING INTELLIGENTLY?    205

7.3.1    The Turing Test    207

7.3.2    Computers Can Only Solve Problems That Have Clear-Cut Answers    208

7.4    IS THE TECHNOLOGICAL SINGULARITY THE REAL THREAT?    209

7.4.1    Consciousness and the Chinese Room Experiment    209

7.4.2    Being a Maverick Is a Very Human Trait    210

7.5    THE TROLLEY PROBLEM    211

7.5.1    Reinforcement Learning, the 4th Learning Paradigm    213

7.5.1.1    A Simple Example with an Autonomous Vehicle    215

7.5.1.2    Autonomous Driving in the Real World    216

7.5.2    Is the Trolley Problem a Real Problem?    218

7.5.2.1    Disentangling the Statistics Also Helps with Acceptance    219

7.5.2.2    Unanswered Ethical Questions    220

7.6    ROBOTS REFLECT OUR OWN HUMANITY    220

7.7    FURTHER READING    221

7.8    CHAPTER REVIEW QUESTIONS    227

Appendix–Answers to Chapter Review Questions    229

Chapter 1. A Bird's-Eye View and the Art of Asking Questions. 229

Chapter 2. Descriptive Analytics.    232

Chapter 3. Predictive Analytics.    234

Chapter 4. How are Predictive Models Trained and Evaluated? 237

Chapter 5. Are Our Algorithms Racist, Sexist and Discriminating?    239

Chapter 6. Personal Data, Privacy and Cybersecurity.    241

Chapter 7. What Are the Limits of Artificial Intelligence?    243

Bibliography    247

Index    271

# Foreword

What is the difference between a regular cook and a chef? A cook may follow recipes and create edible dishes. However, knowing what ingredients should be used and how they should be prepared, combined and presented makes all the difference. What really adds value here is knowing the right tools, ingredients and processes and how they should be orchestrated to create a terrific dish. Data science is no different: Anyone can run a clustering algorithm or train a neural network with minimal effort, but what really matters is knowing, for a specific dataset, what questions should be answered, what algorithms should be used to answer each one of these questions, as well as the ethical and data privacy issues that must be contemplated. The data scientist who can answer these questions can not only follow recipes but is also capable of applying the right algorithms to answer the right questions while minimising potentially discriminating outputs. This book focuses on these relevant questions; if you wish to cook a terrific dish, this book will undoubtedly help you.

Jordi Conesa i Caralt, PhD
Associate Professor of Computer Science
Universitat Oberta de Catalunya

# Preface

Data science is an exciting and fast-evolving field that is no longer the exclusive domain of computer scientists and mathematicians. Today, many other professionals such as engineers, physicists, security experts, lawyers and hospital administrators approach this field and often make very valuable contributions thanks to their unique perspectives and backgrounds.

Despite the abundance of excellent books and resources on data science (many of which I reference here) the standard focus is on solving specific problems programmatically while ignoring the bigger picture. My goal with *How to Think about Data Science* is to present the field of data science in a critical, conceptual and holistic manner where all the relevant facets (technical, social and philosophical) are integrated. Data science is made up of many straightforward ideas whose combination gives rise to an ecosystem consisting of multiple, interconnected elements. These include topics as important as the rational choice of algorithms, the nature of data bias and algorithmic discrimination, data privacy and cybersecurity, as well as being able to understand the risks involved in the deployment of artificial intelligence tools.

This book contains no programming code – there are already plenty of 'how to' books and online courses out there detailing algorithms and their implementation. Here, we become literate in data science by asking the *why* behind data science problems and by learning to reason about these problems holistically instead of following recipes. Thus, we take the scientist's approach of focusing on asking the right question as this is the single most important factor contributing to the success of a data science project. We discuss key concepts and how they are linked together, the pros and cons of various methods, all while abstracting away from the minutiae of the implementation. Developing a holistic understanding is a most valuable skill that will survive specific programming fashions, working styles and computing platforms.

This book is accessible to readers without a strong computational background (although you should be numerically literate), but it is also of much interest to data science practitioners. For example, a programmer in a start-up who wears many different hats might benefit from reading the chapter on algorithmic bias (Chapter 5) or the chapter on cybersecurity (Chapter 6). Likewise, a regulator working on data privacy will benefit from having a critical understanding of the different types of supervised learning methods, their limitations and areas of applicability (Chapter 3).

The advice I give here is the distillation of my experience, both as a practitioner and as a mentor of the many data scientists I have trained in my career. I hope you enjoy reading this book as much as I have enjoyed writing it.

# Acknowledgements

First and foremost, my gratitude goes to Jordi Conesa for pushing me to write this book and for all his insightful advice and feedback. Having Jordi by my side has been a fantastic experience and I am forever grateful for his generosity.

I also wish to thank others who also provided constructive suggestions and support, including Josep Curto, Subhajyoti De, Pedro Ballester, Michael Fernandez-Llamosa, as well as the anonymous reviewers who challenged me to clarify my thinking, examples and exposition.

Randi Cohen is an excellent publisher, and I am grateful for her support and guidance. The Taylor & Francis editorial team members have also helped make this book a reality. To you all, a heartfelt thank you.

And last but not least, there are a number of people I wish to thank for their help during this tumultuous year. These include (in alphabetical order):

My family, including my extended family at BN Arquitectos, for their unconditional support.

Ingelise Gerrand for being the best at what she does as well as a beautiful human being.

Don Paco Gómez for teaching me some very important things that I could not have learnt in any other way.

Aaron G., my dear friend from Oxford, for his always sound advice and support.

Ricardo Martín and Luis Ngale for the opportunities as well as for broadening my horizons.

Silvana Martorell because, out of all of life's chance encounters, she is my favourite one.

Jorge Skinner-Klée for his camaraderie and for showing me the world through his eyes.

# List of Figures

1.1    The scientific method for learning objective truths has a rather linear structure.    3

1.2    Different mental models for learning.    7

1.3    Margaret Hamilton was the lead software engineer in the Apollo 11 mission.    8

1.4    A linear representation of the data life cycle.    9

1.5    Evolution of Uber's data assets and Big Data platform performance.    13

1.6    A simplified representation of Uber's Generation 3 Big Data architecture (2017–present).    14

2.1    Descriptive analytics is historical, whereas predictive analytics tries to infer future (unseen) values.    22

2.2    Snapshot of the Johns Hopkins University Coronavirus Resource Center dashboard.    23

2.3    Weighted moving averages prediction of the number of airline passengers.    24

2.4    The different data variable types.    25

2.5    Anscombe's quartet, a dataset built for the sole purpose of illustrating the importance of plotting data instead of relying on simple statistical measures.    27

2.6    Northern European tourists travelling to Spain (fictional dataset).    28

2.7    The box-plot and its summary of a distribution.    28

2.8    Miles per gallon that a sample of four-, six- and eight-cylinder cars can do.    29

2.9    Florence Nightingale's chart displaying the causes of soldiers' deaths during the Crimean war (1853–1856).    31

2.10    John Snow's map depicting the numbers of deaths from cholera in London's Soho.    32

2.11    Charles Minard's representation of Napoleon's French invasion of Russia (1812).    33

2.12    A clustering algorithm uncovers three natural groups and an outlier (toy example).    36

2.13    Heatmap displaying the distances among all US states.    39

2.14    $K$-means clustering of the US states.    40

2.15    Four is the optimal number of clusters to separate all the US states in terms of reported crime.    41

2.16    An intuitive set of clusters (left) and those calculated by $K$-means showing the centroids (right).    42

2.17    The hierarchical clustering result mostly agrees with $K$-means clustering when the cut-off is set to identify the same number of clusters ($K = 4$).    43

2.18 Network representation of the association rules derived for a bakery in Reading (UK). 44

2.19 Combinations of support and confidence levels for association rule mining. 47

3.1 The point of reference is one important difference between descriptive and predictive analytics. 56

3.2 Splitting the original dataset into training and test sets is a characteristic of supervised learning. 57

3.3 The extent of data labelling determines the type of learning that is possible. 59

3.4 The basic flow of a supervised machine learning exercise. 60

3.5 Unlabelled data may be enriched by pseudolabelling to increase the predictive accuracy of a learning model. 62

3.6 The two classes in the 'two moons' dataset cannot be separated by pseudolabelling. 62

3.7 An approximately linear relationship exists between sales and TV advertising expenditure. 66

3.8 A linear model of sales vs TV advertising expenditure. The regression line (blue) is complemented by the 95% confidence interval (thick, grey line) and the LOESS smoother (red line). 67

3.9 The time of data download over the Internet is not a linear function of download speed. 70

3.10 Examples of logistic regressions. 72

3.11 Multiple logistic regression – probability of admission to graduate school. 74

3.12 A simplified example of a binary decision-making process using a tree. 79

3.13 A decision tree to predict survival vs death among the passengers of the Titanic. 80

3.14 The principle of bootstrap aggregating (bagging). 83

3.15 A hypothetical 3-tree Random Forest illustrating node splitting with random feature sets. 84

3.16 Boosting machines improve their performance iteratively. 85

3.17 A hyperplane is a decision boundary that separates two classes. 86

3.18 A hyperplane is a mathematical boundary determined by the support vectors (black triangles and circles). 87

3.19 Kernel-based separation of two classes. 88

3.20 Kernel-based separation of three classes. 88

3.21 Schematic representation of an animal neuron. 90

3.22 The perceptron. 90

3.23 A one-neuron ANN. 91

3.24 A multi-neuron ANN architecture with one hidden layer. 92

3.25 Architectures of the most recurrent types of neural networks [106]. 93

3.26 Inverness Caledonian Thistle FC's AI-powered camera disaster. 94

3.27 An image typical of ILSVRC. 96

3.28 Transfer learning involves reusing previously trained models. 97

3.29   Trade-off between performance and problem types for a specialized algo-
       rithm and a general-purpose one.                                          99
3.30   Domain knowledge and assumptions are key for optimising the performance
       of any algorithm.                                                         99
3.31   Model interpretability can be thought of as a *continuum*.               102
3.32   The typical performance of a learning model against the number of features
       included.                                                                104
3.33   The three types of feature selection methods.                           104
3.34   Some statistical methods for filter-based feature selection.            105
3.35   Two-PC plot of a 30-feature breast cancer dataset (B: benign;
       M: malignant).                                                          107
3.36   Schematic representation of the collaborative and content-based filtering
       approaches.                                                             110

4.1    The general strategy in supervised machine learning.                    122
4.2    Having a diversity of observations is essential for generalisation.      123
4.3    Underfitting vs overfitting.                                            124
4.4    Bias vs variance.                                                       125
4.5    The overfitted line through the 400-year-old earthquake dataset (adapted
       from [139]).                                                            126
4.6    The 10-fold cross-validation strategy.                                  127
4.7    The four possible test dataset classification categories.               129
4.8    A typical precision-recall curve (example).                             133
4.9    A typical ROC curve (example).                                          134
4.10   A range of values for the ROC Area Under the Curve.                     135

5.1    Face ID is Apple's face recognition system.                             140
5.2    Voice assistants help us with an increasing number of tasks at home.     141
5.3    Google search results for Robert Downey Jr. (25 October 2022)           144
5.4    Google search results for Scarlett Johansson. (25 October 2022)         144
5.5    The extremely biased algorithm that predicted exam grades sparked riots
       across the UK (2020).                                                   146
5.6    Hotspots for (a) arrests and (b) drug use in Oakland, California.        147
5.7    Simpson's paradox in action in aggregate data (a) and individual
       groups (b).                                                             150
5.8    The most common types of bias on the Web.                               151
5.9    The Pokémon GO interface with Pokémon in the author's affluent, seaside
       neighbourhood.                                                          154
5.10   Equality and equity try to achieve fairness in different ways.          156
5.11   The basic rates of reproduction for various infectious diseases.        161

6.1    Presidio Modelo (Isla de la Juventud, Cuba), a modern panopticon design. 174
6.2    Screenshot of the output of the Lumen Privacy Monitor.                  183

| | | |
|---|---|---|
| 6.3 | A model of the architecture of the Ada Health app. | 185 |
| 6.4 | A virtual private network (VPN) allows secure communication across public networks. | 190 |
| 7.1 | The protein-folding problem is guessing the 3D structure of a protein from its sequence of amino acids. | 201 |
| 7.2 | Learning models can misclassify adversarial examples with high confidence given the right type of perturbed input. | 203 |
| 7.3 | An illustration of catastrophic forgetting for a binary classification problem. | 204 |
| 7.4 | A representation of the four-colour theorem. | 206 |
| 7.5 | A schematic representation of the Turing test. | 207 |
| 7.6 | The Chinese room experiment claims that machines cannot possess human consciousness. | 210 |
| 7.7 | The trolley problem: Would you save the five people in danger while intentionally killing just one person? | 212 |
| 7.8 | The four machine learning paradigms. | 214 |
| 7.9 | An autonomous vehicle learning to find the exit in a garage. | 215 |
| 7.10 | A simplified deep Q-network for a more realistic autonomous driving scenario. | 217 |
| 7.11 | The different classes of sensors present in autonomous vehicles. | 218 |
| 7.12 | hitchBOT on its way to Neuschwanstein Castle in Southern Germany. | 222 |

# List of Tables

2.1  Visualisations Methods That Tend to Work for Specific Data Types         36

2.2  Values for the First Six States in the USarrests Dataset (1973)          38

2.3  Confidence vs Support in Association Rule Mining                         46

3.1  Expenditure in Television Advertising vs Sales (Sample)                  65

3.2  Probability of Admission to UCLA Graduate School for Various GRE Scores  74

3.3  Probability of Admission to UCLA Graduate School (GPA = 3.8, GRE = 790)  75

3.4  Occurrence of Sepsis-Related Symptoms                                    76

3.5  Passenger Statistics Aboard the Titanic (1912)                           79

3.6  Can You Predict the Output for Input Value = 4?                          89

3.7  Some Characteristics of Interpretable Algorithms                        101

3.8  Incomplete Movie Ratings Table                                          112

3.9  All-Against-All Movie Rating Similarity Matrix                          113

3.10 Known and Predicted Movie Ratings Table                                 114

4.1  A Putative Function Mapping Input Values to Output Values               122

4.2  A More Accurate Mapping Function Given More Training Data               122

4.3  Confusion Matrix of Our Dog-in-Picture Classifier                      130

4.4  Confusion Matrix of Our Classifier for Predicting Terrorists           131

5.1  The Average Grades of Gryffindor and Slytherin Students                150

6.1  The Prices of Various Forms of Identity in the Dark Web                 171

6.2  Summary of the Uses of the Data Collected from the Patient             178

6.3  Summary of the Privacy-Enhancing Tools Discussed Here                  192

7.1  The Set of Updated, Predicted Rewards for Position (1,1)               216

7.2  Characteristics of the Sensor Types Found in Autonomous Vehicles       218

# CHAPTER 1

# A Bird's-Eye View and the Art of Asking Questions

*Il est encore plus facile de juger de l'esprit d'un homme par ses questions que par ses réponses. (It is easier to judge the mind of a man by his questions rather than his answers).*

– Pierre-Marc-Gaston de Lévis (1764–1830), *French politician*

The exponential growth of data in recent years, together with our ability to process, store and analyse it has created a whole new world of opportunities. Today data science applications are found in every industry and affect every single aspect of our lives. If we ask random people (including some data scientists) to define data science, many will say that data science is about finding patterns in the data, extracting data, making predictions and ultimately deriving conclusions from the analyses. While all of these may be part of a data science project, this is not what data science is about. Data science, quite simply, is about asking good questions. This is a simple but a vital concept that puts the focus not on large computers or fancy algorithms, but first of all on our ability to ask the right questions of the data available, in the right context, to solve specific problems. In this chapter we explore key topics such as the data scientific method, what makes a good question and what kinds of question data science cannot answer.

Data is an asset with a characteristic life cycle where each phase is associated with a specific set of questions that must be addressed for the proper exploitation of the data. When dealing with very large datasets, however, single computers are not powerful enough. Multi-computer architectures are designed to handle data with different characteristics (size, speed and complexity) from birth to deletion. We discuss the evolution of Uber's computer architecture in the context of the company's exponential growth and its changing functional requirements.

## 1.1  WHO IS THIS BOOK FOR?

This book is an introduction for anyone wishing to develop a critical understanding of data science.

Data science is a young and vast field at the intersection of many different disciplines, including programming, calculus and statistics, cloud computing, visualisation and story-telling, law, and privacy and security. As a result, data science is no longer the exclusive domain of computer scientists and engineers. Many other professionals such as regulators, lawyers, sociologists, mathematicians, hospital administrators and security experts enter

DOI: 10.1201/b23197-1

1

data science and often make very valuable contributions thanks to their unique perspectives and backgrounds.

One warning, though: this book will not teach you any programming or includes any code. There are already plenty of books out there detailing algorithms and their implementation in the languages of data science (R and Python mostly), but these are 'how to' books. What we are trying to learn here is the *why* behind the problems in data science. We achieve this by discussing key concepts while abstracting away from the minutiae of the implementation. After all, data science consists of many straightforward ideas that are combined in multiple ways. Therefore, developing a holistic understanding is a most valuable skill that will survive specific programming fashions, working styles and computing platforms.

## 1.2   ASKING GOOD QUESTIONS IS THE ULTIMATE SUPERPOWER

The goal of data science is to extract actionable knowledge from data in order to solve real-world problems. Data science is essentially a creative activity that must always start with a **well-defined question**. Two examples of questions that have resulted in key developments include:

- *How can we use data to anticipate a future pandemic?*

  Following the SARS epidemic (2002–2004) Dr. Kamran Khan set up a BlueDot startup (bluedot.global) to anticipate outbreaks by combining text analysis from multiple social networks (in 65 different languages) with flight information. This is how the COVID-19 outbreak was first detected in Wuhan on 30 December 2019 as well as its subsequent spread to Bangkok, Seoul, Taipei and Tokyo [1]. BlueDot was ahead of the World Health Organization by one full month [2].

- *How can I find new and relevant professional connections?*

  This is the question that Jonathan Goldman asked when he started working at LinkedIn in 2006. His efforts were initially dismissed because 'why should you tell me who I should be connecting with?' However, Goldman came up with an experiment where he presented users with the names of three other people they were not connected with but who had worked in the same places or attended the same schools. The custom ads displaying the three best matches for each user had the greatest-ever click-through rate [3].

### 1.2.1   The Data Scientific Method

Goldman's insightful question was just the first (and most important) step of the scientific method that he applied, which is fundamental to doing quality data science (Fig. 1.1).

The basic structure of the scientific method is a process that starts with a *guess*, **the question**, which must be objectively answered by direct observations or with scientific tools. Goldman's formal question was probably along the lines of 'will presenting former classmates and colleagues make valuable professional connections?' A **hypothesis** must then be constructed in a way that facilitates the design of the subsequent experiment. Usually there is a *null hypothesis ($N_0$)* ('the presentation of former classmates and colleagues does not add any value to someone's professional connections') and an *alternative hypothesis* (the opposite of the null hypothesis, i.e. presenting these people does add professional value). Splitting a hypothesis into a null and an alternative one allows the application of statistical tests later on. The effective **experiment** that Goldman designed required collecting data upon presenting the three (ranked) best matches to each user. Finally, the **analysis and**

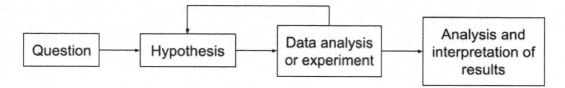

Figure 1.1 The scientific method for learning objective truths has a rather linear structure.

**interpretation of the results** most likely involved comparing the percentage of users that had accepted these personal recommendations with a control group. This allowed Goldman to reject the null hypothesis and conclude that users welcome carefully selected personal introductions into their professional spheres. Following this initial success Goldman kept improving his models of personal relatedness, which eventually were responsible for much of LinkedIn's success.

The story behind Jonathan Goldman is important for various reasons. For one thing, it shows that good data science is about experimenting with ideas and testing them in a measurable and scientific manner. Besides, Goldman had a deep **domain knowledge**, which means he perfectly understood the problem he was trying to solve in that specific context. A question without understanding the characteristics and limitations of the system we are interrogating is useless. This concept brings the application of the analysis into a very strong focus: a fundamental issue in data science is whether you can translate a real-world problem into a data science problem by asking the right questions, knowing what techniques must be applied or developed to solve the question at hand and how you can translate the result of the analysis into a solution that can be fed back into the real world. On top of this, Goldman had the skills to *convincingly communicate his findings* to the stakeholders at LinkedIn. Effective communication should be regarded as the last step in the scientific process, whether it is a Powerpoint presentation, an interactive dashboard, a final product that can be used, or a journal article. No matter how good and solid your conclusions are, if you cannot explain them then they do not count.

Finally, Goldman has a PhD in physics, not computer science or data science. The implication is that an outsider with a good idea can make a real difference in data science. This is what is 'sexy' and exciting about data science, and not necessarily the job prospects or the paycheck [3]. A creative person that is happy playing with ideas and connecting concepts from disparate fields can make an excellent data scientist.

## 1.2.2 What Makes a Good Question?

Unlike at school where we are rewarded by the quality of our answers to the questions that the teacher sets, in data science the most important and difficult task is to ask the right question in the right context. The answer to a question does not necessarily have to involve a very sophisticated analysis: the type of analysis simply must be appropriate for the question. Moreover, complex techniques are not inherently superior if they do not help answer the question or do not facilitate a clear explanation of how the results were produced. Good questions are:

1. **Asked in the right context,** which requires domain knowledge. In fact, there is nothing more useless than a right answer to the wrong question. Also, we must not necessarily rush into asking questions: often good questions become clear after doing some exploratory analyses and basic visualisations of the data.

2. **Tractable,** which means that we should be able to answer it in as few steps as possible while producing a clear experimental result. We must also factor in the time it will take to answer a question and our own level of ability [4].

For instance, 'how can we cure cancer?' is so broad and unspecific that it makes it very difficult to handle and design clear-cut experiments around it. Goldman's question ('will presenting former classmates and colleagues make valuable professional connections?'), on the other hand, is clear, powerful and lends itself to an uncomplicated experimental design.

Dr. Kamran Khan's question ('how can we use data to anticipate a future pandemic?') is also clear but complex. Complex questions must be broken down into smaller sub-questions and worded in a way that facilitates experimental design.

Some types of questions naturally map to existing algorithmic techniques, and with practice one can learn to identify these right away. Some examples include:

- How many kilowatts will be demanded from my wind farm within the next two hours? (Regression, Chapter 3)
- Given a set of financial variables (income, balance, savings, age, marital status), will this customer default on their mortgage? (Logistic Regression, Chapter 3)
- Which are the most relevant variables in my dataset? (Feature Selection, Chapter 3)
- What is a smaller set of variables I can use to describe my dataset? (Dimensionality Reduction, Chapter 3)
- Is there a group of premium customers, or are all customers a homogeneous group? (Clustering, Chapter 2)
- Is this bank transaction fraudulent? (Anomaly Detection, Chapter 3)
- Which animal is in this image? (Multi-Category Classification, Chapter 3)
- How many distinct groups exist? (Clustering, Chapter 2)
- Is this rise in sea temperature abnormal? (Anomaly Detection, Chapter 3)
- Which is the best possible book I can recommend to this customer? (Recommendation Engines, Chapter 3)
- Should I continue driving at the same speed, brake or accelerate in response to that yellow light? (Reinforcement Learning, Chapter 7)

However, there is often more than one way (algorithmic technique) to answer a given question and we should not get locked up with a single approach. For example, many classification problems can be reformulated as regression. In fact, conclusions that are reached from multiple angles using different techniques are always more sound.

The design of an experiment must also include a description of the at least one **independent variable**, which is the one we manipulate and expect to influence the **dependent variable**. Finally, the **control variables** are the experimental elements that remain constant and unchanged during the experiment in order to control for any side effects on the experimental readout.

3. **Not obvious.** Most questions people come up with are rather obvious, and obvious questions are proportionately worthless [5]. We tend to engage in herd thinking ('me too' questions) when we spend too much time in the company of colleagues working in the same area. While having a sound knowledge of a subject is key, so is taking

a certain distance from the field and its practitioners. A good way to avoid being locked-up in a particular frame of mind is to have intermittent social interactions so that we remain curious while also retaining access to collective intelligence [6].

One key difference between a good question and a great one is its degree of unpredictability. Reasonable questions can be posed by many and answered logically using the standard scientific process of experimental design, controls and hypothesis validation (Fig. 1.1). Great questions, on the other hand, lie outside of our current frame of knowledge and require an illogical step that is often the product of letting one's mind wander freely [7]. Great questions have the power to transform our reality – a classical example of this is when Einstein was trying to modify Maxwell's equations so that they were no longer in contradiction with the constant speed of light that had been observed. After years of trying to modify these equations, Einstein eventually realised that it was not Maxwell's fault. Rather, our notion of time was incorrect. Einstein thus stumbled upon the very question that led to the idea that the rate at which time passes depends on one's frame of reference.

4. **They can arise from a combination of already existing concepts.** Truly novel and revolutionary questions are rare, but we can also work on a higher dimension where we try to combine concepts to come up with a new idea or application of existing ideas. This is very important because *new ideas give rise to new questions, and questions give rise to experiments*. For example, Darwin was a geologist who collected various bird species from the Galapagos islands. When Darwin showed ornithologist John Gould his drawings and the annotations of the islands where those species were found, Gould immediately realised the importance of his findings and this marked the beginning of Darwin's Theory of Evolution [8].

The observation that disruptive innovation often comes from outsiders has been called 'the Medici effect' [9]. Another example is the Cretaceous-Paleogene extinction event that wiped out three-quarters of plant and animal life on Earth (including dinosaurs). The theory was first put forward by geologist Walter Alvarez and his father, experimental physicist Luis Walter Alvarez [10]. Computer scientist, entrepreneur and investor James Altucher refers to the Medici effect as 'idea sex' and offers a more mundane but practical example: girls like playing with dolls and boys with guns. What would be the result of combining dolls with guns and action, Stan Weston asked? The result is called G.I. Joe which has sold over one billion US dollars' worth of merchandise [11].

## 1.2.3   What Kinds of Questions Can Data Science Not Answer?

Computers are unable to answer most types of questions, including those that require empirical evidence (e.g. in physics or chemistry), mathematical reasoning (with the exception of the four-colour theorem, Chapter 7) as well as those related to love, family, democracy, ethics, aesthetics and faith. Among the problems that data science can solve we must watch out for situations where no matter how much you torture the data, data science will never yield any meaningful insights. We can refer to these as the limits of data science [12]:

- **When we do not know what value should be predicted or optimised.**

  For instance, Goldman's goal was to *optimise the number of connections* that were made when LinkedIn users were presented with former colleagues and classmates. This is as clear a goal as it gets.

Another interesting example is the 2011 film *Moneyball* [13]. Billy Beane (Brad Pitt) was the manager of the uncompetitive Oakland Athletics. The question on the table was how to beat much richer Major League Baseball (MLB) teams on a tight budget. Yale economics graduate Peter Brand (Jonah Hill) convinced Beane that he had to steer away from buying players by applying conventional criteria, and instead focus on the players' statistics: *'Your goal shouldn't be to buy players. Your goal should be to buy wins. In order to buy wins you need to buy runs'.*

Brand used a formula to score each player by taking into account their statistics (hits, walks, total bases, stolen bases, etc.). Thus, with a limited budget they managed to hire unconventional talent that had been overlooked for reasons such as age, appearance and personality that were unrelated to their statistical performance. In the 2002 MLB season the Oakland Athletics finished first in the American League West with a record 20-game win streak [14].

Brand was able to ask the right question and focus on one specific value that had to be optimised (the number of runs). Focusing on a less tangible concept such as 'the value of winning games' would have been a mistake because it can be defined in different ways (e.g. maximise profits) and also because there are many confounding variables involved instead of just one variable that had to be optimised. The message here is that without a clear, quantifiable goal, any data analysis is pointless.

- **When dealing with subjective data.**

  Subjective data is data that depends on a person's interpretation of a particular situation instead of an empirical measurement. Two key questions to ask here are:

  – *Is it possible to remove the subjective element from the data?*
  – *Is any of this data usable?*

  If the subjective element cannot be removed from the data, taking the measurements at face value could be an option. For example, although different people perceive pain differently, if most patients rate the pain experienced when using a medical device as 8/10, would you keep prescribing it?

  Some subjective data are outright unusable: for example, it is a fact that police officers take race and ethnicity into account (either implicitly or explicitly) when deciding who should be detained. Can you imagine the bias and discrimination introduced in an algorithm trained with this dataset with the goal of preventing crime (PredPol, Chapter 5)?

- **When several people do not share the same mental model of a process.**

  It is easy for people to disagree even on simple mental models of the world. For example, one reason why many students give up programming quickly is because they believe progress is linear, when in fact the reality for most people learning to program from scratch is a steep learning curve punctuated by a few eureka moments (Fig. 1.2).

  Can you imagine a situation where various stakeholders cannot agree on, for instance, how to interpret a complex operations model of a factory with its many feedback loops? What about an even more complex model such as global climate with its many variables even if the values to predict are clear? A shared mental model is key for agreeing on the results of the analyses and predictions. Another important aspect is, when we have a complex model that must be shared and discussed by many people, how can it be validated?

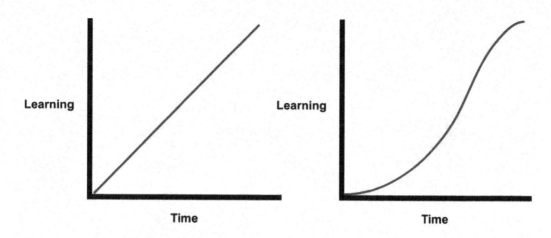

Figure 1.2 Different mental models for learning.

### 1.2.4 The Apollo 11 Mission: Raw Processing Power Is Not as Important as Asking the Right Questions

Asking the right question is the first and most important consideration in a data science project. We also need to have access to quality and often huge amounts of data that may require processing in real time. Although our computational power has increased tremendously, the data that is generated in the world grows even faster. This makes us wonder: Is having access to raw computational power an indispensable condition in data science?

One answer to this question can be found in the design of the Apollo Guidance Computer, the machine that managed to guide the Apollo 11 spaceflight to the moon and back in 1969. Although this is not a data science problem (e.g. in the sense of making predictions), but one of large-scale computation, its planning is a fascinating exercise in design thinking guided by scientific questioning.

The team led by Margaret Hamilton (1936–) engineered a marvel that managed to work out the right course to the moon by continuously recalculating the position of the spacecraft (Fig. 1.3). Information on the position was regularly fed into the machine by the astronauts who took astronomical measurements during flight using a sextant (a navigation tool invented in the 18th century). Besides this efficient human-computer interaction, the Apollo computer also communicated with about 150 different devices in the spacecraft while prioritising the computational tasks it had to accomplish [15]. Thus the Apollo computer was incredibly reliable and capable for the tasks it had been set up to, even though your smartphone is millions of times more powerful [16].

This feat of engineering could not have been achieved if Margaret Hamilton and co-workers had not been able to ask the right questions and put the solutions together in the most optimal way. Key questions likely included: How often does the course need to be recalculated, and how will the system manage the memory available? In case of a general electrical failure, how shall we prioritise the communication of the computer with the spacecraft's devices? If an astronaut inputs the wrong number, how can the wrong course be identified and corrected?

The story of the Apollo 11 computer illustrates how beyond a certain point having access to a certain amount of raw computational power is rather secondary. A well-designed system will always be more capable than a more powerful one that is poorly engineered. In the context of data science, raw processing power definitely helps, but it also becomes irrelevant if the analytical question is not well defined, if the dataset is too small or of poor

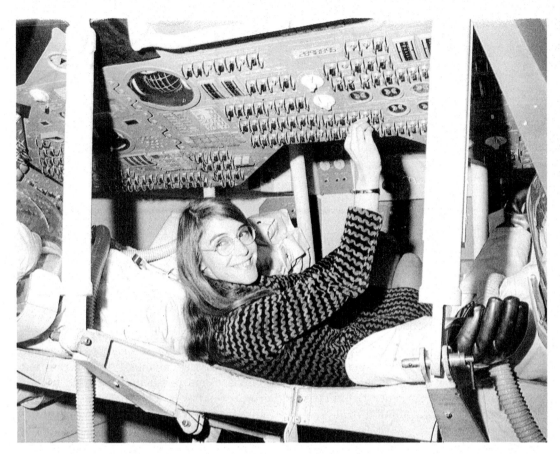

Figure 1.3 Margaret Hamilton was the lead software engineer in the Apollo 11 mission.

quality, or if the algorithm of choice is not appropriate for the specific question and dataset. We will repeatedly discuss throughout the book how focusing on the analytical question is the first and most important part of a data science project. Only once we have a well-defined question can we start adding specific layers of technology (e.g. complex algorithms and computer architectures) as if it were an onion.

## 1.3 THE DATA LIFE CYCLE

Data is the raw material of data science and has a characteristic life cycle, from its generation to the final production of its (volatile) value and its final disappearance. As such, data must be considered an asset which, if of sufficient quality and given the right questions and analyses, can yield tremendous insights and ultimately great value. The various phases of the data life cycle may be described as follows (Fig. 1.4):

1. **Data generation**: No matter the origin, the 'three V's' of the big data paradigm are still useful when asking questions about raw data:

   - *Volume:* How big is your dataset? How many files are there? Will you be able to store and analyse it in your laptop or will you need a large computer cluster such as Amazon Web Services (AWS) or the Google Cloud Platform?

   - *Velocity:* Does your data come in a continuous stream and therefore must be captured and analysed in real time?

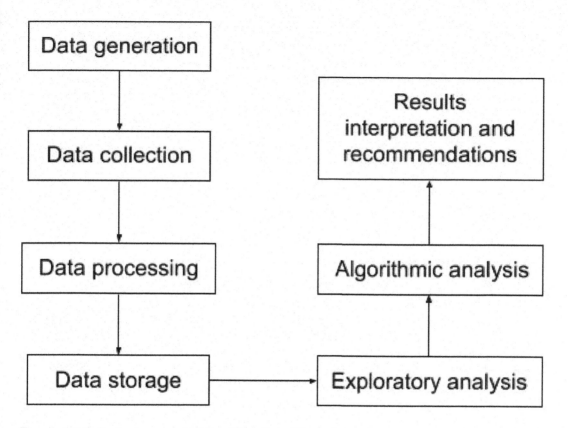

Figure 1.4 A linear representation of the data life cycle.

An example of this would be an application for taxi companies to assign the closest car to a given customer in real time. Another example is an e-commerce application that seeks to combine mobile device location and user data to make location- and time-sensitive offers.

- **Variety:** Is all your data available in the same format (e.g. text, audio or video) or will you have to combine their information? Is your data available in one database or will you have to combine various sources into a unified data scheme?

  For example, we are testing a new drug and want to understand its side effects. For this we will probably have to integrate (i) (anonymised) patient data from various hospitals where the drug trials have been carried out (structured data but perhaps in different formats); (ii) interview data on how patients feel (unstructured text that needs to be processed); and (iii) data from social networks (unstructured too) to learn through automated sentiment analysis whether a correspondence exists between what patients report and what they tell their relatives and friends.

2. **Data collection**: It is key to think carefully about how the data will be collected and the complexity associated with each system. For example, will the data be scraped off the web? Is the data available in one or more databases—all relational or a combination of relational and NoSQL? Will the data come from questionnaires and surveys or from

Excel files produced with different Excel versions? Is the data available in text files, in which case are the fields uniformly separated by tabs, commas, or a mixture of these?

Moreover, we must only collect the data that is relevant. For example, the Large Hadron Collider experiments at CERN (home.cern) collect data from some 150 million intelligent sensors. At a rate of 600 million collisions per second and data being delivered 40 million times each second, the resulting amount of data is colossal. In practice, only 0.001% of all this data is retained for further analysis [17]. Still, the data eventually kept translates to about 200 PB of data every year (properly stored and replicated). This is equivalent to the data contained in the British Library, four-thousand times over.

Knowing which specific data must be collected is a key aspect of any data science project. A good data scientist should be asking the following questions:

- What data should be acquired for this project and why?
- When should this data be acquired?
- What is the difference between the various available datasets?
- How complex is the data import process?
  *For instance, are the data available as CSV (comma-separated values) files that can be put together? Or do I need to build a complex pipeline to extract data from various data warehouses? Will I need to use an API to extract the data from a remote, online server? If there is no API available, how will I scrape data from a website? Is scraping that website legal?*
- What implications are there to storing this or that dataset of size $x$ over the next few months or years?

Simply collecting all the data that is available 'just in case it might be useful one day' is a rookie mistake that shows that you have not really thought deeply enough about the research question that you should be trying to answer. Unless you can justify every aspect of a data collection decision, you do not really have a data investment strategy.

3. **Data processing** involves the cleaning and preparation of data as raw data can never be effectively used for analysis. For example, does the data have consistent formats (geographical, dates, etc.) and structural errors (e.g. inconsistent capitalisation, typos)? What is the level of cleaning required, including the removal of duplicate entries? Can you identify and remove the data that is of no relevance to the question? And most importantly, can you describe the data quality in terms of the six dimensions of data quality?

   - *Accuracy:* How accurately does our data describe the real-world objects and events at that point of time? Do the values make sense, or can you spot some strange ones?

   - *Completeness:* How much of the entire dataset do we have access to? For example, would you try to predict the next US President from a poll taken among New York's Upper East Side residents? Can we estimate *how incomplete* and *biased* our sample is?

     We may also encounter the situation where we have access to the complete dataset but with issues at the record level, e.g. missing values, rows and columns. Shall we throw away the rows and columns with missing data, or try to *impute* the missing values [18, 19]?

- **Consistency:** If data about a specific entry is distributed across various sites (e.g. databases), is the data consistent and verifiable? For example, customer data that is selectively updated in certain databases but not others ends up having different contact details and preferences for the same user. Which one is right?

- **Timeliness:** An air traffic controller needs access to real-time data, not data about flights that is made available twice a day. Is the timeliness of our data an accurate representation of the reality we want to understand?

- **Uniqueness:** Each data point representing a real-world object or event (or part thereof) should only be represented once in any given dataset. Primary Keys (PKs) in relational databases were defined to avoid duplicate entries.

- **Validity:** How valid is our data. For example, do all email addresses contain the '@' symbol? Are values realistic within a given range (e.g. nobody lives to 200 years, no month is longer than 31 days) and conform to a particular syntax (e.g. dd:mm:yyyy or mm:dd:yyyy)?

Data preparation also includes formatting a stream of data from car sensors into a data structure to which machine learning algorithms can be applied more efficiently (e.g. a table). Large datasets might have *low value density*, and here the goal of the processing and analysis steps is to increase the value density of the data.

4. **Data storage**: Here key questions to ask include, for example, the optimal type of database and its design for different dataset types. Moreover, data that are collected at different velocities require a specific architecture for their combined collection, processing and storage.

   And if the data we have collected and processed is too large for the computers in our organisation, shall we store and process it in the cloud? How will we keep the data secure? To prevent losing all our valuable data, how, where and how often will we back up our data?

5. **Exploratory data analysis**: A statistical description of the data and the application of statistical tests together with key visualisation techniques (e.g. probability distributions, bar charts and various other plots) are key for getting a feel of our dataset (Chapter 2). Exploratory data analysis can help us decide which data to keep by asking key questions such as:

   - Should outliers (extreme values) be kept or not?
     *Here a sound understanding of the question (domain knowledge) is key. For instance, are outliers required because we are trying to build an anomaly detector? Or are outliers dispensable because we are only interested in the most common values?*

   - How should missing data be handled?
     *If a vector is missing a data point, do we get rid of this data or try to calculate the missing data point (imputation)?*

   - How should categorical data be treated?

When we do understand the data at this level of intimate detail we can gain the first insights into which analytical techniques might work, and which probably will not. Exploratory data analysis can also help us identify bias that can lead to discriminatory outcomes (Chapter 5).

6. **Data analysis** involves the application of specific algorithms and methods and is the stage where the data is transformed into potentially useful information.

   The goal of the analysis might be to yield a descriptive result (by simply summarising and mining historical data, Chapter 2) or a predictive result, e.g. by building a model that tries to predict unseen values (Chapter 3). The performance of a predictive model must always be evaluated by choosing the most appropriate metric for each context (Chapter 4). Moreover, as described earlier many questions yield themselves to specific types of algorithm (e.g. classification, clustering, regression), and a question may also be answered using more than one type of algorithm.

   The most basic definition of an algorithm is *a set of steps that describe how to solve a particular problem*, such as *sorting* a set of numbers into increasing order. The three characteristics of a good algorithm include **correctness** (solving the task intended without error), **efficiency** (the algorithm uses as little time and/or space as possible) and **interpretability** (can you easily understand how the algorithm generated those predictions?). A model that cannot be interpreted easily must be *explained*; the interpretability vs explainability dilemma is presented in Chapter 3.

   Many modern algorithms such as Google's search service are so much more complex to the point where they should be rather described as 'complex software systems' because they integrate many layers with many sub-algorithms, each of which is managed by teams of developers and scientists.

7. **Results interpretation and recommendations**: At this stage the various hypotheses are accepted or rejected. We must then ask: What are the main conclusions and how should they be summarised? Should we use static or interactive visualisations? How about using a dashboard where we can play with the data? Once we can summarise and prioritise the main findings follow-up actions can be implemented to address the original question. What are the high-priority areas in which action will yield the most valuable result?

   In practice, however, the various phases of the data life cycle *almost never run this linear*. For example, upon visualisation of the data at the exploratory stage we may decide that a better or a different question should be asked, and this might lead to modifying how the data are processed and stored, as well as to a different choice of algorithm. The data that are not useful are ultimately destroyed because storage capacity is an asset too. Finally, if the model is to be implemented at scale in a large company it will need to go into production. This phase normally involves collaborating with software and data engineers to discuss issues like what the best production language is as well as the best choice of computer architecture. Latency issues (how fast the system responds to a request) as well as any dependencies with other applications must be tested throughout too.

## 1.4 DATA VOLUME AND PROCESSING REQUIREMENTS DETERMINE LARGE-SCALE COMPUTER ARCHITECTURES

Data is being generated at an exponential rate, and by 2025 the world will be producing some 175 zettabytes annually [20], of which we will only be able to store between 3% and 12% of it [21].

With this avalanche of data, traditional computer and software systems (e.g. storage servers, relational databases and desktop software packages) have encountered serious limitations. For example, they cannot efficiently process or analyse datasets that are heavily streamed, or are too large or too complex. To accomplish these tasks, a great diversity of

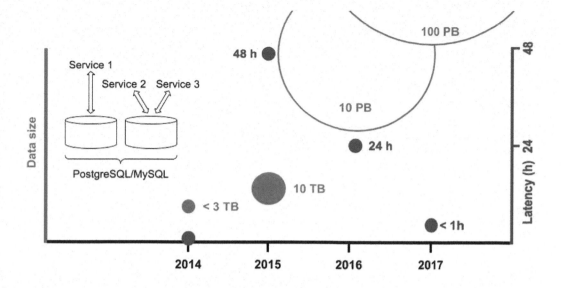

Figure 1.5 Evolution of Uber's data assets and Big Data platform performance.

technological solutions have been developed over the years. These solutions are combined into computer architectures designed to handle data with specific characteristics, and no two architectures are the same. For example the system required to capture and analyse the data from an airport traffic system is different from the architecture needed for dealing with large patient datasets. The flight traffic data is likely to be structured, streamed at very high speed and needs to be analysed in real time but perhaps is not particularly large or needs to be stored indefinitely. On the other hand, patient data is not streamed and can be analysed in batch (in chunks) once a week, but the machine learning (ML) algorithms to be applied are very memory-intensive and the data itself might be massive and have very specific requirements (such as data anonymisation and permanent data storage). Therefore, if we can ask the question of what is the most important requirement for our project and dataset, we can find various architectures that are designed to extract the maximum value from different types of data.

### 1.4.1 The Evolution of Uber's Data Science Needs

*Big data* architectures are rarely designed from scratch but they typically evolve with increasing requirements for data processing and analysis. The evolution of Uber's Big Data Platform is a compelling example of how an architecture organically develops in parallel with data growth and changing business requirements [22]. Here the overarching question that guided its development was: How can we handle and analyse more data, faster?

Today Uber's business model relies heavily on the fast processing and analysis of petabytes of data. Back in 2014, however, the total data size was only a few terabytes. This data was stored in non-centralised relational databases that were accessed and manipulated by data scientists as needed (Fig. 1.5).

Uber's exponential growth called for the centralisation of all data in an analytical data warehouse. Multiple technologies were incorporated and despite the huge success and the increased functionality, one negative side was that the latency went from sub-minute to somewhere between 24–48 h.

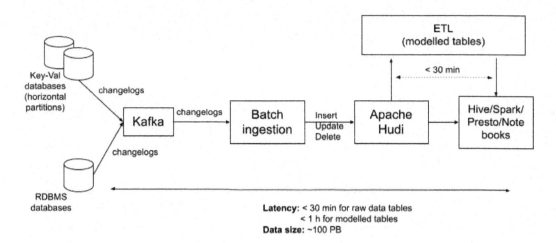

Figure 1.6 A simplified representation of Uber's Generation 3 Big Data architecture (2017–present).

From 2015 to 2016 the amount of data to be processed increased about one thousand times to petabytes of data. By then the analytical data warehouse was not only slow but also presented some data reliability issues and could not be scaled horizontally at a reasonable cost (would imply buying larger and larger database servers, but there is a limit). In its second incarnation, the Uber Big Data platform was re-architected into a scalable Hadoop ecosystem that introduced many technical improvements and facilitated the handling of increasing amounts of data slightly faster.

The increasingly large datasets that were being handled on a daily basis introduced functional bottlenecks into this first Hadoop architecture. Besides, latency was still about 24 h and did not allow making business decisions in real time. This led to the third incarnation of the Uber Big Data platform with some truly sophisticated solutions (Fig. 1.6, [22]). The changes introduced now allow all users of the platform to access the company data both quickly and reliably. Further improvements to the Uber architecture are being made to, for instance, improve the quality of the data, reduce the latency for mini-batch processing even further (from less than one hour to ideally less than 5 minutes), and in general make the system more scalable and reliable for the future to come.

## 1.5  FURTHER READING

- **General programming courses**

  An extensive list of technical resources are referenced in each chapter of this book. For those new to programming I can recommend a number of sites that include courses and certificates where one can learn the languages of data science (Python, R and SQL mainly). Some of these courses are freely available or are otherwise reasonably priced. There are other popular sites featuring programming courses and certificates such as Udemy (udemy.com) and DATAQUEST (dataquest.io) that are not listed below simply because I am not familiar with them.

  - **Coursera (coursera.org)**
    *Coursera is a provider of massive open online courses (MOOC) founded by Andrew Ng and Daphne Koller of Stanford University in 2012. A popular*

*certificate is John Hopkins University's Data Science Specialization (https://bit.ly/32Gu0v1).*

– **Datacamp (datacamp.com)**
*Founded in 2013, Datacamp hosts a number of well-designed courses and certificates with an interactive programming interface that helps you learn from your mistakes in real time.*

– **edX (edx.org)**
*edX is a MOOC provider created by Harvard and MIT in 2012. Two particularly popular certificate programs are MIT's MicroMasters Program in Statistics and Data Science (https://bit.ly/3sCrFfh) and UC San Diego's MicroMasters Program in Data Science (https://bit.ly/3EA3Nvj).*

- **Websites**

  – **Data Science Central**
  URL: datasciencecentral.com
  *A community resource for data scientists, including discussion forums, blog posts, books, cheat sheets and jobs.*

  – **Data Science @ TheConversation.com**
  URL: https://bit.ly/2QJJwgn
  *The data science section of The Conversation has articles written by academics (a requirement) for the general public, so the standard is rather good.*

  – **Deepmind.com/blog**
  *Founded in 2010 and acquired by Google in 2014, DeepMind are world leaders in AI.*

  – **The Right Question Institute**
  URL: rightquestion.org/
  *The RQI is a non-profit that has developed their own tools (e.g. the Question Formulation Technique) to build people's skills to ask better questions by combining thought processes that occur at different levels.*

  – **Kdnuggets.com**
  *KDnuggets is a comprehensive website covering all aspects and applications of data science with the contents conveniently divided into sections (e.g. Blog/News, Opinions, Education, Tutorials).*

  – **TowardsDataScience.com**
  *This site contains interesting articles with a technical twist by data science practitioners. Articles are usually well referenced.*

- **Podcasts**

  – **Super Data Science Podcast**
  URL: https://www.superdatascience.com/podcast/
  *A fun and eclectic collections of podcasts across all domains and applications of data science. There is something here for everyone.*

  – **The Banana Data Podcast**
  URL: https://banana-data.buzzsprout.com/
  *Podcasts on the latest and most impressive trends and developments in data science. Also available in text format.*

  – **Towards Data Science Podcast**
  URL: https://towardsdatascience.com/podcast/home
  *An equally diverse and entertaining set of interviews on all things data science.*

- Videos

  - **Artificial Intelligence Needs All Of Us (Rachel Thomas, TEDx)**
    URL: https://bit.ly/3s46hvK
    *In her empowering and inclusive message Rachel Thomas disproves the myth that one needs to have the finest machine, degree, or a sophisticated knowledge of mathematics to do data science that makes a difference. A discussion of the triumphs and misconceptions of AI includes how having a fair representation of society in the software teams is the most effective way to tackle algorithmic bias.*

  - **Data Science 101 (Data Professor)**
    URL: https://www.youtube.com/c/DataProfessor
    *Some really good videos by bioinformatics professor Chanin Nantasenamat covering fundamental concepts in data science as well as recommendations on how to learn and free learning resources.*

  - **Intro to Data Science (Steve Brunton)**
    URL: https://bit.ly/3cKCuTG
    *This is Prof. Steven Brunton's excellent introductory course in data science. The videos are short and the explanations are clear and focused on one specific item at a time.*

  - **Introduction to Computational Thinking (MIT)**
    URL: https://computationalthinking.mit.edu
    *An incredibly popular course that teaches the process of computational thinking (decomposition, pattern recognition, abstraction and algorithms) by coding real-world applications using the Julia programming language.*

  - **Idea Sex (James Altucher Series Episode 7)**
    URL: https://bit.ly/3cz32an
    *Truly novel and original ideas came by rarely. Here computer scientist, investor and entrepreneur James Altucher discusses his concept of 'idea sex' where combining already existing ideas can lead to even better ideas. The more you exercise your 'idea muscle', the better you will get at it.*

  - **Light Years Ahead | The 1969 Apollo Guidance Computer (Robert Wills)**
    URL: https://bit.ly/3bU1zvB
    *This is Robert Wills's outstanding introduction to the Apollo Guidance Computer's pioneering design principles. Wills discusses specific problems that occurred during the landing of the spacecraft and the role of the Computer in saving the mission.*

  - **The Future of Data Science—Data Science @ Stanford**
    URL: https://bit.ly/2Z8YVOY
    *An early and interesting debate on the promise, applications and future of data science by leaders in computer science and other disciplines where data science is of key importance.*

  - **We're All Data Scientists (Rebecca Nugent, TEDx).**
    URL: https://bit.ly/32KO63k
    *In this excellent and empowering TEDx talk Rebecca Nugent demystifies data science while explaining how each one of us carries a data scientist inside.*

- Articles

  - Alon U. How to choose a good scientific problem. Molecular Cell 35(6):726–728, 2009.
    *An interesting perspective on how to choose any scientific problem in terms of its interest, difficulty and career stage, and why you should always take your time to ponder about what problems to work on.*

  - Breiman L. Statistical Modeling: The Two Cultures (with comments and a rejoinder by the author). Statist. Sci. 16 (3), pp. 199–231, 2001.
    *A historical paper by Leo Breiman on how machine learning differs from statistical learning.*

  - Davenport TH and Patil DJ. Data Scientist: The Sexiest Job of the 21st Century (Harvard Business Review, October 2012).
    URL: https://bit.ly/359N2ZW.
    *An interesting 10-minute read that provides an account of the early developments that shaped the field of data science in the context of the big data revolution. For example, did you know that Hadoop was developed by Doug Cutting while working at Yahoo!? The other co-founder of Hadoop, Mike Cafarella, was at the time starting his PhD at the University of Washington. 'Hadoop' was actually Doug's son's toy elephant—and today Hadoop being the most popular framework for distributed data storage and processing is synonymous with big data. Most importantly, however, is how Davenport and Patil describe the creative process in data science.*

  - Garcia Martinez A. No, Data Is Not the New Oil (WIRED, 26 February 2019).
    URL: https://bit.ly/3k0BEXc.
    *An interesting reflection on how monetising from one's own data is not as straightforward as some people claim it is.*

  - Lum K and Chowdhury R. What is an "algorithm"? It depends whom you ask (MIT Technology Review, 26 February 2021).
    URL: https://bit.ly/3cyeRNR
    *An up-to-date discussion on the definition of what constitutes an algorithm, how an algorithm differs from a model and whether we should rather change the focus from the design of these systems to their impact.*

  - Madrigal AC. Your Smart Toaster Can't Hold a Candle to the Apollo Computer (The Atlantic, 16 July 2019)
    URL: https://bit.ly/37C6jCR.
    *An insightful analysis of the Apollo Guidance Computer and the tasks it had to accomplished to take the first men to the moon and back.*

  - Nantais J. Data science or Statistics? (Towards Data Science, 27 September 2019).
    URL: https://bit.ly/2YPTCAR.
    *A fun debate on the extent to which statistics does include data science and vice versa.*

  - Press G. A Very Short History of Data Science (Forbes, 28 May 2013).
    URL: https://bit.ly/34MQmd1.
    *A well-researched and lucidly written account of the short (but distinguished) history of data science.*

- Shiftehfar R. Uber's Big Data Platform: 100+ Petabytes with Minute Latency (Uber Engineering, 17 October 2018).
  URL: https://ubr.to/2Z5Xi1h.
  *A detailed and technical explanation of the evolution of Uber's big data architecture over the years as the company's needs shifted with more and faster data and more customers to serve.*

- Vale R. The value of asking questions. Molecular Biology of the Cell 24(6): 680-682, 2013.
  *Biochemist Ronald Vale reflects on the practice of asking questions that has roots in ancient Greece and the Buddhist schools of thought. Although not easy to teach or learn, being able to ask good questions remains the most effective tool of independent learning and inquiry.*

- Yanai I and Lercher M. What is the question? Genome Biology 20(1):289, 2019.
  *A lucidly written and entertaining account on the true nature of the scientific process and how the hallmark of first-class science is the generation of unpredictable questions that lead us onto uncharted territories.*

- **Books**

  - Grus J. *Data Science from Scratch: First Principles with Python (2nd edition* O'Reilly Media Inc., Sebastopol (CA), USA, 2019. ISBN-10: 1492041130.
    *A very well written introduction to the Python programming language as well as to some of the most common techniques in data science.*

  - Irizarry R. *Introduction to Data Science. Data Analysis and Prediction Algorithms with R.* Chapman & Hall/CRC, Boca Raton (FL), USA, 2019. ISBN: 9780367357986.
    *An outstanding, practical introduction to data science using the scientific approach of asking questions on case studies. The R programming language is taught alongside key concepts in probability, statistics, machine learning, data wrangling and visualization, and version control with Git and GitHub.*

  - Johansson F. *The Medici Effect: What Elephants and Epidemics Can Teach Us about Innovation.* Harvard Business School Press, Boston (MA), USA, 2006. ISBN-10: 9781422102824.
    *The Medici Effect describes how innovative ideas often come from people who have no experience in a given field as well as by mixing experts working in completely different domains.*

  - Lewis M. *Moneyball: The Art of Winning an Unfair Game* W. W. Norton & Company, New York, USA, 2004. ISBN-10: 0393324818.
    *The book that describes the data-driven transformation of the Oakland A's into a major challenger in the baseball league by finding value in (and hiring) players that had been overlooked. The film with Brad Pitt and Jonah Hill is based on this book.*

  - Stephens-Davidowitz S. *Everybody Lies: What The Internet Can Tell Us About Who We Really Are.* Bloomsbury Publishing, London, UK, 2017. ISBN-13: 9781408894736.
    *Did you know that people usually lie in surveys and when facing other people, but not when they search online. This wealth of data can be used to understand who we really are in terms of human behaviour, preferences and emotions.*

– Thiel P. *Zero to One: Notes on Start Ups, or How to Build the Future* Virgin Books, London, UK, 2014. ISBN-10: 9780753555194.
*Peter Thiel is one of the most famous entrepreneurs of our time, but besides talking about start-ups he has a unique and interesting point of view on what are really good questions and how to articulate them.*

– Wylie C. *Mindf\*ck: Inside Cambridge Analytica's Plot to Break the World.* Profile Books, London, UK, 2020. ISBN-13: 9781788165006.
*An interesting account on how the established power uses online social media and Big Data technologies to change our perceptions and manipulate us.*

## 1.6   CHAPTER REVIEW QUESTIONS

1. **The prominence and success of data science today is due to:**

   (a) The exponential growth of data.

   (b) The development of novel methods and algorithms.

   (c) The development of faster computers and cheaper storage.

   (d) All of the above.

2. **A successful data science project or initiative rests on:**

   (a) Having as much computational power as possible.

   (b) Finding cheaper storage in the cloud so that we have access to all data available.

   (c) Asking the right question.

   (d) Hiring the right people.

3. **'Data science' means:**

   (a) It is a fancy name for statistics.

   (b) Same thing as 'Big Data'.

   (c) It is a field whose goal is to extract actionable knowledge from data.

   (d) Machine learning.

4. **What sort of questions can data science answer?**

   (a) Mathematical theorems like Fermat's Last Theorem.

   (b) Questions for which the answer is a moving target.

   (c) Questions that can naturally map to existing algorithms.

   (d) Only questions that require complex analytical techniques.

5. **A basic definition of an algorithm is 'a set of steps that describe how to solve a particular problem'. Select some key characteristics of a good algorithm:**

   (a) Interpretability and legibility.

   (b) Simplicity.

   (c) Correctness, efficiency and interpretability.

   (d) Efficiency and interpretability.

6. Can you name and briefly describe the six dimensions of data quality?

7. Uber's Big Data Platform is a central piece in the evolution of Uber's data analysis requirements. Select all statements that are true.

(a) Back in 2014 Uber was already dealing with petabytes of data stored in non-centralised relational databases.

(b) The Hadoop ecosystem was introduced because it was a trendy technology.

(c) Kafka is a fancy name for a relational database.

(d) Spark and Hive were introduced into the architecture of Uber's Big Data Platform because both are provided by the Apache Software Foundation as open source projects.

# CHAPTER 2

# Descriptive Analytics

*The greatest value of a picture is when it forces us to notice what we never expected to see.*

— John Tukey (1915–2000), *American mathematician*

Transforming data into value is the overarching goal of data science. To achieve this we must be able to ask the right question from the data available, in the right context. Questions in data science belong in descriptive or predictive analytics. Descriptive analytics is the exploration of historical data to summarise its main features and uncover its intrinsic structure, the goal of a predictive method is to use some of this historical data to predict unseen values. Descriptive and predictive analytics are closely linked for without a good understanding of a dataset (e.g. its distribution, an understanding of outliers and the intrinsic structure of the data) it is not possible to build accurate predictive models.

Data visualisation is essential because, for one thing, it can reveal fundamental truths about the data that would otherwise remain hidden to numerical analysis. Moreover, humans excel at processing complex visual information, and therefore it is easier to convey a message using the right visualisation rather than using statistical summaries. In this chapter we learn how to think about the visual representation of data, the advantages and limitations of various methods, and how to deal with outliers. Every visualisation problem must be considered in the context of the question and the message to be communicated. While we discuss a set of general guidelines for choosing the right visualisation for exploring, analysing, interpreting and communicating datasets and models, there are no set-in-stone rules and much of visualisation relies on the creativity of the data scientist. This is exemplified here with historical examples of visualisations that saved millions of lives and opened entire fields of research.

Finally we also discuss specific techniques such as cluster analysis and association rule mining whose goal is to uncover the intrinsic structure of data but which are also relevant in predictive analysis.

## 2.1 DESCRIPTIVE AND PREDICTIVE ANALYTICS: WHAT IS THE DIFFERENCE?

The goal of data science is to transform data into value. We can only achieve this by focusing on asking the right question for the problem at hand with the data available. Thus, the focus is put first on the data scientist and their creativity rather than on any computational infrastructure or specific algorithms. One important advantage of focusing on the question is that tasks are easier to discuss than complex algorithms. It is a rookie mistake to start discussing specific methods or algorithms as soon as some data is available.

DOI: 10.1201/b23197-2

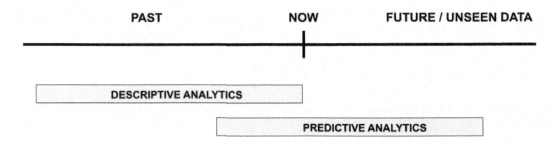

Figure 2.1 Descriptive analytics is historical, whereas predictive analytics tries to infer future (unseen) values.

There are usually multiple ways to achieve an analytical goal given the breadth of methods and algorithms that today exist.

The questions that can be asked in data science can be ascribed to one of two categories: those that fall in the realm of descriptive analytics and those that belong in predictive analytics. A practical way to think about the difference between these two categories is the time point of reference (Fig. 2.1).

- **Descriptive analytics** is the exploration of existing (historical) data to summarise its main characteristics and uncover hidden relationships in the data.

Some of the most common descriptive analytics tasks include being able to simply describe your data in detail (descriptive statistics) and to uncover any naturally occurring groupings in entire datasets (cluster analysis) as well as in transaction data (association rule learning). Inferential statistics is an extension of descriptive analytics and consists of a number of techniques developed on the basis of probability theory whose goal is to generalise the descriptive statistics about a given dataset (the sample) to make estimates and inferences about a wider population. These techniques include confidence intervals to estimate population parameters, and hypothesis tests to answer questions like: 'Are the means of two populations significantly different from each other?'

The result of a descriptive analytics exercise often is a **table of results** or a **visual plot**. Complex projects often use **dashboards** that help visualise elaborate data summaries and also manipulate them for further exploration and analysis. A good example here is the COVID-19 Dashboard by the Center for Systems Science and Engineering (CSSE) at Johns Hopkins University (https://coronavirus.jhu.edu/map.html). These dashboards skillfully integrate massive amounts of information with multiple data visualisation tools such as table summaries, stacked bar plots, Shewhart X-bar charts, coloured maps and infographics to convey a lot of important information yet are easy to navigate (Fig. 2.2). The Global Map of the COVID-19 pandemic provides a quick, up-to-date overview of the coronavirus cases worldwide (split by active and cumulative cases, deaths, recovered, case-fatality ratio and testing rate). The U.S. map portrays all this information in a coloured map of the 50 states, split by county. Clicking on any one county provides access to a status report where the basic information of the pandemic is extended to detail the population by age, race, ethnicity, type of medical insurance, as well as the evolution of the infection and the number of hospital beds (staffed, licensed and ICU).

- **Predictive analytics**, on the other hand, involves the use of historical data to predict unseen or future instances.

Although descriptive analytics is all about exploring and summarising existing data, it is a necessary step for any subsequent predictive analysis. This is because unless we have

Figure 2.2 Snapshot of the Johns Hopkins University Coronavirus Resource Center dashboard.

an understanding of the distribution and intrinsic structure of our data we will not be able to model it appropriately (more on this topic in Chapter 3).

A typical example of predictive analytics is the (time series) forecasting of the value of a stock, the temperature in Barcelona next week or the number of airline passengers (Fig. 2.3). In time series analysis we use historical data with temporal resolution to predict regular fluctuations in the short term as well as general trends over longer periods. Time series analysis is used in almost every domain, including business, climate change research, earthquake prediction, astronomy, weather forecasting, economic history and medicine (e.g. electroencephalography). Clearly, the further into the future that we try to predict, the less accurate that our predictions will be. For instance, with the temperature prediction example the importance of the time variable cannot be ignored because, as we all know, tomorrow's temperature is more dependent on today's temperature than on last month's temperature. Likewise, the values of a stock tomorrow are more dependent on its value today than on last week's values.

The prediction of future values in a time series is often given as an example of predictive analytics because it is easy to visualise the idea that we use values from the past to try to predict future values (Fig. 2.3). However, a prediction is also any situation in which historical data are used to build a model that can predict unseen values that the model has not been trained with, and independently of when these values were generated. For example, let us imagine that we have produced a new anti-cancer drug. There will be some patients for whom the drug will work, and others for whom it will be better to use a different drug. The question here could be: 'Is it possible to accurately predict whether the drug will be effective on new patients?' Any new patient is a 'future' patient, but the time variable is not relevant here in the same dependent way that it is in the time series examples.

Finally, consider too how many different patient features may be used to build such a predictive model. Would height, weight, or eye colour be relevant for predicting the efficacy of an anti-cancer drug? Or perhaps the disease progression state is a better predictor? This is the problem of **feature selection** (Chapter 3): A predictive model should be made up of the most predictive features, and be as simple as possible. For some modern algorithms, such as deep neural networks, feature selection is not a necessary step. It is also possible

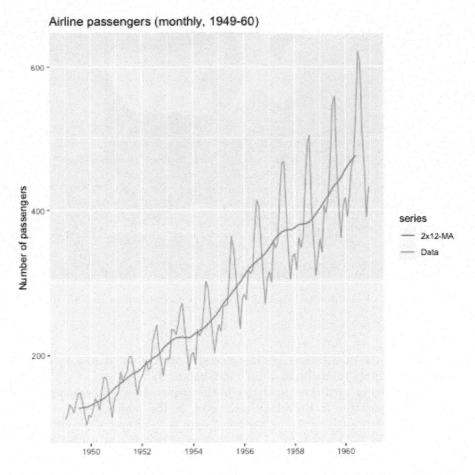

Figure 2.3 Weighted moving averages prediction of the number of airline passengers.

to train complex algorithms with obscene amounts of data with today's fast computers. However, an unnecessarily complicated model is always less *interpretable* than a simpler model (Chapter 3), and rarely superior when the data are structured and have a good representation of meaningful features [23].

## 2.2 DESCRIPTIVE STATISTICS

The goal of a descriptive statistics analysis is to summarise and present the general features of a dataset through numerical calculations and visualisations. This is an essential, unavoidable first step to understand the basic properties of our data. Data variables can be either numerical or categorical (Fig. 2.4). Numerical variables are either discrete (integers) or continuous (decimals), and can be thought of as measurements, such as someone's height or weight, or the number of books they own. Categorical (qualitative) variables are used to represent characteristics such as a person's gender (nominal) or whether they have passed their driving test (Boolean: Yes or No, True or False). It is not possible to add categorical variables together. A special case among the categorical variables is the ordinal variables, which sometimes may be treated mathematically. An example of this are the categorical star ratings of movies (e.g. 1–5 stars).

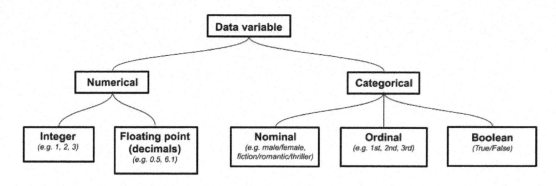

Figure 2.4 The different data variable types.

Just to recapitulate, the basic statistical metrics include:

- **Measures of central tendency**

    - Mean—the sum of observed values divided by the number of observations.
    - Median—the central value in an ordered distribution, also called the 50th percentile.
      *The median is much less affected by outliers (extreme values) and skewed data than the mean is.*
    - Mode—-the most common value in a distribution.
      *In a perfectly normal distribution the mean, median and mode are the same. Nearly all statistical tests require normally distributed data and it is possible to transform non-normally distributed data to fit a normal distribution.*

- **Measures of dispersion (or variability)**

    - Range—the difference between the minimum and maximum values of a distribution.
    - Interquartile range—the difference between the upper (75th) and lower (25th) quartiles (quartiles split a distribution into four equal parts).
    - Variance—a measure of how far each value in a distribution is from the average.
    - Standard deviation—the square root of the variance.
      *The standard deviation is the most commonly used measure of dispersion. Data points of distributions with a low standard deviation tend to cluster around the mean, whereas distributions with high standard deviations have data points spread over a wider range. In a normal distribution ∼34% of data points lie between the mean and one standard deviation above or below the mean. The z-score tells you how many standard deviations from the mean a given data point lies.*

- **Modality**

    - Unimodal—a one-peak distribution.
    - Bimodal—two peaks in a histogram suggest the existence of two groups of observations.
    - Multimodal—three or more peaks.

- **Skewness—a distribution's measure of symmetry**
  *A perfectly normal (symmetric) distribution has a skewness of zero.*

- **Kurtosis—a distribution's measure of 'tailedness'**
  *Distributions with high Kurtosis present heavy tails and more outliers (extreme values) compared to a normal distribution. A normal distribution has a Kurtosis of zero (mesokurtic).*

## 2.3   WHY IS DATA VISUALISATION ESSENTIAL?

The various descriptive statistics, as important as they are for describing datasets, are necessary but never sufficient. We cannot do without properly visualising the datasets. But how did we come to this conclusion?

English statistician Francis Anscombe (1918–2001) while teaching at Yale University asked the following, insightful question: 'Is it possible to produce a series of datasets that look identical in terms of descriptive statistics but which are actually entirely different?'

The answer to this question is what is known as Anscombe's quartet. This group of 11-point $(x,y)$ datasets share identical or nearly-identical means, variances (and therefore standard deviations), $x$-$y$ correlations, slopes of regression lines and the $R^2$ coefficients of the linear regressions yet the four datasets are completely different (Fig. 2.5) [24]. Therefore, this is the proof that the numerical summaries provided by the measures of central tendency and variability above can only go so far to describe a dataset, and may even be deceiving.

We can see how the linear regression models fit to each one of the Anscombe quartet datasets look alike (blue lines in Fig. 2.5), but they are inappropriate for different reasons. For example, *dataset 1* seems to be nicely approximated by a linear model, but *dataset 2* is probably better approximated by a polynomial function. The linear model is also inappropriate for *dataset 3* because only one data point passes through the fitted line whereas another data point is a clear outlier that biases the regression analysis. *Dataset 4* is an example of how a single data point is enough to produce a high correlation coefficient even though the other data points (clustered at the same $x$ value) do not indicate any relationship between the $x$ and $y$ variables.

Therefore data visualisation can reveal a truth that may hide behind simple numerical analysis. Although there are many ways to represent a dataset (e.g. histograms, pie charts, scatter plots), the most important consideration when choosing a type of graphical representation is asking the following question: 'Which type of plot will summarise the most important aspects of the dataset in the context of the question we are asking?'

Data is only as good as it is presented, and our representation must not be confusing or misleading. Sometimes we can choose among different types of plot. If we consider the bar and the pie charts that display the same dataset (Fig. 2.6), which representation do you think will help you compare the tourist nationalities more easily?

## 2.4   THE BOX PLOT: EXTENDING VISUALISATION OF KEY STATISTICS TO MULTIPLE SAMPLES

The types of plots that most people know about (e.g. histograms, pie charts and scatter plots) describe a limited aspect of a dataset. There are other, very powerful representations that are capable of representing additional dimensions, which can provide important insights. For example, American mathematician John Tukey (1915–2000) asked the question of how he could represent key descriptive statistics in a single plot that would allow the quick visual comparison of multiple datasets. The answer was the box plot [25], which at

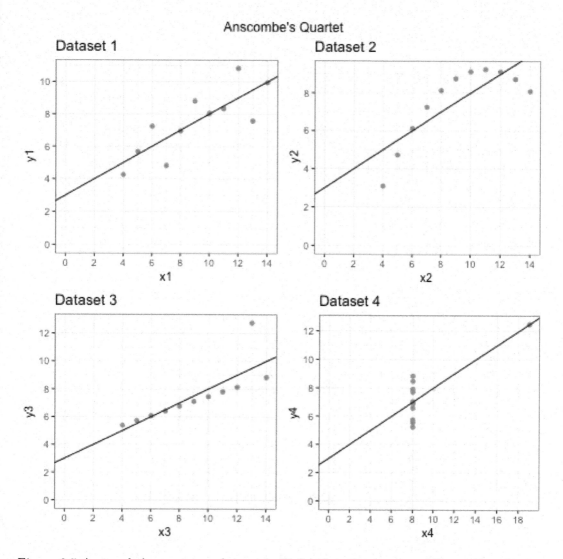

Figure 2.5 Anscombe's quartet, a dataset built for the sole purpose of illustrating the importance of plotting data instead of relying on simple statistical measures.

a glance provides information on key values of a distribution as well as an indication of its degree of normality (Fig. 2.7).

- Min: The smallest data point (excluding outliers).

- Lower whisker: The lower 25% spread.

- $Q_1$: The lower quartile (or 25th percentile) is the median of the lower half of the dataset.

- Median: The middle value of a dataset. The median can also be referred to as $Q_2$ or the 50th percentile.

- $Q_3$: The upper quartile (or 75th percentile) is the median of the upper half of the dataset.

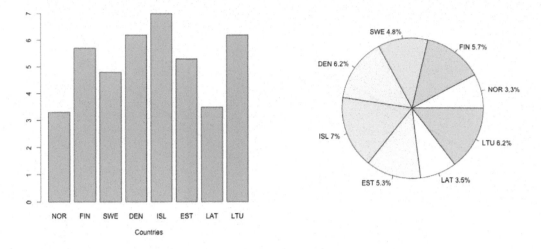

Figure 2.6 Northern European tourists travelling to Spain (fictional dataset).

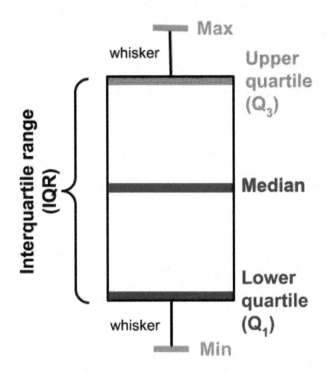

Figure 2.7 The box-plot and its summary of a distribution.

- Upper whisker: The upper 25% spread.

- Max: The largest data point (excluding outliers).

- Interquartile range (IQR): The distance between $Q_3$ and $Q_1$.

Besides getting a quick, visual understanding of a dataset's basic statistics, box plots facilitate the side-by-side comparison of multiple datasets. For example, if we focus on the

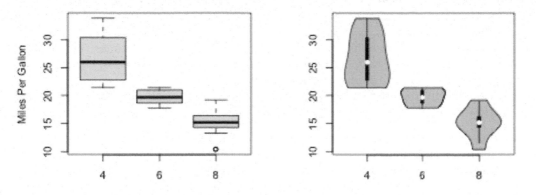

Figure 2.8 Miles per gallon that a sample of four-, six- and eight-cylinder cars can do.

following three datasets detailing how many miles per gallon four-, six- and eight-cylinder cars can do (Fig. 2.8) you will notice that (i) the more cylinders your car has, the less efficient use of petrol it will make; (ii) the spread of the four-cylinder dataset is much larger than the other two datasets, with minimum and maximum values of around 22 and 34; and (iii) the distribution of the six-cylinder dataset appears to be symmetrically centred around the median. The distributions of the two other datasets seems skewed. Skewness is important because many data analysis methods only work with normal distributions. However, skewed datasets may be transformed into normal-looking distributions by taking logarithms.

For all the advantages that box plots have, one disadvantage is that they provide relatively low resolution information. Finer analysis is often required, especially for any follow-up predictive analytics. Moreover, the median of the box plot tells you nothing about fluctuating averages, which might be better visualised with Shewhart X-bar charts. It would also help if box-plots included additional details such as the size of each sample. Finally, a violin plot is similar to a box plot with the addition of a density plot to visualise the shape of the distribution. Here the violin plots of the same datasets reveal that actually only the eight-cylinder dataset (and not the six-cylinder dataset) presents an approximately normal distribution (Fig. 2.8).

This example has considered the relationship between two different variables: The miles per gallon that cars with different cylinders can do. This is called a bivariate analysis. In many cases we will be analysing even more variables at the same time. Additional techniques for bi- and multivariate analysis include *contingency tables, scatter plots, measures of correlation and dependence* and *conditional probability distributions.*

### 2.4.1 Outliers: Keep or Drop Them?

You might have noticed that the box plot of the eight-cylinder dataset presents a single, separate data point represented by a circle with a value of about 11 (Fig. 2.8). This eight-cylinder car model is particularly inefficient when it comes to fuel use and is called an **outlier**, i.e. an extreme value that is clearly different from the rest of the data. An outlier can be a real observation like this one, a false one such as a measurement error (e.g. a flaw in the instrument or an ambiguous answer misinterpreted by the interviewer) or a sampling frame error (a measurement that is not part of the population but which somehow is included in the sample) [26]. It is crucial to understand the nature of outliers and be able to identify them. This is not only because most parametric methods are sensitive to outliers (and therefore affect a model's predictive accuracy) but also because outliers often convey crucial information. For example, a *genuine outlier* might mean some sort of problem such as a medical condition (e.g. too high blood pressure), a security incident (who comes into work at 1 a.m.?) and even bank fraud (why did they wire money 25 times this month?). Anomaly detection is a very important field combining descriptive statistics, clustering, and also a number of predictive analytics techniques [27].

Outliers in univariate data can be detected by sorting the data, clustering (see below), by using data plots (such as box plots, bar charts and scatter plots), as well as by:

- Applying common sense: nobody is 3 meters tall, 200 years old and still alive (wrong values), or runs the 100 meters at the summer Olympics in 10 minutes (wrong units). Sometimes only when we consider multiple variables at once can we spot outliers. For example, being 2 years old is a valid age, and so is being 2 meters tall, but a 2-meter tall child is an outlier.

- Using statistical tests: relatively simple tests are Peirce's [28] and Chauvenet's criteria [29], as well as Dixon's [30] and Grubb's tests [31], but all of these assume that the data comes from a normally distributed population. Dozens of sophisticated tests for outlier detection in all data types have been developed [27].

*Non-genuine outliers* are discarded, but most important of all is to go back to the data source and try to figure out the reason for a bad outlier: Under what circumstances will this type of outlier happen again and how often? There are various approaches to dealing with *genuine outliers*, including keeping them, eliminating them and *winsorising* it (modify its value to make the data point more similar to the other values). The last two options invariably introduce statistical bias [26]. If we decide to retain the genuine outliers for any subsequent analysis, it is key to run the analysis both with and without the outliers and ask how the results and assumptions have changed as a result. Do genuine outliers skew a statistical relationship? Do genuine outliers generate new statistical relationships and are these justified? Most important of all is to bear in mind that *one or more outliers should never constitute the basis for your results.*

## 2.5  FAMOUS HISTORICAL VISUALISATIONS

Thus far we have presented relevant albeit straightforward visualisations. Despite their simplicity, however, the development of each one of these plots always required asking the key question of how to represent a given feature of a dataset. For inspirational purposes and to illustrate how much creativity goes into data visualisation, below we discuss several truly outstanding visualisations that have opened new fields of research and provided major insights into modern history.

### 2.5.1  Florence Nightingale's Soldiers

John Tukey famously said that 'the greatest value of a picture is when it forces us to notice what we never expected to see'. Perhaps one the best demonstrations of this is Florence Nightingale's chart depicting the causes of English soldiers' deaths during the Crimean War (1853–1856). Nightingale (1820–1910) was at the time a nurse organising the care for wounded soldiers when she realised that the major reason for the death of soldiers was their unhygienic living conditions: Clothes infested with lice and fleas, dirty linens and rats running around meant that soldiers were dying more of infections than from battle wounds.

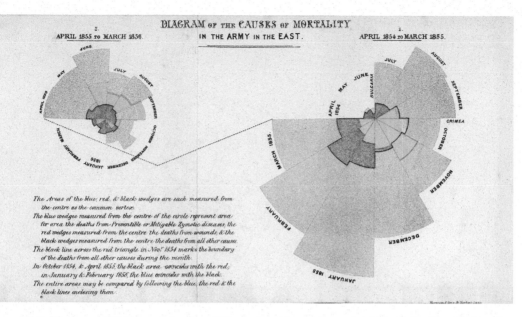

Figure 2.9 Florence Nightingale's chart displaying the causes of soldiers' deaths during the Crimean war (1853–1856).

Clearly, Nightingale had to let this be known, not only because of the medical implications but also because her findings could change the fate of the war. Using data that Nightingale herself collected she developed a type of pie chart (known today as a polar area chart) that she used to convey her findings to the chief doctors with the hope that they would implement the necessary changes. Nightingale's visualisation unequivocally shows at a glance that many more soldiers were dying from cholera, typhus and dysentery (blue areas) than from battle wounds (red areas) (Fig. 2.9). The subsequent introduction of sanitation measures (like hand washing) prevented the spread of infectious diseases and unnecessary deaths (Fig. 2.9, left diagram). Her ideas were completely revolutionary at the time, and Nightingale passed down in history not only as an statistics and data visualisation pioneer but also as the founder of modern nursing. Russia ended up losing the Crimean war to the alliance of the United Kingdom, the Ottoman Empire, Sardinia and France.

### 2.5.2 John Snow and the Transmission of Cholera

Around the same time as Florence Nightingale, physician John Snow (1813–1858) was also doing far-reaching work. In 1854 London was experiencing a deadly cholera epidemic. Back then, cholera was believed to be passed on by breathing in 'bad air' from rotting organic matter. Snow's medical training and his experience with patients led him to believe differently. He likely asked himself: 'How can I prove that cholera is not transmitted by air and thus its spread can be controlled?'

Snow then set himself to the task of quantifying and mapping cholera deaths onto a London street map while interviewing local residents. Snow's famous map shows that the Soho outbreak could be mapped to a single (contaminated) water pump on Broad St (Fig. 2.10) [32]. This indirect evidence sufficed Snow to persuade the local council to disable the Broad St. water pump, which in turn limited the spread of the disease. By using a single visualisation Snow managed not only to gain key insights into cholera's method

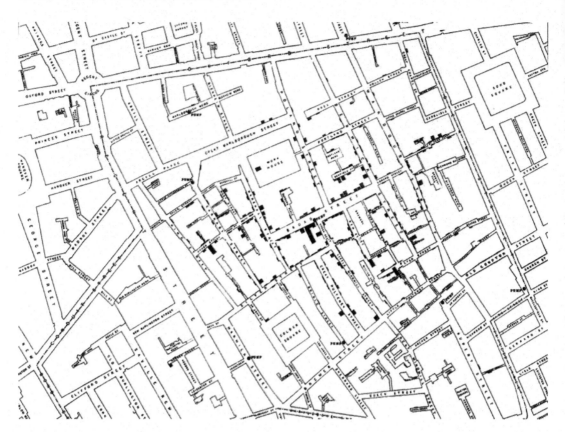

Figure 2.10 John Snow's map depicting the numbers of deaths from cholera in London's Soho.

of transmission but also influenced worldwide changes in public health policies (e.g. the construction of improved sanitation facilities) that have saved many lives since then.

Nightingale and Snow were two of the most creative individuals in Victorian medicine. They showed once and for all how by asking the right question and combining measurements with relatively simple albeit ingenious visualisations it is possible to answer questions of global importance. Their dedication and creativity eventually resulted in the creation of two fields, nursing [33] and modern epidemiology [34].

### 2.5.3   Napoleon's Defeat or the Most Brutal Military Tactic in History

Charles Minard's story is very different from those of Nightingale and Snow. Minard (1781–1870) was a talented engineer and cartographer working for the French government who set himself the task of teaching a lesson that nobody would ever forget.

In 1812, Napoleon led the world's largest army in an attempt to conquer Russia. This enterprise, however, turned into one of the greatest disasters in military history [35]. Minard's map (drawn in 1869) stands as one of the most impressive statistical visualisations ever made (Fig. 2.11). It shows Napoleon's Grande Armée departing the Russian-Polish border towards Moscow, and their way back. The information represented in this map includes:

- The number of men, represented by the width of the lines (1 mm = 10,000 men).

- The direction of travel (yellow towards Moscow; black for the way back).

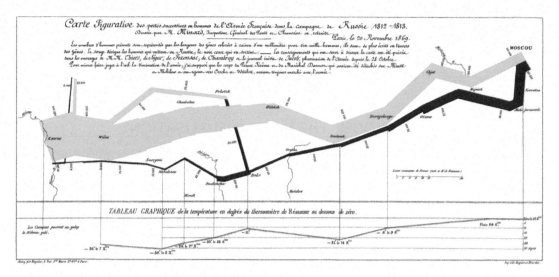

Figure 2.11 Charles Minard's representation of Napoleon's French invasion of Russia (1812).

- The distance travelled.

- The latitude and longitude (Minard's map can be superimposed onto a map of Europe and it will stretch from Kaunas (Lithuania) to Moscow.

- The location relative to specific cities.

- The location relative to specific dates.

- The temperature.

A function in two dimensions normally represents two variables ($x$ and $y$). Minard managed to represent seven different variables on two dimensions—a beautiful example of how graphics can be used to explain complex events.

What most people do not know is that Minard's superior visualisation is also an account of one of the most brutal military tactics in history. Despite Napoleon having conquered Moscow and the Tsar having fled Russia, the Russians still refused to surrender. In this situation, Napoleon realised that there was no point in extending the conflict over the upcoming winter months for which they were not prepared. Thus in late October 1812 Napoleon decided to retreat his remaining 110,000 men. The Russians would not waste this opportunity to decimate the Grande Armée. But how did they achieve this? Simply by letting the French walk back the way they came during their retreat. There was not a single encirclement of the French army, although the Russians kept bleeding the troops with regular raids. Most importantly, however, in each of these confrontations the Russians always gave the French the possibility to escape towards the west. The value of this tactic is rooted in human psychology: In the face of danger we can either *fight* or *flight*. A brutal encirclement would have achieved less because when you remove the flight option, fighting for your life is the only possibility and this would have given the French a psychological edge. However, if you have the choice to escape or surrender, soldiers always take the latter because fighting is unpredictable. Fighting and likely dying is worse than surrendering and staying alive. This is the reason why professional armies never massacre their prisoners. The Russians made the French think that walking west while being hungry and plagued by diseases in the middle of the Russian winter was safer than facing the Russian army. By giving them hope to escape is how the Russians made the French lose the only advantage they still had.

At the start of the French invasion of Russia, Napoleon's army consisted of about 685,000 soldiers. Only about 10,000 (or 1.5%) returned. This single event driven by the exploitation of human psychology marked the beginning of the end of Napoleon's empire [35].

## 2.6  HOW CAN WE CHOOSE THE RIGHT VISUALISATION?

Without visualisations we rely on numerical analyses which, as we learnt with Anscombe's quartet, may not tell the truth about the data. Moreover, statistics are poorly understood by most people. Humans, however, are exceptional at processing complex information when presented in visual form. This is because in the course of evolution the brain structures involved in visual processing have expanded dramatically in all primates, including specific anatomical and functional specialisations not seen in other mammals [36, 37]. Our eyes are able to distinguish subtle variations in shape, size, orientation, position, hue and brightness across multiple dimensions. Therefore, choosing the right visualisation is key for exploring, analysing, interpreting and communicating datasets and models from which informed data-driven decisions can be made.

Data visualisation is a large and active field of research, and it would be simplistic to give a number of set-in-stone recommendations. Besides, there is much room for creativity when it comes to presenting one's data and results. There are already excellent and more extensive resources that discuss the principles of data visualisation over a few pages [38], or as books written for business people [39], for computer scientists looking to dive into mathematical theory and algorithms [40], and for beginners wishing to use R and the powerful ggplot2 package [41]. In the 'Further reading' section at the end of this chapter a number of useful websites are listed that will help you become familiar with standard solutions and tricks for visualising specific types of data (Beautiful News Daily, The Economist's Graphic Detail, The Tableau Blog) as well as poor visualisation solutions from which we may learn even more (Reddit's Data Is Ugly, WTF Visualizations).

However, when facing a data visualisation problem, or the presentation of data before an audience, there are a number of questions that we must always ask:

1. **What is your audience like?**

   Thinking about your audience will help you focus on your message and the level at which it should be delivered. Does the audience have any expertise in the field, or even any exposure to statistics and data visualisation?

   Giving a talk at your children's school is different from giving a TEDx talk, which is again different from giving a seminar at a scientific meeting where experts in your field will scrutinise every word you say. You must learn to split your audience, for example by:

   - Background knowledge: What can we assume they already know and understand about the topic? We should not explain basic concepts unnecessarily, or dive into concepts that are too complex without providing a gentle introduction.

   - Statistical and data visualisation literacy: How much statistical and visualisation detail can we provide before our audience gets lost? What is the minimum amount of detail necessary?

   - Job role: Are we presenting before technically-oriented people or executives? Managers typically only want to hear the high-level summary without too many details.

Finally, it is also a good idea to let a colleague look at your visualisation: Can they understand the message you are trying to convey right away?

2. **What message do you want to convey?**

For this it is useful to use just pen and paper and think about the particular aspect of the data that tells the key story. For example, is the goal of the visualisation to compare amounts, proportions, distributions or relationships?

If multiple visualisations are necessary, then there must be a logical thread joining them together, both in the message and the logic behind the plots used, including using the same colour codes. Also, is there a particular context in which the data should be presented to facilitate their interpretation?

3. **What is the most appropriate type of chart?**

As discussed above, using the right chart can reveal a truth that would otherwise remain hidden behind simple numerical analysis. Of all the different types of graph that exist there is usually more than one type that can be used for representing specific messages (amounts or value comparisons, proportions, distributions and relationships [38]).

However, there is not always a textbook answer to the question of which type of plot will best summarise the most important aspect of a particular dataset. Every visualisation problem must be considered in the context of the question and the message to be communicated. Still, some universal truths include: Pie charts are only useful when dealing with a maximum of three of four segments of really different sizes. Otherwise, using a bar chart is normally the better choice (Fig. 2.6). However, when representing the variation of multiples values over time line plots are superior to bar charts. Scatterplots are effective for representing relationships between variables, especially when size and colour are added to the symbols to make the plot more information-rich. Table 2.1 includes some standard and advanced visualisation methods that might be appropriate for specific types of data.

Further tips include:

- The use of **colour** is incredibly powerful as humans find it easier to remember colourful visualisations [42].

  Different colours and intensities can be used to highlight relevant aspects of the data. For example, the graph representing the association rules mined from a transaction dataset (Fig. 2.18) combines directionality (all items point towards coffee) with colour intensity and (circular) item size to convey key statistical metrics of the association rules such as their support and lift.

  We must never represent data in a way that contradicts standard conventions. For example, darker always means higher density and the colour of the sea is blue, not brown.

  We must use a colour scheme that is friendly to the colour-blind, for which the ColorBrewer resource (colorbrewer2.org, [43]) is of great help. ColorBrewer's colour system is available as libraries for both Python (seaborn [44]) and R (RColorBrewer [45]).

- Our representation must not be **confusing** or **misleading**, for example by cherry picking data to show a misleading trend that fits a specific message. Other equally bad practices include focusing only on a narrow set of values to make the differences appear bigger than they are: for example, if the Y axis only goes from 500 to 520, and the heights of two bars are 500 and 518, it will look like there

TABLE 2.1   Visualisations Methods That Tend to Work for Specific Data Types

| Type of data | | | | |
|---|---|---|---|---|
| Hierarchical | Temporal | Multi-dimensional | Geospatial | Network |
| -Dendrogram | -Timeline | -Histogram, bar chart | -Dot distribution map | -Network diagram |
| -Radial map ('radial tree') | -Gantt chart | -Scatter plot | -Choropleth map | -Matrix |
| -Hyperbolic tree ('hypertree') | -Theme river | -Heatmap | -Cartogram | -Tube map |
| -Wedge stack graph | -Sankey diagram (like Minard's map) | -Treemap chart | -Dasymetric map | -Dependency graph |
| -Icicle chart | | -Marimekko chart ('market map') | -Contour line map | -Alluvial diagram |
| | | -Radar chart ('spider chart') | -Geospatial data map | |

is a large difference. However, if the baseline is not omitted and we also include all over values and see that these fluctuate between 490 and 530, then the real differences are smaller.

Uncertainty (standard deviation, standard error, confidence and credible intervals) must also be shown as these are key aspects of data and models [38].

- When inspecting someone else's visualisations remember that *human vision may be fooled easily*. For example, fraudsters have become very good at anticipating how fraud detection systems analyse and visually present information for inspection. With this knowledge, they can customise the type and size of the fraud to go undetected. Fraud detection is a really hard problem that requires multiple advanced analytical and visualisation techniques [46, 47].

## 2.7   CLUSTER ANALYSIS: MOST DATA HAVE AN INTRINSIC STRUCTURE

All data except random data have an intrinsic structure, and we can learn much from understanding the anatomy of a dataset. Clustering is a key technique for uncovering natural groupings in the data as well as for detecting outliers and is an example of **unsupervised learning** (Fig. 2.12).

Clustering is defined as the organisation of a set of objects into differentiated groups so that objects in the same group are more similar to each other than to objects in

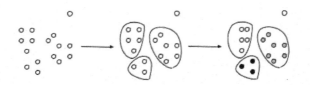

Figure 2.12 A clustering algorithm uncovers three natural groups and an outlier (toy example).

other groups. But what type of questions require understanding how the instances group together?

As a toy example to think about the many different ways of splitting a dataset, let us imagine that you manage an airport that must close because of an imminent snow storm. You still have 100 passengers in the airport that must be taken to hotels for an overnight stay. Assuming that it is more practical to manage smaller groups of people, how would you separate these 100 passengers into groups?

To make the problem simpler, let us also assume that all passengers are travelling individually (without their families). How many different ways of partitioning this group of people into smaller groups can you think of?

- If there are three hotels in the vicinity with 20, 20 and 60 available rooms, that might be a natural way to split the passengers: separate the first 20, followed by the following 20 and then the rest.

- Let us say that four officers are available to take care of these 100 passengers: It might make sense to make four equal groups of 25 people each.

- Let us say that these are international passengers and that the airport officers speak multiple languages, but not all at the same time: Should passengers be grouped by nationality?

- Or should we separate the passengers by their expected time of departure the next day in order to minimise shuttle trips?

Most real-life clustering needs are more complicated than this toy example. However, the example is useful to illustrate the point that there are always multiple ways to define a group, often using multiple criteria. Ultimately it all depends on your specific problem and context, and this is again why asking the right question is the key starting point of any data science exercise.

When we know little about the organisation of our data, clustering typically is the first step. Over one hundred different clustering algorithms exist which differ in how they define a cluster mathematically, and they have been grouped into 19 different categories (e.g. by partition, such as $K$-means, by hierarchy, fuzzy theory, graph theory, swarm intelligence and even quantum theory) [48]. There is no single best clustering algorithm for all problems.

When it comes to evaluating the results of a clustering exercise, there is no single answer either. Different methods have been proposed such as internal clustering quality scores and the evaluation of the results on artificial or benchmark datasets [49]. However, none of these are satisfactory as a universal metric because clustering results cannot be treated as independent mathematical problems but must always be analysed in the context of the question [49]. Perhaps if our data are labeled in some way (pre-classified by some criteria) we can use this information to determine if our clusters match this labelling criteria (should they match, anyway?). And most importantly: Are the resulting clusters any useful for the intended application?

A typical strategy is to start off with a clustering algorithm that we think would be appropriate, then do the analysis and perhaps modify some of the parameters, evaluate the resulting clusters, and iterate until we come up with a set of clusters that makes sense in the context of the question we are asking.

## 2.7.1 Clustering in Practice: What's the Most Dangerous State in the USA?

We will illustrate clustering using the $K$-means algorithm and a well-known dataset from 1973 called 'USarrests' listing all the violent crimes per 100,000 residents in every state of

TABLE 2.2   Values for the First Six States in the USarrests
Dataset (1973)

|            | Murder | Assault | Urban population | Rape |
|------------|--------|---------|------------------|------|
| Alabama    | 13.2   | 236     | 58               | 21.2 |
| Alaska     | 10.0   | 263     | 48               | 44.5 |
| Arizona    | 8.1    | 294     | 80               | 31.0 |
| Arkansas   | 8.8    | 190     | 50               | 19.5 |
| California | 9.0    | 276     | 91               | 40.6 |
| Colorado   | 7.9    | 204     | 78               | 38.7 |
| ...        | ...    | ...     | ...              | ...  |

the USA. Violent crimes include murder, assault and rape. A fourth column includes the percent of the population living in urban areas (Table 2.2).

What sort of questions can be asked with this dataset? One obvious question would be: 'What is the state with the largest number of murders?'

In 1973 it was actually Georgia (17.2 murders/100,000 persons). If we look at the statistics for rape, however, Georgia appears to be much safer than Nevada (25.8 vs 46.0 rapes/100,000 persons).

However, picking the largest number from a table is trivial and we do not need a computer to do that. But what if the question were: 'What was the most *dangerous* state in the USA in 1973?' To answer this question we would have to compare all the crime statistics for all states, and group the states accordingly, which we cannot easily do by hand.

*K*-means is the most popular clustering algorithm for splitting a dataset into a pre-specified number ($K$) of clusters. Each cluster is characterised by a *centroid*, which is the middle of the cluster (the mean of all observations assigned to the cluster). Two additional conditions that must be optimised are:

- The observations within the same cluster must be as similar to each other as possible, which mean they have **high intra-class similarity**

- The observations in foreign clusters must be as dissimilar as possible, which mean they present **low inter-class similarity**.

The steps of a *K*-means clustering exercise include:

1. Calculation of the distances between all observations in the dataset. This step is common to all clustering algorithms.

   Many different distance functions exist, such as the (default) Euclidean distance, the Pearson's correlation distance, the cosine distance and the Mahalanobis distance. The choice of distance metric is key because it has a strong influence on the clustering results. For example, when dealing with outliers Spearman's correlation might be a better choice than Pearson's correlation. However, when clustering gene expression data Pearson's correlation might be preferred because the correlation is performed over thousands of genes and here the effect of outliers is minimised [50].

   If we display the distances between all the observations in the USarrests dataset on a matrix and colour them by values of distance, we can start to see blocks of similarity (Fig. 2.13). That is, states with similar crime rates are displayed as blocks of similar colour.

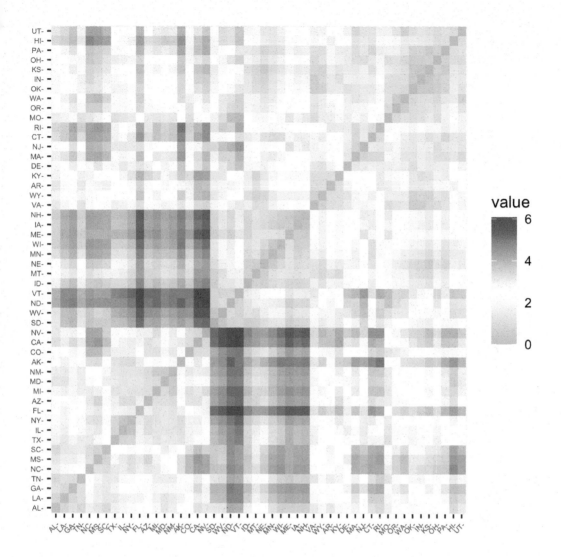

Figure 2.13 Heatmap displaying the distances among all US states.

2. Once we decide the number of clusters $(K)$ into which the dataset will be split, the algorithm randomly selects $K$ observations from the dataset to serve as the initial centroids.

3. In the **cluster assignment step** the $K$-means algorithm assigns the remaining observations to its closest centroid.

4. **Centroid update** is a particular step in $K$-means clustering where the algorithm calculates the new mean value of each cluster. The observations might be reassigned to different clusters as a result.

The cluster assignment and centroid update steps are repeated until observations are no longer reassigned to new clusters (i.e. when convergence is achieved). Steps 2, 3 and 4 constitute the core definition of the $K$-means algorithm.

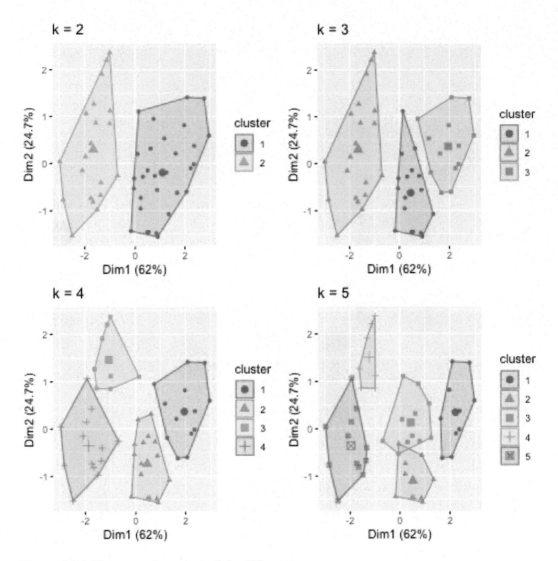

Figure 2.14 *K*-means clustering of the US states.

5. **Cluster evaluation and visualisation** is the final step where the resulting clusters are evaluated in the context of the specific question.

The visualisation of the various clusters of states by danger is useful because it helps us to start thinking right away. Although with *K*-means we can divide the data into as many clusters as we want (Fig. 2.14), there are also ways to determine the optimal number of clusters, e.g. by plotting a chart showing the *within sum of squares* values for different *K* values (calculation not shown). Here we must find the point where the within sum of squares value is minimised against a maximum number of resulting clusters. In this example, four is the optimal number of clusters, suggesting that the USarrests dataset has an intrinsic structure consisting of four groups of data. Therefore there are no simply 'dangerous' and 'safe' states, but various groups of states with different levels of danger for citizens. In the following figure, without going into too much detail, the states in the blue polygon are the most dangerous and those in the green polygon are the least dangerous (Fig. 2.15).

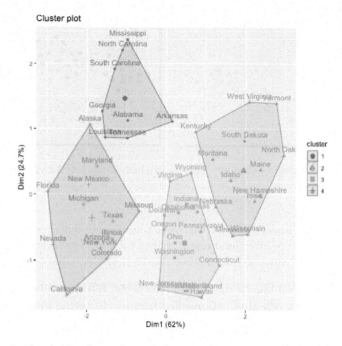

Figure 2.15 Four is the optimal number of clusters to separate all the US states in terms of reported crime.

## 2.7.2 Advantages and Limitations of $K$-Means Clustering

$K$-means has the advantage of being simple and fast, and scales well to large datasets with a limited number of dimensions (features). As with any algorithm, we must also take into account its limitations and possible solutions in the context of our question and dataset:

1. The choice of $K$ in advance assumes prior knowledge of the data. As we learnt above, there are ways to calculate the optimal number of clusters. Alternatively, we can always run $K$-means multiple times for as many values of $K$ as we wish and compare the resulting clusters.

2. The resulting clusters are dependent on the initial random choice of centroids. Another implication of this initial random choice is that rearranging the order of the data will likely produce different results.

   Since multiple runs of the $K$-means algorithm might produce slightly different clustering results, an idea is to select the solution with the lowest total within-cluster sum of squares. As the number of clusters $(K)$ increases, performing $K$-means *seeding* might be a good idea [51].

3. $K$-means is sensitive to outliers because all observations are treated the same when it comes to calculating distances. There are other clustering algorithms that are less sensitive to outliers such as the PAM algorithm ('partition around medoids').

4. $K$-means has trouble dealing with clusters of different sizes and densities (Fig. 2.16).

   When dealing with naturally imbalanced clusters (Fig. 2.16) we can try and modify the cluster boundaries and their shapes ('generalisation').

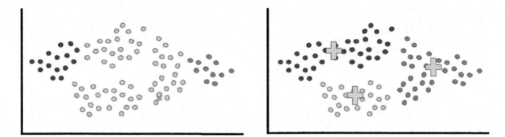

Figure 2.16 An intuitive set of clusters (left) and those calculated by $K$-means showing the centroids (right).

5. $K$-means does not scale well with increasing number of features (dimensions). In such cases we may try to reduce the dimensionality by applying techniques such as spectral clustering [52] or Principal Component Analysis (PCA, Chapter 3).

The USarrests is a well-known dataset to which the $K$-means clustering algorithm can be applied. Other well-known applications of $K$-means clustering include:

- Document classification, where we classify documents into a predefined number of categories by tags or topics, as well as by content.

- Customer segmentation: Given a database of customers, it is possible to discretise them into groups according to specific variables such as age, spending habits, income, or level of education. Understanding a particular segment and being able to target it is very important when trying to launch new products (e.g. luxury products targeting specific customers).

- Insurance fraud detection: Given a list of past fraudulent insurance claims, any new claim can be compared against these and see if by content or form it clusters anywhere close to previous fraudulent patterns. This has important applications in healthcare and car insurance programs.

Even though it is possible to determine the 'optimal' number of clusters for a $K$-means clustering exercise, it is always worth comparing the results to those of another clustering algorithm such as **hierarchical clustering**. Hierarchical clustering does not need a pre-specified number of clusters and the output is a *dendrogram*, i.e. a tree-like representation of the observations showing how they group by distance and mode of clustering (e.g. single-linkage or complete-linkage clustering) [53]. The downside is that we must have a way to set a cut-off in a dendrogram and thus decide what are clusters (below the cut-off value) and what are outliers (above the cut-off value) (Fig. 2.17).

## 2.8 ASSOCIATION RULES

In the previous example of grouping US states by their recorded level of danger we used $K$-means clustering to uncover the structure inherent in the data. Like clustering, **association rule mining** can also uncover hidden relationships in large datasets in the form of naturally occurring combinations. Association rules are one of the best studied models for data mining and another example of unsupervised learning.

For example, it is not difficult to imagine how the various crimes in the USarrests dataset (murder, assault and rape) can occur in combinations. However, with only three features there is a limited number of combinations. Association rule theory (also called

**Cluster Dendrogram**

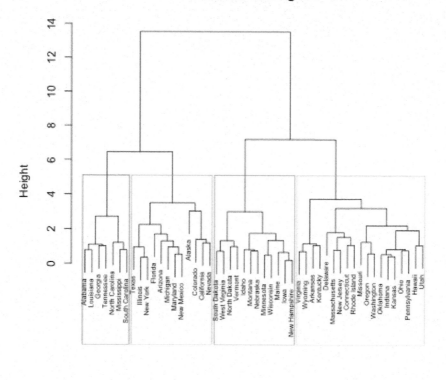

dist
hclust (*, "ward.D2")

Figure 2.17 The hierarchical clustering result mostly agrees with $K$-means clustering when the cut-off is set to identify the same number of clusters ($K = 4$).

market basket analysis) was developed to take advantage of transaction data recorded by point-of-sale systems in supermarkets [54]. The question that association rule mining seeks to answer is: 'What products are typically bought together?' For example, customers that buy a pencil and paper are likely to buy a rubber or ruler too. This is called an IF-THEN rule.

Another well-known example is the famous association between beer and diapers: the analysis of 1.2 million market baskets from some 25 stores revealed that between 5 and 7 p.m. men were buying diapers and beer, or beer and diapers. The explanation was that as their wives sent them to the Osco Drug store for diapers in the evening (or on the way back from work), they would also grab a 6-pack of beer. There are doubts as to how much of this story is true [55], but it is still a useful reminder of how association rules can uncover unexpected relationships.

Knowing which items occur in specific combinations can provide tremendous insights for formulating marketing, sales, operational and customer support strategies, including:

- In-store promotion and strategic placement of products throughout the store.

- Development of *cross-selling* (selling an additional product or service to an existing customer) and *up-selling* strategies (offering the customer more expensive items or upgrades to generate extra revenue).

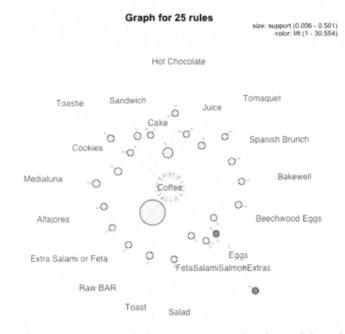

Figure 2.18 Network representation of the association rules derived for a bakery in Reading (UK).

- Launching inbound marketing strategies on social networks, for example by sending out promotional coupons to customers for products related to items they recently bought.

- Development of new products with combined functionalities.

- Web clickstream analysis for website optimisation: The analysis of web logs can provide much knowledge on user behaviour, which can be used to optimise websites and present pages that other users with a similar behaviour have viewed [56].

- Inventory optimisation to decrease storage costs and optimise profits.

- Complaints and customer reviews: These can be discretised and analysed for associations with specific products, time of day or week, promotions and salespeople.

- Fraud detection: Credit card transaction datasets are mined to identify normal and abnormal patterns of behaviour [57].

In a typical application of association rule mining, a real dataset containing $\sim 25,000$ transactions from a bakery in Reading (UK) showed that coffee is the number one product and that customers order coffee in combination with a number of other products, such as toastie, cake, alfajores and salad. The graph plot draws relationships between the various items with the arrows indicating the direction of the relationship (Fig. 2.18). Color intensity and circle size aid in the interpretation of the data.

A number of marketing recommendations for this bakery included setting up combos for breakfast (e.g. eggs + coffee, toast + coffee, cookies + coffee), lunch (e.g. Spanish brunch + coffee) and the afternoon (e.g. media luna + coffee, cake + coffee). Also, anyone buying coffee alone, at any time of the day, should actively be offered a combo.

Another application of the analysis of transaction data is in medical diagnosis where rare combinations of symptoms can provide useful leads for doctors, both in a descriptive and in a predictive manner [58] (a short note on predictive rule learning is provided below). For example, think of a population with a high incidence of a condition that cannot be diagnosed and which we are trying to prevent, such as sarcopenia (muscle weakening) in senior people. Patients with weak muscles can easily lose balance, fall and injure themselves, which brings a whole new set of problems to the health system. Since there are no predictive tests for sarcopenia, an idea might be to record all symptoms and ask the following question: 'Which symptoms are found in sarcopenic patients that can help anticipate muscle weakening?' By recognising these symptoms in those aged over 65 (e.g. diabetes, obesity, bone fracture), these patients might be put on specific programmes to proactively delay the onset of sarcopenia and thus prevent a number of associated health problems.

## 2.8.1 Quantifying the Relevance of Association Rules

An association rule always has an **antecedent or body** and a **consequent or head**. In the example below {bread,eggs} are the antecedent and {milk} is the consequent.

$$\{bread, eggs\} \rightarrow \{milk\}$$

The first step in building a set of association rules involves determining the optimal thresholds of **support** and **confidence** that will work for our dataset [54, 59] and question. Let us say that the $\{bread, eggs\} \rightarrow \{milk\}$ association has the following support and confidence values:

$$\text{Support} = 10\%; \ \text{Confidence} = 50\%$$

- **Support** is the percentage of transactions that contain both the antecedent and the consequent, that is the entire **itemset**. Here a support of 10% means that 10% of the customers' baskets contain bread, eggs and milk. The higher the support the better: For example, we may only want to consider as significant those itemsets that are present in, say, 100 out of every 10,000 transactions (i.e. have a support of 0.01).

$$Support\ (\{X\} \rightarrow \{Y\}) = P(X \cap Y) = \frac{Transactions\ containing\ both\ X\ and\ Y}{Total\ number\ of\ transactions}$$

- **Confidence** is the percentage of transactions containing both bread and eggs that also contain milk, i.e. the likelihood of buying milk if a customer already has bread and eggs in the basket. Here a confidence of 50% means that of all the customers that buy milk, only one out of two will also buy bread and eggs. In other words, confidence measures the conditional probability of the occurrence of the consequent given the antecedent.

$$Confidence\ (\{X\} \rightarrow \{Y\}) = P(Y|X) = \frac{Transactions\ containing\ both\ X\ and\ Y}{Transactions\ containing\ X}$$

In practice a support of 10% indicates is that if we have 1,500 customers per day, an average of 150 of those will buy bread, eggs and milk together. Thus, the support provides an idea of the market size. Confidence, on the other hand, is an indication of how popular specific itemsets already are in the customers' minds. Every rule is different and must be understood in its precise context and interplay of support and confidence, for a particular type of clientele (Table 2.3).

TABLE 2.3   Confidence vs Support in Association Rule Mining

|  | **High confidence** | **Low confidence** |
|---|---|---|
| **High support** | The ideal situation. However, a rule that has both high confidence and support is most likely already obvious. | These are the rules for popular products, which most likely pair with many other products. The precision of the recommendation will be limited. |
| **Low support** | These rules represent less popular products but the associations are robust. | Rules of no interest. |

One drawback of the confidence measure is that it tends to misrepresent the importance of an $\{X\} \rightarrow \{Y\}$ association. For example, if $Y$ (milk in this case) is also a very popular item, there will be a higher chance that a transaction containing $X$ (bread and eggs) will also contain $Y$, thus inflating the confidence measure. A third measure called the **lift** is used to account for the base popularity of both the antecedent and the consequent:

$$Lift\ (\{X\} \rightarrow \{Y\}) = \frac{Support\ (X \cup Y)}{Support\ (X)\ x\ Support\ (Y)}$$

- A **lift > 1** means that the relationship between the antecedent and the consequent is more significant than would be expected if the two sets were independent and therefore the rule is likely to be genuine.

- A **lift < 1** means this is most likely a spurious association.

Whenever we need to find the optimum combination of two or more parameters, such as support and confidence here, a practical approach is to first get a feel for how many rules are obtained for various combinations of thresholds (Fig. 2.19). Too few rules convey limited information, and too many rules with limited confidence are difficult to implement. A question that may be asked in the context of this bakery is: 'What is an appropriate level of support and confidence for this dataset and how many rules can be implemented in practice?'

For a relatively small dataset of this size (25,000 transactions) a support level of 0.1% will contain transactions with at least 25 itemsets, which may seem 'enough', but this is really a low support threshold. Such low support values are more prone to producing spurious associations, i.e. random events that occur with unexpected frequency in the data.

A support level of 10% returns only a few rules, all with low confidence levels and no rule with a confidence of at least 50% (Fig. 2.19). This means that there are very few associations that are relatively frequent (at 10%) which present a reasonable degree of confidence. For a support level of 5% only two rules are identified with a confidence level of at least 50%.

With a support level of 1% we find 12 rules with a confidence level of at least 50%, whereas with a support level of 0.5% we obtain 25 rules with a confidence of at least 50%. However, these 25 rules represent less popular transactions, which makes them less optimal for the implementation of cross-selling strategies.

Therefore, the answer to the question of what the optimal set of association rules is not straightforward and must be answered in the context of their specific implementation. One valid question here would be: Given a set of rules with a confidence of at least 50% and a lift greater than 1, how many would I be able to implement in practice?

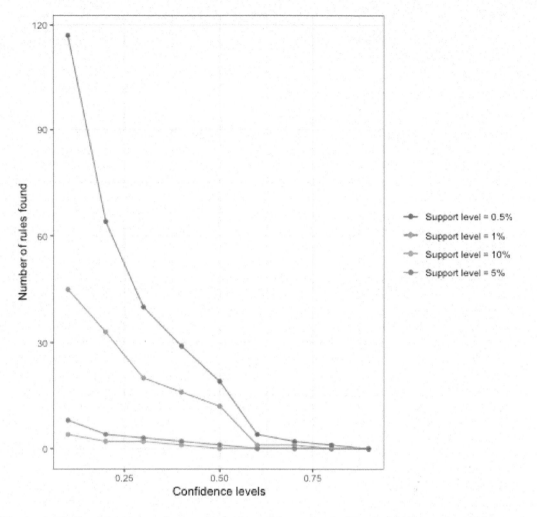

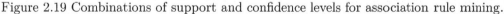

Figure 2.19 Combinations of support and confidence levels for association rule mining.

Rules with relatively high support will be applicable to a larger number of transactions. However, if instead of a bakery the business is a long-tail retailer such as a hardware store, it might be impossible to derive rules with high support. High confidence rules normally lead to recommendations that drive a higher response rate, but we still need a large enough transaction dataset to derive statistically meaningful rules.

Fig. 2.18 includes a set of 12 rules with a support level of at least 1% and a confidence level of at least 50%. All such rules have lift values greater than 1, but none of these rules is overwhelmingly superior to any the others. Moreover, all rules converge towards coffee, which is not particularly illuminating because this must be a known fact for the employees. It does not make sense for a small establishment to launch 12 combo offers at the same time as this might lead to *cognitive overload* and thus end up repelling customers. What can be done in such situations?

Besides collecting more data, the same type of analysis can be repeated while segmenting the data and asking more specific questions (called *differential analysis*):

- Are there any rules that stand out on specific days of the week?

- What about specific times (e.g. morning vs afternoon)?

- What about specific seasons (when enough data is available)?

- Are there store-specific rules (e.g. for shops with a clientele that differs by age or ethnic origin, for example)?

### 2.8.2 Limitations of Association Rule Mining

One practical limitation is that a large number of transactions (for example, in the millions) are needed if statistically significant rules are to be found.

Another limitation of association rule mining is its simplicity as it basically involves counting items and their associations. The most popular algorithm for association rule mining, the **Apriori algorithm** [54], is a *heuristic*, that is an approximation that is not optimal but which can give a good-enough answer in a realistic time frame. Apriori makes the efficient search for association rules possible by first filtering out all pairs that contain non-frequent items before trying to work out the association rules. That is, Apriori applies the principle that *if an item-set is rare, then all of its subsets must be rare too*. Without a heuristic, the brute-force approach for finding out association rules involves listing all possible association rules and computing the support and confidence for each rule followed by pruning the rules that do not meet the threshold. The computational complexity of the brute-force approach grows exponentially with the number of items, which becomes prohibitive for even a relatively modest number of items. For example, for $n$ distinct items, the set of possible pairs is $2^n - 1$.

Still, the Apriori algorithm can be limiting with large inventories or when the support threshold is set too low. In this case, it would be possible to improve the Apriori algorithm and reduce the number of comparisons further by using advanced data structures, but this is usually not worth the trouble if we can have access to individual customer identifiers and build a *personalised* recommender system (Chapter 3). Association rule mining is not personalised since the unit of analysis is the transaction. It does not matter who the customer is or what their past purchase history is: If two separate customers buy bread and milk, they will get the same recommendations regardless of what they have bought in the past.

Alternative algorithms for performing association rule mining include ECLAT and FP-growth, but they are not inherently superior to Apriori. They simply employ different tricks to reduce the computational complexity of the starting problem but basically they are all counting beans [59].

Another limitation of all these algorithms is that they are not attached to a sophisticated probabilistic model that would make a better assessment of the confidence in the rules. For analysing correlations between features other techniques like mutual information would probably work better. Association rule mining algorithms also lack the ability to learn from experience and recognise serendipitous associations like a latent variable model would do in a recommender system. Thus association rule mining can be regarded as a primitive form of a recommender system.

### 2.8.3 Predictive Rule Learning

The goal of association rule mining is to find individual IF-THEN rules that capture patterns in the data. While this is a *descriptive* exercise, the goal of predictive rule learning is to generalise the training data to enable classification predictions on new data. The two most popular strategies for learning rule sets may be regarded as extensions of standard association rule algorithms like Apriori, and include **classification by association** (e.g. the CBA, CMAR, CPAR and FARC-HD algorithms) and **separate-and-conquer or covering algorithms** (e.g. the AQ, CN2, FOIL, RIPPER, OPUS algorithms) (reviewed in [59]). One advantage of predictive rule learning over more complex predictive methods such as Support Vector Machines (Chapter 3) is that they are *interpretable*. An interpretable model is one that we can inspect and understand how the predictions were calculated, and this is a very desirable quality of any predictive method (Chapter 3) [60].

## 2.9 FURTHER READING

- **Websites**

  - **Beautiful News Daily**
    URL: informationisbeautiful.net/beautifulnews/
    *Beautiful News Daily is an interesting project that publishes a new visualisation every day.*

  - **College Statistics @ Khan Academy**
    URL: khanacademy.org/math/ap-statistics/
    *An excellent introductory statistics course from Khan Academy.*

  - **Graphic Detail (The Economist)**
    URL: https://econ.st/3p2d62t
    *This is The Economist's blog with hundreds of examples of insightful visualisations we can all learn from. Each visualisation is accompanied by a short analysis indicating the data source used.*

  - **Probability and Statistics in data science using Python**
    URL: https://bit.ly/32wIET4
    *An introductory probability and statistics course using the Python programming language.*

  - **Quick-R by Datacamp**
    URL: statmethods.net
    *This website is a reference site for R and has extensive sections on statistical methods.*

  - **Reddit's Data Is Ugly**
    URL: https://bit.ly/3sd7Z1l
    *A humorous yet serious website listing terrible visualisations and what is wrong with them. Because we also learn from others' mistakes.*

  - **Statistics – The Science of Decisions by UDACITY**
    URL: https://bit.ly/3iwmEgA
    *An excellent, free introductory statistics course with two parts: descriptive and inferential statistics.*

  - **Statistics How To**
    URL: statisticshowto.com
    *A website dedicated to elementary statistics with thousands of articles and videos and interesting sections on probability and statistics and experimental design.*

  - **The Tableau Blog**
    URL: tableau.com/about/blog
    *The Tableau Blog includes visualisation powered by Tableau with extended explanations detailing the impact and insights derived from such visualisations.*

  - **WTF Visualizations**
    URL: viz.wtf
    *Like Reddit's Data is Ugly, WTF Visualizations is dedicated to seriously awful and misleading visualisations with explanations of what is wrong about each visualisation. Because we also learn from others' mistakes.*

- **Podcasts**

  - **Data Stories**
    URL: DataStori.es
    *Podcasts on data visualization with Enrico Bertini and Moritz Stefaner.*

  - **Data Viz Today**
    URL: https://dataviztoday.com/
    *Data visualisation designer Alli Torban discusses the latest methods and tools through her own work and interviews with other visualisation experts.*

- **Tools**

  - **Tableau**
    URL: tableau.com
    *Tableau is a powerful analytics platform that facilitates data manipulation, combination and visualisation, results reporting, and the building of live dashboards and even some uncomplicated clustering and forecasting models.*

  - **Google Data Studio**
    URL: datastudio.google.com
    *Google Data Studio is like the free but less powerful version of Tableau, but still an excellent choice for creating relatively simple visualisations.*

- **Videos**

  - **The Beauty of Data Visualization (David McCandless, TEDGlobal 2010).**
    URL: https://bit.ly/3bXdUxu
    *A fascinating talk on powerful visualisations as a way to understand the world we live in. David McCandless is a London-based data journalist and information designer.*

  - **The Best Stats You've Ever Seen (Hans Rosling, TED2006).**
    URL: https://bit.ly/3ku6chB
    *Hans Rosling is a statistics guru who has pioneered visualisation techniques to help him convey his ideas.*

- **Articles**

  - **Berinato S. Visualizations That Really Work (Harvard Business Review, June 2016).**
    URL: https://bit.ly/35BFcZ2
    *A thoughtful analysis on the importance of good data visualisation for decision-making in a business context.*

  - **Fürnkranz J., Kliegr T. A Brief Overview of Rule Learning. In: Bassiliades N., Gottlob G., Sadri F., Paschke A., Roman D. (eds) Rule Technologies: Foundations, Tools, and Applications. RuleML 2015. Lecture Notes in Computer Science, vol 9202. ISBN: 9783319215419.**
    *A thorough introduction to the problems of descriptive and predictive rule discovery and the algorithms involved.*

  - **Grentzelos C., Caroni C. and Barranco-Chamorro I. A comparative study of methods to handle outliers in multivariate data analysis. Computational and Mathematical Methods 3(3): e1129, 2021.**

*An excellent comparative review on the techniques available for detecting outliers in multivariate data, with worked examples in R including specific packages and datasets.*

– Marmolejo-Ramos F. and Tian S. The shifting boxplot. A boxplot based on essential summary statistics around the mean. International Journal of Psychological Research vol. 3(1): 37–46, 2010.
*The authors describe the development of a new type of box plot to meet a specific type of data visualisation need.*

– Midway SR. Principles of effective data visualization. Patterns 1(9): 1–7, 2020.
*A short and clear set of guiding principles to make the most of your visualisation efforts.*

– von Luxburg U, Williamson RC, Guyon I. Clustering: Science or Art? In Proceedings of ICML Workshop on Unsupervised and Transfer Learning (PMLR), 27:65–79, 2012.
URL: https://bit.ly/3J2AeWt
*It is not possible to compare the quality of the results of different clustering algorithms objectively as if they were independent mathematical problems. The results must always be analysed in the context of their end use. Here the authors introduce a taxonomy of clustering problems in an attempt to start comparing the performance of clustering algorithms.*

– Xu D. and Tian Y. A Comprehensive Survey of Clustering Algorithms. Annals of Data Science vol. 2, pp. 165–193, 2015.
*An excellent review of the different classes of clustering algorithms compared side-by-side in terms of their complexity (time of execution), scalability, suitability for both large-scale and high-dimensional data, and their sensitivity to noise and outliers, and to the sequence of inputting data).*

● Books

– Aggarwal C.C. *Outlier analysis (2nd Edition)* Springer International Publishing AG, Cham, Switzerland. ISBN: 9783319475776.
*This is an excellent and up-to-date reference to outlier analysis and anomaly detection. The book is not heavy on the mathematics, but it is not a beginner's book either.*

– James G, Witten D, Hastie T, Tibshirani R. *An Introduction to Statistical Learning: with Applications in R.* Springer, New York, (NY), USA, 2021. ISBN-10: 1071614177.
*This authoritative textbook is a great introduction to unsupervised and supervised learning. This book is the younger sibling of 'The Elements of Statistical Learning' by Hastie, Tibshirani and Friedman (Springer) where the topics are treated in greater detail.*

– Healy K. *Data Visualization: A Practical Introduction.* Princeton University Press, Princeton, (NJ), USA, 2018. ISBN-10: 0691181624.
*A superb, critical introduction to the principles and practice of data visualisation using R and the powerful ggplot2 and tidyverse packages.*

– Nussbaumer Knaflic C. *Storytelling with Data: A Data Visualization Guide for Business Professionals* John Wiley & Sons, Hoboken, (NJ), USA, 2015. ISBN-10: 1119002257.

*This book teaches data visualisation and effective communication (storytelling) in a very practical way using real examples. The target readers are business people rather than UI designers. They have an interesting blog too that is worth following: storytellingwithdata.com/blog*

- Posavec S. and Lupi G. **Dear Data.** Particular Books, London, UK, 2016. ISBN-13: 9781846149061.
*A very unique book of the postcards the two authors sent each for a year to explain particular aspects of their lives. To do this they combined their knowledge of data science and visualisation skills in very masterful and creative ways.*

- Rowntree D. **Statistics Without Tears.** Penguin Books, London, UK, 2018. ISBN-13: 9780141987491.
*A short and authoritative introduction to statistics for the general reader.*

- Sugiura K. **Experiments in "Time Distance Map" : Diagram Collection by Kohei Sugiura.** Kajimashuppankai, Japan, 2014. ISBN-13: 9784306046061.
*Kohei Sugiura has produced some of the most beautiful modern visualisations.*

- Telea A.C. **Data Visualization: Principles and Practice (2nd Edition).** CRC Press, Boca Raton (FL), USA, 2015. ISBN-10: 9781466585263.
*This is an excellent technical reference for computer scientists looking to learn about data visualisation problems and techniques, with a focus on mathematical theory and algorithms.*

## 2.10 CHAPTER REVIEW QUESTIONS

1. You are a teacher and have been trying to implement a number of changes in your school to promote more interactive learning. If you were to analyse the posts on your school's online discussion board and split them by year, class, student gender and any other factor, would this be a descriptive or a predictive analytics exercise? For either answer, please explain your reasons.

2. You are an engineer in a Formula 1 team and want to find out when a particular set of tyres will burst until specific conditions of temperature and rain. For this you collect historical data first. Would this be a descriptive or a predictive analytics question? For either answer, please explain your reasons.

3. What are some descriptive statistics measures?

    (a) The optimal number of clusters in a dataset as determined by $K$-means clustering.

    (b) The mode.

    (c) The standard deviation.

    (d) Skewness.

4. What does Anscombe's quartet prove?

5. Clustering is

    (a) The random grouping of data points that at least data are a bit more organised.

    (b) The discovery of natural grouping patterns in the data which may not become apparent otherwise.

(c) The differentiation of data into 'good' and 'bad'.

(d) A technique for getting rid of useless data.

6. **Can you list the sequential steps in a $K$-means clustering exercise?**

7. **Which of the following can be solved using association rule analysis?**

(a) Discover new symptoms associated with a particular disease.

(b) Identify the customers that spend the most so that these can be targeted in a campaign for a new, luxury product.

(c) Optimise the inventory in your business.

(d) Find out the height structure of students in a school that are taller than 170 cm.

# CHAPTER 3

# Predictive Analytics

*I think the brain is essentially a computer and consciousness is like a computer program. It will cease to run when the computer is turned off. Theoretically, it could be re-created on a neural network, but that would be very difficult, as it would require all one's memories.*

– Stephen Hawking (1942–2018), *English theoretical physicist*

The starting point of any data science problem is being able to ask the right question of the right data in the right context. In Chapter 2 we examined some unsupervised learning algorithms, such as clustering and association rule learning. Here we discuss predictive, or supervised learning algorithms, which seek to solve one of two problems: **Regression** (predicting a continuous value) or **classification** ('what class does this observation belong in?'). In fact, most of data science is about making predictions on unseen values.

The focus of this chapter is on illustrating each algorithm's domain of applicability, their relative strengths and limitations, trade-offs, and any alternative methods. We first examine linear regression for its applicability and also because it serves to illustrate the fundamental principles of interpretability and explainability. Many modern algorithms like deep learning networks can achieve extraordinary performance but cannot be explained or even tweaked easily. These 'black-box' algorithms are not ideal in, for instance, the legal and medical contexts. Moreover, when the data is structured and the features represented are meaningful, there is often no significant difference in performance between complex models and simpler ones.

The No Free Lunch Theorem explains why there is no algorithm that dominates over all other algorithms or all possible datasets, and why for every method that we use we must always make sensible assumptions. Thus, without an understanding of the inner workings of each algorithm it is impossible to select the optimal one. Moreover, beyond a certain point changing the algorithm, selecting the right features, or adding more features to a predictive model does not improve performance, in which case we must resort to engineering new features from our original data. Feature engineering is as much an art as it is a science and this illustrates once again how the insight of the data scientist is central to the success of any data science project. When a problem is well-understood and enough quality data is available, achieving a solution is a no-brainer in most cases. However, when the question is not clear and the data are imperfect, the only two in the ring are the problem and the data scientist's creativity.

Finally, we discuss recommender systems as they combine elements of supervised and unsupervised learning, and are neither but a concept on another level. Complex recommender systems illustrate the creative design and application of families of algorithms ('ensembles') over single methods to boost predictive performance.

DOI: 10.1201/b23197-3

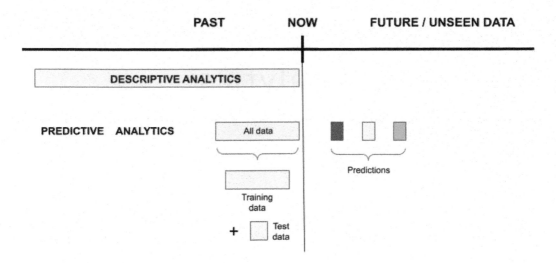

Figure 3.1 The point of reference is one important difference between descriptive and predictive analytics.

## 3.1 WHAT IS PREDICTIVE ANALYTICS?

Whereas the goal of descriptive analytics is to answer the question of 'what happened?', predictive analytics focuses on the question of 'what is likely to happen?' The difference between these two questions is the point of reference. Descriptive analytics uses only historical data to generate data summaries and reports, but predictive analytics uses historical data to try to anticipate what future data values might be. The most important question before embarking on a data analysis project is 'What is the question I want to ask of this dataset, and is it possible?'

Simply put, the goal of predictive analytics is to find a mathematical function that most accurately predicts unseen values given a set of inputs. In other words, a properly trained predictive algorithm must fit historical data well and also be able to generalise to similar, but non-identical values. To assess how well a given algorithm can generalise, we use some (but not all) of the historical data and train a predictive model, which is then tested on some of the data that the model has not been trained with, called the 'test dataset' or the 'holdout dataset' (Fig. 3.1). In a time-bound context, with predictive analytics the closer the period of the historical data to the period for which the values are to be predicted, the more accurate the prediction will be. In other words, given an algorithm that has been trained with a specific dataset, we can only make predictions on other data that are not too different from the training data. For example, given a weather dataset of this week for the city of Barcelona, it is easier to forecast the temperature tomorrow than the temperature next month. The prediction of a continuous value, like temperature or the price of a stock, is an example of a **regression problem**.

Besides regression problems, we also have **classification problems** where the goal is to predict the categories of input values. For example, we could use a library of animal pictures to train a model that can identify dogs in photographs. Being able to tell whether a photo has a dog in it is an example of a binary classification problem as the answer can only be 'yes' or 'no'. For this, if we have 100 photographs of various animals, as a first approximation we could train the algorithm with 90 photographs (the *training set*) and test the resulting model on the remaining 10 photographs (the *test set*) (Fig. 3.2). For the model to be able to discriminate dogs beyond the examples it was trained with (that is,

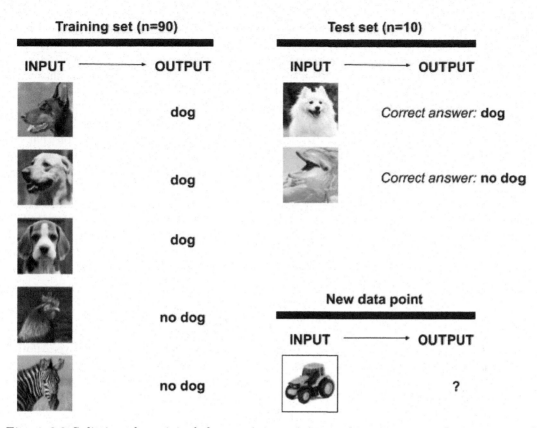

Figure 3.2 Splitting the original dataset into training and test sets is a characteristic of supervised learning.

*generalise*) the examples in the training set need to be varied enough—if all the training set photos were of dobermans and giraffes, would you expect the model to identify a labrador as a type of dog?

One essential concept in classification problems is that for the training to be meaningful the examples must be labeled. That is, if we want the model to learn that this photo of a labrador actually represents a dog, I must tell it so since we cannot expect the algorithm to know these things at the training stage. Also, since the test data photographs are equally labeled, at the test stage it is easy to tell which photographs have been classified correctly.

Finally, once our predictive model is built and tested, if we feed it with the photo of a yellow tractor (Fig. 3.2), should we expect it to yield any meaningful results? Not really because the nature of this input data is way too different from the data the algorithm was originally trained with. In other words, a predictive method can only make reliable predictions if the data being classified bear some resemblance to the data it has been trained with. In computational chemistry this is known as the applicability domain problem [61]; other fields where supervised learning algorithms are extensively applied call it differently.

The example of classifying pictures into two categories ('contains dog' and 'does not contain dog') is called a binary classifier. Multi-category classification problems are also common. For instance, we could extend the previous model to predict which type of breed a dog belongs to.

Predictive analytics is not inherently superior to descriptive analytics—the most important point when choosing one class of algorithm over another is being able to ask the right question about your data in the context of your analytical needs. Sometimes you will need to understand historical data, and sometimes you will need to use some of this historical data to make predictions about the immediate future or unseen data.

Predictive analytics cannot truly be separated from descriptive analytics because without a good understanding of the working dataset it is often not possible to build a robust predictive model. For example, understanding the distribution of a dataset determines whether we should apply parametric or non-parametric methods. **Parametric methods** make the assumptions that the data to be modelled originates from a population that can be described by a probability distribution with a known set of parameters, such as a normal distribution. **Non-parametric models**, on the other hand, do not assume an explicit form for the underlying distribution.

Moreover, understanding how the observations of a dataset segregate into groups (Clustering, Chapter 2) is often relevant to the successful development of multi-level classifiers [62]. Clustering can also help identify outliers in our dataset, and deciding how to deal with outliers is also key for the sensible application of most algorithms: Some like linear regression are particularly sensitive to the presence of outliers, whereas other algorithms such as Support Vector Machines are not.

## 3.2   THE THREE MAIN LEARNING PARADIGMS

So far we have divided the algorithms of data science into descriptive and predictive. Another way to think about learning algorithms is by how much we know about the input data as this conditions the questions that we can ask. Whenever we embark on a data science project we must always ask the following:

- Where does the data come from and how reliable is it?

- How much data is available?

- What proportion of the data points is labelled?

- Is it possible to label the unlabelled observations?

**Machine learning** has three principal learning paradigms: **unsupervised, supervised** and **semi-supervised** learning (Fig. 3.3). A fourth paradigm called **reinforcement learning** is discussed in Chapter 7 in the context of autonomous vehicles.

(a) **Unsupervised learning** problems belong in **descriptive analytics** and are characterised by unlabelled input data. The goal here is to understand the underlying structure in the data for which two main types of analysis exist:

- **Clustering analysis**, where the aim is to identify naturally occurring groupings for the observations (Fig. 2.12, Fig. 3.3). In the context of market segmentation, a typical clustering problem is the identification customers with high purchasing potential so that they can be specifically targeted in a new marketing campaign for a luxury product. Another example is the optimal division of US states into groups according to their murder, assault and rape statistics ($K$-means clustering, Chapter 2).

   An extension of clustering is the identification of abnormal observations (outliers): If we know that data typically cluster into a number of well-described groups, an observation that does not cluster into any of the known groups is an outlier. This has many practical applications, for example if employees check in around 9 a.m. and 4 p.m. for the different shifts, would you investigate someone that checked in around 11.30 p.m. on Friday night?

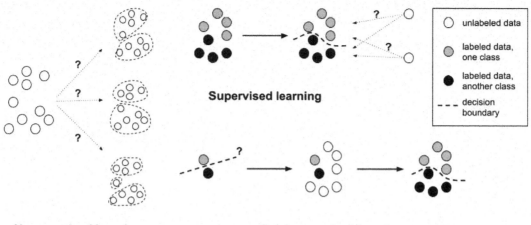

Figure 3.3 The extent of data labelling determines the type of learning that is possible.

Clustering resembles classification problems because we end up putting obser-vations into different categories, but there is a fundamental difference here: In clustering the number of groups (categories) is not predetermined. This is because the clusters are identified as part of the model creation process.

- **Association rule analysis**, where the aim is to extract rules that describe specific combinations in the dataset. Examples here are the compilation of a list of symptoms related to a new disease or the identification of products that are frequently bought together in a supermarket (Chapter 2).

(b) **Supervised learning** is synonymous with **predictive analytics,** and is charac-terised by having all the observations (input data, $x$) labelled with output values ($y$, the associated response). Therefore, only if our data is labelled can we ask predictive questions.

Formally, the goal of supervised learning is to use an algorithm to discover the function $y = f(x)$ that connects the input variable to the output variable (e.g. photograph $x$ 'contains dog' or 'does not contain dog'). This is doubly important: For one thing the function $y = f(x)$ allows us to understand the relationship between $x$ and $y$ (inference), which we can then use to predict $y$ from new values of $x$. In the case of a class-based predictor the goal of the function is to identify a decision boundary that can adequately separate the classes (Fig. 3.3). Once we can relate the response measurements to the predictors (input) we can use this model for predicting the response of future observations.

Making predictions from data is called supervised learning because the process is sim-ilar to the interaction between a student and a teacher: The teacher knows what the right answers are, and during the learning process the algorithm (student) builds a model from the training data and its predictive accuracy is determined on the test dataset. The result is fed back during the learning step and therefore when the predic-tions are wrong, the model is corrected by the teacher. This iterative learning process stops when the algorithm achieves an acceptable performance on the test dataset (Fig. 3.4). Besides the classification of photographs into 'contains dog' and 'does not contain dog', other examples of binary classification include predicting whether a

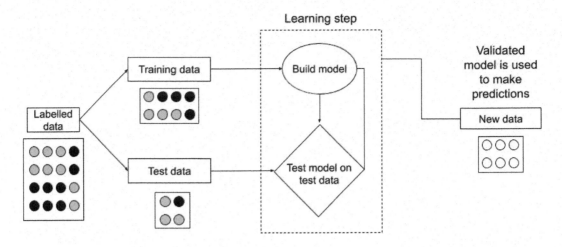

Figure 3.4 The basic flow of a supervised machine learning exercise.

biopsy image indicates disease or not, and something as common as an email spam detector: The algorithm is trained with examples of both spam and normal emails and must accurately decide the class to which new (unseen) incoming emails belong. As discussed earlier, supervised learning is also used to model regression problems where the output value is not a category but a continuous value, such as tomorrow's temperature or the future value of Tesla stocks.

(c) **Semi-supervised learning** is the situation where we wish to build a predictive model but only have a small set of labeled observations and a vast majority of unlabeled data. Here the labelling of the unlabeled data points and their incorporation into the learning model often improves its classification accuracy. For example, when we only have two labeled data points the decision boundary separating the two classes could be a straight line, but the incorporation of new data points to each class might help build a more precise decision boundary, resulting in a more robust learning model (Fig. 3.3). The labelling of unlabelled data in this toy example may include various assumptions, e.g. that the data points that are located in close proximity must belong in the same class (the 'continuity assumption'), and the same for those within the same cluster (the 'cluster assumption').

The great importance of semi-supervised learning is that most real-world learning problems are of this type. These situations where we have a few labeled data points and a majority of unlabeled data points always occur whenever the collection and storage of observations is cheap and easy but their labelling (the associated response) is much more expensive, perhaps because it requires human annotation. For example, we may want to extend the binary classifier of photographs to a multi-class classifier for the identification of not just dogs but of different dog breeds. To do this we need much more data. We may collect dog photographs from the Internet easily, but how would we go about labelling every dog breed in, say, 10 million dog photographs? By hand?

In a creative use of alternative sources of information, Guillaumin, Verbeek and Schmid (2010) found that the tags associated with both labelled and unlabelled images can be used to annotate unlabelled images and thus improve an image classifier's accuracy. Starting with a small set of labelled photographs and a much larger set of unlabelled images from the Flickr.com site (an image and video hosting service and online community), the authors simply extracted and compared the public (tag) annotation of both labelled and unlabelled images to build a semi-supervised learning system whose performance was much better than that obtained using labelled images only [63]. This clever approach to enrich a dataset for a classification problem is an example of **feature engineering**.

Semi-supervised learning has also been applied to text data exclusively, for example to identify the trafficking of humans for the purpose of sexual exploitation. A challenging problem for law enforcement officers is the real-time identification of advertisements that may involve human trafficking since the total amount of sex advertisements published daily is immense. In 2017, Alvari, Shakarian and Snyder extracted advertisements from the Backpage website (the largest sex marketplace, seized in 2018) and annotated a small portion of these with the help of a human trafficking expert. There are certain words that are clearly indicative of human trafficking. For example, although sex with children is never mentioned explicitly, those who have this inclination tend to use keywords such as 'sweet', 'candy' and 'new to the game', and advertisements detailing a body weight below 115 lbs (ca. 52 Kg) also correlate with underage girls. Mention of multiple women at the same time is suggestive of organised human trafficking. Starting just with a small set of labelled examples and a much larger set of unlabelled advertisements, the researchers managed to train a semi-supervised learning method that was particularly effective in flagging advertisements related to human trafficking [64].

## 3.2.1  Pseudolabelling

A key ingredient for the success of semi-supervised learning is being able to label the unlabelled data as well as possible. A simple method to do this is pseudolabelling—here a predictive model is first built with the labelled data and used to predict the labels for the unlabelled data. The newly pseudolabelled data is then combined with the original, labelled data to learn a new predictive model (Fig. 3.5). Pseudolabelling works iteratively—in each round the algorithm labels only those observations it is most confident about (that is, those above a given cutoff). The decision boundary is then recalculated for the next iteration in order to accommodate the newly labelled points until no more unlabelled observations can be relabelled.

Pseudolabelling has been shown to outperform supervised learning models in the classification of images [65, 66]. However, there are many situations where the method's *cluster assumption* (that data points cluster according to class) does not hold even if the observations that belong in the same class clearly cluster together. In the two moons dataset there are only a handful of labelled points and those observations from different classes are not always clearly separated (Fig. 3.6). In this context pseudolabelling is unable to find the correct decision boundary unlike other semi-supervised learning algorithms such as Virtual Adversarial Training and the Π-model [67]. Pseudolabelling typically requires rather extensive labelling, in the order of 1,000 labelled examples in the early days of pseudolabelling (the SVHN image dataset [65]), and at least 100 labelled examples in a more recent classification exercise on the MNIST dataset (handwritten digits) using deep neural networks [66]. Thus, pseudolabelling will not work when the number of labelled examples is critically small, or when the location of these labelled examples is uninformative. If data points that are too distant from the decision boundary are used to learn the supervised classifier, pseudolabelling will go awfully wrong. This is analogous to the situation with Support Vector Machines where the only important data points are the support vectors that define class boundaries.

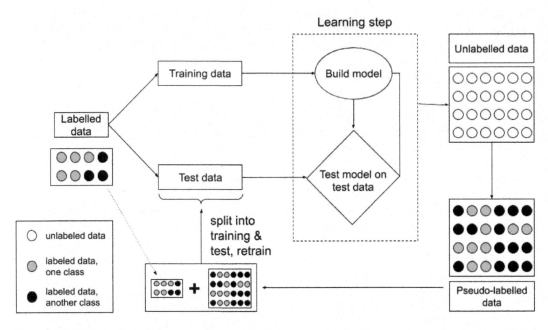

Figure 3.5 Unlabelled data may be enriched by pseudolabelling to increase the predictive accuracy of a learning model.

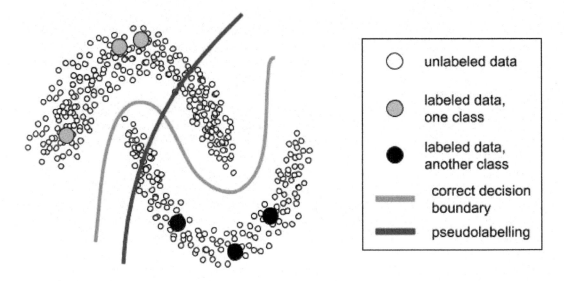

Figure 3.6 The two classes in the 'two moons' dataset cannot be separated by pseudolabelling.

Despite its shortcomings, pseudolabelling is still an important method because it not only illustrates the challenges with semi-supervised learning, but also how its mechanistic and visual simplicity can actually be rather misleading. For starters, most real-world problems are not two-dimensional like the ones we have discussed here, and high-dimensional spaces behave differently in many ways—how could we visualise a three-dimensional decision boundary that shifts with every iteration? Also, rather than using a single supervised classifier, some sophisticated implementations of the algorithm may include multiple classifiers, each being learned with specific subsets of labelled data. This strategy would be similar to Random Forests, which seek to prevent high degrees of correlation when some data points are dominant predictors.

Finally, why have we placed so much emphasis on semi-supervised learning? As we discussed above, most real-world learning problems are semi-supervised as we typically only have a minority of labelled examples and a vast majority of unlabelled observations. More importantly, have you noticed that the human mind also learns in a semi-supervised way? We do not need to explore every road in the world to become confident drivers; we do not need to do every possible differentiation exercise to become confident at calculus; we do not need to become fully bilingual in a language before we start combining the newly learnt words to try to explain complex concepts. The human mind only needs a few guiding points to identify the underlying pattern. Likewise, if progress in artificial intelligence is to come faster (Chapter 7) we must find a way to teach machines to learn from a few (or no) labelled examples instead of being so heavily dependent on tons of labelled data (supervised learning) and on our own, rigid interpretation of the world around us [68]. Semi-supervised learning is an incredibly hot topic of research and will remain so for the foreseeable future: For ~17,000 papers on semi-supervised learning published in 2010, ~67,000 were published in 2020.

## 3.3 AN OVERVIEW OF MACHINE LEARNING ALGORITHMS

We have just discussed the three main learning paradigms. Another useful way of classifying algorithms is not by how they learn from data, but by their general strategy. Below we present a classification of the main types of algorithms. The first two classes (clustering and association rule learning) are exclusively unsupervised and were presented in Chapter 2. Certain advanced classes of algorithm have intentionally been left out of the discussion. These include reinforcement learning (discussed in Chapter 7), computer vision, evolutionary algorithms and natural language processing. We are only scratching the surface here, but this classification scheme is a useful guide for discussing the most common classes of machine learning algorithms.

1. **Clustering**

   Clustering algorithms seek to uncover the groupings inherent in the data so that we can better organise the observations by some measure of relatedness. In Chapter 2 we learnt about $K$-means clustering whereby the data is split into a fixed number ($k$) of clusters determined by their central points (centroids). Other common clustering algorithms are hierarchical clustering and Expectation Maximization (EM).

2. **Association rule learning**

   Like clustering, association rule learning algorithms seek to uncover relationships in the data in the form of naturally occurring combinations such as items that are bought together (Chapter 2).

3. **Instance-based**

   These algorithms learn the training instances (examples) by heart and then generalise to new examples based on some similarity measure to find the best match and thus make a prediction. Instance-based methods are also referred to as 'winner-take-all', 'memory-based learning' or 'lazy-learning methods'. Some of the most popular instance-based algorithms are classification techniques such as Support Vector Machines (discussed below) and $K$-Nearest Neighbours (KNN).

4. **Dimensionality reduction**
   Their goal is to summarise a dataset using less information, a key pre-requisite for many learning algorithms. Principal Component Analysis (PCA) and Linear Discriminant Analysis (LDA) are typical algorithms in this context. Feature selection (see below) is a form of dimensionality reduction, but not all dimensionality reduction is feature selection.

5. **Regression**
   Regression algorithms are among the most basic predictive methods. All regressions model the relationship between variables including linear regression for continuous value predictions and logistic regression to model a binary output. LOESS (Locally Estimated Scatterplot Smoothing) is briefly discussed in the context of linear regression as a way to estimate the quality of a linear model.

   **Regularisation algorithms** (e.g. LASSO, Ridge Regression) are an extension to regression methods that penalise complex models in favour of simpler ones (which are normally better at generalising). We mention these as examples of embedded methods in the context of feature selection. We must note, however, that LASSO can also work as classifiers (e.g. [69]).

6. **Bayesian**
   Algorithms based on Bayes' theorem of conditional probability can be applied to both classification and regression problems. We discuss naïve Bayes classifiers as these are very fast, scalable, and may outperform more sophisticated methods. Other Bayesian algorithms include averaged one-dependence estimators, and bayesian networks which represent conditional dependencies through a directed acyclic graph.

7. **Trees**
   Single trees are mostly used in classification problems (called decision trees) because neural networks and standard regression models typically outperform regression trees for the prediction of continuous values. We discuss the well-known algorithm CART and important extensions to basic trees like Random Forests, which today are one of the most powerful predictive methods available.

8. **Artificial Neural Networks (ANNs)**
   ANNs are inspired by biological neurons and are used for both classification and regression problems. Here we discuss the single-neuron classifier (the perceptron), the backpropagation algorithm as well as diverse ANN architectures suited to different problems. We also learn about deep learning, a modern ANN paradigm characterised by networks with complex, hidden layers which exploit today's large computational resources. Deep learning networks are responsible for the most spectacular advances in machine learning in recent years.

9. **Ensembles**
   Ensembles are a powerful class of techniques where the goal is to combine many weak models into a supermodel in order to outperform any single model. Here we discuss important ensembles such as Bootstrap Aggregating (bagging) and Random Forests, as well as heterogeneous ensembles comprised of different methods that have won major competitions including the Netflix Grand Prize. The combination of weak learners that should make up any one ensemble is a very active area of research.

The focus of the discussion of the different algorithms in the rest of this chapter is on each algorithm's domain of applicability, strengths and limitations, alternative methods and especially their degree of interpretability. When given a choice between a simpler and a more

TABLE 3.1  Expenditure in Television Advertising vs Sales (Sample)

| TV advertising expenditure | Sales (thousands of dollars |
|:---:|:---:|
| 17.2 | 9.3 |
| 44.5 | 10.4 |
| 181.0 | 12.9 |
| 152.0 | 18.5 |
| 230.0 | 22.1 |
| ... | ... |

complex but perhaps marginally more accurate algorithm, the simpler one is usually the better choice because it is more interpretable. We will learn how complex algorithms are powerful, but also impossible to comprehend or even finely adjust beyond a certain point.

## 3.4  LINEAR REGRESSION

Linear regression is a technique that models the relationship between a response ('dependent') variable and one or more explanatory ('independent') variables. For linear regression to make accurate quantitative predictions of the dependent variable, the dependent and independent variables must hold an approximately linear relationship. Bear in mind that the variables are 'naturally labelled' as they represent continuous values.

As an example of linear regression we have data on expenditure on television advertising for a given product, and its sales volume in 200 different markets (from the well-known TV, Radio and Newspaper advertising dataset (Table 3.1) [70, 53]). If we plot the TV advertising expenditure on the $X$ axis (the independent variable) and the sales on the $Y$ axis (the dependent variable) we see that the two variables hold an approximately linear relationship (Fig. 3.7). Therefore the question here is: Could we use the values on TV advertising expenditure to predict the sales volume?

Given that a linear relationship exists between the two variables, fitting a simple linear regression line seems an appropriate method for predicting future sales from the TV advertising expenditure. A linear model has the standard formula of a straight line that we learnt at school ($Y = \beta_0 + \beta_1 X + \epsilon$). Thus, the goal of a linear regression exercise is to approximate the coefficients of the formula $\beta_0$, $\beta_1$ and $\epsilon$ as accurately as possible. In a linear model the straight line is fitted through the points often by minimising the sum of the squared errors—the approach that Legendre and Gauss developed independently (although other methods exist). In other words, if you had two points on the $X$ axis, you would draw the straight line in a way such that the perpendicular distance of the point north of the line is identical to the perpendicular distance of the point south of the line (equidistant). Thus the distance between the two points is maximised. Now imagine this strategy being systematically applied to hundreds or thousands of data points.

For the full TV advertising expenditure vs sales dataset, the result of fitting a simple linear regression produces the formula $Y = 7.03 + 0.047X + \epsilon$ as plotted in Fig. 3.8. Here two key parameters are the slope coefficient of 0.047 (i.e. the average increase in $Y$ for every one-unit increase in $X$) and the intercept coefficient (i.e. the expected value of $Y$ when $X = 0$) of 7.03. The latter means that in the absence of TV advertising we can expect sales of about 7 units. An slope coefficient of 0.047 means that for every \$1,000 increase in TV advertising we can expect an average increase in sales of 47 units. The variable ($\epsilon$) is an all-inclusive term for anything that this linear model misses. This is because with real data the relationship between any two variables is almost never perfectly linear, only

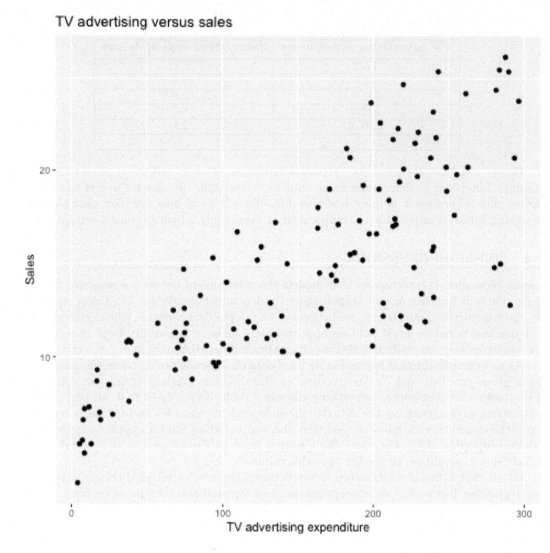

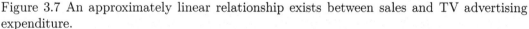

Figure 3.7 An approximately linear relationship exists between sales and TV advertising expenditure.

approximately. Making assumptions about the data is a fundamental part of choosing the right algorithm for our problem.

### 3.4.1 How Good Is Our Linear Model?

Before we apply any statistical model we must not only understand it in as much detail as possible, but also question its validity and the assumptions made.

One advantage of a simple model like linear regression is that it is interpretable and therefore requires little explanation. For example, we would like to know how confident our model is about these 47 units for every $1,000 spent on TV advertising. In other words, did we get the intercept and slope coefficients right? How statistically significant are these coefficients? For this we can compute the standard error (SE) and then calculate the 95% confidence interval for the $\beta_1$ slope coefficient—in this case it is [0.042–0.052]. This means

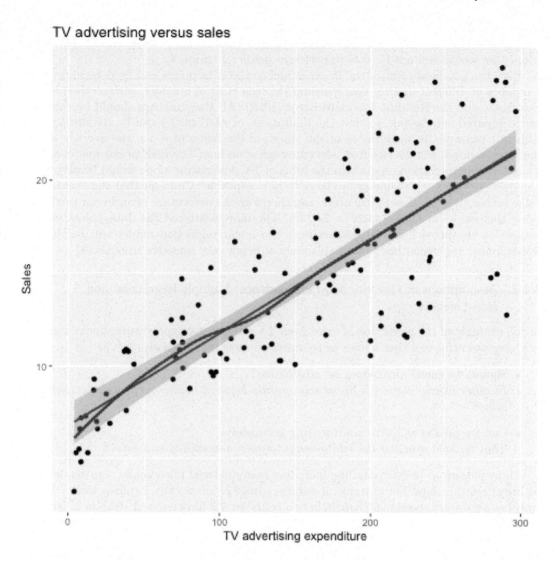

Figure 3.8 A linear model of sales vs TV advertising expenditure. The regression line (blue) is complemented by the 95% confidence interval (thick, grey line) and the LOESS smoother (red line).

that with 95% probability the increase in sales units for every $1,000 spent will lie somewhere between 42 and 52 units. This 95% confidence interval is shown in Fig. 3.8 as the shaded extension on either side of the blue regression line. The red line that runs essentially parallel to the regression line is the LOESS (locally weighted smoothing) smoother that helps us to visualise the general trend of the data. LOESS is non-parametric and does not assume any linearity relationship between the two variables; it only seeks to fit a smooth curve between two variables. Here the LOESS smoother suggests that a linear relationship between the two variables exists [53].

Besides having a measure of confidence for the coefficients of the linear regression (i.e. 'did we get the intercept and the slope right?'), we also need to understand how tight the regression line fits the data. The reason for this is that if we look at Fig. 3.8 we can see how spread out the data points are around the regression line. It is exactly because the regression line does not pass through all the data points that we have an error, $\epsilon$. Therefore even if we could calculate the true regression line coefficients $Y = \beta_0$ (intercept) and $\beta_1$ (slope) we would still not be able to perfectly predict $Y$ from $X$.

Here the goodness-of-fit of the linear model to the data points can be determined using a number of different metrics that measure the lack of fit of a model, such as the $(R^2)$, the F-statistic and the Residual Standard Error (RSE). All these metrics should be calculated and compared side-by-side so that the limitations of each model can be understood. The RSE, for example, is an estimate of the standard deviation of $\epsilon$, i.e. the average amount that the response will deviate from the true regression line. The RSE of our model is 3,259. Therefore any prediction on sales on the basis of TV advertising alone would be off by 3,259 units *on average*. Is this number too large to be acceptable? Consider that the average sales value across all markets is 14,022 units, and therefore the percentage error in our predictions using this model is 3,259/14,022 = 23.24%. The more scattered the data points are with respect to the fitted line, the less accurate the linear regression model will be. In other words, linear regression has the disadvantage of being very sensitive to outliers.

### 3.4.2 Assumptions of Linearity and Independence, Multiple Regression and Non-Linearity

In the example of the prediction of sales from TV advertising expenditure, linear regression is a very powerful tool that allows us to answer important questions such as:

- Should we spend any money on advertising?
  *In other words, is there a linear relationship between money spent on advertising and sales?*

- Can we predict sales from advertising accurately?
  *That is, how strong is the relationship between advertising and sales?*

Many situations in everyday life, including many natural phenomena, can be described by linear relationships. For example, if a coffee costs \$2 you can buy 5 coffees with \$10. If we travel at a constant speed of 50 Km/h, in two hours we will have covered 100 Km (Distance = Speed $\times$ Time). Alternatively, if we double the speed, we will also double the distance covered per unit time. Newton's second law is also an example of a linear relationship. This law (Force = Mass $\times$ Acceleration) says that the acceleration of an object depends upon two variables, the net force acting upon it and its mass. Therefore if we double the mass of the object, we must also double the force applied upon it to maintain the same acceleration.

A key assumption that is made in linear regression besides assuming that a linear relationship exists between the variables, is that the data points are independent. We must be careful here because lack of independence between the data points can arise easier than we think: For instance, in a linear model of height $\sim$ weight any one person might have been weighed multiple times. Although their weight might have changed, clearly the weight of that person today is not independent of that person's weight of last month. Moreover, a very strong correlation (which does not necessarily mean causation) might also be hiding an effect where both the dependent and the independent variables are affected by an external factor. This might be problematic because such a factor might affect each variable within a certain range only and our model might not be able to generalise well.

Up until now we have discussed situations with two variables only. In many real-life scenarios there are often multiple variables to consider. As an example of multiple linear regression, the original TV, Radio and Newspaper advertising dataset [70, 53] also includes data on radio and newspaper advertising expenditure, all of which should be considered in the same context as the TV expenditure. This is because although the TV advertising $\sim$ sales relationship is linear, when we incorporate additional predictors the various relationships are not necessarily independent from each other. For example, radio advertising might have a priming effect on consumers that listen to the radio (while driving to work, for example) such that when we combine radio advertising with TV advertising the combined effect is greater than the sum of the parts. Thus, radio advertising increases the slope of the TV regression line. Whenever this type of statistical interaction effect is observed (called the 'synergy effect' in marketing) allocating 50% of the advertising budget to each channel may increase sales more than allocating the entire budget to either TV or radio commercials. This type of situation opens up additional questions such as 'Do all media contribute to sales and how much?', or 'How accurately can we predict the level of sales from advertising in the various channels?'

Finally, many relationships between variables appear linear but really are not, in which case it would not make sense to force a straight line through the data points. There are multiple ways to take non-linear relationships into account, for example by transforming the variables (by taking the square root of logarithm of the values) or by introducing polynomial regression.

### 3.4.3  Linear Thinking or How We Can Be Easily Fooled

Despite all the powerful tools that exist for manipulating linear relationships, one very important limitation of linear regression lies in the cognitive bias that we humans have for it. Our brains prefer to think in linear terms because it is easier. However, not every situation is linear and the inability to recognise this leads to making poor decisions. For example, everyone knows the formula for constant speed:

$$\text{Speed} = \frac{Distance}{Time}$$

When people have to travel from A to B the vast majority will think: 'oh, right, if I travel at a speed of 100 Km/h I will cover 100 Km in an hour. Then, if I speed up to 200 Km/h I will arrive in half the time'. As a result, most people will speed while burning a disproportionate amount of fuel and increasing their risk of having an accident. The question they should be asking, however, is not how much they can speed up but how much time they will be saving by speeding. Surprisingly, this is an example of a non-linear relationship. If we rearrange the formula above to calculate the time as a linear function of distance and speed we get this:

$$\text{Time} = \frac{Distance}{Speed}$$

Let us imagine that we are travelling from Bordeaux to Paris (500 Km). If we travel at a constant speed of 100 Km/h, it will take us 5 h to cover the distance. Increasing our speed from 100 Km/h to 130 Km/h will save us $\sim 1.16\ h \sim 70\ min$.

$$Time = \frac{500\ Km}{130\ Km/h} \sim 3.84\ h \qquad (1.16\ h\ difference \sim 70\ min)$$

However, increasing our speed from 130 Km/h to 160 Km/h will not save us 140 min but only 112 min (while increasing the risk of having an accident several times):

$$Time = \frac{500\ Km}{160\ Km/h} \sim 3.125\ h \qquad (1.875\ h\ difference \sim 112\ min)$$

Our fixation with linear relationships is often exploited in marketing campaigns. Do you remember how Steve Jobs said that marketers should focus on consumer benefits rather than

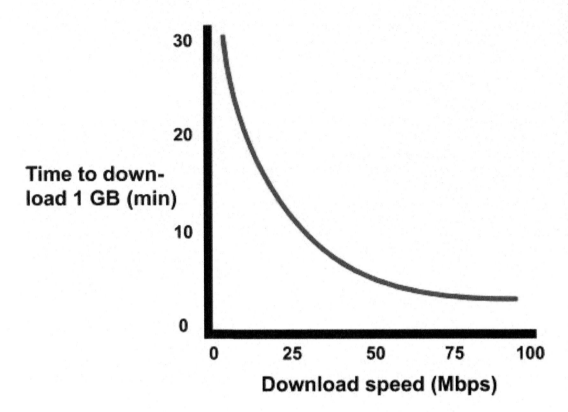

Figure 3.9 The time of data download over the Internet is not a linear function of download speed.

on product attributes? This is because it is easier for people to grasp the benefits of storing 1,000 songs in an iPod instead of trying to work out how many songs could be stored in 5 gigabytes of memory. However, given of our tendency to think linearly it is sometimes easier to fool consumers by focusing on a product's attributes. The packages offered by Internet Service Providers (ISP) are normally priced rather linearly: Twice the speed, twice the price. However, the relationship between download speed and download time is not linear as additional factors come into play (Fig. 3.9). In other words, beyond a certain bandwidth (download speed) the download time does not improve, but the price of the connection does. Here ISPs take advantage of our tendency to think that the relationship between benefits and attributes is linear. A mid-priced Internet connection is often preferable to the most expensive option.

In summary, linear regression is a simple but incredibly powerful technique for predicting a quantitative response. Besides, other important methods such as logistic regression are extensions of linear regression. The main caveat with linear regression, as with any other statistical learning technique, is that we must understand its domain of applicability and its inherent limitations. Being a relatively simple technique, however, does not mean that it is inferior to other techniques as there are situations where linear regression is the appropriate tool. Quantum mechanics, for instance, is all about linear algebra.

### 3.4.4 And a Short Historical Note

Historically, linear regression is the first predictive method, developed in 1805 by French mathematician Adrien-Marie Legendre (1752–1833) to describe comet orbits [71]. German mathematical giant Carl Friedrich Gauss (1777–1855) had apparently discovered it before Legendre did, but did not report it then because he deemed the method simplistic. However, Gauss became furious upon learning of Legendre's publication, and eventually published his own account [72]. Gauss was eventually recognised as the father of linear regression at the cost of one of the most famous disputes in the history of mathematics. Given the ubiquity of linear relationships, Legendre and Gauss were not the only ones to independently discover the method of least squares that is still used today to fit a straight line through the observations. English polymath Sir Francis Galton (1822–1911) also reported linear regression to explain variations in height patterns across generations [73].

## 3.5 LOGISTIC REGRESSION

The goal of linear regression is to make a quantitative prediction between two numerical variables that hold an approximately linear relationship. But what if the response variable is categorical? There are many situations where the response variable is not quantitative, for example:

- Will this person (age, sex, ethnic origin, state, etc.) vote republican or democrat? (yes/no)

- Given a set of financial variables (balance, savings, income, age, marital status), will this customer default on their mortgage? (yes/no)

- Is this online transaction a credit card fraud? (yes/no)

- Will I be admitted to Graduate School? (yes/no)

- Is this email spam? (yes/no)

Logistic regression is an extension of linear regression whose goal is to answer the following question: Given one or more input features what is the probability of getting either type of categorical response? This simple but powerful question applies to many other situations beyond the examples above, including the well-known prediction of survival of seriously injured patients [74] and other clinical events [75]. The wide applicability of logistic regression is linked to its distinguished history: It was first developed in the 1830s as a model of population growth and, like linear regression, was subsequently re-discovered multiple times in various fields of research, such as chemistry [76].

Probabilities range from 0 (low probability) to 1 (the event will most likely happen), and logistic regression models present this characteristic S-shaped probability curve (Fig. 3.10, upper plot). This curve results from applying the logistic function to model the response variable from the input features such that the resulting probabilities are kept within 0 and 1—negative values and values larger than one are perfectly valid in linear regressions.

In summary, logistic regression simply models the probability of output in terms of input, and when we set a cutoff to this probability we can easily build a classifier. For example, if the probability is $> 0.5$, then we may say that the classification result is, for example, 'A'; otherwise it is 'B'.

### 3.5.1 Interpreting Simple Logistic Regression

The upper plot in Fig. 3.10 shows a logistic regression fitted to model key variables of the mtcars dataset, a popular dataset that comes with the standard distribution of the R programming language and which details key characteristics of 32 different car models. Our model here describes the probability that a car has manual or automatic transmission

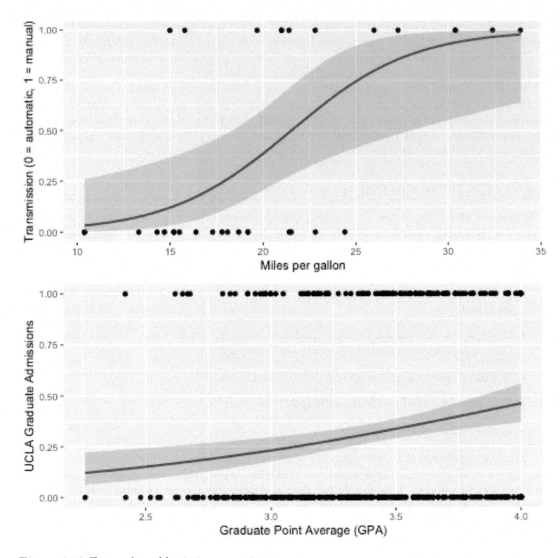

Figure 3.10 Examples of logistic regressions.

given its fuel efficiency. If we look at the data points closely, we see that the fuel efficiency of automatic cars stays below 25 miles per gallon (mpg). Fuel efficiency for manual cars starts at 15 mpg and goes up to about 34 mpg. This is expected as manual cars are more economical to run. Given this dataset of only 32 different vehicles and the fact that a substantial overlap exists between manual and automatic cars in the 15–25 mpg range, the 95% confidence interval is particularly wide. This is typical of small sample sizes as there is an inverse square root relationship between confidence intervals and the size of the sample. In other words, if we wish to reduce our margin error by 50% we need to quadruple our sample size.

The lower plot in Fig. 3.10 shows the probability of being admitted to graduate school at the University of California, Los Angeles (UCLA), given a specific GPA (your average undergraduate score) [77]. Why does the logistic regression curve not go all the way from 0 to 1 as in the example above? If we focus on the data points in the plot we can see that there is an extensive overlap in GPA scores between the students that were admitted (top line, probability = 1) and those that were rejected (lower line, probability = 0). Some students with really impressive GPA scores were turned down, whereas students with modest GPA scores were accepted. Therefore when there is not a clear difference between the two groups the predicted probabilities will not fluctuate between the two probability extremes and the result is the approximately linear curve that we see over the range of values. This actually makes a lot of sense because as important as undergraduate grades are, they are not the sole factors determining admission to graduate school.

The confidence on the coefficients of a logistic regression equation can be determined in a way similar to that of linear regression. The goodness-of-fit is calculated with another set of metrics, including the Likelihood Ratio Test ('Does adding another predictor improve the model?') and various pseudo $R^2$ metrics such as Cox and Snell's $R^2$, McFadden's $R^2$ and Tjur's $R^2$.

### 3.5.2 Multiple Logistic Regression

As with multiple linear regression, multiple logistic regression (also called multivariate logistic regression) considers additional predictor variables. For instance, besides the GPA scores, the UCLA Graduate Admissions dataset [77] contains two other key variables: the GRE score (a specific exam taken for access to graduate school in the US) and the rank of the undergraduate school a student attended (ranging from 1—most prestigious-to 4—least prestigious). GPA and GRE are numerical variables with continuous values, whereas the rank variable is categorical. Thus we can model the probabilistic relationship between admission to graduate school and GPA, GRE and rank (Fig. 3.11). This is a very standard way of thinking in data science: First we build a simple model and gradually build it up by adding additional variables. Most importantly, the results obtained from a regression model using a single predictor might be very different from those obtained using multiple, relevant predictors. This is called 'confounding' and can happen if, for example, the predictors are correlated.

When dealing with multiple predictors we also want to know how relevant each one is in predicting the response. For the UCLA graduate admissions dataset rank is nearly twice as important as the GPA. The GRE is the least important variable of these three in determining admission to graduate school at UCLA. However, the combination of these three predictors is still unable to predict entirely whether an applicant will be admitted to UCLA (Fig. 3.11). Therefore, additional factors are involved, such as the interview and the personal statement that is included in the application. If we could translate the quality of an applicant's statement into a numerical feature (feature engineering) this might help improve accuracy the model.

Once we have built a regression model we can start making predictions with our own input values. On top of this, with multiple regression models we can run interesting experiments to understand the effect of each variable on the final outcome. Remember that during any experiment (in any scientific field) we can only change one variable at a time while keeping all other variables constant. For example, let us say that a student that attended a rank-2 university has a GPA of 3.5. How good their performance at the GRE test must be to have a 50% probability of getting admitted to UCLA graduate school (Table 3.2)?

Now let us compare four equally outstanding applicants (GPA = 3.8, GRE = 790). How much of a drag would you say the rank of their undergraduate school is? The answer is that if you have such good scores and also attended a rank-1 school, essentially you already have a foot in the door. If you attended a rank-3 or rank-4 school, your chances of getting into UCLA graduate school are only half as good (Table 3.3).

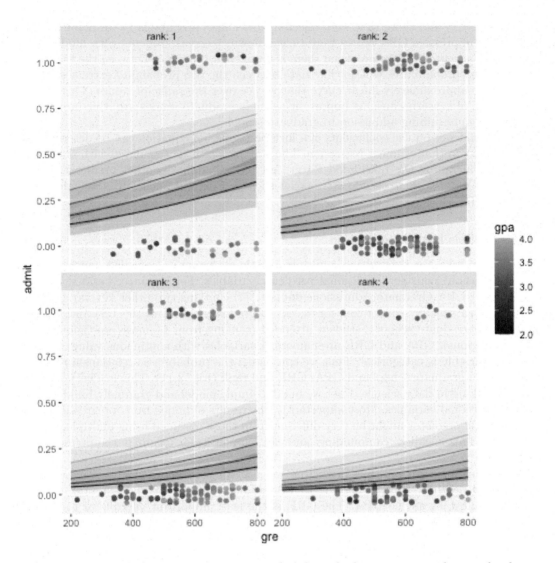

Figure 3.11 Multiple logistic regression – probability of admission to graduate school.

TABLE 3.2   Probability of Admission to UCLA Graduate School
for Various GRE Scores

| GRE | GPA | Undergraduate school rank | Probability |
|-----|-----|---------------------------|-------------|
| 600 | 3.5 | 2 | 37.92 |
| 650 | 3.5 | 2 | 40.62 |
| 700 | 3.5 | 2 | 43.38 |
| 750 | 3.5 | 2 | 46.18 |
| 800 | 3.5 | 2 | 49.00 |

Does this mean than an exceptional student who did not have the good fortune of attending a prestigious university in the first place will never get into graduate school at UCLA? Of course not, it only means that the cards are a bit stacked against them, but that is all. The logic behind attaching so much importance to the prestige of universities is the following: If an applicant has previously passed a tough selection process then there is limited

TABLE 3.3 Probability of Admission to UCLA
Graduate School (GPA = 3.8, GRE = 790)

| Undergraduate school rank | Probability |
|:---:|:---:|
| 1 | 0.70 |
| 2 | 0.54 |
| 3 | 0.38 |
| 4 | 0.33 |

risk in accepting this student. The downside of this conservative approach clearly is that it is easy to miss out on unconventional but very gifted students. One very important advantage of regression models (linear or logistic) is that they are completely transparent methods and the contribution of each variable to the outcome is well understood. Therefore anyone with access to admissions statistics (which many universities provide) could devise a strategy derived from the analysis of the data. For example, if I were the exceptional student who did not attend a prestigious university as an undergraduate, in my application statement I would not focus too much on why I did not get a perfect GRE score on the test day or a 4.0 GPA. I would just focus on explaining my choice of undergraduate university and how I went above and beyond the curriculum. This might include any research undertaken (which must be explained in detail), publications (journals, newspapers) and outreach activities. Finally, let us not forget that besides the bias introduced by admissions officers, we also have other important biases in the dataset. For example, the UCLA admissions data are from different graduate schools, and thus the probability of admission might differ a lot from the most selective to the least selective schools. Moreover, the dataset includes 400 applicants but these are heavily biased towards those that were rejected (274/400 or 68.5%) [77]. In Chapter 5 we discuss the importance of bias in training learning algorithms and how to correct it.

Logistic regression is only one technique that can be used to model a binary output from numerical features. Besides its many advantages, an obvious disadvantage is that it is rather sensitive to outliers (unlike Support Vector Machines, for example). Thus, the data must be properly inspected (and perhaps even curated) before fitting both linear and logistic regression models. Useful variations of logistic regression include the possibility of producing a categorical output from mixed input (continuous and binary) as well as from binary input alone; and the output of more than two outcome categories, called multinomial regression (or ordinal logistic regression if the categories are ordered as in exam results: A, B, C, D, F). Other classification techniques that may serve the same purpose as logistic regression include $K$-Nearest Neighbours (KNN), Linear Discriminant Analysis (LDA, perhaps a more popular method for multinomial regression), Support Vector Machines (SVM), and regression trees and ensembles of trees such as Random Forests.

## 3.6 NAÏVE BAYES CLASSIFICATION

Naïve Bayes is a simple probabilistic classifier whose goal is to learn the likelihood of event A happening given that event B has occurred, that is $P(A|B)$. These classifiers have been typically applied to specific problems such as spam detection and document classification, but they can be generally used for all binary and multi-class classification tasks. Naïve Bayes is super-fast, can perform really well when trained with limiting amounts of data, and yet it remains fast on large datasets (it is linearly scalable). Naïve Bayes might be outperformed by more sophisticated methods, yes, but since it works so well and is so easy to implement, naïve Bayes is often one's first port-of-call for classification problems. Any other method that is subsequently tried (e.g. logistic regression, KNN or SVM) should

TABLE 3.4    Occurrence of Sepsis-Related Symptoms

| | Blood pressure | | Pulse rate | | |
|---|---|---|---|---|---|
| | Low | Normal | Normal | High | Total |
| Sepsis | 21/25 | 4/25 | 5/25 | 20/25 | 25 |
| Non-sepsis | 4/75 | 71/75 | 70/75 | 5/75 | 75 |
| Total | 25/100 | 75/100 | 75/100 | 25/100 | 100 |

substantially outperform naïve Bayes to justify the greater computational complexity. Thus naïve Bayes is a baseline against which other classifiers are measured.

Bayes' theorem for conditional probability calculates $P(A|B)$ (properly called the posterior probability) by taking into account the likelihood, $P(B|A)$, the class prior probability, $P(A)$, and the predictor variable probability, $P(B)$:

$$P(A|B) = \frac{P(A) \times P(B|A)}{P(B)}$$

And now for a simple example: if we have a 52-card deck of cards, what is the probability of randomly picking a queen card if you know it is a face card?

$$P(Queen|Face) = \frac{P(Face|Queen) \times P(Queen)}{P(Face)}$$

The probability of simply picking a queen card ($P(A)$) is $4/52 = 1/13$ since there are four queens in every deck. The probability is picking a face given that it is a queen ($P(B|A)$) is simply 1 because a queen is always a face card. The probability of a card being a face ($P(B)$) is $12/52$ since there are 12 faces in each deck: Four jacks, Four queens and Four kings. Therefore, the probability that a card is a queen given a face card is 0.3:

$$P(Queen|Face) = \frac{1 \times (1/13)}{(12/52)} = 0.3$$

In this example we only had one predictor variable (the face card). Naïve Bayes classifiers are often used in clinical settings with multiple predictors. For example, let us say that we wish to implement a quick test in hospital admissions to determine whether a patient might be suffering from sepsis. Sepsis is a generalised infection throughout your body which, if left untreated, will kill you. Two of the most common symptoms in septic patients are low blood pressure and a very high pulse. Table 3.4 details the frequencies of low vs normal blood pressure, and normal vs high pulse rates, for a group of 100 patients (of which 1/4 are septic). Based on this dataset we can use a naïve Bayes classifier to predict the likelihood that a given patient might be septic. One question we could ask is, for a patient presenting low blood pressure but still a normal pulse rate, what are the chances that they might be septic?

Here we have two predictors instead of one (blood pressure and pulse rate), in which case the posterior probability $P(A|B)$ can be calculated as the product of the probability distribution for each individual variable conditioned on the response category (septic or non-septic). The class prior probabilities are:

$$P(sepsis) = 25/100$$
$$P(non\text{-}sepsis) = 75/100$$

The predictor prior probabilities are:

$$P(lowBP) = 25/100$$
$$P(normalBP) = 75/100$$
$$P(normalPulse) = 75/100$$
$$P(highPulse) = 25/100$$

The individual conditional probabilites are:

$$P(normalBP|sepsis) = 4/25$$
$$P(lowBP|sepsis) = 21/25$$
$$P(normalBP|non\text{-}sepsis) = 71/75$$
$$P(lowBP|non\text{-}sepsis) = 4/75$$
$$P(normalPulse|sepsis) = 5/25$$
$$P(highPulse|sepsis) = 20/25$$
$$P(normalPulse|non\text{-}sepsis) = 70/75$$
$$P(highPulse|non\text{-}sepsis) = 5/75$$

In order to classify our patient as septic or non-septic we must separately calculate the probabilities of the two events. First we work out the likelihood of our patient being septic. The symbol ∩ indicates the intersection of the two sets.

$$P(sepsis|lowBP \cap normalPulse)$$
$$= \frac{P(lowBP|sepsis) \times P(normalPulse|sepsis) \times P(sepsis)}{P(lowBP) \times P(normalPulse)} = 0.224$$

The likelihood of non-sepsis for our patient presenting low blood pressure but still a normal pulse rate is:

$$P(non\text{-}sepsis|lowBP \cap normalPulse)$$
$$= \frac{P(lowBP|non\text{-}sepsis) \times P(normalPulse|non\text{-}sepsis) \times P(non\text{-}sepsis)}{P(lowBP) \times P(normalPulse)} = 0.199$$

Since the likelihood that a patient with low blood pressure and a normal pulse rate being septic is greater than that of being non-septic ($0.224 > 0.199$), on the basis of this classification the patient should be inspected for additional signs of sepsis.

### 3.6.1 The Assumption of Predictor Variable Independence

One problem with diagnosing sepsis in this way is that we have only used two predictor variables. Sepsis really is a heterogeneous syndrome for which no standard diagnostic tests are available, and we should be taking other known symptoms into account such as high temperature, high respiratory rate and, in elderly people, an altered mental status [78, 79]. Would adding more predictor variables make the computation more complex? Yes, but only in a linear (proportional) way. This is because naïve Bayes makes an assumption that makes it possible to process large amounts of data very fast. Naïve Bayes assumes that the predictor variables are all independent from each other (hence the name *naïve*), which is almost never the case in the real world. A generalised infection of the body affects all organs, which are in turn interconnected through the blood and immune systems—it is not difficult to see how any one effect is conditionally dependent on others. Correlations between variables are normally determined with correlation plots.

For $m$ classes and $p$ predictor variables, predictor variable inter-dependence would mean making $m^p$ computations. For $m = 2$ (e.g. sepsis and non-sepsis) and $p = 2$ (blood pressure and pulse rate) the calculations are only $2^2 = 4$. However, what if we had a multi-class classification problem with more predictor variables? These problems are not difficult to imagine. For example, let us say that we want to build a classifier that takes written text and outputs the language it is written in. There are about 6,500 different languages in the world [80], and we could use a subset of 25 predictor words, which might be too few as many words are common to many languages. The computations here would be $6,500^{25} \sim 2.1 \times 10^{95}$, which is larger than the number of atoms present in the observable universe [81] and thus an intractable calculation. Under the assumption of predictor variable independence the calculations would only be $6,500 \times 25 = 162,500$, which then becomes a solvable problem. The predictor independence assumption is the main disadvantage of naïve Bayes classifiers, but it also is the blessing that makes them so fast. Is there a disadvantage to assuming variable independence? Yes. The problem is that the calculation of the posterior probability will be much less accurate. However, since the goal of a naïve Bayes classifier is not to be accurate but to determine which of the two (or more) likelihoods is greater (e.g. sepsis > non-sepsis), at this level it usually works very well.

The output calculated here by the naïve Bayes classifiers is binary (sepsis vs non-sepsis) and the predictor variables are equally categorical (blood pressure low vs normal, and pulse rate normal vs high). The predictor variables may also be continuous—for example if we had been given the patients' pulse rates as continuous measurements we could have discretised the values into normal ($\leq 100$ bpm) and high ($> 100$ bpm).

## 3.7 TREES

Trees are one popular method for making decisions or predictions about data characterised by many different variables that do not necessarily hold linear relationships. An example of such a situation is given by the following financial question: 'Should this person be granted the loan?' The data scientist in a bank can gather historical data and determine the profiles of those customers that pay their loans on time vs those that do not. For a relatively homogeneous customer population the decision process can be straightforward and even intuitive (Fig. 3.12):

In the tree in Fig. 3.12 the boxes with the final decision (loan granted/declined) are the terminal nodes or leaves of the tree. In a city with a more heterogeneous customer population we would try to incorporate additional variables as these might help make finer decisions. These variables might include the applicant's nationality, how long they have been living in the country for, whether they work for a local company or one in their country of origin, and whether they can produce a credit rating history. The resulting tree will learn a richer set of decision rules from the training data, but it will also be a deeper tree that will most likely require *pruning* (see below). In this example of the bank loan the target variable is categorical (loan granted/declined), and this type of tree is called a classification tree. Trees can also be built to estimate the value of a continuous target variable (e.g. price, weight, height), but such regression trees are rare these days because standard regression models and neural networks tend to outperform them in terms of prediction accuracy (Chapter 4).

Another example of a categorical classification involving a complex dataset is the prediction of passenger survival in the Titanic. In 1912, 60% of the passengers aboard the Titanic died when the ship hit an iceberg in the North Atlantic ocean. Besides giving rise to a great film, this fateful trip also produced a very interesting dataset [82] containing detailed information on over 1,300 passengers (Table 3.5):

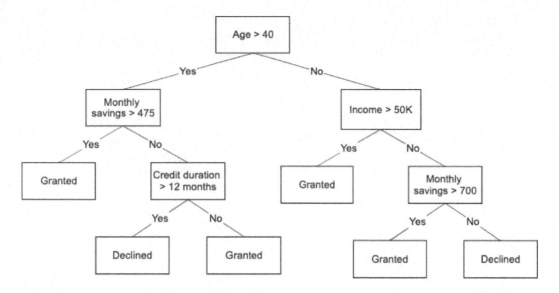

Figure 3.12 A simplified example of a binary decision-making process using a tree.

TABLE 3.5  Passenger Statistics Aboard the Titanic (1912)

| Survived | Pclass | Sex | Age | SibSp | Parch | Fare | Embarked |
|---|---|---|---|---|---|---|---|
| 0 | 3 | male | 22 | 1 | 0 | 7.2500 | S |
| 1 | 3 | female | 26 | 0 | 0 | 7.9250 | S |
| 1 | 1 | female | 35 | 1 | 0 | 53.1000 | S |
| 0 | 3 | male | 35 | 0 | 0 | 8.0500 | S |
| 0 | 1 | male | 54 | 0 | 0 | 51.8625 | S |
| 0 | 3 | male | 2 | 3 | 1 | 21.0750 | S |
| ... | ... | ... | ... | ... | ... | ... | ... |

Besides Sex, Age and Fare, the other variables include: Survived (0 = No, 1 = Yes), Pclass (Passenger Class: 1st, 2nd or 3rd), SibSp (Number of siblings or spouses aboard), Parch (number of parents or children aboard) and Embarked (Port of embarkation: (C)herbourg, (Q)ueenstown or (S)outhampton). In contrast to the bank loan example, here the relationships among the data are not as obvious. Would you be able to predict who would have survived? Would you say that the passenger cabin class was a relevant factor? Or perhaps the age of the passenger?

The application of the well-known CART (Classification and Regression Trees) algorithm [83, 84] on the Titanic dataset yields the tree shown in Fig. 3.13.

The top (root) node of the tree contains 100% of the dataset, which is progressively partitioned as we travel down the various branches of the tree. The top node states that 60% of the passengers died, with the zero at the top indicating how the node is voting (0 = death, 1 = survival). The CART algorithm found that the first, most important consideration for the passenger population is whether one is male or female. Note how trees are also helpful in a descriptive manner for exploring the structure of a dataset and uncovering dependence relationships among the variables.

Males (down and left of the top node) make up 64% of the passenger population and have an overall survival rate of only 20%. If you are a male over 13 years of age (like me), then

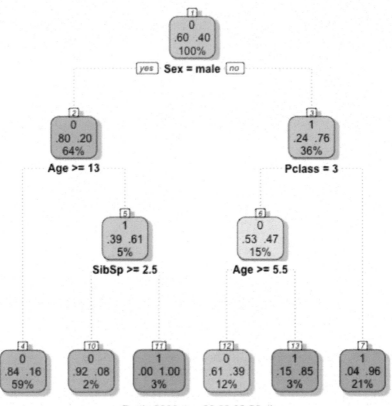

Rattle 2020-Jun-28 23:08:58 diego

Figure 3.13 A decision tree to predict survival vs death among the passengers of the Titanic.

your chances of survival are only 16% (left-most terminal leave, at the bottom). Finally, the best chances of survival were for boys under 13 years of age travelling with both parents and no siblings (100% survival rate), but this group only represents 3% of the entire population aboard the Titanic.

But how is each node partitioned in order to create the whole tree? Deciding what data has to be at the root and at each subsequent node is the main challenge in building reliable decision trees. The algorithm first considers all the variables and then decides on the best one to split on. In the *information gain* approach the goal is to split on the variable that results in the most pure nodes, thereby maximising information gain (i.e. reducing the level of entropy) as you travel downwards from the root node. For example, a decision that splits the data into 90% and 10% is better than one that splits the data into 50% and 50%. The process of splitting the original datasets until no more splits can be done (e.g. when the subset at a node has all the same values of the target variable) is called *recursive binary partitioning*.

Trees are easy to understand because the graphical representation of trees mimics how the human brain works. In fact, early philosophers recognised the hierarchical classification of categorical information. A clear example of this can be found in Aristotle's (384–322 BC) *Categories*, a book on how to categorise and think about the world around us. This work not only encapsulates much of Aristotle's philosophy but has also been incredibly influential in much of Western philosophy ever since.

Another key advantage of trees is that they make it clear what the most important decision-making variables are. Moreover, the statistics detailed in each node makes them intuitive and easy to explain to anyone. Being able to understand and explain in detail how a classifier works is a very important point in data science: For many algorithms (e.g. neural networks) it is not possible to explain why a particular instance was assigned a given predicted value. Trees are also fast and can handle very large numerical and categorical datasets. Moreover, running a tree algorithm requires relatively little effort on the part of the data scientist as the data typically needs little or no pre-processing.

One important limitation of trees is that beyond a certain point the optimal tree cannot possibly be learnt in an acceptable amount of time. This type of search problem is described as *NP-complete* in algorithmic theory. The practical approach to modelling a tree in an acceptable amount of time is to use a *heuristic* (an approximation that is not optimal but which can give an good-enough answer in a realistic time frame) like CART's recursive partitioning approach [83]. The CART algorithm is also a type of greedy algorithm as it focuses on finding the locally optimal solution at each node, one node at a time. Not considering all the possible solutions at once makes it impossible to find the optimal solution, but it makes the computation so much faster. This strategy also means that a partition done early in the tree cannot be optimised later based on subsequent partitions. Therefore a greedy algorithm like CART trades optimality for efficiency. To illustrate how greedy algorithms work with a different example, imagine you live in a country where the coins are worth 1, 15 and 25 cents. Let us say that you buy something in a shop and the cashier algorithm has to give you 30 cents back using the smallest number of coins possible (the splitting strategy). A greedy algorithm would start with the coin that leaves the smallest amount of change left to pay $(25 + 1 + 1 + 1 + 1 + 1)$, whereas we all know that the optimal solution would be $15 + 15$ as this minimises the number of coins you have to carry in your wallet. Trees work in the same way: They give you a solution fast, but it may not be the globally optimal solution.

### 3.7.1 Tree Pruning

The purpose of modelling a tree is to be able to use it for predicting outcomes on new data. However, a dataset containing very specific attributes will render a tree unable to generalise to new data. That is, it will make poor predictions. For instance, if we had information about which deck of the Titanic each passenger's room was on, this could be included in the model. But would this attribute be useful for predicting passenger survival in a similar type of accident? This would probably be as useful as knowing the home town of each passenger. A tree cannot classify attribute value combinations that are not present in the training data. This is called *high variance* and is a major cause of poor predictive performance (Chapter 4).

Depending on the number of attributes and their combinations, the complete partitioning of a dataset can result in very deep trees. If $n$ is the number of instances the minimum and maximum depth of a binary tree is $log_2(n)$ and $n - 1$, respectively. There are manual ways to limit the growth of a tree, for example by setting an upper limit to the number of nodes or a lower limit to the number of data points required before another split is made (otherwise resulting in a terminal node). However, using a systematic method like tree pruning is preferable. The pruning of a tree has the effect of limiting its variance and thus prevent the overfitting to specific attributes. The tree is made smaller by snipping some of the lower ends (starting from the terminal leaves). The final size of the tree can be controlled by a cost complexity parameter that balances the depth of a tree against its complexity in order to optimise predictive performance. Very simply, if the cost of adding another attribute to the tree from the current node is greater than the value of the cost complexity parameter, then that node becomes a terminal node. The bias introduced by pruning a tree helps stabilise the ability of the tree to generalise on new data.

## 3.8 ENSEMBLE LEARNING: INDIVIDUAL MODELS ARE WEAK, FAMILIES ARE NOT

Most supervised learning methods, including linear and logistic regression, naïve Bayes and Support Vector Machines, are based on a single, predictive model. The disadvantage of this approach is that there will always be an upper limit to the performance of any single model. We can only go this far by tuning an algorithm's hyperparameters. The next question then becomes: How can we overcome any method's intrinsic limitations?

By combining multiple, weak models into a family of models it is often possible to overcome the predictive limitations of single models. Ensembles tend to give better results when the models being combined are particularly diverse. We must note, however, that the design of ensembles is both a science and an art; not surprisingly, some superb ensembles like the one that won the Netflix Grand Prize in 2009 are poster children in predictive analytics [85].

It has been shown that it is possible to determine the optimal number of models to combine (both for batch and online ensemble classifiers), and that this depends on the majority voting technique that is used to generate the final prediction (see below). For example, for majority voting ensembles the predictions become more accurate the more strong models that are combined. However, if the majority voting is weighted, the optimal number of models is close to the number of class labels as long as the models are strong and independent from each other [86]. The individual models can represent different algorithms, but in practice many ensembles are made of trees because trees are easy to train and generally fast to run. Bagging, Random Forests and boosting machines are some of the most popular approaches to building ensembles that result in particularly robust learning methods.

### 3.8.1 Bootstrap Aggregating (Bagging)

Single trees typically present high variance and their pruning helps reduce it. Another way to explain high variance is the following: If instead of modelling a tree from your entire training data you split it into two equal parts and use each part to model a tree, the two trees will be quite different. This is because there will be an uneven distribution of attribute combinations, and any tree can basically adjust its predictions to every single input.

In other words, the variance is the error introduced when an algorithm is particularly sensitive to tiny fluctuations in the training dataset. Not all algorithms are equally affected by fluctuations in the dataset: Linear regression, for instance, tends to present low variance as long as the number of data points is larger than the number of attributes.

One limitation of the tree pruning technique is that high variance is reduced by essentially getting rid of some data (data that might be useful!). Bootstrap aggregating (bagging) is an ingenious technique developed by Leo Breiman [87] that circumvents the problem of having to get rid of data. Bagging consists of generating multiple, similar, models from the original training set and averaging the results at the end. Like this we take advantage of all the tiny particularities of the data but we only take them into account if they are statistically significant.

During bagging we first create hundreds (or thousands) of sets of instances (bags) from the training data (Fig. 3.14). These bags are generated by bootstrapping, that is each bag must have the same number of observations as the training set but any one observation from the training set can be included in the bag more than once (that is, there is replacement).

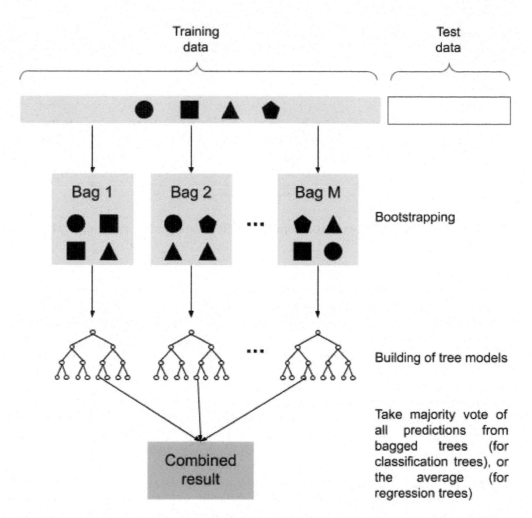

Figure 3.14 The principle of bootstrap aggregating (bagging).

Next, we model a tree on each bootstrapped set of instances. Trees are grown as deep as needed but are not pruned, and thus present high variance. The individual predictions from all trees are averaged (for regression trees) or the majority vote taken (for classification trees), and these will be the final, predicted values. Bagging typically improves the predictive performance of a single tree as it takes advantage of the entire dataset. Moreover, it is easy to determine the contribution of each specific predictor, as well as the test error of a bagged model if we have a hold-out dataset. However, the two main limitations of bagged models are (i) they are less easy to explain than single trees and (ii) since all models are built from the same dataset, they may be highly correlated.

### 3.8.2   Random Forests or the Wisdom of the Crowd

A fundamental problem with bagged trees is that they can present a high degree of correlation. This arises whenever there is one or more strong predictors in the dataset. For example, in the Titanic dataset out of the eight different predictive features (Table 3.5) the most important one is the passenger's gender (Fig. 3.13). This is not surprising given that

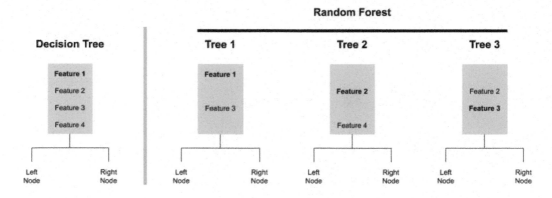

Figure 3.15 A hypothetical 3-tree Random Forest illustrating node splitting with random feature sets.

most of the passengers aboard the Titanic were adults and whenever the rescue lifeboats are rolled out women and children always go first. Here the gender is a strong predictor.

The problem with these dominant predictors is that if you end up with such a predictor in your bag, that predictor will always be chosen. This is why in the presence of strong predictors many bagged trees will look very similar (especially at the top). Predictions from similar trees will be equally similar, or correlated. Averaging the results of many highly correlated trees does not lead to a reduction in variance.

The improvement introduced by Random Forests (RF) involves limiting the number of predictors that can be used at each split. RFs are identical to bagged trees except that in a RF you cannot use all the predictors for making the split at each node. In a RF, each time a split in a tree is considered, the algorithm randomly chooses a sample of predictors from the full set of predictors. From this sample, only one predictor is eventually chosen for the split. For example, if the total number of predictors $(p)$ is, say $n = 8$ as in the Titanic dataset (Table 3.5), at each split of a RF tree typically only $p = \sqrt{8} \approx 3$ predictors are considered. This introduces even more diversity among the trees and ultimately results in lower correlation across trees and more robust predictions (Fig. 3.15). The original idea for the random subsetting of predictors came from Tin Kam Ho in 1995 [88], and the bagging improvement was later introduced by Adele Cutler and Leo Breiman [89].

RFs exploit a statistical phenomenon known as 'the wisdom of the crowd'. In a social context, this is the situation where the collective opinion of a group of people (among which there might be domain experts) is on average more accurate than the opinion of any single person. Although first mentioned by Aristotle (384 BC – 322 BC) in his opus *Politics*, the statistical description of the wisdom of the crowd phenomenon was first reported by Sir Francis Galton (1822–1911) in 1906. While visiting the Annual Show of the West of England Fat Stock and Poultry Exhibition (Plymouth), Galton witnessed a weight-judging competition whereby entrants had to guess the weight of an ox. Those whose estimate was closer to the real weight would win a prize. Upon examination of the 800 tickets that were entered for the competition, Galton realised that the median value of all tickets (1207 pounds) was only 0.8% larger than the real weight of the dead animal (1198 pounds) [90].

What is the logic behind the wisdom of the crowd? Very simply, each person's prediction is biased, either as an underestimate or an overestimate of the real weight of the ox. By taking a central value of all the individual judgements it is somewhat likely that the noise asociated with the predictions will cancel out since not everyone will err in the same

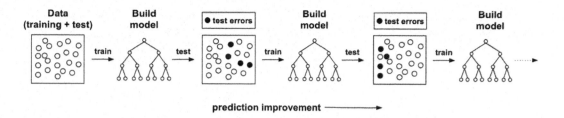

Figure 3.16 Boosting machines improve their performance iteratively.

direction. The wisdom of the crowd is also the principle behind criminal trials by juries as well as collaborative filtering recommender systems (see below).

Like all trees, RFs can be applied to both categorical and continuous target variables, are able to handle outliers and imbalanced data, and also have the advantage of being less prone to overfitting (Chapter 4). On the other hand, RFs lose interpretability next to normal trees where you can see the individual node splits. Thus, like other complex predictive methods such as Support Vector Machines and Neural Networks, RFs too become some sort of 'black boxes'. However, they are particularly good black boxes to consider since in a recent experimental evaluation of classification algorithms against over a hundred datasets, RFs turned out to be the best all-round family of classifiers [91].

### 3.8.3 Boosting Machines

Boosting ensembles are among the best families of classifiers [91] and they also use many trees (although other base learners can also be used). A fundamental difference with the bagging method is that whereas bagging produces many, non-identical copies of the training dataset to fit as many independent decision trees, the trees produced in boosting are not independent. Each tree is built from the previous tree in a sequential process to correct the errors from the previous model and up until some predetermined limit is reached (Fig. 3.16). The first boosting algorithm, AdaBoost (short for Adaptive Boosting), was developed in 1995 by Yoav Freund and Robert Schapire to boost the performance of decision trees on binary classification problems [92].

Boosting is a very flexible method, which also complicates finding the optimal combination of hyperparameters (e.g. the depth of the trees and their optimal number, which can be thousands, and the learning rate). One advantage of this slow process, however, is that the potential for model overfitting is lesser. Moreover, because each tree is the product of a progressive learning exercise, smaller trees typically suffice, which helps with their interpretability.

## 3.9 SUPPORT VECTOR MACHINES

The goal of a Support Vector Machine (SVM) is to separate observations into classes. SVMs were originally conceived in 1963 by Vladimir Vapnik and coworkers for classification problems [93, 94]. Some 30 years later the SVM method was extended for regression challenges (called Support Vector Regression) [95, 96].

To separate observations into classes, an SVM first plots the labelled data points and then determines the best way to separate them using either a line, or a more complicated shape. For example, in Fig. 3.17(a) we have two different classes: The red circles and the blue triangles. The two classes could represent anything that you like, such as disease vs

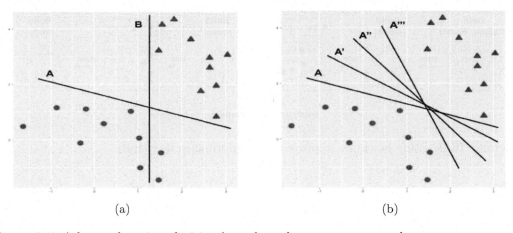

Figure 3.17 A hyperplane is a decision boundary that separates two classes.

non-disease, sunny vs rainy, male vs female, etc. How would you separate these two classes, by using line A or line B?

Line A is the better linear decision boundary here because it achieves the perfect separation of the two classes. The plots in Fig. 3.17 are on a two-dimensional plane ($X$ and $Y$ coordinates), which is characteristic of datasets with two features. More complicated datasets with $n$ features are plotted in $n$-dimensional space, which is often impossible to represent visually although the principle is the same. In $n$-dimensional space the linear separator is properly called a **hyperplane**, which in an $n$-dimensional Euclidean space is a flat, $n-1$ dimensional subset of that space that divides the space into two disconnected parts. And now, if we focus on Fig. 3.17(b), which of the four hyperplanes would you choose, A, A', A" or A"'? The most rational choice of hyperplane is the one that represents the largest separation (called the *hard margin*) between the two classes. One way to visualise this is to think of the widest possible brick that you can insert between the two classes—the midline of the brick is effectively your optimal hyperplane. Fig. 3.18 displays the optimal hyperplane for this dataset (called the 'maximal margin hyperplane'), which in fact is quite similar to the almost vertical A"' line from Fig. 3.17(b). This more sophisticated representation shows that the maximal margin hyperplane really is a mathematical boundary with a given slope that is centered around zero (or the white colour in Fig. 3.18). Naturally, changing the hyperplane's slope also means un-optimising the margin.

The black, filled-in triangles and circles in Fig. 3.18 are the **support vectors** that determine the position and slope of the maximal margin hyperplane. The hyperplane is solely dependent on the position of the support vectors and not on any of the other data points. This algorithmic feature confers the important advantage of making SVMs particularly robust to the presence of outliers (unlike linear regression). The disadvantage, on the other hand, also is that the hyperplane is very sensitive to even small changes in any of the support vectors.

Therefore, the goal of an SVM is to find the hyperplane that best segregates the labelled data. The rationale for selecting the hyperplane with the higher margin is robustness because a lower margin hyperplane that is then used as a classifier (called a *maximal margin classifier*) is more bound to mis-classify new data points. Fig. 3.18 shows a nice and wide maximal margin hyperplane that allows for the perfect separation of the two classes. Thus it qualifies as a maximal margin classifier. There are other cases, however, where instead of such a comfortable, hard margin we find what is called a *soft margin* [97]. In soft margins some of the observations are allowed within the margin (the whiteish stretch between the

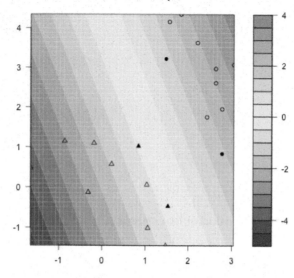

Figure 3.18 A hyperplane is a mathematical boundary determined by the support vectors (black triangles and circles).

support vectors in Fig. 3.18) when they should really be outside of it, or even allowed on the wrong side of the hyperplane. A soft margin hyperplane is advantageous when the two classes cannot be perfectly separated by a line (but still a line is the simplest boundary that allows to generalise beyond the training set), as well as in situations where a separating hyperplane might not be sensible. For example if the margin of the fitted hyperplane can actually separate the two classes but is really narrow then the confidence of the subsequent classifications will be equally narrow. Here the implementation of a soft margin hyperplane where some of the training data points are naturally allowed to be misclassified makes a better classifier. The extension of a maximal margin classifier to the soft margin classifier (which is still linear but allows some misclassification) is also known as the *support vector classifier*.

## 3.9.1 The Kernel Trick

Most real datasets, however, will not be fully separable by the linear maximal margin nor the soft margin classifiers. Non-linear classification is done by using a technique called the *kernel trick*, which is essentially a complex mathematical function that can take almost any shape (polynomial, Gaussian, sigmoid, hyperbolic, etc.) and which transforms the input data into a higher dimensional space that facilitates their separation (Fig. 3.19). The modification of the feature space using kernels is properly called the SVM. The key aspects of an SVM are the choice of kernel and its parameters (Gaussian is standard) and the soft margin parameter $C$. One way to find the best combination of these two is by exploring all the possible combinations and then testing by cross-validation (Chapter 4). One important extension of the kernel trick is its application to cluster analysis (Chapter 2): Since the data are mapped to a higher dimensional feature space to facilitate their separation, this also makes it possible to discriminate clusters of data [98].

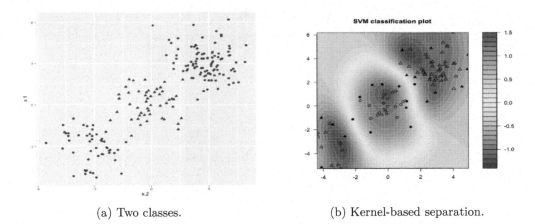

(a) Two classes. (b) Kernel-based separation.

Figure 3.19 Kernel-based separation of two classes.

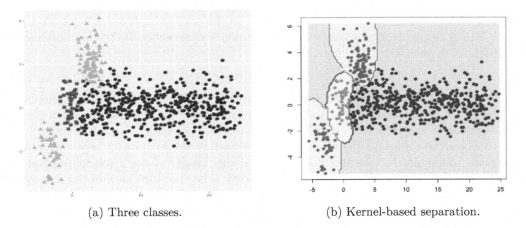

(a) Three classes. (b) Kernel-based separation.

Figure 3.20 Kernel-based separation of three classes.

### 3.9.2 Multi-Category Separation by SVMs

So far we have discussed classifiers for separating two different classes, either using a linear boundary (Fig. 3.18) or a non-linear one (Fig. 3.19). SVMs can also be used in a robust manner to separate data consisting of multiple classes (Fig. 3.20). The extension of a binary classification SVM into a multi-category (multi-class) one can be achieved by reducing the problem into many different binary classification problems, which can in turn be done using various strategies (e.g. one vs all and one vs one).

### 3.9.3 Advantages and Disadvantages of SVMs

Generally SVMs can be used with any type of data and can be useful in high dimensional spaces and for the classification of data whose number of features is greater than the number of examples. On the other hand, if there is too much noise in the data (e.g. when target classes overlap), SVMs will not perform that well and here logistic regression might be a better choice. Traditionally SVMs have been extensively used for classifying images and text, but some detractors will say that deep neural networks will perform better in this

TABLE 3.6  Can You Predict the Output for
Input Value = 4?

| Input | Output |
|-------|--------|
| 1 | 2 |
| 2 | 4 |
| 3 | 6 |
| 4 | ? |

area. On the other hand, deep learning requires much more data for learning a model, which might not always be available.

One clear disadvantage of SVMs is that the number of key parameters that must be carefully tuned for optimal results for a given problem will be different from those for a different problem. Also, complex kernels cannot be interpreted easily and SVMs are not that efficient computationally with really large datasets (unlike deep neural networks).

## 3.10   ARTIFICIAL NEURAL NETWORKS

Artificial Neural Networks (ANNs) are a class of supervised learning algorithms used both for classification and regression problems; in both cases the input may be numerical or categorical, and the output may only be categorical (classification) or numerical (regression) [99].

The role of an ANN is to take a series of inputs and outputs and derive a function that maps the two. That is, ANNs are function approximators. For example, given the series of inputs and outputs in Table 3.6, what would say is the output value for 4?

Most people would say that the output value for 4 is 8 because for every other input, the corresponding output is twice its value. Thus, we can say that the function mapping input $x$ to output is $f(x) = 2x$.

ANNs are so called because their design is inspired by biological neurons (Fig. 3.21). An animal neuron consists of three main parts: A cell body (where the nucleus and most of the cellular machinery is located), a number of dendrites that receive information, and a number of axon terminals that transmit a response to this information onto the next cell(s). When enough input signals reach the dendrites, the cell body generates a response signal that travels down the cell's axon to the synaptic terminals where certain chemical signals are released to affect the adjacent cell.

The concept of the artificial neuron was first proposed in 1943 in McCulloch and Pitts's working model of the human brain [100]. Then, in 1948 Alan Turing proposed the concept of a neural network, which he referred to as 'B-type unorganised machines' [101]. However, it was not until 1957 that the mathematical description of the single artificial neuron (called the *perceptron*) was completed by a young and brilliant research psychologist called Frank Rosenblatt [102]. The perceptron is a simple binary classifier that takes inputs, adds them, applies an activation function and produces an output (Fig. 3.22, [103]).

### 3.10.1   The Perceptron

In Fig. 3.22 the inputs $X = \{x_1, x_2, x_3, ..., x_n\}$ correspond to the dendrites (and the weights signify the importance of each input), the activation corresponds to the axon terminals, and the transfer function, net input and activation function are equivalent to the cell body where the output response is computed. As with animal neurons, only when a specific activation threshold is reached does the activation function produce an output signal. The activation threshold for signal propagation is neuron-dependent. Despite its simplicity, the

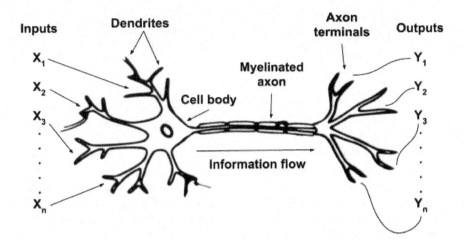

Figure 3.21 Schematic representation of an animal neuron.

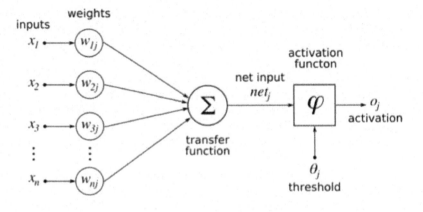

Figure 3.22 The perceptron.

perceptron might still find its application niche today for linearly separable problems because it is very fast [104].

As an example of how a single artificial neuron works, let us return to the example of TV advertising expenditure vs sales that we examined in the context of linear regression. A linear relationship exists between the two variables, and thus the amount of sales may be approximated by a linear regression function taking the amount of TV advertising expenditure as the input variable (Fig. 3.8). A one-neuron ANN would approximate this relationship by using a linear activation function (Fig. 3.23).

In this one-neuron ANN (Fig. 3.23) the input layer reads input data, whereas the *transfer function* adds all the inputs together to calculate a net input. This transfer function is also referred to as the *net input function*. The *activation function* is then applied to the net input to generate an output given a particular threshold. There are many different activation functions, including linear, binary step, sigmoid, softsign and the Rectified Linear Unit (RLU). When non-linear functions are used in a neural network, the entire network behaves like a very large and complex non-linear function.

Bear in mind that sometimes the combination of the net input and activation functions is collectively called the *transfer function*. This terminology goes back to the machine

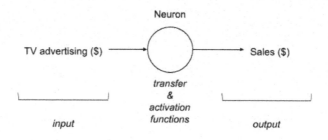

Figure 3.23 A one-neuron ANN.

learning books of the 80's and 90's when the discipline was not yet mainstream and many practitioners had a background in electrical engineering.

### 3.10.2 Beyond the Perceptron

A single neuron, however, has limited intrinsic approximation capability and would not be able to map input-output relationships that are more complex than this simple, linear example. Since ANNs can be of any size and structure, the real power of ANNs comes from having many neurons working together into a defined architecture. Such a neural network allows accommodating more complex input space where the variables might be related not only linearly but in many different ways. For example, for the sales prediction example we might want to include marketing expenditure not only on TV but also on other venues such as Google and the radio, and also throw in people's perception of your product on social networks (e.g. Facebook) as all of these are known to influence sales. The resulting ANN with four features has an input layer, a three-neuron hidden layer where the learning occurs, and an output layer (Fig. 3.24).

### 3.10.3 How Do ANNs Learn?

This multi-neuron ANN is also a great starting point to illustrate the following question: How do ANNs learn? As with any other supervised learning technique, ANNs must be trained with labelled data. In ANNs the weighted sum of the input features is fed into the activation function which then gives random weights to the connections between the neurons. This first training pass (called the *forward pass*) produces an output that is recorded. Do you think that this first output will be close enough to the labelled output values? The answer is no for the vast majority of forward passes. Since the goal is to minimise the difference between the predicted output values and the labelled output values, the weights between neurons (positive values for activation, negative for inhibition) must then be adjusted during a process called *backpropagation* [105] and the neural network rerun until the network converges towards a pre-determined performance value. A parameter called the *learning rate parameter* (*r*) gives an indication of how close we are to the optimum weight values.

Since there are not only various hyperparameters that help you tune the performance of an ANN, but also a multitude of activation functions, no universal tuning strategy exists. However, certain activation functions are known to work well in specific situations. Given enough training data and the right activation function, ANNs are capable of learning approximately any function. However, this does not mean that ANNs can by virtue of their design outperform just any other learning algorithm.

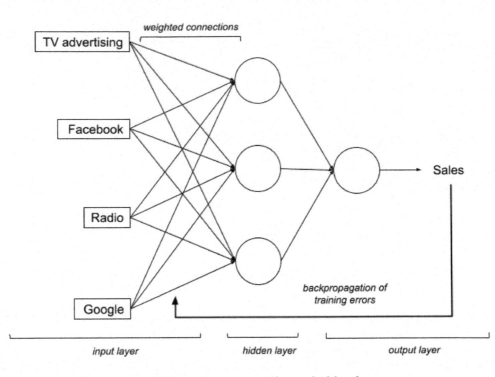

Figure 3.24 A multi-neuron ANN architecture with one hidden layer.

An extra degree of complication is introduced by the ever-growing range of network architectures (Fig. 3.25, [106, 107]). In theory, those networks with a larger number of hidden layers are capable of learning more abstract concepts, and therefore approximate more complex problems. In practice, however, most existing problems can be solved with networks presenting a single hidden layer (plus the input and output layers). The most important take-home message here is that each ANN architecture tends to be suited to a specific sets of problems. Building up from the simplest architecture (the perceptron), a well-known topology is the Convolutional Neural Network (CNN), which is designed specifically for computer vision. Recurrent Neural Networks (RNN) are applicable to time series or sequences of data and form the basis of forecasting and language models, and the Deep Feed Forward (DFF) network is an adaptation of the Feed Forward networks of the 1950s but with more than one hidden layer. DFFs were responsible for key early developments in deep learning in the early 1990s (Fig. 3.25).

### 3.10.4 Advantages and Disadvantages of ANNs

The main advantages of ANNs are that (i) they are able to map any complex relationship (e.g. highly non-linear) between input and output values and (ii) ANNs can handle high-dimensional problems such as image classification.

One serious disadvantage of ANNs is that they are so complex that they essentially function as black boxes. This makes them difficult to explain, tune or correct. A funny example of how things can go wrong with neural networks happened during a football match of Inverness Caledonian Thistle FC (Scotland) in October 2020. The COVID-19 pandemic prevented supporters from attending the matches and the local club decided to live stream its matches using a camera system powered by deep learning technology. Such a camera must follow the ball, which is not such an easy problem because the ball must be

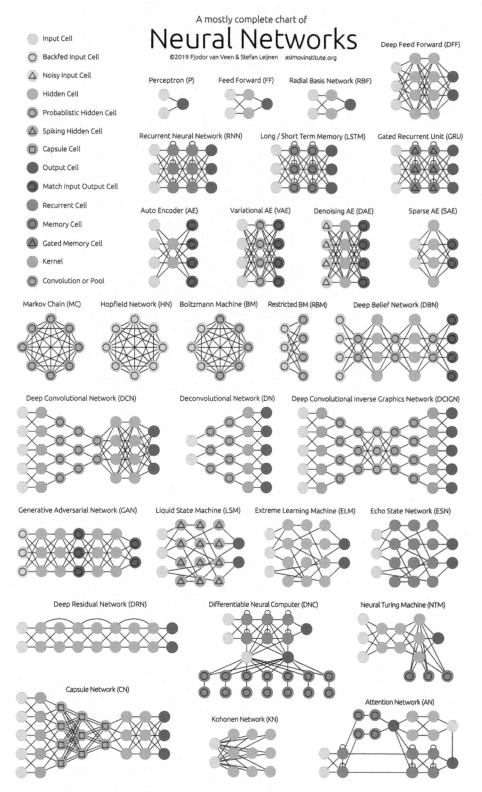

Figure 3.25 Architectures of the most recurrent types of neural networks [106].

**Tom Cox**
@seagull81

Inverness Caledonian Thistle don't employ a cameraman as
their camera is programmed to follow the ball throughout the
match. The commentator had to apologise today as the
camera kept on mistaking the ball for the linesman's head...

12:36 AM · Oct 25, 2020                                    ⓘ

♡ 10.9K   ♡ 2.4K people are Tweeting about this

Figure 3.26 Inverness Caledonian Thistle FC's AI-powered camera disaster.

identified against many different backgrounds, e.g. it could be on the ground, in the air, or
in the hands of a player or the goalkeeper. Instead of following the ball on the pitch the
camera kept focusing on the lineman's bald head (Fig. 3.26, [108]). How would you tweak
a deep neural network with possibly hundreds of connected layers? [109].

Besides the finesse required to tune a network's hyperparameters, another disadvantage
of ANNs is that they are very sensitive to the weights initially given prior to learning.
Particularly inappropriate initial weights may not allow the ANN to improve its performance
beyond a certain point. However, the greatest disadvantage of ANNs probably is their all-
round applicability and power, especially in the context of deep learning: Data scientists
tend to overuse ANNs for almost any classification and regression problem these days. This
practice often results in overly-complicated models that are difficult to explain and reason
about when the problem at hand may have been solved using simpler methods. Despite
the tremendous power and flexibility of ANNs they require much more data than simpler
methods. When it comes to choosing between two algorithms that perform equally well for
a given problem, unnecessary complexity is not a virtue.

## 3.11   DEEP LEARNING

Following the development of the perceptron in 1957 [102], Marvin Minsky (1927–2016)
provided sound theoretical proof of its limitations [110]. This cooled down the development of the field during the 1970s and 1980s until John Hopfield suggested the concept of
*backpropagation* to make networks learn, and which led to overcoming the limitations of the

perceptron [105]. The rebirth of ANNs in the first decade of the this century was due to a few key influential papers. For example, the group of Geoffrey Hinton at the University of Toronto presented an algorithm that allowed the efficient training of deep belief networks [111] and other groups like those of Yoshua Bengio (University of Montreal) and Yann Le-Cun (New York University) published similar methods [112, 113]. It was at this time that the name 'deep learning' became a popular way to refer to our new ability to train deeper networks. Jürgen Schmidhuber has also produced many fundamental contributions to the deep learning field, the most popular of which are the Long Short Term Memory (LSTM) networks. LSTMs are a type of recurrent neural network architecture (Fig. 3.25) with feedback connections, allowing them to remember the most relevant information in a sequence and make it available for future use. LSTMs are applied to tasks as varied as speech and handwriting recognition, voice assistants, robotics and music composition. They are used by all major software companies and power millions of devices around the world [114].

An ANN is called a deep neural network (DNN) if it contains at least one hidden layer between input and output. For example, the network in Fig. 3.24 contains just one hidden layer, but the Deep Belief Network (DBN) in Fig. 3.25 contains five hidden layers. Hidden-layer architectures are behind some of the most exciting developments and innovations in natural language processing, computer vision, personalised medicine, finance, speech recognition and self-driving cars.

The number of hidden layers in a DNN is potentially unlimited. For example, Inception-ResNet-v2 is a Convolutional Neural Network (CNN) trained on over a million images from the ImageNet database [115]. This CNN is 164 layers deep and can classify images into one thousand different object categories [116]. However, although deeper networks make better learners than shallower ones, they also require more training data. Another key decision when building a DNN is how many neurons should be allocated to each layer.

### 3.11.1  AlexNet and the ImageNet Competition

Despite the influential papers that the groups of Hinton, Bengio and LeCun published around 2006–2007, the real 'Big Bang' that put the field of deep learning in the limelight happened in 2012 with the reporting of the AlexNet DNN developed by Alex Krizhevsky, Ilya Sutskever and Geoffrey Hinton that won the ImageNet challenge in 2012 [117].

ImageNet (image-net.org/) is an image database that is used in research on object recognition [115]. An image in ImageNet is annotated to indicate the presence or absence of a particular object (e.g. 'image contains dog'), and on a deeper level with a bounding box around the object in question (Fig. 3.27). ImageNet runs a competition every year called the ImageNet Large Scale Visual Recognition Challenge (ILSVRC) where programmers compete in the detection and correct the classification of objects from images.

Predictors in ILSVRC are evaluated by their top-5 error rate. That is, for every image, each predictor is allowed to submit its top five predictions, of which only one has to coincide with the real label of the image.

Up until 2011 a good top-5 error rate was $\sim 25\%$, that is the best predictor could annotate 75% of the images correctly according to the top-5 rule. In 2012 the AlexNet CNN achieved a 15.3% top-5 error rate, or $\sim 11\%$ better than the runner-up [117]. This single, spectacular improvement in classification performance for such a difficult problem as object recognition in realistic settings marked the start of the deep learning revolution. How did Alex, Ilya and Geoffrey achieve this?

CNNs had been previously applied very successfully for the identification of hand-written characters, but the problem of general object classification is much harder given the greater diversity of objects in the real world (22,000 different class labels for 15 million images in ImageNet). In 2012 the application of CNNs to high-resolution images was still very challenging as well as prohibitively expensive computationally.

Figure 3.27 An image typical of ILSVRC.

AlexNet is an eight-layer CNN consisting of five convolutional layers and three fully connected layers. AlexNet's improvements applied to both network architecture and to how the network dealt with the overfitting problem. Since all of these improvements existed before, the success of AlexNet lied in how they were masterfully combined to improve the network's performance and reduce its training time.

- Architectural improvements.

  - *Graphical Processing Units (GPUs)*: These are specialised processors that fit the nature of the training data (images). AlexNet was spread over two GPUs—half of the neurons were kept on one of the GPUs, the other half on the second GPU. A key point is that the GPUs can read and write to each other's memory directly (without going through the main memory of the machine) but only for certain layers. This highly optimised GPU implementation allowed the faster training of bigger models.

  - *Overlapping pooling*: This is a technique used to downsample images by projecting information from image pixels onto a smaller grid while retaining the key features required for classification. Pooling reduces the computational cost, but typically CNNs only pool the output of neighbouring neurons. The introduction of overlapping also helps reduce the problem of overfitting during training.

  - *The Rectified Linear Unit (ReLU)* was the activation function of choice over standard non-linear functions (e.g. sigmoid). This made the training of the model much faster.

  - *Local Response Normalisation (LRN):* Input normalisation is not required when you use ReLUs, but AlexNet still uses Batch Normalisation (BN) as the authors found that it helps reduce overfitting.

- Improvements to reduce overfitting.
  Overfitting is the situation when a model learns its training data too well and finds it difficult to generalise to new, unseen data (Chapter 4). AlexNet is a network with 60 million parameters, and thus reducing overfitting was key to for performance optimisation.

  - *Data augmentation* was randomly performed to artificially increase the training dataset. The effect of having a more varied dataset is that it reduces overfitting.

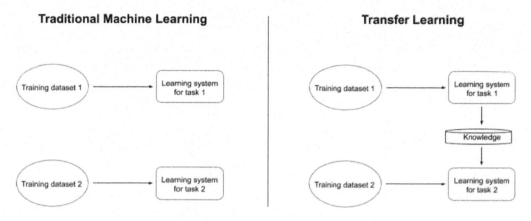

Figure 3.28 Transfer learning involves reusing previously trained models.

— In the *dropout technique* the model selectively 'drops out' specific neurons during training (e.g. those below a certain probability threshold). Such dropped neurons do not contribute to the forward pass or are involved in backpropagation. The net effect is a reduction in the network's potential to overfit.

## 3.11.2  Transfer Learning

DNNs being a special class of ANNs have the same advantages and disadvantages discussed earlier. On top of these, one remarkable advantage of DNNs is that they are scalable: In principle the larger the DNN and the more training data, the better its performance. However, like all other machine learning algorithms DNNs eventually reach a performance plateau as the amount of training data increases, even with noise-free data due to the increasing complexity in identifying the global optima of the cost function.

One problem with using huge amounts of data to achieve superior performance is that the training of the network becomes very expensive in terms of time and resources. This is particularly true for computer vision and natural language processing tasks. Transfer learning allows overcoming this limitation by using a model previously trained (the *base model*) for a similar task (Fig. 3.28). The concept of transfer learning is very intuitive: if we can ride a motorcycle on the road and want to learn to drive a car, we do not need to learn everything from scratch. We can take advantage of the knowledge we already have about driving in general and adapt it to the new context of a car.

For transfer learning to work the features of the base model must be rather general and appropriate for both the base and target tasks [118]. The base model can be used in its entirety or only parts of it, and it may also be tuned for specific tasks [119]. Tuning a pre-trained model is a complex process, and the right strategy is determined by how much data we have and how similar it is to the data the base model was trained with. For instance, if we wish to identify birds and frogs in a small dataset, and the images of these animals in ImageNet are quite similar, we may simply adjust the output of a model trained on ImageNet by modifying the softmax and the Fully-Connected layers to end up with two categories instead of thousands.

Transfer learning can be implemented with any learning algorithm (not just DNNs). It is also an empirical activity and we might not always succeed, but as long as we can identify a similar task in one of the many repositories of pre-trained models, like Model Zoo (https://modelzoo.co/), transfer learning might be worth a try. Moreover, for some problems we do not have access to sufficient data or resources, in which case resorting to pre-trained models often is our only chance of success.

## 3.12 WHY THERE ARE SO MANY DIFFERENT LEARNING ALGORITHMS AND HOW TO CHOOSE

Thus far we have discussed a number of supervised and unsupervised algorithms in detail, and mentioned a few more in passing. Since it is possible to carry out both regression and classification tasks using a number of approaches, an obvious question here is: Why has nobody invented one type of algorithm that can be universally applied?

This is because it is not possible to design one learning algorithm that is optimally suited for all classification and regression problems, and datasets. As an example, let us imagine that we have two quantitative variables that hold an approximately linear relationship and we wish to predict $Y$ from $X$ (as in the TV advertising $\sim$ sales example). Here we may fit a linear regression line. This is an example of an algorithm that is optimally suited for this type of dataset and predictive question. If, however we had a dataset of Tesla stock values against time, would you use a linear regression to decide when to buy and sell your own Tesla options? I hope not because the stock market is highly non-linear, difficult to predict and many other unknown variables are often at play. Therefore, whereas a linear regression algorithm might be optimally applied to some problems, it cannot be used universally while expecting to get consistently good results. In more general terms and as put by David Wolpert in 1996 'for any algorithm, any elevated performance over one class of problems is offset by performance over another class' [120]. This is another way of saying that the average performance of any two classifiers across the board of all possible problems and datasets is the same (equally mediocre), but each individual algorithm might excel when applied to specific problems.

### 3.12.1 Why Making Assumptions Is Good and the No Free Lunch Theorem

We must note how in the linear regression example we are making the assumption that the relationship between the two variables is linear. This is called a *structural assumption*. The other two types of assumption are *distributional* (about the values of a variable or the distribution of measurement errors) and *cross-variation assumptions* (joint probability distribution). All learning algorithms must make some assumptions (also known as learning biases) between the predictor and target variables; otherwise a predictive model could never be built. This is because a learning model must be a simplified representation of reality where we focus on the main trend of the data while ignoring certain aspects of the data. In the linear regression example (Fig. 3.8) we can easily see how the relationship between the two variables is not perfectly linear because not all data points pass through the regression line. Still, we decide to model it as a linear regression. By doing this we are trading the power and simplicity of linear regression for the loss of some prediction accuracy.

A by-product of making assumptions is that certain algorithms will fit certain datasets better (a good model) but will not fit most datasets at all. Therefore the advantage of one algorithm on one class of problems is offset by its poor performance on virtually almost any other type of problem. This is popularly known as the **No Free Lunch Theorem** because there is always a cost. Making certain assumptions to model a dataset with a specific algorithm has the cost that the same algorithm will not perform for other problems and datasets (Fig. 3.29).

Wolpert extended his proofs on classifiers to problems of search and optimisation the following year. A search algorithm is a method that tries to retrieve information (stored in some data structure) in an efficient manner, that is, without engaging in an exhaustive search (for which no method is needed). Wolpert and Macready equally concluded that the performance of any two given search algorithms over all possible problems in the same [121]. The proof of the No Free Lunch Theorem to search and optimisation problems offers

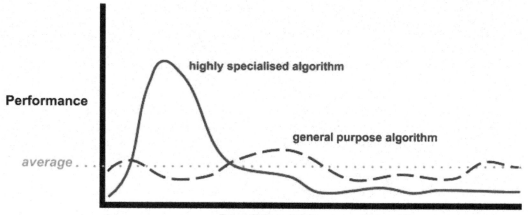

Figure 3.29 Trade-off between performance and problem types for a specialized algorithm and a general-purpose one.

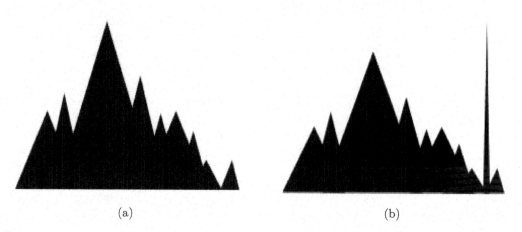

(a)                                                    (b)

Figure 3.30 Domain knowledge and assumptions are key for optimising the performance of any algorithm.

a very memorable representation of how in the absence of assumptions it is not possible for an algorithm to do better than average. Let us imagine that we are on a blind climbing quest to identify the highest peak on Earth. Having the knowledge that mount Everest is part of a mountain range consisting of various eight-thousanders, perhaps we could make the assumption that choosing to walk in the direction that elevation increases is an optimal strategy (Fig. 3.30 (a)). If, however, we were on a planet where the highest peak is surrounded by the lowest points (the exact reverse), then an algorithm that searches among the smallest points would be better (Fig. 3.30(b)). This is actually a description of the Mauna Kea volcano in Hawaii, and it is not on another planet. Its height of 4,207 m is smaller than that of mount Everest. However, the base of Mauna Kea is on the floor of the Pacific ocean, about 6,000 m below the surface, making the overall height of Mauna Kea over 10,000 m. Unless you knew this fact about the Mauna Kea volcano, you will probably have imagined an algorithm similar to that in Fig. 3.30 (a). Without detailed knowledge of our system we cannot make reasonable assumptions. Without prior assumptions no algorithm can be expected to perform better than chance.

### 3.12.2   Some Families of Algorithms Are Better than Others

According to the No Free Lunch Theorem no algorithm is better than another across the entire board of problems and datasets. In practice, however, the design of some algorithms appears to be better suited for classification problems. In a key paper from 2014, Fernandez-Delgado and co-workers presented the result of evaluating 179 different algorithms (belonging to 17 distinct families) in the classification of all the datasets (n = 121) of the UCI Machine Learning Repository (https://archive.ics.uci.edu/) [91]. It turned out that Random Forests (RF) are the best family of classifiers across the board, followed by SVMs, ANNs and boosting ensembles. The poorest classifiers presented average classification accuracies below 50% (that is, for binary classification problems flipping a coin is as good). Surprisingly, many of the worst classifiers also are ensemble methods like some of the best classifiers. Clearly ensembles are a growing trend, but not all ensembles appear to be generally applicable and their design is as much an art as it is a science.

### 3.12.3   How Can We Choose the Right Algorithm for Our Problem?

In practice what one usually does when presented with a problem is to first carry out a descriptive analysis of the data in order to get a feel for it. We can then start considering what type of algorithms may work for the given problem. Reading the literature to find out what others have done in similar situations can be incredibly helpful. It is crucial to be familiar with the knowledge domain as well as with how the data were generated, recorded and any other particularities. This information will help us make certain assumptions about the nature of our data, as well as engineer novel features. Moreover, we must not forget that having quality data is always more important than having a cutting-edge algorithm. High-dimensional datasets often require feature selection too so that at least we start off with a smaller number of variables.

**Feature scaling** tends to be necessary too because continuous variables can have very different ranges. A variable presenting very large and very small numbers (a wide range), for instance, can have a large impact on the final prediction simply because of its scale. Therefore, unscaled data may lead to useless results, and there is not a single technique for feature scaling. Rather, the choice of technique depends on both the nature of the data and the type of algorithm to be used. Some well-known methods include:

- **Min-max normalisation**, whereby we rescale the range of features to a scale in the range $[0, 1]$ or $[-1, 1]$ (the choice depends on the type of data). This method retains the original distribution of the data points, but on the downside is not robust as it is very sensitive to outliers.

- **Z-score normalisation (standarisation)** uses the calculated mean and standard deviation of each feature and is probably the most used scaling method in many learning algorithms (e.g. SVMs and ANNs). One key disadvantage is that both the mean and the standard deviation are so sensitive to outliers. Standarisation does not guarantee a common numerical range for the resulting scores, and if the data points are not normally distributed, then the original distribution is not retained at the output either.

- More robust techniques include scaling on the **Median** and the **MAD (Median Absolute Deviation)** because they are insensitive to extreme values. *Tangent hyperbolicus (tanh) estimators* are also robust and highly efficient but they are not so easy to calculate compared to the most commonly used methods [122].

TABLE 3.7   Some Characteristics of Interpretable Algorithms

| Algorithm | Linear | Monotone | Task |
|---|---|---|---|
| Linear regression | Yes | Yes | Regression |
| Logistic regression | No | Yes | Classification |
| Trees | No | Some | Regression, classification |
| Naïve Bayes | No | Yes | Classification |

Next, the data is prepared into basic, randomised training and test sets to quickly test the predictive accuracy of models of varying complexity. Normally the simpler algorithms are tried first, such as naïve Bayes before logistic regression, or KNNs before SVMs, but you have to understand which assumptions are being made in each case and how these assumptions condition the method's ability to answer the question at hand. One type of algorithm will hopefully work better than the others, which makes it a starting point for parameter optimisation and testing through cross validation (Chapter 4). The more sophisticated algorithms (like DNNs) are very attractive but they also are more difficult to tune as their internal structures are less transparent. However, beyond a certain point increasing an algorithm's performance through parameter tuning is not possible and we must then resort to engineering new features from the original data attributes.

The reason why the simpler learning models should always be tried before proceeding with the more complex ones is not because simpler does better in the tradition of Occam's razor ('entities should not be multiplied without necessity', after William of Ockham (1287–1347)). In fact there are many counterexamples, including the impressive performance of DNNs and ensembles. Also, although adding more random features typically leads to overfitting, there is not always a connection between the two as exemplified by SVMs, which can have an unlimited number of parameters without overfitting. The reason why the simpler methods should be our first port of call is because simplicity is a virtue in its own right [123]. Simpler methods are *interpretable*, easier to tune and less opaque than the more complex ones, and it is only when we develop an intimate relationship with the data that we can get the most creative insights. Finally, beyond a certain point it becomes very difficult to tune any given algorithm. Thus, whenever we hit a performance wall with any one approach we should focus on engineering new features and perhaps building different, complementary approaches that might be later combined into an ensemble [85].

### 3.12.4   Interpretability vs Explainability

The complexity of supervised learning methods ranges from the simple and straightforward such as linear regression to complex ones such as DNNs. When discussing the choice and practical application of learning methods, two additional key concepts are *interpretability* and *explainability*:

- An **interpretable** model is one that we can inspect and understand how the predictions were calculated, such as linear regression and trees. Table 3.7 lists the characteristics of some of the interpretable algorithms we have discussed so far. *Linearity* means that the association between features and target values is modelled linearly, whereas *monotonicity* means that an increase in a feature value leads to either an increase or a decrease in the target value (but not both) over the entire range of feature values [60].

- In opposition to interpretable models, an **explainable** model is one that requires a second (post hoc) model for understanding how the predictions were generated. This type of algorithms are the black boxes that are impossible to explain beyond a

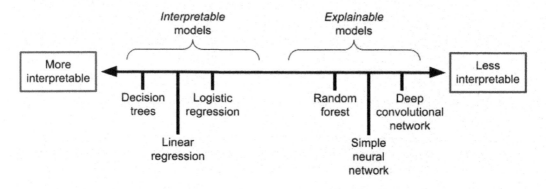

Figure 3.31 Model interpretability can be thought of as a *continuum*.

certain point such as the Inception-ResNet-v2 convolutional neural network (CNN) with hundreds of hidden layers [116]

In practical terms we can think about interpretability as a *continuum:* The more naturally interpretable a model is the less of an explanation that is required, and *vice versa* (Fig. 3.31). The general recommendation is that given a choice between a simpler yet more interpretable model, and a more complex but less interpretable black box that performs slightly better, the simpler model is the better choice. Moreover, it is a myth that there is a trade-off between predictive performance and interpretability: When the data are structured and have a good representation of meaningful features there is often no significant difference in performance between complex models and simpler ones [23]. Therefore, black boxes are not necessarily indispensable for achieving top predictive performance.

Another problem with black boxes is that they require a second model to provide an explanation, which in itself might be an inaccurate representation of the black box. Moreover, some black box models might not be that complicated for a human to understand, but they are proprietary software that can only capitalise from the intellectual property rights given to a black box method. An example of this is the inaccurate COMPAS algorithm that predicts the tendency of a convicted criminal to reoffend (Chapter 5) as well as models used in medical care that can make serious errors depending on the data they are trained on [23]. Thus, there are many situations where using overly complex, uninterpretable models not only does not lead to superior performance but is outright unsafe. Hence, we must always consider the context of application and the consequences of using black boxes. For example, if we can develop a sophisticated stock value prediction method for day trading, does it really matter understanding how the predictions are generated as long as they remain accurate? And how about a movie recommendation system? Wasting some viewing time is probably the worst thing that can happen while we find another film.

## 3.13  FEATURE SELECTION AND ENGINEERING IS WHERE A LOT OF MAGIC HAPPENS

In any predictive modelling exercise we always have a response or dependent variable (the target of the prediction) and usually a much larger number of attributes (independent variables) that we can use to build a predictive model. For example, in the section on linear regression we built the TV advertising expenditure ~ sales, but the original dataset also contains information on the the radio and newspaper expenditures [70, 53]. Ideally, all three attributes should be considered in a multiple regression model as they are likely to have combined effects.

Today it is too easy to collect massive amounts of features and data, but not all attributes are ever relevant. For instance, if besides the expenditure on TV, radio and newspaper we included the expenditure of the company on electricity and pencils, would you expect these variables to have an effect on the response variable? Me neither.

In modelling we should only consider attributes that help solve the modelling problem, and we refer to these attributes as *features*. An attribute that does not contribute to solving the problem is not part of the problem and therefore not a feature. Therefore, being able to select the right features in a dataset is easily one of the most important factors contributing to the predictive power of a model. In other words, the inclusion of irrelevant variables in any learning model usually has detrimental effects. For one thing, a large number of variables increases the computational cost of developing, training and running predictive models. More importantly, irrelevant features normally lead to overfitted models, that is models that do better on a training dataset than on a test dataset. An overfitted model ends up learning the random noise in the data instead of focusing on the relationship between the relevant features and the response variable, leading to a degradation in performance (Chapter 4).

### 3.13.1 The Curse of Dimensionality

The curse of dimensionality describes the difficulties that arise when training a predictive model with increasing amounts of features (dimensions). Specifically, the number of observations required to calculate a given function (for a given level of performance) increases exponentially with respect to the number of input features in the training dataset [124].

In other words, it is not possible to keep adding features at will: The more features we wish to include, the more data we must have for training the algorithm. A rule of thumb in machine learning is that for every feature there should be at least five training examples, although these may not be sufficient [125]. Also, while adding features (and observations) that are associated with the response variable typically results in a peak of performance of the model, beyond a certain point this performance drops [126]. This is because even if these features are relevant, and the training dataset is correspondingly larger to accommodate more features, the statistical variance introduced by the new variables makes the model weaker (Fig. 3.32).

### 3.13.2 Feature Selection Methods

The goal of feature selection is to reduce the number of features needed to train a model by identifying the most relevant ones. The simplest approach consists of identifying highly correlated variables to retain only one and discard the others. A typical rookie mistake here is to think that two variables that have a correlation score of 0.8 are identical, when in practice we should set the bar much higher, for example at 0.99. This correlation-based approach is unsupervised because the response variable is not being considered.

The most relevant feature selection methods are supervised. Filter-based, wrapper and embedded methods all evaluate the relationship between each feature and the response variable but differ in the choice of evaluation metric (Fig. 3.33).

- **Filter-based** methods choose features by their positive correlation with the response variable (a proxy measure because the error rate is what should really be tracked). The assessment of this correlation is performed by various statistical tests, the choice

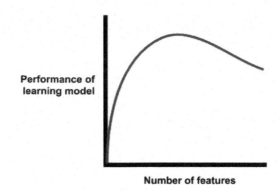

Performance of
learning model

**Number of features**

Figure 3.32 The typical performance of a learning model against the number of features included.

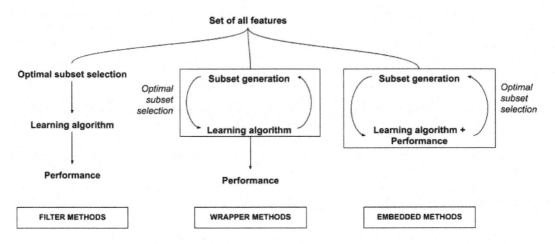

Figure 3.33 The three types of feature selection methods.

of which depends on the nature of the response variable and the features, either numerical or categorical. Recall that the type of response variable indicates the type of predictive problem: If the response (output) variable is numerical we are dealing with a regression problem, whereas a categorical response variable indicates a classification problem. As a quick introduction to the statistical tests available, if both the features and the response variable are continuous we could use either Pearson's correlation coefficient or Spearman's rank-order correlation. In a typical logistic regression where the features are numerical and the response variable is categorical (e.g. 'Will this customer default? (yes/no)'), the choice of method includes Kendall rank correlation coefficient and ANOVA (Fig. 3.34).

Filter-based methods have the distinctive advantage of being very fast next to wrapper methods. On the down side, since the fitness of a feature with the target variable is calculated one feature at a time (univariate statistics), these methods are not trying to solve the real problem of optimising the performance of the classifier like wrapper methods do. As a result, filter-based methods might fail to identify the better subset of features on many occasions. Another limitation of filter-based methods is that since they only consider one feature at a time, they have no way of detecting multicollinearity, i.e. when two or more features are highly linearly related. Multicollinearity is a

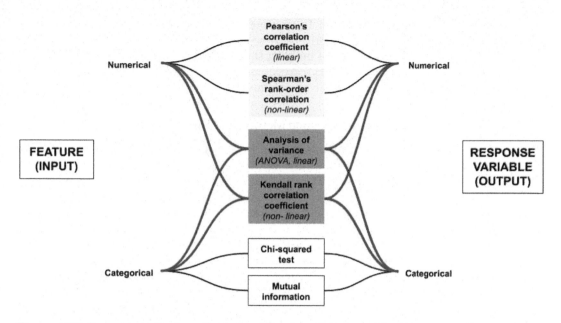

Figure 3.34 Some statistical methods for filter-based feature selection.

problem because it undermines the statistical significance of each feature and therefore must be dealt with before training the algorithm.

- **Wrapper** methods measure the fitness of a subset of features not by their correlation with the response variable (like filter-based methods do), but by actually training a learning model with such features and then testing it on a left-out dataset. With large numbers of features, this search problem becomes computationally prohibitive and so a number of heuristics (approximations or shortcuts) have been developed. These include:

  – *Forward selection* starts with no features and keeps adding positive features at each iteration until no further improvement is recorded.

  – In *backward elimination* the opposite process is performed—we start off with all the features and remove the least significant features at each iteration until additional subtractions no longer help improve the model.

  – In *recursive feature elimination* a model is first created from which the best and worst-performing features are identified, which are then put aside. In the next iteration another model is built with the remaining features, and again the best and worst performers are identified and left out. Features are finally ranked in order of elimination.

  One advantage of wrapper methods is that they nearly always guarantee the identification of an optimal subset of features. On the downside, recursive feature elimination methods are computationally expensive, and being greedy algorithms (like the CART algorithm for building trees) they can only make the optimal choice at each iteration. This means that they cannot guarantee the overall optimal solution as the entire dataset is never considered at once. A further disadvantage when compared with filter-based methods is that upon performance evaluation the learning model built from these features is more prone to overfitting (Chapter 4).

- **Embedded** methods are similar to wrapper methods in that they also optimise the performance of the learning algorithm. However, embedded methods perform feature selection as part of the process of building the learning model. Examples of embedded methods are LASSO and RIDGE regressions, as well as trees (and ensembles of trees like Random Forests) and genetic algorithms [127].

### 3.13.3 What Is the Best Feature Selection Method and How Many Features Are Enough?

With all the different methods available for feature selection, which is the best one? Just like there is no 'best dataset' or 'best algorithm', there is no best feature selection method. Different selection methods will produce different sets of features. The trick always lies in trying various methods (that is, by performing careful experimentation) and see which one works best. This will vary from one problem to another, and even within the same problem if you are given a different set of features.

The question of how many features suffice is equally open-ended as it also depends on the problem domain—for example, for the problem of identifying dogs in photographs, maybe a resolution of $500 \times 500$ pixels per photo will do. This results in 250,000 features per image. However for the problem of predicting house prices using known variables (e.g. house size, number of bathrooms, past selling prices in the area, etc.) 250,000 features are not only excessive but also inexistent.

Sometimes we get lucky with a good number of features that correlate well with the response variable. However, if the class is a very complex function of the features, most algorithms will have serious problems with it.

### 3.13.4 Dimensionality Reduction

When your dataset includes too many continuous variables to consider that are also correlated, you may want to consider a dimensionality reduction technique such as **Principal Component Analysis (PCA)**.

PCA is an unsupervised algorithm and its goal is to summarise the information contained in the original (standardised) attributes into a smaller number of variables called Principal Components (PC). In other words, PCA projects the data found in all the original attributes onto a lower-dimensional space called PCs. Therefore, PCA is not a form of feature selection for it won't reduce the number of features, but simply a different way of representing the original attributes.

Each PC is a mathematical (linear) combination of the original attributes that is meant to contain as much of the relevant, original information as possible. PCA's uses variance as the measure of how relevant a specific dimension is. For example, in Fig. 3.35 PCA has managed to reduce the variation found in a breast cancer patient dataset to just two PCs that collectively explain as much as 63.3% of the variation found in the original 30 attributes [128, 129, 130]. The first PC always presents the maximum variation; the second PC encapsulates the most of the remaining variation (and so on). Including additional PCs would increase the representation of the original variation, but it is already remarkable that two-thirds of the variation found across 30 attributes can be summarised by just two PCs. Moreover, the representation of the original dataset into PCs helps with the visualisation: in the figure it becomes clear that a combination of attributes found in the original dataset allows the separation of the majority of cases of tumours into benign and malignant. Thus, by using a simpler representation of the original dataset in the form of PCs it is now possible to build a classifier for the two types of tumour.

One clear limitation of using PCs to build such a predictor is that since each PC is a combination of various original attributes, we immediately lose out on interpretability.

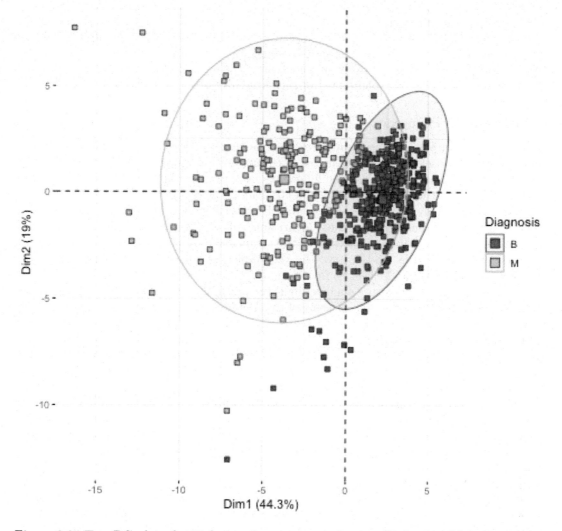

Figure 3.35 Two-PC plot of a 30-feature breast cancer dataset (B: benign; M: malignant).

Moreover, even though just two PCs can explain two-thirds of the variability, it is often the case that capturing nearly all of the variation (at the expense of adding more and more PCs) is key for building a robust classifier.

Today PCA is definitely used in the context of visualising complex datasets, but for building robust classifiers it is difficult to beat the convenience and performance of ensemble methods like RFs.

One serious trap that many data scientists fall for when using PCA is thinking that the first PCs are the most relevant ones as these encapsulate most of the variability. In the context of breast cancer, for instance, all the thirty attributes are descriptions of digitised images of breast cell nuclei (e.g. area, radius, texture and symmetry of the nuclei). However, if we included an (genetic) attribute detailing whether the DNA in the cells' nuclei contains a specific mutation in either the BRCA1 or the BRCA2 gene, this single feature alone with limited variance (0 or 1) would make a better predictor for cancer since we know that germline mutations in BRCA1/BRCA2 predispose to breast and ovarian cancers [131].

However, the negligible variance found in this genetic attribute would have been treated as noise by the PCA algorithm.

Therefore, PCA is only useful when capturing variability is key. For example, if we wish to predict the volatility of stocks in an index fund, the companies whose stocks present the largest fluctuation in closing price would contribute the most to the first components, which in turn should be able to explain most of the variability of the index fund.

### 3.13.5 Feature Engineering

Beyond a certain point trying to improve an algorithm's performance by tuning its hyper-parameters or by selecting a different set of features will not work. When we hit this type of performance wall, we must ask the following question: 'Are the features we used to train our model the best way to present our dataset for this prediction problem?'

Our model is only as good as our features. Even with sub-optimal features it is possible to get good performance because most algorithms will pick up on the underlying structure in the data. However, well-engineered features can make even simple algorithms perform remarkably well. Simple models have the very desirable advantages of being more interpretable, faster to run and easier to maintain.

A famous example of feature engineering is the paper that won the KDD Cup 2010. This competition is held at the annual meeting of the ACM Special Interest Group on Knowledge Discovery and Data Mining. In the year 2010 the goal was to predict student performance from past behaviour. The secret sauce of the Taiwanese group that won the competition was to simplify the structure of the dataset by performing an extreme binarisation on it to create millions of features. This resulted in a huge, but simple dataset to which linear methods were successfully applied [132].

Binarisation means assigning all the values of a variable to one of two values. For example, the three possible values red/yellow/no_colour could be binarised to colour/no_colour. When we have more than two categories this is the general case and is called quantization or binning. For example, a range of body mass indices (BMI) such as 17.1, 18.6, 19.4, 20.6, 24.5, 29.0, 32.7 can be binned as *underweight* ($<18.5$), *normal* ($18.5–25$), *overweight* ($25–30$) and *obese* ($>30$).

Feature engineering can also be achieved by combining features and by decomposing them. Feature combination can be done by adding, multiplying, or performing any mathematical operation on them. A typical instance of feature decomposition is when we take a computer-based timestamp such as '2021-06-01 20:05:43 CET' and extract the hour of the day if our intuition tells us that it might be related to another feature. The hours may also be discretised to various parts of the day (morning/midday/afternoon/evening).

Besides *benchmarking* (e.g. doing the proper data selection, understanding how relevant the training-test partition is for the problem at hand, and model selection), feature engineering is a key strategy despite being less well documented because there are no hard rules. It is part experimentation and creativity, part domain knowledge, and part intuition and experience. All we can say about feature engineering is that it is as much an art as it is a science, and that it is always an iterative process, like all machine learning: (i) think hard about your features; (ii) decide what features to create; (iii) implement a model with those features and test their impact on the model's performance; (iv) combine features and repeat the entire process until you can improve no more.

Finally, **feature learning** is a more recent approach to engineering features automatically where some deep learning approaches like Boltzmann machines and autoencoders have achieved some success.

## 3.14 HOW DOES AMAZON RECOMMEND BOOKS THAT YOU WILL ACTUALLY LIKE?

Can you imagine what it would be like if every time you walk into the supermarket your grocery list is arranged before your eyes, thus saving you the hassle of walking through every aisle?

This is effectively what Amazon.com does for you—each person sees the Amazon.com store differently because it is individually personalised to their interests. How amazing is it that an algorithm picks a few items from the hundreds of millions available, and quite often these recommendations are useful? This is the job of information filtering systems called *recommender systems*. Internet giants like Amazon, Facebook, YouTube, LinkedIn, Ebay, Netflix, Spotify and Google have shown that the item being recommended can be of any sort, including books, friends, videos, jobs and professional contacts, films and series, music, restaurants, places to visit, financial products and even jokes. Since the search space that recommenders can inspect in real time is so vast, personalised recommendations typically result in the user being opened up to a whole new range of products and possibilities that they may not have considered otherwise. In other words, the goal of personalised recommendations is to maximise the value for both the buyer and the seller. A recommender system basically tries to solve the following problem:

What you like → What you might like

The most primitive type of recommender system is a popularity-based one whereby users are recommended the best-sold products or services. However, this type of recommendation has zero personalisation. The two main families of recommender systems are *collaborative filtering* and *content-based filtering* (Fig. 3.36) [133]. These two approaches are applied differently depending on how much we know about the user:

- **Collaborative filtering** methods are used when we have extensive information on a customer's preferences, for example from a store loyalty card or from their online shopping or navigation pattern.

  A collaborative filtering recommender system compares the profile of the user in question to those that are most similar to them, and then recommends new items that have been bought by similar users. One important advantage of collaborative filtering methods is that they require zero understanding of the item and thus can recommend complex items without expert intervention.

- **Content-based filtering** methods are used when we do not have an extensive history of a customer's transactions but we do know a lot about this one item that they just bought or are considering.

  For example, let us pretend that we own a bookshop and this new customer comes in through the door asking for authors similar to Junot Diaz. Junot is a hip author that writes about the immigrant experience of Puerto Ricans in the USA. Perhaps a good recommendation for this person would be a book by Toni Morrison, who also writes about the outsider experience. This is perhaps all we can come up with because we have read both Diaz and Morrison, but what if we could search all published books that have been tagged by other readers with the words 'hip' and 'immigrant experience'? Content-based recommender systems rely on the extensive annotation of the products such as those that can be found in book documentation and reviews. The main advantage of content-based recommenders is that they work when no customer information is available, thus overcoming the *cold start* problem. One clear

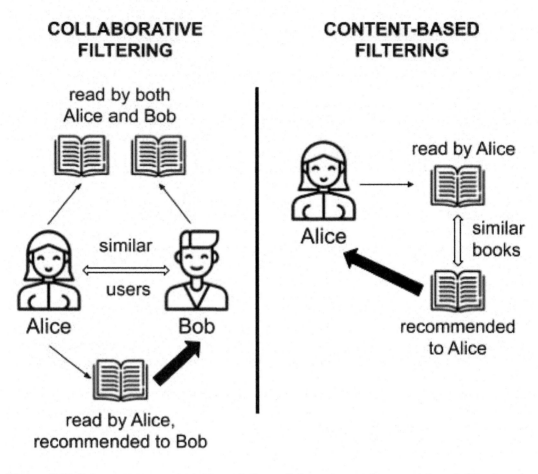

COLLABORATIVE FILTERING     CONTENT-BASED FILTERING

read by both Alice and Bob

similar users

Alice     Bob

read by Alice, recommended to Bob

Alice

read by Alice

similar books

recommended to Alice

Figure 3.36 Schematic representation of the collaborative and content-based filtering approaches.

disadvantage is that the products must be very well annotated using a uniform vocabulary so that the similarities among the products can be computed.

Therefore the choice of recommender system ultimately depends on whether we have access to (large enough) historical transaction data for specific customers. In such a case, through collaborative filtering it might possible to make good recommendations thanks to the *wisdom of the crowd* (the same principle underlying Random Forests). When no transaction data is available (the *cold start* problem) recommendations from content-based filtering approaches are customary but only until enough transaction data starts to accumulate, at which point the power of collaborative filtering usually is introduced. This is because content-based filtering approaches tend to be over-specialised on similar items while neglecting the very important wisdom of the crowd. After all, we choose our friends for a reason.

**Hybrid methods** are a third type of recommender systems that combine both collaborative and content-based filtering approaches. Hybrid recommenders typically provide more accurate recommendations [133]. For instance, Netflix is a typical example of a hybrid method since it combines the watching and searching habits of similar users (collaborative) and more general movie characteristics such as genre and actors (content-based).

### 3.14.1 Item-to-Item Collaborative Filtering Is Faster and More Scalable

To give an idea of how globally important recommender systems are, when the journal IEEE Internet Computing had to choose the most important article published in the first 20 years of the journal, the paper selected by the editorial board was 'Amazon.com Recommendations. Item-to-Item Collaborative Filtering' [134]. **Item-to-Item collaborative filtering** is a variation of standard collaborative filtering developed by Greg Linden, Brent Smith and Jeremy York while working at Amazon.com. Their algorithm is a great example of how a smart algorithm has evolved and adapted over decades to accommodate key insights derived from the analysis of Amazon.com's customer data.

Item-to-Item collaborative filtering was initially developed to overcome an important limitation of traditional collaborative filtering methods, namely the fact that they do not scale well with the number of customers and items [135]. The Item-to-Item collaborative filtering algorithm does not focus on comparing customers but on matching each of the user's items to similar, rated items. Similar items are then combined into a recommendation list that is actually calculated offline. The only task that the Item-to-Item collaborative filtering algorithm does online is to look up similar items for a given user's transaction history and ratings. Traditional collaborative filtering algorithms, on the other hand, do almost none of the calculations offline, and so the computational complexity scales with the number of customers and products, making it impractical when you have millions of customers and products. Therefore the advantage of Item-to-Item collaborative filtering is not only its speed and scalability for extremely large datasets, but also its simplicity and interpretability. Not surprisingly the original algorithm has been adopted and adapted all over the Internet and today is one of the most popular recommendations algorithms. Some of the insights that have been coded into Amazon.com's Item-to-Item recommender over the years include the concepts of (i) time—three books bought at the same time is stronger evidence of relatedness than if each one is bought separately; (ii) directionality of purchases—if you buy a photo camera it makes sense to recommend a memory card, but not the other way around; (iii) life stages—if you buy a baby pram today, it makes sense to recommend a pushchair a few months down the line (sounds simple but this is not so easy to formalise into an algorithm); and (iv) some item-to-item similarities tell you so much more about a customer (e.g. a book) and can lead to higher quality recommendations [135].

### 3.14.2 Are Recommender Systems Supervised or Unsupervised Learning?

This is a question that often puzzles data science enthusiasts. The truth is that, although recommender systems can integrate both supervised and unsupervised methods, it is neither. This is because a recommender system properly is an *information filtering system*, and therefore a concept at a different level.

The goal of a recommender system is to make the best possible recommendations and in order to accomplish this it often integrates a variety of techniques. For example, whenever a prediction is made (either by collaborative or by content-based filtering) the accuracy of these predictions is always tested on a hold-out set of customers to see if the products that they eventually bought match some of these recommendations. The unsupervised part of recommender systems can come in various flavours too: For instance, a collaborative filtering system may cluster the customers in its database according to some criterion and then target everyone in the same cluster with a similar type of offers or products. Again, the validity of this approach could be tested using a supervised learning approach: By making an offer to 90% of the customers in the cluster, how many of these bought the product being offered, and how many in the remaining 10% bought it in the absence of an incentive? Was this the right incentive? Was this a homogeneous cluster, or should we have split the customer population according to a different criterion? There are many experiments like this that combine supervised and unsupervised learning in creative ways to ask different questions that teach us much about the preferences and behaviour of a particular customer population.

### 3.14.3 Democracy of Choice, the Real Potential of Recommender Systems

Beyond their commercial applications recommender systems have the potential to improve our lives by helping us manage information and eventually make not more, but better choices. More information always means a wider range of choices, and in this world of information overload being able to make the right choice can have important consequences. We are not talking about choosing movies or books, but about choices that can have a lasting impact in our lives. Think about job searches, educational and learning opportunities and even finding the soulmate that is just right for you. The focus and attention of the human brain is limited, and when faced with so much choice we consistently fail at choosing what is best for us. Human experts will never be able to keep up with machines when it comes to sifting through mountains of data and make very specific recommendations. For this reason recommender systems have the potential to democratise many important life choices in society. The ultimate, future goal of recommender systems is to provide any one user with a fully personalised interaction to the point where even the timing of the recommendations, the specific words used and perhaps even the colour of each interface is customised for every person.

## 3.15  BUILDING A MOVIE RECOMMENDER SYSTEM MANUALLY

Building a simple but functional and useful collaborative filtering recommender system is easier than we think. We will see how straightforward the mathematics are and how the information derived can be used for making recommendations. Let us pretend that we have a dataset of four different people who have rated up to three movies. The most important consideration here is that every single movie has not been rated by every single person as otherwise there would be no recommendations to be made. Thus with limited information on movie ratings from a set of users the goal is to recommend specific movies to other users depending on their first interests. For example, if Peter is looking up or has recently viewed *Spiderman*, the goal is to recommend one or more closely related movies such as *Spiderman 2*, *Spiderman 3* and *Superman*, but not *Pretty Woman*. The movies that have been rated by our four fictional users include two science fiction ones (*Avatar* and *Jurassic Park*) and *The Godfather* (1972), with Marlon Brando and Al Pacino (Table 3.8). All three movies are excellent in their own right, and whereas perhaps user 4 is more into science fiction movies the case might be different for user 1.

Next, the building of any recommender system has three basic steps:

1. Calculation of an item-to-item similarity matrix.

TABLE 3.8  Incomplete Movie Ratings Table

|        | Avatar | Jurassic Park | The Godfather |
|--------|--------|---------------|---------------|
| user 1 | ?      | 5             | 3             |
| user 2 | 2      | ?             | 5             |
| user 3 | 3      | 3             | 4             |
| user 4 | 4      | 5             | ?             |

TABLE 3.9   All-Against-All Movie Rating Similarity Matrix

|  | Avatar | Jurassic Park | The Godfather |
|---|---|---|---|
| Avatar | 1 | 0.99 | 0.95 |
| Jurassic Park | 0.99 | 1 | 0.93 |
| The Godfather | 0.95 | 0.93 | 1 |

2. Prediction of the ratings for items that have not yet been rated.

3. Making of recommendations based on the complete rating matrix that we have just built.

### 3.15.1   Calculation of an Item-to-Item Similarity Matrix

To calculate the similarities between any two items we need a similarity measure such as cosine similarity (although other distance measures may be used). Cosine similarity is a popular measure to assess the similarity between items because it is magnitude-independent. In other words, the purchase of one particular book by a user is more relevant than the number of copies of the book the user has purchased.

$$\cos(\mathbf{A}, \mathbf{B}) = \frac{\mathbf{A}\mathbf{B}}{\|\mathbf{A}\|\|\mathbf{B}\|} = \frac{\sum_{i=1}^{n} \mathbf{A}_i \mathbf{B}_i}{\sqrt{\sum_{i=1}^{n} (\mathbf{A}_i)^2}\sqrt{\sum_{i=1}^{n} (\mathbf{B}_i)^2}}$$

Now we need to calculate the degree of similarity between all pairs of movies. The comparisons to be made are *Avatar* vs *Jurassic Park*, *Avatar* vs *The Godfather* and *Jurassic Park* vs *The Godfather*. When it comes to deriving the cosine similarity between any two movies, A and B, we can only consider the users that have rated both A and B. For example, for the *Avatar* vs *Jurassic Park* comparison we create two item vectors with information on their ratings:

- Avatar (A) = 3 (user 3) + 4 (user 4)

- Jurassic Park (B) = 3 (user 3) + 5 (user 4)

$$\cos (A,B) = \frac{(3x3) + (4x5)}{\sqrt{(3^2) + (4^2)}\sqrt{(3^2) + (5^2)}} = 0.99$$

Cosine similarity values range from zero (no similarity) to one (identity). Therefore the similarity between *Avatar* and *Jurassic Park* from the scores given by users 3 and 4 is extremely high at 0.99. If we do the same type of calculation for the remaining pairs (*Avatar* vs *The Godfather* and *Jurassic Park* vs *The Godfather*) we end up with a complete item-to-item similarity matrix (Table 3.9).

### 3.15.2   Prediction of the Ratings for Items That Have Not Yet Been Rated

Here for each user we predict the ratings for the items that they have not yet rated. In our specific example this means estimating specific ratings for user 1 (*Avatar*), user 2 (*Jurassic Park*) and user 4 (*The Godfather*) (Table 3.8). For user 1 we first need to acknowledge all that other items that this user has already rated (*Jurassic Park* and *The Godfather*). We take the ratings that user 1 gave to these two movies and multiply these by the cosine similarity distance between *Avatar* and *Jurassic Park*, and *Avatar* and *The Godfather*. Finally, we scale this weighted sum with the sum of similarity measures so that the calculated rating remains within specific bounds:

$$\text{rating (user 1, Avatar)} = \frac{(5x0.99) + (3x0.95)}{(0.99 + 0.95)} = 4.02$$

Thus the predicted rating for (user 1, *Avatar*) is 4.02. Clearly the disadvantage of this approach is that we are assuming that new, estimated ratings are likely to be bounded by previous ratings. The larger the dataset, however, the more likely this assumption will be true. After estimating the ratings for each film that each person has not yet seen we end up with the information in Table 3.10:

TABLE 3.10   Known and Predicted Movie Ratings Table

|        | Avatar | Jurassic Park | The Godfather |
|--------|--------|---------------|---------------|
| user 1 | 4.02   | 5             | 3             |
| user 2 | 2      | 3.45          | 5             |
| user 3 | 3      | 3             | 4             |
| user 4 | 4      | 5             | 4.49          |

### 3.15.3   Making Movie Recommendations

Once we have populated the tables of movies × users with the estimated ratings for all movies, making recommendations is as easy as recommending, for each user, all the movies they have not yet watched in decreasing rating order. In the simple example above each user has at most one movie that they have not yet watched, so at most we can only recommend one movie per user. A more realistic, bigger table with a larger set of movies will uncover more unwatched movies per user and therefore more opportunities for making recommendations.

## 3.16   THE NETFLIX GRAND PRIZE WAS WON BY AN ALGORITHM THAT WAS NEVER IMPLEMENTED

The Netflix Grand Prize was an open competition between 2006 and 2009 that really highlighted both the importance and the difficulty of building strong recommender systems. The goal of this competition was to develop a collaborative filtering algorithm that would improve the accuracy of Netflix's Cinematch algorithm by at least 10%. Netflix provided a training dataset of over 100 million 1–5 star ratings on ~18,000 movies by ~480,000 users. The average user had rated over 200 movies and the average movie had been rated by ~5,000 users. On June 26, 2009, the BellKor's Pragmatic Chaos team achieved a 10.06% improvement (measured by Root Mean Square Deviation (RMSE), see Chapter 4) over Cinematch and was awarded the $1,000,000 Netflix Grand Prize.

BellKor's Pragmatic Chaos won the Netflix Grand Prize with an algorithm that (expertly) blended 107 different algorithmic approaches including Singular Value Decomposition (SVD), $K$-Nearest Neighbours (KNN), Asymmetric Factor Model (AFM), Restricted Boltzmann Machines (RBM) and Global Effects (GE) [85]. There are specific reasons for combining so many different predictive methods: For example, RBMs are especially useful when the movie or user has a low number of ratings. However, the BellKor's Pragmatic Chaos algorithm was never implemented for the following reasons.

First of all, the algorithm was too expensive to implement. The improvement provided by the algorithm over Cinematch did not seem to justify the engineering costs of bringing it into production. The implementation would have required a computer and software architecture that could handle large volumes of data and run computationally very expensive algorithms. Additionally the method should have been to be responsive to users in real time and be able to accommodate various recommendation approaches. None of this would have been technically trivial or inexpensive.

Secondly, by the time the Netflix Grand Prize was awarded the company's business model had transitioned from DVD rental to online streaming. Video streaming changed the way that users interact with the Netflix platform, which in turn generated more and new types of data. With the availability of movies over the Internet we do not pick a movie today in the same way we would select a movie on Monday to watch it on Saturday night. As a result, the recommendations that were made based on DVD rental data did not work well anymore. Moreover, whereas with DVDs Netflix relied on explicit ratings provided by the users, with streaming data we have access to so much more real-time information that called for the implementation of different methods.

Finally, online movie streaming resulted in a smaller catalog. When Netflix's business model relied on DVD rental the law was you could buy a DVD and rent it out as many times as you wanted. This prompted the creation of a huge Netflix catalog. However, when Netflix transitioned to online streaming the lack of mandatory licensing meant that Netflix had to negotiate with the studios, which were hoping to compete with Netflix. As a result the Netflix catalog became much shorter and the need for very sophisticated algorithms that work with a colossal number of titles subsided.

An ensemble of methods like the one that the BellKor's Pragmatic Chaos put together was a strategy already known in the machine learning community to improve upon any single method [136]. In other words, in many cases the quantifiable improvement in RMSE (see Chapter 4) is a function of the number of methods combined. However, truly excellent systems that still perform really well can be built with just a few selected models. In fact, having quality data is more important than having a very sophisticated algorithm. The focus for any machine learning exercise, therefore, should first be on collecting abundant, quality data and then build a method that works reasonably well and which can be tested quickly. In the real world it does not matter how good the predictions are if implementing a complex method will cost more than the revenue it will generate.

## 3.17  FURTHER READING

- **Websites**

  - **3Blue1Brown**
    URL: https://bit.ly/3uBsAvs
    *An extremely popular channel focused on teaching higher mathematics from a visual perspective. Some topics are quite hardcore (e.g. geometry, topology, number theory), but there are some excellent videos on concepts essential to supervised learning such as linear algebra and calculus.*

  - **Fast AI - Making neural nets uncool again**
    URL: https://www.fast.ai/
    *This site is a gold mine for all things data science, especially because it includes the most widely used deep learning course in the world: Practical Deep Learning for Coders (https://course.fast.ai/).*

  - **Machine Learning @ Quora**
    URL: https://bit.ly/3f0zdBZ
    *This section on Quora is an interesting resource for all things Machine Learning. The quality of the answers varies because the content is not peer-reviewed, but at the same time you have a lot of world-class researchers like Yoshua Bengio*

*contributing their thoughts. There are other Quora sections specific for Computer Science, Artificial Intelligence, Deep Learning, Natural Language Processing, etc.*

– **Tidy modeling with R (Max Kuhn and Julia Silge)**
URL: tmwr.org
*This is an important resource and online book that teaches model building and good statistical practice using the Tidyverse interface to the R programming language.*

- **Podcasts**

  – **Learning Machines 101**
  URL: https://www.learningmachines101.com/
  *A friendly introduction to machine learning and artificial intelligence.*

  – **Linear Digressions**
  URL: soundcloud.com/linear-digressions
  *A series of interesting podcasts on some unusual and interesting applications of machine learning that make learning so much more fun.*

  – **O'Reilly Data Show Podcast**
  URL: https://bit.ly/3vKxCGc
  *A very interesting and eclectic combination of data science topics.*

- **Videos**

  – **Deep learning, self-taught learning and unsupervised feature learning (Andrew Ng)**
  URL: https://bit.ly/3gimBED
  *This is an influential seminar on deep learning by Andrew Ng.*

  – **Feature engineering (Ryan Baker)**
  URL: https://cutt.ly/blZU7xu
  *Excellent practical advice on how to perform feature engineering using tools like Excel and Google's OpenRefine.*

  – **Machine Learning Methods (Uwe Aickelin)**
  URL: https://bit.ly/3jyCmHD
  *This is an excellent explanation about the difference between supervised, unsupervised and semi-supervised learning by Prof. Uwe Aickelin of Melbourne University.*

- **Articles**

  – **Agrawal A, Gans J and Goldfarb A. How to Win with Machine Learning (Harvard Business Review, September-October 2020).**
  *Building a predictive method is all fine and dandy, but what does it take to build a prediction-based business? And what does it take to compete with established players in machine learning?*

  – **Alom MZ, Taha TM, Yakopcic C, Westberg S, Sidike P, Nasrin MS, Van Esesn BC, Awwal AAS and VK Asari. The History Began from AlexNet: A Comprehensive Survey on Deep Learning, 2018.**
  URL: https://arxiv.org/abs/1803.01164
  *An outstanding review on the many different deep learning approaches discussed in the context of their application domains.*

– de Langhe B, Puntoni S and Larrick R. Linear Thinking in a Non-Linear World (Harvard Business Review, May-June 2017).
*An interesting reflection on how pervasive non-linear models are and how we insist on thinking in linear terms.*

– Domingos P. A Few Useful Things to Know About Machine Learning. Communications of the ACM vol. 55(10): 78–87, 2012.
*Domingos gives a lot of relevant, practical advice for building machine learning solutions.*

– Gomez-Uribe CA and Hunt N. The Netflix recommender system: Algorithms, business value, and innovation. ACM Trans. Manage. Inf. Syst. 6 (4): Article 13, 2015.
*This is an excellent account of the different algorithms that make up the modern, online streaming Netflix recommender system, and how they are tested and improved in a business context.*

– Hernandez D. Facebook's Quest to Build an Artificial Brain Depends on This Guy (WIRED, 14 August 2014).
*This article reflects the excitement of the early days of deep learning, especially in the context of Yann LeCun's convolutional neural nets in computer vision.*

– Jordam MI. Artificial Intelligence—The Revolution Hasn't Happened Yet. Harvard Data Science Review 1(1), 2019.
*An interesting perspective on the historical development and future of machine learning as an engineering discipline.*

– LeCun Y, Bengio Y and Hinton G. Deep learning. Nature 521, pp. 436–444, 2015.
*An outstanding review on deep learning by the Turing Awards recipients of the year 2018.*

– Rudin C. Stop explaining black box machine learning models for high stakes decisions and use interpretable models instead. Nature Machine Intelligence 1, pp. 206–215, 2019.
*This is a very important paper describing the perils of using black box models instead of interpretable ones. The challenges of interpretable machine learning are described as well as example applications where black box models could be replaced.*

– Schmidhuber J. Deep learning in neural networks: An overview. Neural Networks 61, pp. 85–117, 2015.
*A monumental review on deep learning by one of its founding fathers. A general opinion in the community is that the 2018 Turing Award unfairly left out Schmidhuber.*

– Smith B and Linden G. Two Decades of Recommender Systems at Amazon.com. IEEE Internet Computing vol. 21(3):12–18, 2017.
*An excellent review of the historical development of recommender systems at Amazon.com by the data scientists that developed the first collaborative filtering method.*

– van Veen F. The Neural Network Zoo. The Asimov Institute.
URL: https://www.asimovinstitute.org/author/fjodorvanveen/
*An interesting article providing an overview of the major architectures of neural networks and deep neural networks.*

- **Books**

  - Allaire J. *Deep Learning with R.* Manning Publications, New York (NY), USA, 2018. ISBN-10: 9781617295546.
    *This book is an excellent introduction to deep learning using the uber-famous and useful Keras library. Joseph Allaire is the creator of ColdFusion and co-author François Chollet is the developer of the Keras library in Python. Hence this book is the translation into the R programming language of Chollet's book 'Deep Learning with Python' (Manning Publications).*

  - Grus J. *Data Science from Scratch.* O'Reilly Media Inc., Sebastopol (CA), USA, 2015. ISBN: 9781491901427.
    *A practical introduction to data science with examples provided in the Python programming language.*

  - James G, Witten D, Hastie T, Tibshirani R. *An Introduction to Statistical Learning: with Applications in R.* Springer, New York (NY), USA, 2021. ISBN-10: 1071614177.
    *This authoritative textbook is a great introduction to machine learning and the one from which the linear regression example was derived. This book is the younger sibling of 'The Elements of Statistical Learning' by Hastie, Tibshirani and Friedman (Springer) where the topics are treated in greater detail.*

  - Kuhn M, Johnson K. *Applied Predictive Modeling.* Springer, New York (NY), USA, 2013. ISBN-10: 1461468485.
    *A well-written and practical reference textbook on machine learning with examples in R.*

  - Molnar C. *Interpretable Machine Learning - A Guide for Making Black Box Models Explainable,* 2021.
    URL: https://bit.ly/2NCvrmR
    *An unconventional, important and lucidly written book that discusses what humans think is a good explanation and focuses on the interpretability of machine learning models.*

  - Siegel E. *Predictive Analytics.* John Wiley & Sons, Inc., Hoboken (NJ), USA, 2013. ISBN: 9781118356852.
    *Published in 2013, Siegel's book is one of the first, most popular and engaging accounts of how predictive analytics impacts every aspect of our lives.*

  - Wickham H, Grolemund G. *R for data science.* O'Reilly Media Inc., Sebastopol (CA), USA, 2017. ISBN: 9781491910399.
    *A practical introduction to data science with examples provided in the R programming language by gurus Wickham and Grolemund.*

  - Zheng A, Casari A. *Feature Engineering for Machine Learning: Principles and Techniques for Data Scientists.* O'Reilly Media Inc., Sebastopol (CA), USA, 2017. ISBN-13: 9781491953242.
    *This is a good reference book on feature engineering with examples in Python.*

## 3.18   CHAPTER REVIEW QUESTIONS

1. **The goal of predictive analytics is**

   (a) To use historical data to generate reports using descriptive statistics techniques.

   (b) To use animal photographs to classify new photographs intro dog breeds automatically.

(c) To improve upon the limitations of descriptive analytics.

(d) To use historical data to train a learning model so that unseen values may be predicted within the same domain.

2. **In a decision tree, how are the top and subsequent nodes partitioned?**

(a) Randomly.

(b) Using a strategy that splits the tree in the most uneven way possible.

(c) By splitting the dataset on the variable with the largest values.

(d) By splitting the dataset with the smallest values.

3. **The goal of an SVM is to**

(a) Make labelled data from unlabelled data.

(b) Separate the labelled data into their classes using a straight line.

(c) SVMs have no place today because DNNs will always do better.

(d) Find the hyperplane with the higher margin.

4. **The advantage of Transfer Learning is that**

(a) You can use a pre-trained SVM for another SVM classification problem.

(b) You can re-use part of a pre-trained DNN for another classification or regression problem.

(c) It makes DNNs faster.

(d) It facilitates feature learning.

5. **Machine Learning is**

(a) The same thing as Artificial Intelligence.

(b) The ultimate goal of the Turing test.

(c) The study of how computers can learn from data.

(d) The combination of descriptive and predictive analytics.

6. **Briefly describe the difference between model interpretability and explainability.**

7. **Explain the purpose of feature selection and briefly describe the main types of methods.**

# CHAPTER 4

# How Are Predictive Models Trained and Evaluated?

*When the number of factors coming into play in a phenomenological complex is too large scientific method in most cases fails. One need only think of the weather, in which case the prediction even for a few days ahead is impossible.*
   – Albert Einstein (1879–1955), *German-born theoretical physicist*

The goal of supervised learning is to find a function that maps input values to output values most accurately. In this chapter we discuss the main principles behind the training and evaluation of a predictive model. These include how the function must not model the data neither too closely (overfitting) nor too loosely (underfitting) but achieve an optimal balance between these two types of error. Besides modelling the training data properly, a good model must also be able to generalise to new observations it has not been modelled on.

The evaluation of a model's performance using a test set alone has the limitation that not all the available data is used in the training step. Cross-validation training is a strategy that overcomes this problem at the expense of others issues. We review the metrics most commonly used to evaluate the performance of both **classification** and **regression** models while discussing their limitations and optimal areas of application. The training and evaluation of a model are intimately linked processes that must be treated as a whole and in the context of the specific question.

## 4.1   HOW DO PREDICTIVE METHODS LEARN?

As discussed in Chapter 3, the goal of a predictive or supervised machine learning method is to model a set of input-output pairs via a mathematical function such that this function can be used to accurately predict output values for novel (unseen) observations. Prediction problems are either **regressions**, i.e. the prediction of continuous values such as tomorrow's temperature of the value of a stock, or **classification** problems. An example of a classification problem is the identification of dogs in photographs (Fig. 3.2).

A model is normally trained with the majority of the data available (except in settings with extremely large datasets), and its performance tested on at least one test dataset (Fig. 4.1). Moreover, for classification problems the dataset must be labelled with positive and negative examples, both for the training and the testing steps. Otherwise the model will not learn to discriminate and it will not be possible to tell whether an observation from the test dataset has been classified correctly. In regression problems, the observations are

DOI: 10.1201/b23197-4

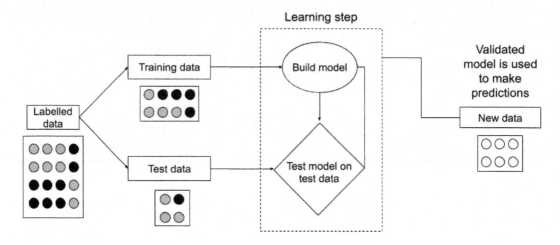

Figure 4.1 The general strategy in supervised machine learning.

TABLE 4.1   A Putative Function Mapping Input
Values to Output Values

| Input | Output | Function |
|-------|--------|----------|
| 2 | 4 | |
| 3 | ? | $f(x) = 2x$ |

TABLE 4.2   A More Accurate Mapping Function
Given More Training Data

| Input | Output | Function |
|-------|--------|----------|
| −1 | 1 | |
| 1 | 1 | |
| 2 | 4 | $f(x) = x^2$ |
| 3 | 9 | |
| 4 | ? | |

naturally labelled as these are continuous values. For instance, let us imagine that we have a magic box that multiplies money such that if you put in 2 coins, it returns 4. Now, how many coins would you get back if you put in 3 coins? Since 4 is two times 2, most people would probably say that if you put in 3 coins you will get 6 coins back. Therefore, the continuous function mapping the very limited training data that we have would be defined as $f(x) = 2x$ (Table 4.1).

The **first rule of supervised learning** is that if we do not have sufficient training data we will not be able to build a good predictor. If we now look at Table 4.2 we see the original training data from Table 4.1 plus three additional data points. Here the function $f(x) = 2x$ does not appear to be valid any longer: For input −1 the output is 1, and for input 1 the output is 1. Given this new training data it looks like a more appropriate function mapping the input values to output values would be $f(x) = x^2$. If we had built our predictive model with a single data point (Table 4.1) while ignoring the rest of the data available (Table 4.2) our predictions would have been seriously flawed. For example, if we put in 4 coins, under the new model the machine would give 16 coins back, not 8 as the first model would have predicted. Therefore the goal of a supervised learning model is to find the function that maps input values to output values most accurately.

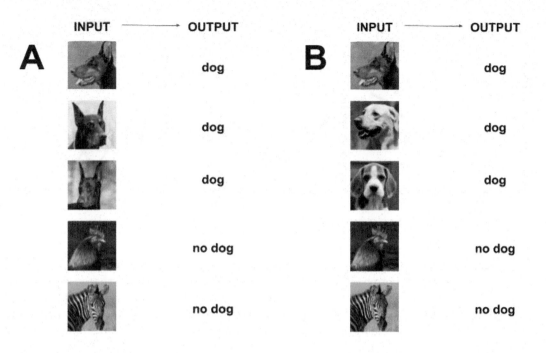

Figure 4.2 Having a diversity of observations is essential for generalisation.

Besides having enough training data, the **second rule of supervised learning** is that a robust predictive method should be able to *generalise* beyond the examples it was trained with. To achieve this, the training examples must be varied enough. There is little point in training a predictive algorithm with lots of identical data. To illustrate this, let us return to the classification problem of identifying dogs in photographs that we introduced in Chapter 3 (Fig. 3.2). Now, training set A contains three dobermans, a rooster and a zebra (Fig. 4.2). Training set B contains three examples of dog breeds (a doberman, a labrador and a beagle), and again the rooster and the zebra. Given the same image classification algorithm, which training dataset do you think is more likely to identify a bulldog in a photograph, A or B?

Answer: The image classifier trained with dataset B. This is because dataset A is too focused on identifying dobermans, whereas dataset B has a richer diversity of different dog breeds and thus should be able to generalise better to new breeds that it has not yet seen but which nevertheless possess general canine features.

## 4.2 UNDERFITTING AND OVERFITTING

The function mapping input to output training data $f(x) = x^2$ (Table 4.2) is, nevertheless, a very simple function. In real life data is always more messy and a perfect predictor on a training set is sub-optimal as it will not be able to generalise or predict new values. One should expect a predictive model to make predictions errors on test data and understanding which type of errors you can afford to make is the key to designing a good predictive model. Below we examine key concepts in supervised learning such as underfitting and overfitting, cross-validation, and the various types of classification errors.

When fitting a model to a training dataset there is always a tension between building a model that is complex enough to capture the main features of the training data as well

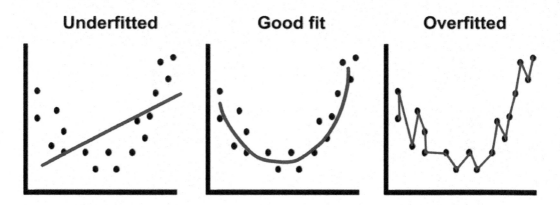

Figure 4.3 Underfitting vs overfitting.

as its inherent variability, but not so complex that the noise in the training data is also included in the model. Let us consider the example in Fig. 4.3, a dataset that is represented by the black dots and which is parabolic in nature. We wish to fit a model to this dataset so that we can use it to predict future values of $Y$ given a value of $X$. The two types of mistakes that occur when fitting a model to a dataset are called underfitting and overfitting (Fig. 4.3):

- An *underfitted* model is a simplistic model that does not capture the trends in the dataset. The example here is given by a linear function (magenta line) which if used, would make very poor predictions most of the time.

- An *overfitted* model is the opposite of an underfitted model as it has too many parameters fitting the training data. Although the training data here describe the trend of a parabola, it is not a perfect parabola. In other words, the data contains noise or deviations from a perfect parabola. The overfit model here employs a higher order polynomial that fits every single data point, instead of fitting the trend of the data points. An overfitted model will always perform better on a training set than a simpler model, but will do worse on test data as it is not able to generalise.

The better function to describe the training dataset is given by the pink line that describes the trend of a parabola instead of passing through every single data point like the overfitted model does (center figure in Fig. 4.3). An underfitted model is said to have *high bias*, whereas an overfitted model is said to have *high variance* (Fig. 4.4). Thus the goal of predictive model building is to minimise these two types of error, otherwise known as the **bias-variance dilemma**. In complex models like ensembles it is possible to combine the base models in a way that reduces either the bias or the variance, depending on the weakness of these base models.

In general a predictive model should be as simple as possible. For example, if logistic regression yields a classification accuracy of 93% on a dataset, it is rarely justified to employ a much more complex model such as a support vector machine (SVM) that might perhaps improve the accuracy of the model by 1%. An exception here are Kaggle competitions (kaggle.com) where absolute performance is more important than anything else. In a real-life setting with real business constraints, however, we must remember that the more complex models are more difficult to interpret and explain, and will always run more slowly (implementation latency constraints).

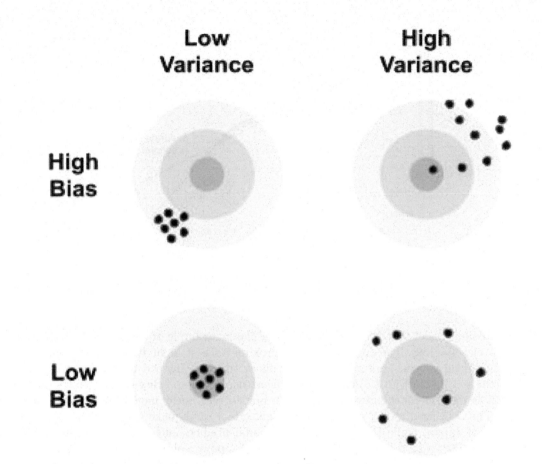

Figure 4.4 Bias vs variance.

## 4.3 OVERFITTING IN THE CONTEXT OF THE FUKUSHIMA NUCLEAR PLANT DISASTER

In 2011 I was a professor at Osaka University. In the early afternoon of March 11 a colleague and I were discussing a set of results. Suddenly, the walls of our building started to shake for what we thought was an abnormally long period of time. We quickly checked this Japanese website to find out where the epicenter was, and when we learnt of a location some 300 Km north of Tokyo, we immediately knew something serious had happened.

The Fukushima nuclear disaster is the accident that occurred at the Fukushima Daiichi Nuclear Power Plant in Okuma, Japan, immediately preceded by the Tohoku earthquake and tsunami that took place on March 11, 2011. It is classified as the second most severe nuclear accident after Chernobyl (1986) [137].

Part of the problem with the Fukushima nuclear plant disaster had to do with its poor construction. In an area known for frequent earthquakes, the engineers had to design a nuclear plant that would withstand a large earthquake. The Gutenberg-Richter Law predicts the probability of a very strong earthquake from the frequency of the unnoticeable, weak earthquakes that occur all the time. It states that the relationship between the magnitude of an earthquake and the logarithm of the probability that it happens is linear [138]. Therefore, the goal should have been to fit a linear model through the 400-year-old earthquake dataset.

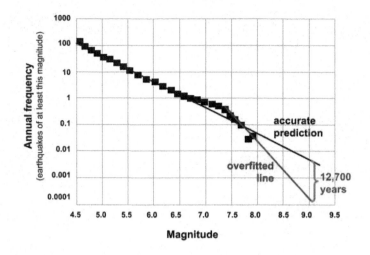

Figure 4.5 The overfitted line through the 400-year-old earthquake dataset (adapted from [139]).

The regression model that was fit (Fig. 4.5) is a classic example of overfitting as it fits the data too closely [139]. The training data approximates a straight line, and therefore the trend should have been approximated by a linear function instead of the more complex model (the red line in Fig. 4.5) that the engineers used to map every single data point.

What is the difference between the simple but correct linear model and the overfitted model? The overfitted model predicts one magnitude-9 earthquake every ~13,000 years in that area of Japan, while the correct, linear model predicts such an earthquake to happen every ~300 years [139]. The Fukushima nuclear power plant was built to withstand an earthquake of magnitude 8.6. The 2011 earthquake that wrecked the Fukushima plant had a magnitude of 9.1 or 2.5 times stronger than a magnitude 8.6 (the Richter scale is logarithmic).

Surely a number of additional factors contributed to the catastrophe, including the tsunami as the earthquake happened on the seabed, and therefore ascribing the Fukushima nuclear disaster to a linear regression problem is an oversimplification. However, working on a different set of expectations regarding the frequency of large earthquakes must have had an influence on some of the decisions that were taken during the construction process.

## 4.4 EVALUATING MODEL PERFORMANCE BY CROSS-VALIDATION

All predictive methods must be trained with a *training set*, and then be evaluated on a left-out dataset called the *test set* (Fig. 4.1). The partitioning of a dataset into training and test sets is a very important topic because a test set must provide an honest assessment of the predictive model. Therefore, data partitioning must be done in the right way to avoid introducing any systematic bias between the training and the test sets. For example, some datasets are ordered by size, and so it would be a terrible idea to take the first half for learning and the second half for testing because one set will always end up with the largest or the smallest possible values. In general a random assignment is the simplest way to avoid introducing bias in the training and test sets. However, no matter how much care we take in selecting a validation set, two problems still remain [53]:

(i) Depending on which observations are included in the test and training sets, the test error rate can be highly variable;

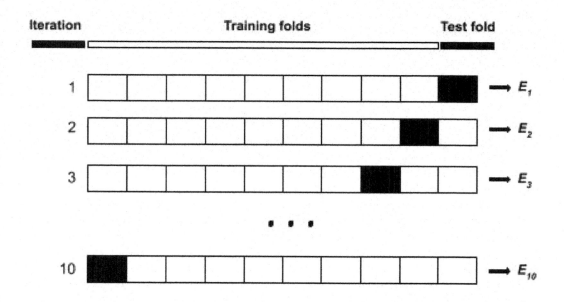

Figure 4.6 The 10-fold cross-validation strategy.

(ii) Keeping a holdout set for testing means that not all the observations are used to train the model. This can be a problem if the amount of data is limited as statistical methods always perform better when trained on more data. The net effect is that the error rate of the model as calculated on the test set can be overestimated.

A much better way of partitioning the data is to do cross-validation. In $k$-fold cross-validation we partition the original dataset into $k$-1 training sets and one test set of equal size. We then build $k$ predictive models and perform their evaluation (Fig. 4.6). The composition of the training and test sets changes and the final evaluation is averaged over $k$ models and their evaluations. The advantage of $k$-$fold$ cross-validation is that all the observations are used for both training and testing, and so the effect of the inherent variability in the dataset is minimised. Ten-fold cross-validation is the most common type of cross-validation strategy as it presents an optimal bias-variance trade-off [53], but it is by no means the only valid strategy [140].

### 4.4.1 Beyond the Test Set: The Validation and Final Testing Sets

The performance of a predictive model on its own training set alone cannot possibly be representative of its actual performance because of the overfitting problem. There are various ways to reduce overfitting, for example by adding a regularisation term to the function in order to penalise overly complex models (since simpler models tend to generalise better). However, the introduction of the test set (e.g. in the form of cross-validation) is the most popular way to combat overfitting by providing an impartial assessment of the model's skill. But is this assessment really impartial?

There is a catch in using a test set because the test set is somehow also used to optimise the performance of the model in the learning step (Fig. 4.1). For instance, in linear regression the method of least squares is most commonly used to fit a straight regression line through the training data. A test set can then be used to assess the performance of the linear model. However, one important disadvantage of linear regression is that it is very sensitive to outliers. There are a number of solutions to this problem [141], the easiest of which probably is to remove the outliers. But what if outliers are also present in the test set (which is a reasonable expectation)? This is an example of how the test set is not completely independent of the training process if it is being used to determine the *parameters* of the linear model (the slope and intercept coefficients) during training.

Other methods have an even more intimate relationship with the test set. For instance, a neural network is trained on the test set until the performance starts to deteriorate. Thus, the weights among the neurons are heavily influenced by the test set. And besides network parameters, we also have *hyperparameters* we can adjust, such as the learning rate controlling how quickly a neural network adapts to the test dataset. Therefore, in the same way that the parameters can be overfit to the test set, so can the hyperparameters. As long as we use the test set results to optimise the model we are effectively overfitting to the training and test set combo.

One solution here is to keep a small *validation set* aside to continuously monitor the performance of the model during the training process. The training is carried out until the validation set error starts to deteriorate.

When building models that do not require iterative training a validation set is also useful as a *final testing set* that provides an additional evaluation of the performance of a classifier. In this type of situation, once we obtain the evaluation on a *final testing set*, one of three things can happen:

(i) The performance of the model on this set is similar to that on the test set. This means that the model is stable and is probably what most of us would expect naturally.

(ii) The performance of the model is better on the final testing set than on the test set. If the difference is not too great, this might be due to the validation set being more similar to the training set than the training and the test sets are. This type of situation can arise by chance.

(iii) The performance of the model is worse on the final testing set than on the test set. This is the most worrying scenario as most likely there is some degree of overfitting in the model. This might be due to a high intrinsic variability of the training set, in which case it would be worth trying to use much more data for training since the introduction of redundancy often reduces variability.

Finally, if I am allowed to play the devil's advocate, what would you say is a potential problem with using a final testing set? If the source of all the datasets is the same, perhaps we should question whether our model has been properly evaluated beyond a purely theoretical exercise.

Depending exclusively on the application domain of the model, a posterior performance could be done on data of the same type but which has been sourced from a different, but equivalent system. For example, if a classifier's goal is to predict a particular disease and all the datasets come from the same patient population, a better test to assess the true performance of the classifier could be to use data from patients who are genetically distinct (a different ethnic origin, perhaps). In a different example, if we have a speech recognition system that translates (classifies) spoken English words into text and it has been trained with recordings of native speakers from the UK and the USA, perhaps a better way to test its performance could be to see how well it does when interpreting the spoken English of non-native speakers. Therefore, the specific details of the training, validation and implementation of a predictive model in a real context are heavily dependent on the specific problem. The solution, once again lies with the data scientist and their ability to ask the right questions, in the right context, with a healthy dose of skepticism.

**Positive examples**  **Negative examples**

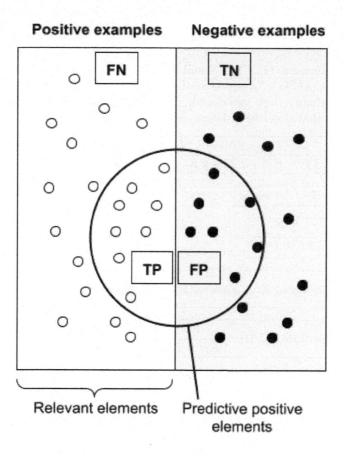

Relevant elements    Predictive positive
elements

Figure 4.7 The four possible test dataset classification categories.

## 4.5  WAYS TO DESCRIBE THE PERFORMANCE OF A CLASSIFIER

The evaluation of a model will always present errors. To illustrate how we can think about these errors let us return to the image classification problem where the goal is to build a classifier that can tell whether a photograph contains the image of a dog.

When a photograph of the test dataset is subjected to the image classifier, the data in the photograph (in the form of coloured pixels) is analysed by the model: If the result of the computation is above a particular threshold, the photograph will be classified into one of two possible categories (either 'contains dog' or 'does not contain dog'). Thus the photographs that make the cut according to some criteria constitute the predicted positives elements (Fig. 4.7). The rest of the data are the predicted negatives. When we examine the predictions on the test dataset, since the data is labelled in the form of positive and negative examples, every predicted data point must belong to one of four possible categories (Fig. 4.7):

- True Positive (TP): A positive example identified as positive (a hit)

- True Negative (TN): A negative example identified as negative (a correct rejection)

- False Positive (FP), or Type I error: A negative example mistakenly classified as positive (a false alarm)

- False Negative (FN), or Type II error: A positive example mistakenly classified as negative (a miss)

The interplay between TP, FP, FN and TN is more easily visualised in what is called a **confusion matrix** (Table 4.3), which can be easily extended to accommodate classification problems involving more than two classes. TP, FP, FN and TN are then combined into a number of metrics that describe different aspects of a model's performance:

- $\boxed{\text{Accuracy} = \dfrac{TP + TN}{TP + FP + TN + FN}}$

- $\boxed{\text{Error rate} = 1 - Accuracy}$

- $\boxed{\text{Precision} = \dfrac{TP}{(TP + FP)}}$

- $\boxed{\text{Recall, sensitivity or True Positive Rate (TPR)} = \dfrac{TP}{TP + FN}}$

- $\boxed{\text{False Positive Rate (FPR)} = \dfrac{FP}{FP + TN}}$

Now let us illustrate how these metrics are calculated in practice: Our test dataset of 140 pictures contains 100 dog-containing pictures (the positive class) and 40 no-dog pictures. The goal of our classifier is to predict which pictures contain a dog. The test result is as follows: Our classifier predicted 80 dog-containing pictures and 60 no-dog pictures. Of the 80 predicted dog-containing pictures, 75 do contain dogs (the TP) and therefore we have 5 FP among the predictive positive elements. Next, of the 60 predicted no-dog pictures, 35 do not contain dogs (TN), but unfortunately 25 do contain dogs (FN). We can summarise this information in the following confusion matrix:

TABLE 4.3   Confusion Matrix of Our Dog-in-Picture Classifier

|  |  | REAL VALUE | |
|---|---|---|---|
|  |  | Positive | Negative |
| **PREDICTED VALUE** | **Positive** | TP = 75 | FP = 5 |
|  | **Negative** | FN = 25 | TN = 35 |

With the confusion matrix at hand we can easily calculate the various performance metrics:

- Accuracy $= \frac{75+35}{75+5+35+25} = 0.78$

- Error rate $= 1 - Accuracy = 0.22$

- Precision $= \frac{75}{75+5} = 0.94$

- Recall, sensitivity or True Positive Rate (TPR) $= \frac{75}{75+25} = 0.75$

- False Positive Rate (FPR) $= \frac{5}{5+35} = 0.125$

## 4.6 ACCURACY, PRECISION AND RECALL IN PRACTICE

There is no performance metric that works for every predictive method and context because each metric focuses on different aspects of a classifier while ignoring others. This is why we must always understand a prediction in the right context. For example, if we are building a model to predict very large credit defaulting customers (TP) we should be paying the greatest attention to FN errors as these are always more expensive to a company than a FP.

Classification accuracy (the fraction of correct predictions) is the most widely used performance metric because it very intuitive and logical: When we build a classifier we are interested in making as little mistakes as possible, so what could be easier than simply counting the number of mistakes?

One blind spot of the classification accuracy metric is that it does not distinguish between the types of errors it makes (FP vs FN), which normally is not a problem if we have a balanced dataset. A 'balanced' dataset could mean, for instance, 400 observations from class A vs 500 observations from class B. However, it is not difficult to see how the classification accuracy can be seriously biased and give a false sense of high performance if the number of observations belonging to each class are imbalanced. For example, think of a disease that is present in only 5 out of 95 individuals. If we simply predict that everyone in the test dataset is disease-free, we still obtain an impressive accuracy of 95%, but this would be a useless predictor that fails to identify the diseased individuals. When dealing with imbalanced datasets we must consider the recall and the precision.

### 4.6.1 Image-Based Identification of Terrorists

To illustrate the interplay between accuracy, precision and recall let us pretend that we have been given the task of building a predictor from CCTV images in order to tell terrorists from non-terrorists. The fictional situation is that there are 4 terrorists for every 100 people. This is again an example of an imbalanced dataset, a typical problem when building classifiers.

Our classifier singles out 2 people as terrorists (and 98 non-terrorists), of which only 1 is a terrorist (so we are missing 3). The predictions of a model against the actual class labels of the observations is represented in a confusion matrix (Table 4.4):

TABLE 4.4   Confusion Matrix of Our Classifier for Predicting Terrorists

|  |  | REAL VALUE | |
| --- | --- | --- | --- |
|  |  | Positive | Negative |
| **PREDICTED VALUE** | **Positive** | TP = 1 | FP = 1 |
|  | **Negative** | FN = 3 | TN = 95 |

The accuracy of our classifier (the percentage of predictions that it gets right) is 96%. We should be happy, right?

$$\text{Accuracy} = \frac{(1 + 95)}{(1 + 1 + 3 + 95)} = 0.96$$

Although 96 out 100 predictions are correct, the accuracy here is not a useful metric if we can only identify one of the four terrorists. The target here is to identify all terrorists, not just one.

The recall (what fraction of the positives our model identifies) and the precision (how accurate our positive predictions are) are better metrics when we have an overwhelming majority of data points belonging to one class (the non-terrorists):

- Recall—out of all the terrorists, how many terrorists can I identify?

$$\text{Recall} = \frac{TP}{TP + FN} = \frac{1}{1 + 3} = 0.25$$

- Precision—of all the people I select (i.e. think are terrorists), how many of these really are terrorists?

$$\text{Precision} = \frac{TP}{TP + FP} = \frac{1}{1 + 1} = 0.5$$

This model presents a terrible performance because it can only identify 1 in 4 terrorists (low recall), and whenever we select people for screening, only 1 out of 2 is a terrorist (low precision). Clearly we could label all 100 people as terrorists, in which case we would have a 100% recall rate at the expense of precision. However, having everyone in the same bag still does not tell us who the terrorists are.

One thing that precision and recall are completely blind to but which the accuracy metric does consider, is the determination that a negative observation is indeed negative (a TN). This is why the healthiest perspective is to consider various metrics and ponder the relative merits and limitations of each metric in the context of the specific problem.

### 4.6.2 The Precision-Recall Curve

Precision and recall have a very intimate relationship as we can always raise the rate of recall (i.e. be more inclusive) at the expense of precision. Likewise, we can improve our precision to 100% at the expense of the rate of recall.

A precision-recall curve (Fig. 4.8) shows how the precision and recall of a classifier vary with different thresholds. Here a classifier with perfect precision and recall would be a point in the upper, right-hand corner (1.0, 1.0). If a model at a given threshold has a low rate of recall and a high precision rate, it means that its predictions will most likely be correct but it will fail to identify a lot of TP. In the case of predicting a disease, we should choose to have a high recall at the expense of a loss of precision because it is always better to do additional clinical tests than to misdiagnose a patient. Of course this is an oversimplification of a medical situation but the message is that we should always try to understand the costs of making different types of errors with a predictive model.

### 4.6.3 The $F_1$-Score

Besides inspecting a precision-recall curve it is also advisable to consider the $F_1$-score. The $F_1$-score is the harmonic mean of the precision and the recall rates, and ranges between [0,1] (1 being perfect precision and recall).

$$F_1 \text{ score} = 2 \times \frac{Precision * Recall}{Precision + Recall}$$

The $F_1$-score will help us decide on the better classifier in a situation like this: we have classifier A (precision = 95%, recall = 90%) and classifier B (precision = 98%, recall = 85%). Classifier A is slightly better on recall, whereas classifier B is slightly better on precision. Which one is the better classifier?

$$F_1 \text{ score (A)} = 2 \times \frac{0.95 * 0.90}{0.95 + 0.90} = 0.92$$

$$F_1 \text{ score (B)} = 2 \times \frac{0.98 * 0.85}{0.98 + 0.85} = 0.91$$

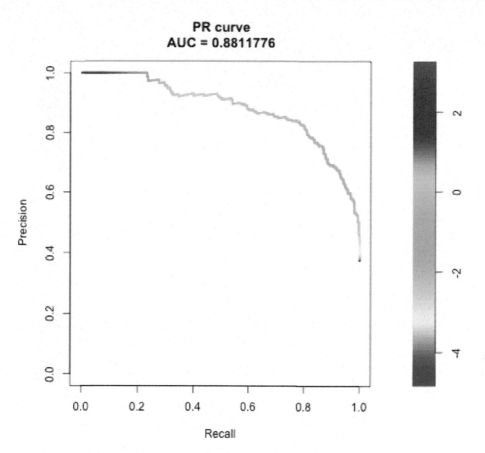

Figure 4.8 A typical precision-recall curve (example).

The $F_1$ score is a conservative metric because it gives equal value to precision and recall, and punishes extreme values. For example, the average of a classifier with perfect precision (1.0) and zero recall is 0.5, but its $F_1$ score is zero. Therefore, we can build a classifier with a perfect balance of precision and recall by optimising the $F_1$ score.

### 4.6.4 The Receiver Operating Characteristic (ROC) Curve

ROC curves display the relationship between a classifier's True Positive Rate or 'hit rate' (also called sensitivity or recall) and its False Positive Rate or 'alarm rate' for a range of threshold values (Fig. 4.9). ROC curves are optimally applied when the observations are balanced between the two classes, whereas precision-recall curves should be used with imbalanced classes.

Like precision-recall curves, ROC curves are useful for selecting the optimal classification threshold for a specific binary classification problem. For example, if we are building a spam filter we should really be selecting a threshold that keeps the FPR really low. This is because it is preferable to let some spam show up in the user's inbox rather than miss important emails because our filter has aggressively labelled some emails as spam. Conversely, if for instance we are building a classifier to predict diabetes given a range of metabolic values and lifestyle indicators, we should tolerate a higher FPR (incorrect diagnosis) just to make sure we do not miss many true positives. Since, it is very expensive to monitor all individuals

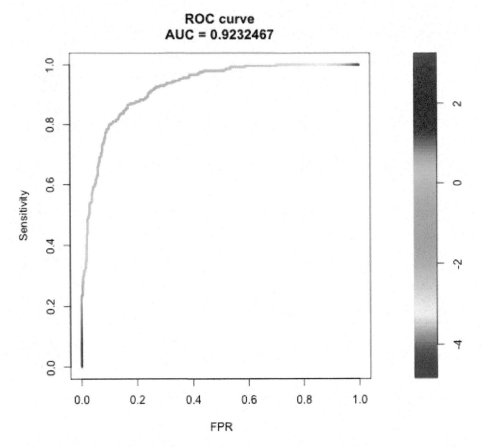

Figure 4.9 A typical ROC curve (example).

of all ages, what would be the problem with recommending a couple of false positive (misdiagnosed) individuals over the age of 35 to eat more vegetables, less carbohydrates and exercise regularly?

The Area Under the Curve (AUC) is the single metric ranging between [0,1] that summarises the area of the square covered by the ROC curve. A perfect classifier (one with a TPR = 100% and an FPR = 0%) has an AUC of 1, whereas a classifier with no predictive power has an AUC of 0.5 or less (Fig. 4.10).

ROC curves are routinely used to compare the performance of different classification methods that are trained and tested on the same datasets. However, using the AUC alone to compare the performance of classifiers is not advised. For one thing, we lose a lot of detail when we substitute the complexity of a ROC curve by a numeric value ranging between [0,1]. Two identical AUC values can present very different ROC curves, and can be especially misleading if the curves cross each other. Another important limitation of the AUC is that it uses different misclassification metrics for different classifiers when this should be an independent property [142].

## 4.7   CLASSIFICATION ERRORS OF CONTINUOUS DATA PREDICTIONS

A confusion matrix and the associated metrics we can derive from it (e.g. accuracy, precision, TPR, FPR) are useful for reasoning about the performance of a classifier. For regression

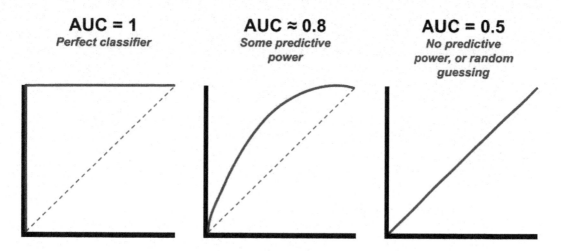

Figure 4.10 A range of values for the ROC Area Under the Curve.

models where the goal is to make a numerical (continuous value) prediction while minimising the prediction error on the test dataset, the most popular metrics include:

- $$Mean\ Absolute\ Error\ (MAE)* = \frac{\Sigma_{i=1}^{n}|(x_i - y_i)|}{n}$$

  The MAE simply is the average difference between the actual values of a test (or validation) set and the values predicted by the model.It is a popular and widely used metric because it is easy to interpret since (i) the units of the MAE score match the units of the target value and (ii) the changes in MAE increase linearly with the number of errors as all predictions are weighed the same.

  A good way to interpret the MAE (or any other metric) is to decide beforehand what an acceptable MAE would be for our specific problem and dataset by taking into account the costs of making such errors, especially when the predictive model is implemented in real life. Additionally, a naïve model may first be run and have the MAE determined: any improvement on the MAE by a predictive model means that the model in question is better than the naïve model and therefore has skill. In theory a perfect MAE is 0.0 (all predictions on the test set match the actual values), but such a score would mean that the prediction problem was trivial to start with.

- $$Mean\ Squared\ Error\ (MSE)* = \frac{1}{n}\Sigma_{i=1}^{n}(x_i - y_i)^2$$

  The MSE simply is the average of the squared difference between the actual values of a test (or validation) set and the values predicted by the model. The squaring of the differences has the effect of overestimating the overall error of the model because large errors (outliers) are magnified. In comparison, the changes in MAE increase linearly with the number of errors as all predictions are weighed the same. Therefore, MAE is a more appropriate metric if we do not wish to penalise outliers excessively.

- $$Root\ Mean\ Squared\ Error\ (RMSE) = \sqrt{MSE}$$

  The Root Mean Squared Error (RMSE) is the square root of the MSE and the most widely used technique for reporting the error of a regression model.

One problem with the MSE is that it is not very intuitive because the error units are squared: For instance, we could have an MSE of 10.4 squared euros, or 4.7 squared degrees Celsius (for the problem of temperature prediction). The RMSE removes this problem by taking the square root of the square (which is the inverse function), which means that the resulting error units are comparable with the actual values (e.g. euros and degrees Celsius). However, like the MSE, the RMSE also penalises large errors.

*Note: $x_i$ indicates an actual value, whereas $y_i$ indicates a predicted value.

## 4.8    FURTHER READING

- **Websites**

    - **The Kaggle Discussion Forum**
      URL: kaggle.com/discussion
      *This is an interesting forum split into groups of interest ('communities') where one can ask for advice and also find interesting threads on virtually every topic.*

    - **Machine Learning @ Quora**
      URL: https://bit.ly/3f0zdBZ
      *This section on Quora is an interesting resource for all things Machine Learning. world-class experts often contribute here.*

- **Videos**

    - **Machine Learning Model Evaluation Metrics|PyData Los Angeles 2019 (Maria Khalusova)**
      URL: https://bit.ly/3cyCCGB
      *An excellent lecture by Maria Khalusova on the various evaluation metrics that exist and to choose wisely.*

- **Articles**

    - **Gopalakrishna AK, Ozcelebi T, Lukkien J and Liotta A. Evaluating machine learning algorithms for applications with humans in the loop, 2017 IEEE 14th International Conference on Networking, Sensing and Control (ICNSC), 2017.**
      *The performance of some classification problems involves human perception and thus cannot be evaluated with a standard dataset with unequivocally mapped input-output pairs. These problems are referred to as 'non-deterministic multiple output classification problems', and here the authors describe a superior metric (the 'Relevance Score') to assess the performance of learning methods in this type of context.*

    - **Japkowicz N. Why Question Machine Learning Evaluation Methods? (An illustrative review of the shortcomings of current methods) AAAI'2006 Workshop on Evaluation Methods for Machine Learning, 2006.**
      *An excellent, practical review on the virtues and blind spots of the most commonly used evaluation metrics in machine learning. Illustration is through examples and I highly recommend reading it.*

    - **Northcutt CG, Athalye A and Mueller J. Pervasive Label Errors in Test Sets Destabilize Machine Learning Benchmarks, 2021.**
      URL: https://arxiv.org/pdf/2103.14749.pdf

*Benchmark datasets are used to train, evaluate and compare algorithsm over time, and therefore are essential for tracking progress in the machine learning field. These MIT scientists found how flawed some of these datasets are, e.g. 6% of the images in the ImageNet database (Chapter 3) are misannotated. The correction of these mistakes changed the performance of previously under-performing methods which are now in the top of their class. Thus this article illustrates how the evaluation of the performance of a method cannot be separated from the quality of the data used for training and testing.*

- **Olson RS, La Cava W, Orzechowski, Urbanowicz RJ and Moore JH. PMLB: a large benchmark suite for machine learning evaluation and comparison. BioData Mining 10:36, 2017.**
  *This article is complementary to that by Northcutt et al. Here the authors discuss the limitations of the various, existing benchmark datasets, and their efforts towards developing a unified resource.*

- **Sokolova MV and Lapalme G. A systematic analysis of performance measures for classification tasks. Information Processing and Management: an International Journal, 45(4), 2009.**
  *In Chapter 4 we discussed how to assess the performance of binary classifiers, but there are three other types of classification tasks (multi-class, multi-labelled and hierarchical). This interesting paper reviews 24 different performance measures for all types of classification tasks while using examples and providing recommendations.*

- **Books**

  - James G, Witten D, Hastie T, Tibshirani R. *An Introduction to Statistical Learning.* Springer, New York, (NY), USA, 2013. ISBN: 9781461471370.
    *Chapter 5 contains an excellent discussion on resampling methods, such as k-fold cross-validation, leave-one-out cross-validation and the bootstrap.*

  - Zheng A. *Evaluating Machine Learning Models.* O'Reilly Media, Inc., Sebastopol (CA), USA, 2015. ISBN: 9781491932445.
    *This short and excellent reference book covers the most important aspects of model evaluation in an accessible way.*

## 4.9   CHAPTER REVIEW QUESTIONS

1. **A supervised machine learning algorithm can be trained to predict**

   (a) The future value of a stock option.
   (b) The weather next week.
   (c) The onset of World War III.
   (d) Depression.

2. **The goal of a supervised learning model is**

   (a) To make good predictions on the training data.
   (b) To fit the training data as closely as possible.
   (c) To find the function that maps input values to output values most appropriately.
   (d) To build a model that has high variance and high bias.

3. **The poor construction of the Fukushima nuclear power plant occurred because**

   (a) The engineers did not have enough training data.

   (b) The engineers should have used a more sophisticated algorithm.

   (c) The engineers overfitted the training data.

   (d) The building was not built with quality materials.

4. **When evaluating a categorical predictor, a model with low recall and high precision**

   (a) Is better than a model with low precision and high recall.

   (b) Will always perform well.

   (c) Will get the predictions right most of the time, but will also fail to identify true positives.

   (d) Is always better than a model with very high accuracy.

5. **When building a predictive model**

   (a) We should always start with the simplest possible model.

   (b) We should always start with complex higher order polynomial functions.

   (c) Partitioning the data properly into training and test data is the only important consideration.

   (d) Our goal should be to minimise the bias and variance errors.

6. **When would you use a precision-recall curve and when would you use a Receiver Operating Characteristic (ROC) curve when comparing binary classifiers?**

7. **Why is using the Area Under the Curve (AUC) alone a bad idea when comparing classifiers?**

# Are Our Algorithms Racist, Sexist and Discriminating?

*The way you see people is the way you treat them, and the way you treat them is what they become.*

— Johann Wolfgang von Goethe (1749–1832), *German writer*

Intelligent algorithms help us everyday with hundreds of tasks from writing emails, movie recommendations, researching restaurants in a new city and even cooking at home. Beyond these harmless examples, algorithms are quickly penetrating every layer of society to the point where they control much more important decisions like who gets hired or fired, who gets a mortgage and who gets released from prison. Algorithms can process huge amounts of data and make decisions faster than any human, but they are also vulnerable to bias, which results in discriminatory outcomes. Here two key questions are: (i) to which extent should we delegate on algorithms for making certain types of decisions? and (ii) what is actually a fair outcome for my algorithm and in which situations?

In this chapter we review various examples of algorithm-based discrimination (including racial, gender and socio-economic) followed by a discussion on the different biases that underlie discriminatory outcomes, and how to reason about them. A universal definition of fairness is unattainable because what is fair varies across individuals, groups and cultures. We discuss how to analyse discrimination creatively from different angles and how to reason about fairness in various contexts. For example, are there any potentially discriminatory features in our data that we should not use at the expense of a loss of accuracy? Are all types of inequality between groups wrong? Should we focus on groups or individuals and is this always possible? In what way are we trying to be fair, by providing equal opportunities (equality) or by providing an equal chance to succeed (equity)? Therefore finding and implementing fairness in machine learning requires combining knowledge of data science with key concepts of moral and political philosophy for specific contexts. A number of sophisticated methods have been developed to identify and address bias and unfairness in machine learning algorithms. Finally, a key ingredient for achieving fairness is to have a design team whose members represent a diversity of ethnic and religious groups, social classes as well as disabilities.

## 5.1 HOW DO SMART ALGORITHMS MEDDLE IN OUR LIVES?

Saturday morning, 07:30 a.m. I always check my social networks and read an article or two before I get out of bed. Face ID, Apple's facial recognition system [143] (Fig. 5.1) unlocks

DOI: 10.1201/b23197-5

Figure 5.1 Face ID is Apple's face recognition system.

my iPhone by first projecting 30,000 infrared dots onto my face which are then scanned to build a three-dimensional map. Next, a supervised learning algorithm compares this 3D map to various stored records of my face. Actually, when I set up my Face ID account I was not sporting a beard, but that is fine because the deep neural networks (DNN) underneath Face ID can adjust for facial hair, age and even wearing the occasional sunglasses.

Like millions of other users, I impulsively log onto my Facebook briefly to check on my friends' updates. The underlying recommender systems continually learn from my viewing history in order to serve me the newsfeed that I might be most interested in. In fact, the goal of Facebook is to personalise the user experience as much as possible [144]. One of the most impressive uses of machine learning on the Facebook platform is the analysis of text by DeepText [145]. The algorithms behind DeepText are different types of DNNs capable of understanding text and content with near-human accuracy in over 20 languages. Text analytics is also used for filtering out fake news and spam, detecting cyberbullying as well as for suggesting services (e.g. an Uber lift) from your written conversation with friends.

10.30 a.m.—my friend Aaron calls to ask if I am up for lunch. As soon as we agree to meet at Union Square at noon, I get on Google Maps to search for restaurants in the area. Until recently, Google Maps was just an application for finding places on a map. Now, however, a sophisticated machine learning platform combines restaurant reviews and photos of dishes and their descriptions [146] and suggests that I might particularly enjoy the rigatoni with vodka sauce at Da Canio's restaurant round the corner from Union Square. What's more, thanks to state-of-the-art natural language processing technology you do not have to worry about the local language anywhere you go.

Before leaving the house I quickly reply to some email with a 'Yes, I am happy to go ahead'. This was Gmail's Smart Reply to Inbox solution that learns from your response patterns so that it can eventually offer you these smart replies without you having to type

Figure 5.2 Voice assistants help us with an increasing number of tasks at home.

them [147]. A different set of learning algorithms for natural language processing checks your spelling and grammar, and yet another type is trained to recognise spam and malware to keep your inbox as secure as possible.

After lunch we go for a short stroll and I end up buying this nice t-shirt. My bank knows my regular locations and purchase patterns and has implemented machine learning-based anomaly detection models to help detect fraud in near real time, therefore saving millions in losses. A credit card transaction that is flagged as abnormal will request additional evidence such as replying to a message sent to your phone for verification (i.e. multi-factor authentication [148]).

As soon as I get back home I throw myself on the sofa and finish watching the last episode of La Casa de Papel (Money Heist). Upon finishing the series, Netflix quickly makes a recommendation: Prison Break. How did this happen?

Inspection of my Netflix history and those of other viewers tells Netflix that I might enjoy watching Prison Break. This is because La Casa de Papel is part of a group of series that are liked by other people like me. I have watched a few series in this cluster but not Prison Break and so Netflix makes this recommendation. This is an example of a recommender system (Chapter 3). In practice the recommender system behind Netflix is much more sophisticated as it can deliver suggestions regarding actors, genres and time periods, all adjusted to the time of day [85].

After watching Prison Break I am feeling creative and decide to make an apple pie. Since I cannot remember the specific ingredients, I ask Alexa for help [149]. Amazon Alexa is a voice-based virtual assistant technology (Fig. 5.2). If I had a more modern kitchen I could even ask Alexa to cook for me. Alexa is an outstanding example of natural language processing combined with machine learning algorithms that can interpret your requests (however you say them, in whichever accent) and suggest a number of possible solutions.

Besides, we can search the Allrecipes database verbally by recipe title, ingredients or by cooking time ('Alexa, what can I cook with mushrooms and eggs in 30 minutes?'). Searching comprises yet another universe of sophisticated algorithms.

### 5.1.1  Outlook

The examples above are a fraction of all the applications in machine learning that are quickly becoming a part of our everyday lives, right from searching information on Google to smart homes to self-driving cars to robot companions that can understand and feel emotions.

Perhaps the most impressive applications are those related to human health as these involve processing huge amounts of complex data whose results impact human lives in a profound way. For example, in 2016 IBM Watson (ibm.com/watson) saved a woman's life by detecting a rare form of leukaemia that had been misdiagnosed. The successful diagnosis was achieved in under 10 minutes as Watson compared the patient's genetic changes against 20 million cancer research papers [150]. Another excellent example is BlueDot's (https://bluedot.global/) algorithm which predicted the COVID-19 outbreak in December 2019. This algorithm uses sophisticated natural language processing capabilities to scan news in real time in different languages, in combination with information on possible outbreaks and commercial flights. BlueDot managed to predict the Wuhan outbreak as well as its subsequent spread to Bangkok, Seoul, Taipei and Tokyo, and was ahead of the World Health Organization by one full month [2].

Relying on algorithms for decision-making can have unfair outcomes too, such as being filtered out for a particular job because we used the 'wrong' wording in our CV, or being denied a mortgage for some reason that cannot be teased apart given the complexity of the algorithm used. Intelligent algorithms are quickly becoming so integrated in our lives that they will eventually constitute the new infrastructure that will power a cognition-based industrial revolution [151]. In this scenario, we must ask ourselves: To which extent should we delegate on algorithms for making key decisions?

In the following sections we first discuss various types of discrimination, followed by a discussion on how the many different types of bias can lead to discriminatory outcomes, how algorithmic bias may be spotted, and finally what we can do to prevent it.

## 5.2  RELEASE ON PAROLE: NOT IF YOU ARE BLACK

Many algorithms that are routinely used to make hugely important decisions in our society are dangerously biased. However, most of the time the algorithms themselves are neither good nor bad, but we make them unfair by introducing our own human biases. A well-known example of a biased algorithm with negative consequences is COMPAS (Correctional Offender Management Profiling for Alternative Sanctions), a method that predicts whether a US convict is likely to reoffend (called recidivism) if released on parole [152]. In 2016 data scientists of the investigative journalism website ProPublica compared the scores given by COMPAS to thousands of convicts and the outcomes in the two years following their scoring [153]. COMPAS managed to correctly predict recidivism for only 61% of the cases (essentially not much better than random guessing). Even worse, for the prediction of violent recidivism, the algorithm's predictions were correct only 20% of the time. In other words, the remaining 80% of predictions were false positives (like when an HIV test is positive on an HIV-negative patient). COMPAS was also found to be racially biased as it incorrectly predicts black convicts to reoffend more often than whites, with whites being incorrectly flagged as 'low risk' more often than blacks too.

A similar study by Julia Dressel and Hany Farid managed to reproduce the findings of the ProPublica team. They also found that despite COMPAS combining an impressive 137 features to make predictions (effectively a 'black box'), the same accuracy can be achieved using linear regression on just two features [154]. And the study led by Cynthia Rudin showed that a simple three-rule IF-THEN-ELSE interpretable model (the CORELS algorithm, https://corels.eecs.harvard.edu/) including only age and prior offences is as accurate as the COMPAS algorithm [155]. However, only by presenting a method as a black box it is possible to profit given the protection of intellectual rights [23].

With 137 features it is easy to sell an algorithm as being 'sophisticated', but the truth is that the predictions made by COMPAS are no better than those made by people with no background in law or the Criminal Justice System. Advocates of methods like COMPAS, however, argue that the predictions made by black box machine learning algorithms that use huge datasets are more accurate and less biased than those made by humans, when this is not necessarily true (interpretability vs explainability, Chapter 3; [23]). Since the Criminal Justice System is relying more and more on predictive methods at the pre-trial, parole and sentencing stages, the amount of unfairness and suffering that incorrectly trained algorithms are bound to introduce in society is alarming.

Another perturbing case where an algorithm was used to predict the likelihood of recidivism is that of Christopher Drew Brooks [156]. Christopher had consensual sex with a 14 year old girl and convicted of statutory rape by a court in Virginia. Typical sentences for this offence are between 7 and 16 months, but given the prediction of recidivism by the algorithm (not COMPAS in this case), the sentence finally given was 18 months. The problem was that Christopher was only 19 at the time and since age was used as a factor for calculating the recidivism score, the algorithm predicted that Christopher being so young was statistically likely to commit another offence in the future. Maybe 18 months in prison is a fair sentence, but had Christopher been 36 years old (or 22 years her senior) the algorithm would have recommended that he not be sent to prison at all. To most people a 36 year old man and a 14 year old girl is much worse than a 19 year old man and a 14 year old girl.

## 5.3   MEN ARE PROFESSIONALS, WOMEN ARE HOT

Gender bias in algorithms is also very common. For example, when you search for images of professionals there is often a gender bias for a variety of occupations as women are typically underrepresented in C-suite positions (when their proportion is in reality much higher) [157].

We can also examine gender bias ourselves: Let us take Hollywood stars Robert Downey Jr. and Scarlett Johansson as an example. When you search for Robert Downey Jr. on Google, the algorithm also returns the most-related searches for the actor, including movies like Iron Man, Sherlock Holmes, Avengers and Tropic Thunder (Fig. 5.3).

So far, so good. But when we search for Scarlett Johansson, however, the topics related to the best-paid Hollywood actress of 2018 and 2019 [158] have to do with her appearance (e.g. 'weight', 'make-up', 'young') (Fig. 5.4). Most interestingly, Robert Downey Jr. and Scarlett Johansson starred together in movies such as Avengers: Endgame (2019) [159], Avengers: Infinity War (2018) [160], The Avengers (2012) [161] and Iron Man 2 (2010) [162].

The searches for Robert Downey Jr. and Scarlett Johansson were done as recently as 25 October 2022. Not only does this type of gender bias conditions our own perceptions, views on equality and opportunities, but people are also more partial to those results that confirm their pre-existing biases. This is known as **confirmation bias** [163], which is exploited by social media algorithms when they present content similar to what you have already visited or 'liked', thus effectively creating an 'echo chamber'. Perhaps there is an evolutionary explanation for confirmation bias being so deep-seated: In primitive societies belonging to one social group had clear advantages, and being able to search, register and

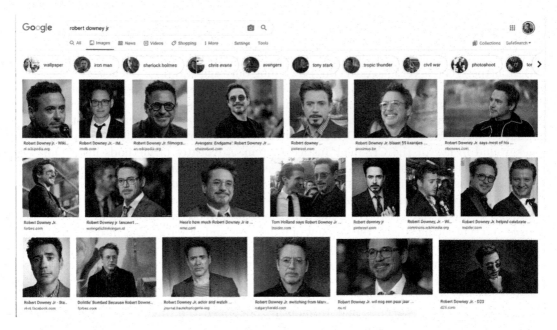

Figure 5.3 Google search results for Robert Downey Jr. (25 October 2022)

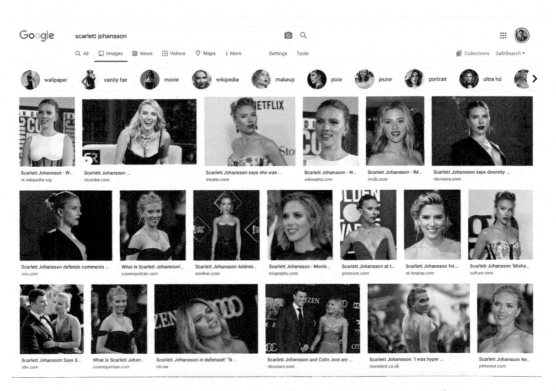

Figure 5.4 Google search results for Scarlett Johansson. (25 October 2022)

remember information that supports the group's values contributed to the cohesiveness of the group. There are many other types of cognitive bias (e.g. self-serving bias, availability bias, hindsight bias, anchoring bias, the framing effect and inattentional blindness), all of which result from our brain's unconscious tendency to simplify the tremendous complexity of the world.

## 5.4 'FUCK THE ALGORITHM'

The COVID-19 pandemic led to the cancellation of the school-leaving exams in the UK. These national examinations, known as A-levels, are of paramount importance because the outcome determines which universities the students will be able to attend. What did the office that regulates qualifications and exams in England (Ofqual) do?

Ofqual developed an algorithm that attempted to predict exam grades in the absence of exams [164]. To do this, for each school and subject the algorithm took the distribution of grades in previous years. The proportion of grades given to specific population segments (gender, ethnicity, etc.) was also kept constant. Once a distribution of grades was available, students were awarded these grades according to the ranking that they had been given by their teachers. For instance, if the class that took Physics in my school the year before produced two A* grades, five A grades, 15 B grades, and so on, and my teacher ranked me in the 8th position, I would be getting a final grade of B. However, my grade predicted for Physics was an A, but tied rankings were not allowed. In fact, the students' predicted grades were completely ignored by the algorithm. Moreover, it is much more difficult to give a student a ranking than a final grade: Whereas there are potentially over 30 different positions to rank in a class, there are only six possible passing grades (A*, A, B, C, D and E).

Another fundamental pitfall of this approach is that the algorithm was not properly tested. There is always much uncertainty regarding the prediction of exam results, and those that developed the Ofqual algorithm should at least have tested their assumptions with data from previous years. If the algorithm works, the ranking of the students of the year before, in the context of the exam results distribution on the same subject in the same school (also the year before), should have matched the final grade that students received (which was known). However, no ranking data was available for the students that graduated in 2019 (or in any previous year) and the inadequate and limited testing that was done did not work very well either [165]. The outcome was that some students received (unfairly) inflated grades, while others (about 40%) had their grades lowered by at least one grade (e.g. from A to B). In hindsight, a better solution would have been to carry out socially-distanced, in-person examinations like other countries did.

*How would you feel if your chances to attend a particular course in your university of choice were determined by some students from the year before whom you never met?*

To make things worse, classes of 15 or less were not assessed by the algorithm and the perceived ranking in any way, but by the teachers' predicted grades. Smaller classes are typical of fee-paying schools, which means that richer students were being insulated against the effects of a biased algorithm. Moreover, the Royal Statistical Society of the United Kingdom offered to help in the design of a predictive model while alerting the government of the many statistical pitfalls that could be incurred, but their good intentions were met with a lack of transparency [166].

Not thinking about algorithm bias and its implications had a major political cost for the UK government as thousands of students protested on the streets with a single mantra: 'Fuck the algorithm' (Fig. 5.5).

Figure 5.5 The extremely biased algorithm that predicted exam grades sparked riots across the UK (2020).

## 5.5 PREDICTIVE POLICING OR HOW TO REPRODUCE THE BIAS OF THE POLICE WITH AN ALGORITHM

PredPol is another infamous example of how biased and unfair algorithms can be. The goal of predictive policing algorithms is to anticipate where and when a crime will take place. If correct, such predictions facilitate law enforcement while reducing crime rates and human bias in policing. PredPol is trained with historical data of the location and time of past crimes, and uses this data to colour city maps by the probability of a crime occurring in that area. One problem with this approach is that the records of criminal offences in police databases are incomplete. Moreover, empirical evidence suggests that police officers take into account race and ethnicity (either implicitly or explicitly) when deciding who should be detained. Training an algorithm with police records that are incomplete and systematically biased towards specific neighbourhoods and non-whites can only lead to a positive feedback loop that amplifies the biases we wish to overcome.

Data scientists Kristian Lum and William Isaac compared predictions made by PredPol in the city of Oakland, California and illicit drug use data from a non-criminal justice data source [167]. PredPol advised focusing on the particularly violent Foster Hoover district, where most arrests have historically taken place. However, illicit drug use actually happens throughout the city of Oakland with a large number of hotspots (Fig. 5.6).

Besides not helping, these erroneous predictions that lead to disproportionate local policing have additional negative effects. These include shifting accountability from humans to machines, as well as having residents develop physical and mental problems as a result of feeling unfairly over-surveilled.

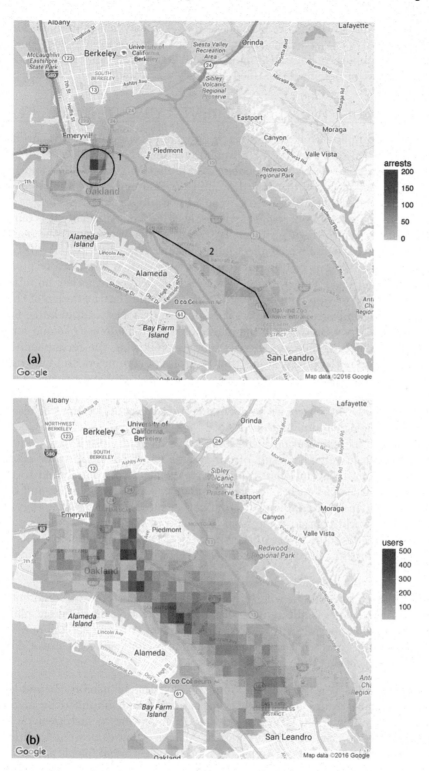

Figure 5.6 Hotspots for (a) arrests and (b) drug use in Oakland, California.

As a result of this, worldwide campaigns such as Amnesty International's 'Ban the scan' (banthescan.amnesty.org) have been started to limit the use of facial recognition technology as it can clearly amplify racially discriminatory policing, with minorities being systematically at greater risk of being misidentified and falsely arrested.

## 5.6 WHOSE FAULT WAS IT? DIFFERENT TYPES OF BIAS

In the previous examples we have showcased only some types of discrimination, including racial (the COMPAS and PredPol algorithms), gender (the Robert Downey Jr. vs Scarlett Johansson example) and socio-economic discrimination (the PredPol and Ofqual algorithms). In the vast majority of cases discriminatory outcomes are the result of training algorithms with biased data. Biased data can potentially originate from systematic data collection errors (for example, a problem with a machine), but normally it is our own cognitive biases that creep into the algorithms. By cognitive bias we refer to the reasoning flaws that we all humans have and which affect our ability to make decisions. As discussed above a well-known human bias is **confirmation bias** where we systematically prefer our own beliefs over external ideas which may nevertheless be correct. Another important type of bias occurs whenever we apply a perfectly logical algorithm but the design of the algorithm and our interpretation leads to a result that is illogical by society's standards. For instance, in the Christopher Drew Brooks case the judge could have made use of some common sense but eventually decided to increase Brook's sentence following the recommendation of the algorithm. Have you noted how it seems that the roles of computers and humans have been reversed over time? Instead of using computers as a tool we have reached a point where it seems that technology is starting to control our most human decisions. We cannot let algorithms take over when it comes to making certain types of decisions or else we will set ourselves for technological domination [168].

Biases are seen as a limitation in reasoning or a 'human design flaw', but they really are not. Biases are merely the result of our brain's effort to simplify the complex world we live in, and from an evolutionary point of view they have contributed to the survival of our species in situations such as danger avoidance, social cooperation and even mating [169]. Since bias is an unavoidable part of human nature, we can assume that all datasets that exist in this world contain some form of bias, and the best attitude one can have to minimise their effect is to be aware of their existence. Dozens of different kinds of bias that affect learning algorithms have been described [170], with most types occurring in different combinations:

- **Behavioural bias** arises when users behave differently across different platforms. For example, emojis facilitate non-verbal communication but different platforms have different emoji repertoires to choose from. Unless two people communicating share the same emojis and what they mean, communication can easily break down because of different reactions to unfamiliar emojis [171].

- **Historical bias** is a type of bias from the past that is usually shaped by prejudice against certain groups and which is perpetuated and amplified by algorithms. An example here is the COMPAS algorithm: Perhaps due to historical racism and inequalities in the criminal justice system, African-Americans were traditionally more likely to be arrested and sent to prison. Since this historical bias is part of the training data, it is no surprise that the COMPAS algorithm makes the same kind of wrong judgements against black citizens, who are predicted to reoffend more often than whites.

- **Incomplete or unrepresentative data.** With small datasets it is possible that some groups of people are better represented than others (a phenomenon called the *Law of large numbers*), thus introducing bias. For example, three different, commercially available facial recognition algorithms were failing to recognise people with darker skin. Researchers from Stanford and the Massachusetts Institute of Technology found that this was due to people with darker-skinned complexions being underrepresented in the training data [172]. This type of racial bias gave rise to the Gender Shades project (http://gendershades.org).

  In a very similar example, the pedestrian recognition algorithms of self-driving cars find it much harder to identify people with darker skin. Again, this was again due to an imbalanced training dataset that is not representative of the context the model operates in [173].

- **Online learning bias** is an emerging type of behavioural bias that has recently been described in online learning platforms. One major goal of online learning is to customise the learning experience for each student as much as possible. In a traditional classroom the teacher has a holistic understanding of the entire class and of each student at the same time. Thus, if a student lags behind the teacher has a lot of information available to provide some form of personalised support. In online learning some tasks of the teacher might be adopted by a Pedagogical Conversational Agent (PCA) designed to provide personalised support. Since progress in online learning is measured not only in terms of assignments completed but also by how a student interacts with the material and the learning platform, those students with a poor Internet connection will generate less data. Having limited information on such students renders the PCA unable to provide personalized support, thus introducing a bias in the system [174]. This is an example of how the digital divide can introduce a bias that leads to favouring some students over others. The digital divide can be seen in countless other contexts: For example someone using a smartwatch that constantly monitors key health data might have access to better medical care.

- **Self-selection bias** occurs when the subjects of the research select themselves. For example, we wish to conduct an online survey on the study habits of successful students. 'Success' can be defined in various ways and it is possible that a student who barely passes their courses will volunteer for the survey whereas 'straight A' students will select themselves out as taking a survey is often seen as a waste of time. This example touches upon the Dunning-Kruger effect, a type of cognitive bias of illusory superiority where those with low ability tend to overestimate their real ability [175].

- **Simpson's paradox**

  Simpson's paradox can be readily identified when a particular trend is observed in discrete groups of data, but disappears or is reversed when all the data is aggregated into a single group. In fact, more than a paradox, Simpson's is a counter-intuitive feature of aggregate data that actually causes a lot of problems on the ways we think about and report on all sorts of statistics.

  As an example, let us examine the average grades of the students at Gryffindor and Slytherin, two houses of the Hogwarts School of Witchcraft and Wizardry of the Harry Potter series (Table 5.1). What house do you think has the better students?

  It is clear that Slytherin boys and girls have the higher average grades. However, when the weighted average is computed by taking into account the size of each group, Gryffindor has the better average [(75x73)/100 + (25x60)/100 = 69.75].

TABLE 5.1 The Average Grades of Gryffindor and Slytherin Students

| | Boys | | Girls | | |
| --- | --- | --- | --- | --- | --- |
| | n | Average | n | Average | Global average |
| Gryffindor | 75 | 73 | 25 | 60 | 69.75 |
| Slytherin | 25 | 76 | 75 | 61 | 64.75 |

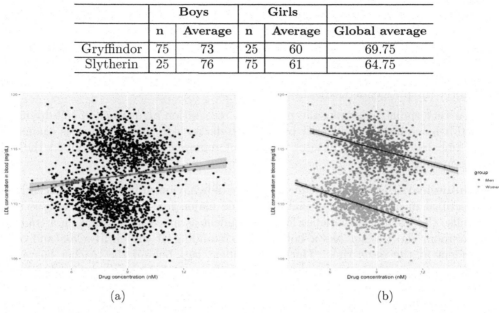

(a)                                        (b)

Figure 5.7 Simpson's paradox in action in aggregate data (a) and individual groups (b).

The effect of weighted averages is very common and nearly always results in incorrect interpretations of the data that may condition public policy. Another well-known example here is that of the US tax rates: Between 1974 and 1978 the tax rate was lowered for each income category, yet the overall tax rate increased from 14.1% (1974) to 15.2% (1978). This resulted from inflation generating more taxable dollars in the higher income (higher tax rate) brackets, and therefore an increased overall tax rate [176].

However, the best-known example of Simpson's paradox is the perceived gender bias in graduate admission to the University of California, Berkeley. Although fewer women were admitted to graduate school, it turned out that women tended to apply to more competitive departments. Once the data was corrected to take differences into account, a small but significant bias in favour of women was found [177].

Finally, another classical Simpson's paradox situation is when individual groups present a strong correlation, but when the groups are combined such correlation is reversed or even vanishes. For example, a new cholesterol-lowering drug is undergoing clinical trials following the successful testing in a cell line in the laboratory. An inexperienced data scientist combines all the data from the clinical trials and, much to his surprise, he finds that the greater the dose given to patients, the more bad (LDL) cholesterol in blood (panel (a), Fig. 5.7). However, then the aggregate dataset is split by gender, we can see how the drug effect in patients mimics the effect observed *in vitro* (panel (b), Fig. 5.7).

In data science a rule of thumb is that, as long as the quality of the data is acceptable, larger datasets not only allow us to draw more reliable conclusions but also are a requirement for training data-hungry methods such as SVMs and DNNs (Chapter 3). Simpson's paradox shows that we must be particularly careful when combining small datasets into a larger one as data (especially big data) is often

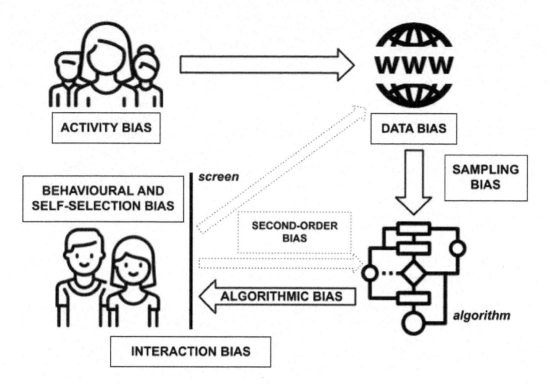

Figure 5.8 The most common types of bias on the Web.

heterogeneous. Also, when presented with a 'large enough' dataset, we should always ask: Could there be independent sub-groups with their own characteristics and behaviour which may introduce an important bias? (Cluster analysis, Chapter 2).

- **Surrogate objectives.** This type of bias is introduced when measuring the intended outcome is not a possibility, usually because it requires human intervention. For example, the goal of recommending certain news and articles should be to keep users informed of events that matter to them in a way that is as neutral as possible. But how do algorithms know which news and articles are truthful as well as impartial? The answer is that they cannot possibly know for computers do not understand these concepts. Instead, recommender systems tend to use the number and frequency of clicks as a measure of relevance hoping that readers will click more on the better articles. In the era of bots and fake news where sensational news collect a disproportionate number of clicks, this is an example of a surrogate objective that does not match the original goal of serving impartial, quality news. Can you think of a similar type of situation during a country's presidential elections and what the outcome could be?

## 5.6.1 Bias on the Web

The Web is not only the world's most active communication channel but also a specific ecosystem where many different biases co-exist in an inter-dependent manner 5.8) [178]:

- **Activity bias.** This phenomenon is also called 'wisdom of a few' because only a limited number of people contribute to the content of the Web. For example, it has been estimated that half of Facebook posts are generated by only ca. 7% of users, and the same can be said for ca. 4% of Amazon users that write product reviews (many of which are paid fake reviews, though) [178]. On Twitter, 5 of every 10,000 users attract 50% of user traffic, an example of what appears to be a scale-free network where a few, select nodes are highly connected and most nodes have a limited number of connections [179, 180].

- **Data bias** on the Web has many origins. For starters, only those that have access to the Internet can possibly contribute to the Web. Besides this educational and economic bias, over 50% of websites are in English despite English speakers amounting to only ca. 13% of the world's population. Moreover, the majority of people do not publish quality, objective information, with fake (malicious, spam) content spreading faster than genuine information [181]. Another important source of data bias is duplicated content, which already in 2003 amounted to as much as 20% of the static web [182].

- **Algorithmic bias** is a more subtle type of bias that comes from poor algorithm design. For example, when we upload a photo to a photo-hosting website, we often get tag recommendations from a collaborative filtering recommender system (Chapter 3). This is perhaps the ultimate example of algorithmic bias because these tag recommendations come only from a limited number of users and the algorithm will never improve unless input from additional users is included. This type of recommender system bias can be reversed by employing an *exploration-exploitation strategy* whereby some users are presented with new items interspersed with genuine recommendations. This is the only way to introduce new recommendations of value, but it often generates a loss of revenue as many of the novel suggestions will remain unpopular [183, 184].

- **Interaction bias** is related to which information is presented to users and how. As exemplified by recommender systems, only those items that are ever presented may be clicked upon. Similarly, a search engine that presents the results in ranked order is asking for bias introduction as the popular sites will become even more popular. Moreover, certain regions of the screen, such as any content near images, attract more clicks. And let us not forget that in Western cultures we start reading from the top-left side, so these areas naturally get more attention.

- **Behavioural and self-selection bias**. Besides the examples of the emojis and the survey for successful students here we might also include the 'herding effect' whereby many people increase their Amazon product ratings once they see that their score is below the average score [185, 186]. Moreover, individual users behave differently before a computer screen: Some scroll down to read the contents in detail, others do not; and some move the mouse where they look, thus attaching different degrees of importance to specific parts of the screen.

## 5.7 HOW CAN WE BUILD FAIRER ALGORITHMS?

This is a simple question with a complex answer. First of all we should ask: What is actually fair for my algorithm and in which situations? The definition of fairness is both culture- and context-dependent, and should it be applied to individuals or to groups? Moreover, if instead of focusing on the equal distribution of resources our definition of fairness involves the equal creation of opportunities, sometimes we can only achieve fairness by not being egalitarian.

Once we have an understanding of what being fair is in a particular context, a bias impact statement can help us analyse a system for bias in a systematic way. Various algorithmic methods have been developed to address bias at all steps of the learning process. However, all of this sophistication can be rendered ineffective if the design team behind the algorithm and its implementation is not diverse enough.

### 5.7.1 What Is Actually 'Fair'?

One fundamental reason why it is so difficult to identify and eliminate bias is because fairness means different things to different people [187]. We could argue that there are large cultural differences when it comes to defining what is fair: In the West we tend to focus on the individual, but in the East the concept of fairness has contextual considerations that transcend the individual and takes the human group into account [188]. Even people of the same ethnic background and nationality disagree all the time on what is fair!

We may even try to adhere to a broad definition of fairness such as 'fairness is the absence of any prejudice of favouritism towards an individual or a group based on their inherent or acquired characteristics' [170]. Even within this context, a fundamental factor complicating the identification of inequalities is that different types of discrimination are visible to some groups of people and invisible to others. For instance, it took a black couple to upload their photo and be automatically labelled as 'gorillas' to realise the limitations of Google's photo tagging algorithm [189]. The explanation behind this event is that Google's classifier was likely trained on the ImageNet dataset (image-net.org/), which in 2014 (the year before the photo mislabelling scandal) contained a mis-classification rate of 7.4% [115]. That is, without any explicit, malicious human bias such as having black men and women mis-labelled as gorillas, the database already contained a substantial number of incorrect annotations. Moreover, about half of ImageNet's images consists of organisms and the other half of man-made objects (such as airplanes, bridges and buildings). When you have a database of about a million photographs split into about one thousand object classes, many objects will be under-represented. A model trained on an incomplete or unrepresentative dataset will not be able to decide whether to categorise a previously unseen black person by colour or physiology. However, there is an advantage to this type of situation: Even if the classifier is a complex black-box such as a DNN, the source of the problem can be found by examining the training dataset.

Now think of a face recognition security system that has been trained on a dataset where certain minorities are under-represented or even absent. It is not difficult to see how a racially biased system will be born in the absence of racist intentions, or of algorithms with intrinsic coding biases. How many times do you think you will be able to justify the alarm going off on your ethnic minority employees? This situation is not unlikely as it sounds: In 2018 Amazon's facial recognition took 28 members of Congress for criminals by incorrectly matching them with police mugshots [190]. For this intrinsic problem of facial recognition software was the 'Ban The Scan' campaign started by Amnesty International (banthescan.amnesty.org).

The mis-labelling of people as 'gorillas' is a form of **direct discrimination** that is easy to spot because it violates so-called 'protected attributes' that should not be included in decision-making. Protected attributes include age, race, colour, nationality, religion, gender and marital status [170]). On the other hand, **indirect discrimination** is much more nuanced because it also affects specific groups but in more subtle ways. An interesting example here is Pokémon GO, the augmented reality mobile game released in 2016 where the players go about the town collecting virtual creatures called Pokémon (Fig. 5.9).

Pokémon GO presents the player with a digital map of the town displaying the available Pokémon physically in the corresponding locations in the real world. The discrimination here is that most Pokémon are found in affluent, predominantly white neighbourhoods. The reason behind this bias is that the developers used the geographic coordinates of an earlier

Figure 5.9 The Pokémon GO interface with Pokémon in the author's affluent, seaside neighbourhood.

game, called Ingress, whose user base was predominantly skewed towards younger, male English speakers. The end result is that people from less affluent backgrounds are being discriminated in the game by virtue of their postcode as it is much more difficult to collect Pokémon that are not within walking distance [191].

Besides direct and indirect discrimination, we also have systemic, statistical, explainable and unexplainable discrimination [170]. In such a complex scenario, how can we conclude that a given algorithm is fair?

- Is an algorithm fair when it does not take into account any of the protected attributes, such as race, gender, religion or nationality?
  *Let us not forget that ensuring universal fairness across groups of people means checking the results against the set of protected attributes, which is in itself unfair.*

- Is an algorithm fair when the results are equally accurate for all the distinct groups?

- Is an algorithm fair when calibrated for all the distinct groups irrespective of the results?

- Is an algorithm fair when similar individuals obtain similar predictions?

One key question here is whether we should focus on evaluating fairness at the level of the group or the individual. It has been argued that drawing generalisations about groups to make inferences on individuals is wrong and a form of statistical discrimination [192]. For example, do you think that all travellers from South America should be uniformly subjected to harsher border checks based on the generalisation that many drug smugglers travel from those countries? What about travellers arriving from Muslim countries and their connection to terrorism? In a way, machine learning is about finding patterns in data and is in principle incompatible with the idea of individuality, although others have argued that only certain types of generalisation are discriminatory [193].

Moreover, it has been proven mathematically that it is not possible to integrate all the different notions of fairness except in unrealistically constrained cases. Therefore, enforcing one type of fairness always comes at the expense of another [194]. Thus, there is no and there will never be a universal answer to what is a fair outcome for an algorithm. One should always ask: what do I think is fair in my specific situation, and how fair could I possibly be given the data available? Are the fairness-to-unfairness constraints acceptable (by you and others) in your given context? Which features in the data are inherently discriminatory? Are all types of inequality between groups wrong? For a given application, should we focus on equality or on equity? Or perhaps we should seek to minimise the damage to the least advantaged? [193]

## 5.7.2 Is Being Fair Enough?

Any discrimination problem must be analysed from different angles beyond the various definitions of fairness and we must always strive to be creative. For example, in the 1970s female musicians made up 5% of the top five symphony orchestras. This type of gender bias was dealt with by doing blind auditions [195]. As a result the percentage of women musicians quickly rose to 25% in 1997 and to 30% in 2019 [196]. But would you say that 30% is a fair proportion of women musicians in symphony orchestras? Would a 50% share be more fair to mirror the general population? Or perhaps a fair number should mirror the percentages of male and female applicants to music schools? There is rarely a straightforward answer to this type of situation. For instance, we may argue that percentages might break down depending on the type of instrument (Simpson's paradox) and that the male-female inequality is likely restricted to a few larger instruments which naturally favour men's larger body sizes? In the latter case perhaps a solution would be to build smaller cellos and contrabasses while continuing to perform blind auditions. Like this, women of all body sizes would have an equal chance. Is this mere speculation? Perhaps, but this is also reminiscent of the story of a young boy who was given a violin made for his body size at age four after his parents

**EQUALITY**          **EQUITY**

Figure 5.10 Equality and equity try to achieve fairness in different ways.

found out about his interest in music. He then went on to perform as a soloist at age 14 with the Philadelphia Orchestra conducted by Riccardo Muti, and made his Carnegie Hall debut at age 17 with the St. Louis Symphony Orchestra. Would Joshua Bell have become one of history's greatest violonists had his parents not provided him with the opportunity to succeed? Thinking creatively is crucial when dealing with discrimination as the right answer might not always be evident or even tractable under established models of fairness.

One fundamental problem with the various definitions of fairness is that they essentially focus on being **egalitarian**, that is in making sure that all parties obtain the same resources, support or outcome, either at the individual or the group level. However, sometimes we can only achieve fairness by not being egalitarian and give each individual or group member whatever they need in order to succeed. This is called **equity**. Thus, the ultimate goal of both equality and equity is to achieve fairness, but they do it in different ways (Fig. 5.10). Sometimes fairness can only be achieved through equity, and a classroom is a clear example of this: All students are initially given the same level of support, but after that some students might need extra (unequal) levels of support to achieve the same level of success as their peers. Here the key question to ask is: In what way are we trying to be fair? Is achieving equal opportunities the end goal, and is it measurable? If so, how unequal but proportionate must the level of support be to encourage equal opportunities? Or simply providing the same support throughout (equality) without a follow-up is all that is required?

Therefore, the operationalisation of fairness in machine learning is not simply a matter for data scientists to reason about. Rather, achieving a solution as to what level and type of fairness is appropriate for a given application requires the input from specialists in the context of ethical reasoning.

## 5.7.3 The Bias Impact Statement

Bias can potentially be introduced in each phase of a data science project, including [197]:

1. **Problem definition.** This situation typically arises from poor algorithmic design or when the end goal is not a straightforward concept, such as trying to determine how truthful and impartial a piece of news is by the number of clicks it receives. Another example is calculating a customer's 'credit worthiness' by integrating multiple metrics. At some point the algorithm must draw a line: Should we set a cutoff that maximises the number of loans that are repaid, or shall we maximise profit even if some of these loans do not get repaid? The latter case can be a form of financial predatory behaviour, especially if collaterals are included in the contract, in which case, which particular group of people is being discriminated against?

2. **Data collection.** As we discussed above, the data may be incomplete, statistically biased, or even reflect our own prejudices (e.g. the COMPAS and PredPol algorithms). Any of these situations will invariably result in poor predictions.

3. **Data preparation.** This can easily happen when selecting certain features to model the problem (Chapter 3). For example, shall we use protected attributes such as gender and nationality for credit worthiness scoring, even if these help maximise the end business goal such as getting the largest number of loans repaid? Selecting certain key features will enhance the performance of the model upon testing, but may it be preferable to select a sub-optimal set of features that do not introduce so much bias?

4. **Code abstraction and modularisation.** From a technical point of view in computer science abstraction and modularisation are considered good practice because they allow re-using the software that we write for similar tasks but in different contexts. An example would be re-using a given interface to present completely different types of data that must be analysed by decision makers. While useful from the point of view of software engineering, abstraction and modularisation are dangerous concepts because they systematically ignore any social context and are referred to as 'the portability trap' [198].

5. **Algorithm testing.** This can occur when we do not use the right metrics that may reveal data bias. Which of the standard metrics described in Chapter 4 (such as accuracy, precision and recall) is likely to identify some form of bias and discrimination in your own problem and context?

Since bias has so many faces and can be introduced at different points, how can we systematically analyse an algorithm for bias? One way to do it is by examining the output an algorithm produces to check for atypical results for different groups. For commercial algorithms this is the only possible way to infer how biased they are since the training data is almost never made available and companies are not forced to regular audits by independent organisations. Here sharing at least the performance of their algorithms when applied to different demographic groups should be a baseline definition of transparency. This is in fact what Joy Buolamwini and Timnit Gebru have done systematically in their

Gender Shades project (http://gendershades.org/) where the goal is to evaluate how biased gender-classification software is [199].

Bear in mind, however, that even when comparing groups not all unequal outcomes are unfair. For example, whenever the COMPAS algorithm assigns a *very high* risk score, both white and African-American defendants actually present equally high recidivism rates, and therefore there is no bias here on the part of the algorithm [200]. Thus, we cannot have equal error rates between groups for all the different error rates, and a requirement for fairness here is to establish which error rate (and in which situations) must be equalised across all groups. Once we have a working definition of fairness -at the level of the individual, the group or the subgroup [170] -, how can we systematically identify and correct for algorithmic bias? One structured approach is to produce a **bias impact statement** that is used as a guide by those designing, implementing and testing algorithms. The set of questions included seem easy when asked but are not equally easy to answer. A thorough discussion of the bias impact statement is described by Lee, Resnick and Barton [201] and a sample of these questions includes:

- Who will be using the algorithm and who will be most affected by it?

- Is the training data sufficiently diverse and reliable? Have you checked for statistical biases, for example? How many groups are represented in the dataset and in what proportions?

- How and when will the algorithm be tested?

- What principles and thresholds will you use to identify bias during the testing phase? What interventions will be made?

- Will the algorithm have implications for cultural groups and play out differently in cultural contexts?

Two additional useful resources to help us build accountable systems are FAT/ML's principles for accountable algorithms [202], as well as the EU Ethics Guidelines for Trustworthy AI, which describes the requirements that an AI application must meet from the legal, ethical, social and technological standpoints in order to be trustworthy and as bias-free as possible [203].

### 5.7.4  Fair Machine Learning

Sometimes the bias does not originate from flawed data, but from poor algorithmic design or implementation. An algorithm's degree of 'transparency' (interpretability vs explainability, Chapter 3) is also crucially important when it comes to understanding bias and discrimination. For example, let us pretend that we apply for a loan to buy a new car. We have been perfect customers, have a steady income and a long-term job with career prospects, but somehow the application is declined. We complain to the bank manager that the algorithm is biased against age (we are too young or too old), ethnic origin or postcode. If the loan approval process had been built using a classification tree, it would be easy to inspect the decision process and understand at which point a bias has been introduced (Fig. 3.12). However, if a DNN is the algorithm responsible for deciding who gets a loan, then it is almost impossible for a human to reconstruct how a given decision was made because for all their sophistication, DNNs function like black boxes. Therefore, algorithms that lack interpretability or clear explainability can easily introduce bias, no matter how great their performance is.

A diversity of methods are available to address bias and unfairness in algorithms (reviewed in [170]). These can be grouped into three different classes:

- **Pre-processing** methods are algorithms capable of modifying the training data to get rid of the underlying discrimination.

  *The main advantage of pre-processing methods is that the classifier needs not be modified and the data can be used for any downstream task. However, these methods tend to perform worse than in-processing and post-processing methods in terms of accuracy and fairness measure.*

- **In-processing** methods try to remove discrimination during the model building process. In practice they do this by imposing constraints or introducing specific changes to the mapping function during the training phase.

  *These are very task-specific methods that require the modification of the classifier (which may not always be possible) but which tend to present good performance on accuracy and fairness measures.*

- **Post-processing** methods are applied whenever the model can only be treated as a black box and it is not possible to modify the training data or the learning function. Here the labels in a holdout dataset (not used for training) get reassigned by a particular function at test time.

  *Post-processing methods are less flexible in selecting an accuracy-fairness trade-off but are universally applicable to any classifier and present decent performance without having to modify the classifier.*

Some classes of algorithm are amenable to more than one class of processing method. For example, fair classification has been discussed in the context of in-processing and post-processing methods, and word-embedding is amenable to both pre-processing and post-processing methods.

De-biasing methods try to achieve fairness in different ways. The majority exclude protected attributes from the decision-making process, and specific types of bias are dealt with in various ways. For instance, exclusion bias might be addressed by including users from key groups. Graph-theoretic approaches are also being used to remove those paths that contain attributes that have an effect in the decision-making process.

## 5.7.5   The Key Is in the Design Team

There are clear advantages to including a diversity of first-time users for any algorithm. For example, the testing of facial recognition software that misidentifies people with darker-skinned complexions more often than whites benefits from having an ethnically and socially diverse set of users as they are able to spot biased outcomes without having to understand the inner workings of the algorithm (http://gendershades.org/).

However the most important and often overlooked consideration when addressing algorithmic bias is having a fair representation of society in the design teams, not just among the set of users [204]. For instance, the absence of black people in the ImageNet database that led to their mis-labelling as 'gorillas' simply mirrors their lack of representation in the computer science field.

Besides having different ethnic groups we should also include people of different gender identities, religions, social classes as well as people with different types of disabilities and mental health disorders. The field of machine learning is particularly exclusive and homogeneous (I have previously counted one or two women for every 10 data scientists, several times, in different research environments). Such a chronic lack of diversity in the technology field can only lead to inequalities no matter how good and noble the intentions of the operators are. This is because whenever a homogeneous group of people is testing an algorithm for bias, this does not mean that they actually understand how bias manifests and operates. If you include someone from a community that has been disproportionately harassed, this person will have a deeper understanding of how technology can be used as a weapon against the most vulnerable, and what safeguards must be implemented. Therefore only by having a sufficiently diverse team from the beginning is the most effective way to build algorithms that are more fair. Only humans have the ability to use common sense and interpret the world in abstract terms.

## 5.8   THE FAILURE TO CONTROL THE COVID-19 PANDEMIC FROM BIASED DATA

Another recent example of how incomplete and biased data have had disastrous effects is the control of the COVID-19 pandemic. For example, the death rate (deceased/infected) following a coronavirus infection was originally calculated at 2.3% [205]. Although the mortality rate is always worked out once an outbreak is under control and a representative part of the population has been systematically tested, there are obvious advantages to having a preliminary idea of the mortality rate. However, by asking the right questions we can see why this number is wrong. According to official statistics from various countries as of March 17, 2020, the death rates fluctuated between 3.6% (United Kingdom), 4.0% (China) and 7.7% (Italy) [206]. If we assume that the initial strain of the virus was the same in every country given the short time since the outbreak was detected, our first conclusion is that the statistics are biased by how many tests are carried out in each country. Although the coronavirus is known to be particularly deadly among senior people and the population of Italy is the most senior in the EU [207], we also know that Italy was particularly thorough and systematic in testing the population [208]. At the start of the pandemic some countries were only testing for coronavirus infection if one was very ill, and not just anyone with a fever. Moreover, since nobody dies immediately from a coronavirus infection a more accurate estimate of the mortality rate would be calculated as [deceased/(deceased + recovered)]. For the numbers available on March 17, 2020, the death rates were: $[7511/(7511 + 80874)] = 0.0849$, which is equivalent to 8.5%. For the numbers available on 5 August, 2020, the global mortality rate is $[705045/(705045 + 11945739)] = 0.0557$ (5.6%). Although 5.6% is lower than 8.5%, it is much higher than the UK's 3.6%. Not surprisingly, the UK's poor predictions from their own biased data were in part responsible for the UK having the dubious honour of being the European country with the largest mortality rate (over 46,000 as of August 5, 2020). Finally, since different countries test to different extents, an even better approximation would be given by calculating the current mortality rates for all countries and plotting them as a distribution from which a more realistic death rate could be estimated.

Another statistic that is key for controlling an outbreak is the *basic rate of reproduction* $(R_0)$, that is the number of people that a carrier can potentially infect. An early estimate for COVID-19 $R_0$ was between 2.24 and 3.58 (March 2020) [209]. This figure is larger than that of the SARS pandemic (2002–2004), the Spanish flu (1918) and the Ebola epidemic (2014) (Fig. 5.11) [210]. However, a July 2020 estimate of COVID-19's $R_0$ was close to 6 [211]. There is a huge difference between a single person being able to infect 3 people or 6 people. Also, since it is possible to be an asymptomatic carrier and thus infect others unknowingly, the implications of providing an incorrect $R_0$ (and mortality rate) estimate from biased data are disastrous because adequate health responses cannot be mounted.

Concealing data has also complicated the management of the pandemic on a worldwide basis. For example, Iran was a major focus of coronavirus from the very start but they tried to deny the existence of the pandemic even when a spokesman for the government gave a press conference with obvious signs that he might be infected (which was later confirmed)

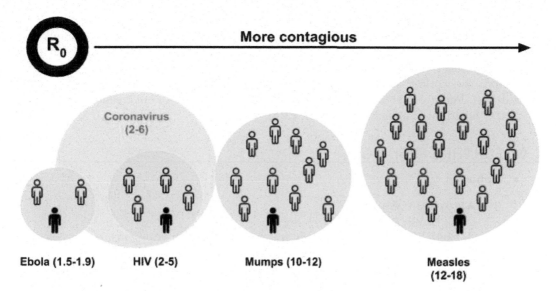

Figure 5.11 The basic rates of reproduction for various infectious diseases.

[212]. It was initially estimated that Iran was reporting only ~25% of the deaths [213], but this is likely an underestimate given the satellite images of mass graves that later became available [214], and the fact that Iran released 85,000 prisoners in an attempt to stop the spread of the virus inside prisons [215]. Iran is visited by five million tourists every year [216]. Had the extent of the epidemic in Iran been known, a flight embargo would have helped contain the spread of the virus.

Therefore, having unbiased data that has been collected in a systematic and thorough manner is the only way to make reliable predictions that can help isolate the pathogen and mount an appropriate response to an outbreak. China understood this very early as the country established an impressive surveillance strategy: Body temperatures were taken on the street and citizens were tracked at all times thanks to the geolocation of mobile phones and the massive crossing of private data with their analyses [217]. The authorities could also find out whether at some point you had been sitting next to an infected person in the train (in which case you would have someone knocking on your door). China's is an example of a 21st century containment strategy for a pandemic where the goal is to identify carriers as well as those potentially infected, and isolate them to prevent the spread of the virus.

The down side of China's strategy is that it has been made possible because the country already has various mass surveillance systems in place. Besides exerting tight controls on Internet traffic (have you tried to access your Facebook account from China?), their facial recognition systems are so advanced that it is possible to follow individuals across entire cities. China's 'Social Credit System' is a national blacklisting scheme where you get points deducted for doing socially undesirable things such as jaywalking, playing loud music in public places, spending too much time playing video games, not paying fines or not stopping before a red light. Once you get blacklisted, you may not be able to get on certain trains, buy plane tickets or apply for credit. This form of mass surveillance is not transparent and does not allow citizens to challenge their own records. What do you think would be the effect of making a mistake like taking someone else for you?

Although effective, the implementation of China's COVID-19 containment strategy is unthinkable in Western countries because it constitutes such a massive violation of human rights. The alternative strategy that most other countries followed involved isolating everyone at home, whether they were infected or not. This plan of action is typical of the Spanish flu pandemic (1918) and has led to a tremendous debilitation of the economy. Major physical and mental health costs have ensued, and the strategy has not turned out to be particularly effective either. Despite the unending criticism towards China, the Asian giant has shown the world that its containment strategy has been most effective because it was data-driven. Perhaps it is time for us to consider giving up a bit of our freedom in exchange for better health and financial prospects? [218].

## 5.9 FURTHER READING

- **Websites**

  - **Algorithm Watch**
    URL: https://algorithmwatch.org/
    *Algorith Watch is a non-profit research and advocacy organisation whose goal is to analyse and explain decisions automated by algorithms and which have an impact on society.*

  - **Ban The Scan**
    URL: https://banthescan.amnesty.org/
    *This is Amnesty International's campaign to put an end to the use of facial recognition software as it can amplify racially discriminatory policing, and minorities always are at a greater risk of being misidentified and falsely arrested.*

  - **FAT/ML**
    URL: https://www.fatml.org/
    *FAT/ML is a relevant community of machine learning researchers and practitioners concerned with building fair and accountable learning systems.*

  - **Gender Shades (Joy Buolamwini and Timnit Gebru)**
    URL: http://gendershades.org/
    *The goal of the Gender Shades project is to evaluate how accurate gender-classification software is as an example of a type of discriminatory bias.*

  - **Survival Of The Best Fit (Gabor Csapo, Jihyun Kim, Miha Klasinc and Alia ElKattan)**
    URL: https://www.survivalofthebestfit.com/
    *An educational game about hiring bias that will show you in a fun and interactive way how your own biases creep into the algorithms you build.*

  - **The Algorithmic Justice League**
    URL: https://www.ajl.org/
    *The AJL is an organisation whose goal is to illuminate and prevent the harmful forms of discrimination that biased algorithms can cause. This project is an extension of the Gender Shades study.*

  - **The Distributed Artificial Intelligence Research Institute (DAIR)**
    URL: www.dair-institute.org
    *A new research institute directed by Timnit Gebru whose goal is to research the downsides of AI and its responsible use, with freedom from corporations and academic politics.*

- **Podcasts**

  - **The Machine Ethics Podcast**
    URL: https://www.machine-ethics.net/

*Interviews with leading figures on the impact of machine learning and AI on society.*

- **Women in Data Science**
  URL: https://www.widsconference.org/podcast.html
  *Brilliant data scientists both from industry and academia discuss their work across a vast range of fields, and also tell us about their journey into data science.*

• **Tools**

- **AI Fairness 360 (IBM) [219]**
  URL: https://github.com/Trusted-AI/AIF360; https://aif360.mybluemix.net/
  *A Python toolkit to evaluate algorithms for different fairness metrics and algorithms to mitigate bias in datasets and models.*

- **What-If Tool (Google) [220]**
  URL: https://pair-code.github.io/what-if-tool/
  *A dashboard interface to help you inspect your predictor performance for different inputs and fairness metrics. Easily integrated with TensorBoard, Jupyter and Colab notebooks, and JupyterHub.*

• **Videos**

- **AI Bias Explained by Google at the Shelly Palmer Innovation Series Summit at CES 2020 (Barak Turovsky)**
  URL: https://bit.ly/3z0acxT
  *Barak Turovsky discusses how Google Translate deal with AI bias.*

- **Artificial Intelligence needs all of us (Rachel Thomas, TEDx)**
  URL: https://bit.ly/3s46hvK
  *In her empowering and inclusive message Rachel Thomas disproves the myth that one needs to have the finest machine, degree, or a sophisticated knowledge of mathematics to do data science that makes a difference. A discussion of the triumphs and misconceptions of AI includes how having a fair representation of society in the software teams is the most effective way to tackle algorithmic bias.*

- **Coded Bias (trailer)**
  URL: https://bit.ly/2Rs8G6V
  *This is the short trailer to the award-winning documentary Coded Bias that explains how technology is effectively managed by a small and homogeneous population whose biases naturally creep into any data-centric technology they develop and create a less fair society for all.*

- **Explaining generalisation and individual justice (Reuben Binns)**
  URL: https://bit.ly/3D1MVhy
  *An excellent lecture on the problem of making decisions about individuals using machine learning.*

- **Health Data Anonymization and Privacy (Khaled El Eman, O'Reilly).**
  URL: https://bit.ly/3hN58En
  *This is an interesting interview with Khaled El Eman on how to properly use health data for scientific research. Open Data has the potential to revolutionise personalised medicine, but being of such a sensitive nature there are many privacy concerns. A trade-off exists between patient data anonymisation and data utility: The more you scramble the data to make it anonymous, the less useful it is. Where should we set the bar?*

    − **How I'm fighting bias in algorithms (Joy Buolamwini, TEDx).**
URL: https://bit.ly/39VgNPy
*This is Joy Buolamwini's TEDx talk of 2017 where she first discusses her ideas on algorithmic bias.*

    − **How the Internet Tricks You Into Thinking You're Always Right (Jason Tanz)**
URL: https://bit.ly/2R9xvo1
*In this 2-minute video Jason Tanz of WIRED discusses how the Internet is fueling confirmation bias and how the self-reflection and the scientific method are powerful weapons to combat it.*

    − **How to Fight the Bad Logic of the Internet (Jason Tanz)**
URL: https://bit.ly/3ukSaDB
*In this 3-minute video Jason Tanz of WIRED explains how to spot flawed arguments on the Internet and question unsupported claims.*

- **Articles**

    − **Baeza-Yates R. Bias on the Web. Communications of the ACM 61(6), 2018.**
*An excellent discussion on the multiple types of bias on the Web and their interplay.*

    − **Binns R. Fairness in Machine Learning: Lessons from Political Philosophy. Proceedings in Machine Learning Research 81:1–11, 2018.**
*An excellent reflection on the meaning of fairness from the point of view of moral and political philosophy, and how some key concepts are incompatible with their application in Machine Learning research.*

    − **Buolamwini J, Gebru T. Gender Shades: Intersectional Accuracy Disparities in Commercial Gender Classification. Proceedings of Machine Learning Research 81:1–15, 2018 Conference on Fairness, Accountability, and Transparency.**
URL: https://bit.ly/3t8vUgb
*This is the core paper of the Gender Shades project to evaluate the accuracy of gender-classification software is.*

    − **Fussell S. This Film Examines the Biases in the Code That Runs Our Lives (WIRED, 15 November 2020).**
URL: https://bit.ly/3201jFN
*An interview with Shalini Kantayya, the director of the documentary Coded Bias on MIT researcher Joy Buolamwini who investigates racial bias in facial recognition algorithms.*

    − **Gebru T, Morgenstern J, Vecchione B, Vaughan JW, Wallach H, Daumé H, Crawford K. Datasheets for Datasets, 2020.**
URL: https://arxiv.org/abs/1803.09010
*This is an influential article reporting a standard process to describe datasets, similar to how machine components are described in technical manuals. The focus is on transparency and accountability, which benefits both the creators and the consumers of datasets.*

    − **Giglio M. Would You Sacrifice Your Privacy to Get Out of Quarantine? (The Atlantic, 22 April 2020).**
URL: https://bit.ly/38qg9Zh

*An interesting reflection on the age-old debate of trading civil liberties for security, in the context of the COVID-19 pandemic.*

— **Hao K. We read the paper that forced Timnit Gebru out of Google. Here's what it says (MIT Technology Review, 4 December 2020).**
URL: https://bit.ly/3dcYoio
*This article summarises the research paper [221] that got Timnit Gebru fired from Google. In this paper Gebru and colleagues report the environmental and financial costs associated with the development and deployment of ever larger language models, which are key to Google's business.*

— **Kievit RA, Frankenhuis WE, Waldorp LJ, Borsboom D. Simpson's paradox in psychological science: a practical guide. Front. Psychol. (12 August 2013).**
*An excellent review on Simpson's paradox with many examples from different fields and practical advice on how to detect it.*

— **Lazer DMJ, Baum MA, Benkler Y, Berinsky AJ, Greenhill KM, Menczer F, Metzger MJ, Nyhan B, Pennycook G, Rothschild D, Schudson M, Sloman SA, Sunstein CR, Thorson EA, Watts DJ, Zittrain JL. The science of fake news. Science 359(6380): 1094–1096, 2018.**
*A discussion on the nature of fake news and how to devise and implement effective intervention strategies, including the empowering of individuals and the development of more sophisticated detection algorithms.*

— **Lee NT, Resnick P, Barton G. Algorithmic bias detection and mitigation: Best practices and policies to reduce consumer harms. Brookings Institute report (22 May 2019).**
*A roundtable discussion on bias detection and mitigation strategies that offers insightful and complementary points of view.*

— **Mehrabi N, Morstatter F, Saxena N, Lerman K, Galstyan A. A survey on bias and fairness in machine learning, 2019.**
URL: https://arxiv.org/abs/1908.09635
*An authoritative review on the many different types of bias and the concept of fairness.*

— **Metz C, Wakabayashi D. Google Researcher Says She Was Fired Over Paper Highlighting Bias in A.I. New York Times (3 December 2020).**
URL: https://nyti.ms/2QGq1sJ
*Having a fair representation of minorities in the technical team is one of the most effective ways to combat algorithmic bias from the start. In this controversial New York Times article the authors discuss the firing of Dr. Timnit Gebru from Google. This action likely reflects a largely undiscussed problem in tech companies that present themselves as the champions of equality.*

— **Mitchell M, Wu S, Zaldivar A, Barnes P, Vasserman L, Hutchinson B, Spitzer E, Raji ID, Gebru T. Model Cards for Model Reporting, 2019.**
URL: https://arxiv.org/abs/1810.03993
*This article describes the fundamental concept of how to detail the performance and characteristics of ML models in order to increase their transparency. Characteristics to be reported include a model's intended use and a benchmark evaluation across the different application conditions*

— **Seneca C. How to Break Out of Your Social Media Echo Chamber (WIRED, 17 September 2020).**

URL: https://bit.ly/3fOO1E6
*An engaging reflection on how the largest social media platforms benefit from increasing your own confirmation bias, and what you can actively do to escape it.*

– **Simonite T. Ex-Googler Timnit Gebru Starts Her Own AI Research Center (WIRED, 2 December 2021).**
URL: https://bit.ly/3otmk7S
*Timnit Gebru opened a new research institute in late 2021 to research the downsides of AI and its responsible use, with freedom from corporations and academic politics.*

– **Thomas R. The Far-Reaching Impact of Dr. Timnit Gebru (The Gradient, 9 December 2020).**
URL: https://bit.ly/3xHsEeE
*An account of Dr. Timnit Gebru's many contributions to diverse fields, including a background to the Gender Shades project and the tremendous impact she has had in AI.*

– **Yagoda B. The Cognitive Biases Tricking Your Brain (The Atlantic, September 2018).**
URL: https://bit.ly/3s6l8Wu
*An excellent discussion on the different types of human bias.*

- **Books**

  – Fry H. *Hello World: How to be human in the age of the machine.* Black Swan, London, UK, 2019. ISBN: 1784163066.
  *In this engaging book Hannah Fry discusses how algorithms are taking important decisions for us in almost every aspect of our lives. The risk of being too dependent on algorithms is explained as well as the huge benefits of using them effectively not to replace humans, but as helping hands to supplement decision-making given our human weaknesses.*

  – Kearns M. and Roth A. *The Ethical Algorithm: The Science of Socially Aware Algorithm Design.* Oxford University Press, USA, 2019. ISBN: 0190948205.
  *A modern and integrative account on how to design socially responsible algorithms by integrating fairness and privacy constraints into algorithm design.*

  – Lippert-Rasmussen K. *Born free and equal?: a philosophical enquiry into the nature of discrimination.* Oxford University Press, USA, 2013. ISBN-10: 0199796114.
  *A philosopher's way to dissect discrimination and what to do about it.*

  – Kahneman D. *Thinking, Fast and Slow.* Farrar, Straus and Giroux, New York (NY), USA, 2011. ISBN: 0374275637.
  *This is Nobel laureate Daniel Kahneman's popular book on how us lazy humans are wired to use short-cuts and trust bad evidence to jump into conclusions.*

## 5.10 CHAPTER REVIEW QUESTIONS

1. **A Type I error in statistical classification is**

   (a) A type of data bias in the training data.

(b) Classifying a True Negative (TN) as a Positive.

(c) Accepting the null hypothesis when it should not have been accepted.

(d) 'A shepherd thinks that there is no wolf in the village and checks this every night for five consecutive nights. Therefore, there is no wolf in the village'.

2. **PredPol is biased because**

(a) It is trained with historical data.

(b) It is trained with biased data.

(c) It seeks to enforce the law.

(d) It is designed to search in very specific areas only.

3. **Cognitive biases result from our brain's unconscious tendency to simplify the complexity of the world around us. The type of bias that tends to reinforces our previously held ideas is known as**

(a) The framing effect.

(b) Inattentional blindness.

(c) Confirmation bias.

(d) Self-serving bias.

4. **Can you define the term 'direct discrimination'?**

5. **What is 'indirect discrimination', and can you provide an example?**

6. **Some good practices to reduce algorithmic bias are**

(a) To have it thoroughly tested.

(b) To implement a bias impact statement.

(c) To use simpler algorithms.

(d) To include a fair representation of society in the team.

7. **In what ways do equality and equity try to achieve fairness?**

# CHAPTER 6

# Personal Data, Privacy and Cybersecurity

*Considerate la vostra semenza:*
*fatti non foste a viver come bruti,*
*ma per seguir virtute e canoscenza*

*Divina Commedia (Inferno, Canto XXVI)*
— Dante Alighieri (1265–1321), *Italian poet and philosopher*

The aggregation and analysis of massive datasets has brought many valuable developments. At the same time, however, mass surveillance has become the business model of the Internet. In a world where the violation of privacy is a daily occurrence and data breaches are on the rise, one key question is: How can we get the individual and group value from our data without sacrificing individual privacy?

In this chapter we examine this question by first discussing the value of data for the individual, for corporations, and for the financially-motivated hackers who sell personal information in the black market. The healthcare sector is extensively targeted by ransomware because the longer it takes to pay, the more compromised the health of patients becomes. Anthem Inc.'s breach of 2015 is presented to illustrate the anatomy of a breach as well as its devastating impact for both the company and the patients, in all its dimensions.

Although the idea of privacy is instinctual and a basic human right, it is also dynamic and context-dependent. We learn how to reason about privacy by conducting the data privacy analysis of a popular health app. The top-down approach used is universally applicable and involves documentation analysis, an assessment of the *Privacy by design* principles, and a straightforward experimental analysis using the freely available Lumen Privacy Monitor. We show how it is possible to appear compliant with the EU's General Data Protection Regulation (GDPR) while violating users' privacy at the same time.

Since privacy cannot exist without security, we discuss the various security controls of the health app analysed. Finally, we present a set of protocols whose implementation greatly enhances our own security and privacy.

## 6.1 HOW MUCH IS YOUR DATA WORTH?

Today data is one of the most valuable assets and it should be managed like any other physical asset in terms of access and storage, protection, expiration date and financial reporting [222]. However, data only becomes useful when it is transformed into information that enables actionable insights, when it is used to build predictive models, as well as when it is strategically combined with other data.

There have been a number of proposals to pay individuals for the data they generate (their 'digital footprints'). However, having individuals monetise from their own data is unrealistic because data is an intangible asset (unlike oil or real estate) whose value can only be extracted by means of sophisticated platforms and algorithms [223]. We get to use Facebook, Google, Amazon, Uber and the like in exchange for our data.

Our Personal Identifiable Information (PII) and digital footprints are of great value in the black market. For instance, in 2021 your credit card details with an account balance up to $5,000 would be sold for $240 [224] (for only $20 in 2020 [225]); your verified Stripe account with payment gateway for $1,000; and your hacked Facebook account for $65 (Table 6.1). PII is used for identity theft and stolen email addresses are key for spam marketing campaigns as well as in phishing attacks for distributing malware [226]. Not surprisingly, data breaches are becoming more and more ubiquitous. For example, whereas in 2010 about 16 million records were stolen in data breaches of 30,000 records or more [227], 36 billion records were exposed in the first half of 2020 alone [228]. Additionally, many organisations do not always report the size of their breaches and smaller data breaches occur all the time.

## 6.1.1   The Cost of a Data Breach

Since we have abundant information on the thousands of data breaches and billions of records that are stolen every year, how can we assess the cost of a data breach in all its dimensions?

This question must be answered from the point of view of both the industry and the individual. The annual report on worldwide data breaches by IBM Security and the Ponemon Institute ('Cost of a Data Breach Report') disclosed that the number of data breaches and their cost for organisations keep increasing every year [229]. This analysis of over 500 organisations across 17 distinct industries shows that data breaches in the healthcare industry have the highest costs of all. For example, whereas the average total cost of a data breach across all industries is $3.9M, it is 65% higher for the healthcare industry ($6.45M). Regarding the average cost per record, the healthcare industry is again the indisputable leader at $429, followed by the financial ($210), the technology ($183) and the pharmaceutical ($178) sectors. This is for two reasons: (i) The cost of a data breach is always higher for organisations that are tightly regulated and (ii) The healthcare industry is extensively targeted by ransonware because without access to medical records the health of the patients is compromised. Therefore the longer the downtime brought about by the ransonware, the more likely that the ransom will be paid [230]. Not surprisingly, the healthcare industry has traditionally had the highest number of data breaches: In the first half of 2021, 238 distinct healthcare data breaches were reported (for 198 data breaches in the finance and insurance industry).

Next, if we consider the cost of a data breach not per record but per employee, smaller organisations always have a disproportionately high cost ($3,533) when compared to larger organisations of over 25,000 employees ($204). On top of this, the healthcare industry presents the largest customer turnover of any industry (followed by the financial and pharmaceutical industries). At the other end of the spectrum the public sector has the lowest customer turnover since it normally has no competitors.

The largest, single healthcare data breach so far is the 2015 hack of Anthem Inc., where nearly 80 million personal records of former and current US policyholders were stolen [229, 231, 232, 233]. Anthem Inc. never were completely transparent but the details that have emerged point towards a sophisticated attack with a strong social engineering component [234]: Following an *intelligence gathering* search on social networks for key staff

TABLE 6.1 The Prices of Various Forms of Identity in the Dark Web

| Category | Product | 2020 | 2021 |
|---|---|---|---|
| Credit card and banking | Cloned American Express with PIN | $35 | $35 |
| | Cloned VISA with PIN | $25 | $25 |
| | Credit card details, account balance up to $5,000 | $20 | $240 |
| | UK hacked credit card details with CVV | Not known | $20 |
| | Spain hacked credit card details with CVV | Not known | $40 |
| | Stolen online banking logins, minimum $100 on account | $35 | $40 |
| | Stolen online banking logins, minimum $2,000 on account | $65 | $120 |
| | Walmart account with credit card attached | $10 | $14 |
| Payment processing services | Stolen PayPal account details, minimum $198.56 | $00 | $30 |
| | Stolen PayPal account details, minimum $1,000 | Not known | $120 |
| | PayPal transfer from stolen account, $1,000–$3,000 | $320.39 | $340 |
| | PayPal transfer from stolen account, $3,000+ | $155.94 | $180 |
| | 50 hacked PayPal account logins | Not known | $200 |
| | Hacked TransferGo account | Not known | $510 |
| | Verified Stripe account with payment gateway | Not known | $1,000 |
| Cryptocurrency accounts | Hacked Coinbase verified account | Not known | $610 |
| | USA verified LocalBitcoins account | Not known | $350 |
| | Crypto.com verified account | Not known | $300 |
| | Cex.io verified account | Not known | $710 |
| | Blockchain.com verified account | Not known | $310 |
| Social media | Hacked Facebook account | $74.5 | $65 |
| | Hacked Instagram account | $55.45 | $45 |
| | Hacked Twitter account | $49 | $35 |
| | Hacked Gmail account | $155.73 | $80 |
| | Instagram followers × 1,000 | $7 | $5 |
| | Pinterest followers × 1,000 | $5 | $4 |
| | LinkedIn company page followers × 1,000 | $10 | $12 |
| Hacked services | Uber driver hacked account | Not known | $14 |
| | Bet365 account | Not known | $50 |
| | Netflix account (1 year subscription) | Not known | $44 |
| | The Telegraph UK Premium | Not known | $7 |
| | Adobe Creative Cloud (1 year subscription) | Not known | $160 |
| | eBay account with good reputation (1,000+ feedback) | Not known | $1,000 |

in the organisation, these key employees were sent phishing messages with links to the *we11point.com* domain (instead of wellpoint.com, Anthem Inc.'s former name). Clicking on those links led to the local installation of the malware that subsequently sent access credentials back to the hackers. Thus, remote access was gained to the victims' machines and at least ninety other systems. From there, 78.8M healthcare records were eventually downloaded and exfiltrated with the following information: Name, date of birth, social security number, healthcare ID number, home address, email address, work information, and potentially also credit card and medical history details. The disclosed cost of this breach was $230M [234], including *direct costs* as well as *indirect costs*. Direct costs include the cleanup of malware and customer turnover. In fact, over 50% of customers affected by a Personal Health Information (PHI) data breach switch their business to a competitor [235]. Indirect costs include making the public announcement and the reputation damage. Moreover, if the company is publicly listed, an effect on the value of its stocks is guaranteed. If the company is not yet established, a data breach is likely to hurt the company at any future investment rounds.

PHI data breaches have been on the rise year after year because as much as $408 is paid on average per record on the black market [236]. PHI records are so detailed and comprehensive that they can be regarded as a window into our souls. Illegitimate access to PHI records always has devastating consequences for the patient, including:

- *Emotionally*, the incident will be a very stressful experience.

- *Medical identities* will be used to purchase medical items, undergo treatment and pay for prescriptions. Medical identity theft can be very difficult to detect, which makes it even more dangerous: 40% of patients found out via letters from creditors for expenses that thieves incurred in their name, and over 50% of fraud victims did not discover that they were a victim until at least one year after the theft [235].

- *Coercion and extortion*: Given specific knowledge of someone's disease or terminal illness, such as a sexually transmitted disease, coercion and extortion are a possibility.

- *Health costs*: In previous PHI breaches 55% of victims had to make out-of-pocket payments to the health plan provider or insurer to restore the coverage, and 32% saw an increase in their insurance premiums [235].

- *Finance*: With access to a social security number and PHI, fraudsters can submit tax returns in the customer's name as well as open new bank accounts. It might take a long time to recover from a low credit score.

## 6.2 WHY IS PRIVACY IMPORTANT?

Privacy is a vital aspect of human dignity that helps us define who we are in relation to the world we live in. Moreover, privacy also is a basic human right upon which other human rights are built.

The idea of privacy is not always easy to articulate because of its dynamic and context-dependent nature. For instance, everyone cares about privacy, but children, teenagers and senior people have different definitions of public and private. The concept of privacy is also instinctual: Although privacy was not an option for the hunter-gatherer societies that existed until around 11,000 years ago (as all activities were performed in public), there is evidence that hunter-gatherers preferred to make love in solitude if given the chance [237]. In ancient Greece not only did Aristotle (4th century BC) make a clear distinction between the public ('polis') and the private ('oikos') life, but also the building style of the early Greeks rested on mathematical principles that allowed to maximise the light available while minimising the exposure to the outside world. The need for privacy was overturned during the Roman Empire where private activities were essentially public, and then changed again during the Middle Ages with the introduction of seclusion and private meditation among the clergy. The popularisation of emotional privacy probably came with the introduction of mandatory confessions (14th–17th centuries AD) and the universal ownership of books following the invention of the printing press. 17th and 18th century plagues also stopped the communal sharing of beds, and the wealth introduced by the Industrial Revolution (1760–1840) further reinforced the concept of privacy with the ownership of separate homes. The publication of 'The right to privacy' by Warren and Brandeis in the Harvard Law Review in 1890 [238] was the first attempt to define privacy as 'the right to be let alone', and constitutes the first legal recognition of solitude and privacy as being essential to an individual's mental well-being. Later developments in communication (mail postcards, telephone, Internet) have helped shape our understanding and expectations of privacy.

A modern, libertarian definition of privacy is that of Alan Westin (1967): 'Privacy is the claim of individuals, groups and institutions to determine for themselves when, how and to what extent information about them is communicated to others' [239]. There are various problems with such a broad definition, including the need to share information on a bureaucratic level in order to have a functional society, as well as the need to survey certain individuals whose behaviour, if left unchecked, would limit others' freedom and privacy. A more recent definition of privacy is Kang's (1998): 'Privacy is an individual's control over the processing, i.e. acquisition, disclosure and use of personal information' [240]. In the Internet era, Kang's definition does not fit very well, and we may prefer a more realistic, working definition of privacy: 'Privacy is the ability to control data we cannot stop generating, giving rise to inferences we cannot predict' [241].

The violation of personal privacy is a daily occurrence, although today it is not as gross as when Scott McNealy (the co-founder and CEO of Sun Microsystems) infamously stated in 1999 that 'you have zero privacy anyway, get over it' [242]. The invasion of privacy continued to be justified, for example when Mark Zuckerberg stated before an audience in 2010 that 'privacy is no longer a social norm' [243]. However, in 2017 Facebook's former vice-president of user growth, Chamath Palihapitiya, confessed in disgust that the tools they had created were so invasive that they were destroying 'the social fabric of how society works' [244]. Former Facebook product manager Frances Haugen went even further in 2021 by being the primary source of a Wall Street Journal investigation on how the social media platform harms children and encourages division in society to the point of weakening the democratic system [245]. Haugen also testified before the US Senate in October 2021 that Facebook executives were aware of all of this but put profits before people [246].

Edward Snowden's disclosures of top-secret NSA documents in 2013 were crucial in exposing how vulnerable people are to privacy invasions and marked an inflection point in how we protect sensitive information. Among other things, Snowden showed how in the name of national security the NSA ordinarily collected phone records of millions of citizens [247]; and how the NSA conducts mass surveillance activities globally and spies on hundreds of world leaders. The metadata collected were not used for the purpose originally intended and thus these operations violated many federal laws. Moreover, most of these data sources were from mobile communications and social media companies who promise to protect our privacy but actually give the NSA access to our data. On top of this, Snowden exposed the casual approach to security that many companies were taking (e.g. by not using SSL encryption) and which routinely exposed user account data. The leaks also highlighted a tool called XKeyscore which is capable of tracking a user's online activities across the world [248].

In 2017, news organisation Quartz carried out an experiment with mobile phones that lacked a SIM card (or a network connection) and showed that Google systematically records each one of our whereabouts [249]. In 2019 we learnt that Google's Nest Guard (a home security system) had been secretly carrying a microphone since 2017, although according to Google they never intended to hide it [250]. How would you feel if you had one of these devices in your living room and found out that the world's largest advertising agency had

Figure 6.1 Presidio Modelo (Isla de la Juventud, Cuba), a modern panopticon design.

been potentially listening to your private conversations for years? American Airlines, United Airlines and Singapore Airlines had hidden cameras installed in the back of the passenger seats, but the airlines stated that they would never be operational and that 'Panasonic manufactured them that way' [251].

Privacy matters for many different reasons, including our right to put a limit on government and corporate power, the management of one's reputation and healthy social boundaries, our right to change and be given second chances, freedom of speech as well as non-discrimination on grounds of race, gender, sexual orientation and political views [252]. Even if we have nothing to hide, even if we choose to believe that we do not care about privacy, one fundamental problem with the invasion of privacy is that knowing that we are being spied upon has a deep psychological effect that ends up conditioning our entire behaviour. This was well understood by English philosopher Jeremy Bentham (1748–1832), who devised a type of circular prison called 'the panopticon' where individual cells face a central watchtower (Fig. 6.1, [253]). As the windows of the tower had shutters, a watchman was not even needed: The fear of feeling watched is enough to control our free will. By the same token we do not run a red light on a deserted street at four in the morning.

The modern concept of flexible working can also be regarded as a type of panopticon since employees lose their privacy and are being observed by *anyone around them* (instead of just a watchman). It has been noticed that constant observation in the workplace makes workers adjust their behaviour to avoid causing unpleasant situations, resulting in the blurring of individual personalities [254]. Furthermore, in an analysis of the modern panopticon that is the WWW, public YouTube comments, videos and playlists of an extensive Greek community were mined and, when aggregated, allowed the researchers to infer the users' political affiliations [255].

Giving up our fundamental right to privacy and autonomy, our right to explore new ideas and be creative even if we only exercise it in our bedroom, is condemning ourselves to our own dehumanisation. Dante already warned us about this in 1320 when he wrote in his *Divina Commedia*:

*'Consider your origins: you were not made to live as brutes, but to follow virtue and knowledge'*

## 6.3  ARE COMPANIES KEEPING OUR DATA PRIVATE? THE ADA HEALTH CASE STUDY

In this section we conduct the data privacy analysis of a well-known app called Ada Health (a virtual doctor). The app is analysed using a top-down approach whereby an increasing degree of detail is gained as we progress through the following steps:

1. Business summary: General description, technical, market and legal, and and usage details.

2. Data audit: What data is collected, for what reason, for how long, and the legal basis for it; how is the data stored and who has access to it; and what security controls are in place.

3. Privacy by design: To what extent has user privacy been taken into account during the design of the system?

4. Experimental privacy analysis.

The analysis is done in the context of the GDPR because, despite its limitations, it is still the world's most stringent privacy law and is uniformly applied across all 27 countries of the EU. Under the GDPR companies are obliged to follow strict guidelines on the collection, processing and storage of personal data. The GDPR, however, does not precisely state how to implement these guidelines and much of the work is left to the imagination and goodwill of the Data Protection Officers. Not all companies play by the same rules, and a goal of data scientists is to understand how and when data privacy is being compromised.

The United States, on the other hand, presents a more complex picture because privacy laws are not identical across states. However, some federal laws exist, such as the HIPPA Privacy Rule which regulates Personal Health Information [256]). Other countries have implemented laws similar to the GDPR [257].

Before proceeding with a thorough analysis of the Ada Health app, could you visit ada.com and write down your notes on the following? You may want to check the documentation on the Ada website, do your own research about this company, and also download the app and play with it.

- How does Ada work and what is the business model?

- Would you say that Ada Health protects your privacy?

- Is the data requested of the user strictly necessary to provide a medical diagnosis?

- Did you try to diagnose yourself and was the result accurate?

### 6.3.1  Business Summary

#### 6.3.1.1  Application Details

- Name of application: Ada - Your Health Companion

- Application website: https://ada.com/

- Price: Free

- Category: Medical

- Description of application: Ada is an AI-powered personal health assistant (a virtual doctor)

- Languages available in: English, French, German, Portuguese, Romanian, Spanish, Kiswahili (Tanzania)

### 6.3.1.2 Technical

- Availability: iOS 9.3 or later (iPhone, iPad and iPod touch) on the Apple App Store (https://cutt.ly/0tT2GiZ); Android 4.3 or later on Google Play (https://cutt.ly/JtT2FXa)

- App size: 20 Mb (iOS), 8.4 Mb (Android)

### 6.3.1.3 Market and Legal

- Company (the 'controller'): Ada Health GmbH, Karl-Liebknecht-Straße 1, 10178 Berlin, Germany.

- Company reach: global

- Employees: 200

- Offices: Berlin (2), Munich, London, New York

- Number of unique users: 8 million

- Health assessments completed to date: 15 million

- Certifications and compliance: GDPR, ISO/IEC 27001, CE Mark (Class I medical devices from the EEA), BiM Badge (German agency for quality management)

- Business model: The app is free to download and use. Ada Health GmbH's revenue model basically consists of selling third party products and services, as well as selling patient data to their business partners [258].

### 6.3.1.4 Application Walk-Through

Following the download of the Ada Health app onto my HUAWEI P smart 2019 running Android 9, at the sign-up stage I confirmed that (i) I am over 16 years old; (ii) I have read the Privacy Policy and the Terms and Conditions; and (iii) I give consent to Ada Health GmbH to analyse my personal health data. After a number of additional, optional consents to which I did not agree, I created my account using a combination of email address and password to avoid supplying any personal details through my Facebook account. Upon login, I had to fill in my health profile (name, gender, date of birth; smoking, high blood pressure and diabetes data). During a medical consultation, Ada asks a large number of questions to finally produce a report indicating the possible causes for your symptoms (a diagnosis). The report becomes part of your medical history and is saved under the user's profile.

## 6.3.2 Data Audit

### 6.3.2.1 Description of Data Collected and Processed

(a) User-provided information includes any information provided at the time of registration, or in any forms and surveys filled on the Ada website or app; any information provided through any correspondence with Ada Health GmbH; when the services are used; and when the user subscribes to the newsletter, promotional emails or other marketing material:

- Name, gender

- Date of birth

- Email address

- Phone number

- Facebook ID; email address and phone number if provided in Facebook account

- Symptoms of illness

- Potential causes of illness symptoms

- Health insurance details

- Medical history, including any allergies

- Medication being taken

- Health background (smoking, diabetes, high blood pressure, pregnancy status, etc.)

- Any other information required to verify user identity

(b) Information collected about the user includes:

- Usage data: device model, operating system, unique device identifiers, mobile network information, geographic location, details of visits to the Ada website and app (including URL clickstream data, with date and time), details of conditions and symptoms searched.

- Analytics data: IP address, operating system and browser type, details of app store where the Ada Health app was downloaded from, duration of visits to certain pages and page interaction information (including scrolling, finger gestures, clicks and mouse-overs).

### 6.3.2.2 Storage of Personal Data

Personal data is stored in the EU in Amazon Web Services (AWS) and Google cloud servers located in Luxembourg and Ireland, respectively. The data may be processed by sub-processors operating outside of the European Economic Area (EEA) that comply with GDPR article numbers 44 (General Principle for Transfers), 46 (Transfers Subject to Appropriate safeguards) and 49 (Derogations for Specific Situations).

### 6.3.2.3 Why Is This Data Held?

The uses of the data that is collected and processed differ by activity (Table 6.2):

TABLE 6.2   Summary of the Uses of the Data Collected from the Patient

| (1) Website access | (2) User account registration | (3) Facebook login | (4) Case creation |
|---|---|---|---|
| To provide access to Ada website. | To provide the user with a user account and access to the services. Otherwise, it is not possible to use the Ada app. | To populate user data and to confirm a user's identity prior to logging in to their account. | To suggest possible causes for the symptoms detailed by the user. |
| **(5) Analysis of case information** | **(6) Analysis of suitability for clinical research** | **(7) Use of health data for statistics and research** | **(8) Use of health data for public health purposes** |
| To guarantee the high quality and safety standards of the app. | To assess suitability for clinical research and potentially invite users to take part in such research. | Analysis of (pseudonymised) data in aggregate statistics on the geographical prevalence of symptoms and conditions. Also to pass summarised statistics to partners in anonymised form. | Pseudonymised data to understand trends, rare diseases and threats. Aggregate data is also presented to the user in the form of clinical advice. Summarised, anonymised statistics are passed to partners. |
| **(9) Direct marketing** | **(10) Provision of safer services** | **(11) Help others with attribution and performance metrics** | **(12) Monitoring of app usage** |
| To send the user information on products, services and surveys. | To monitor usability so that the app continues to comply with the safety and security standards required of medical devices. | To optimise marketing initiatives. | Technical data is used here to ensure the proper functioning, maintenance and improvement of the app. |
| **(13) App performance reports** | | | |
| To ensure optimal functionality of the app | | | |

### 6.3.2.4 Legal Basis for Holding the Data?

The GDPR articles on which the Ada privacy policy rests are:

- Article 6 (1)(a) (consent): *the data subject has given consent to the processing of his or her personal data for one or more specific purposes.*

- Article 6 (1)(b) (contract performance): *processing is necessary for the performance of a contract to which the data subject is party or in order to take steps at the request of the data subject prior to entering into a contract.*

- Article 6 (1)(c) (legal obligation of controller): *processing is necessary for compliance with a legal obligation to which the controller is subject.*

- Article 6 (1)(f) (legitimate interest): *processing is necessary for the purposes of the legitimate interests pursued by the controller or by a third party, except where such interests are overridden by the interests or fundamental rights and freedoms of the data subject which require protection of personal data, in particular where the data subject is a child.*

- Article 9 (2)(a) (consent): *the data subject has given explicit consent to the processing of those personal data for one or more specified purposes, except where Union or Member State law provide that the prohibition referred to in paragraph 1 may not be lifted by the data subject.*

- Article 9 (2)(i) (public interest): *processing is necessary for reasons of public interest in the area of public health, such as protecting against serious cross-border threats to health or ensuring high standards of quality and safety of health care and of medicinal products or medical devices, on the basis of Union or Member State law which provides for suitable and specific measures to safeguard the rights and freedoms of the data subject, in particular professional secrecy.*

- Recital 54: *The processing of special categories of personal data may be necessary for reasons of public interest in the areas of public health without consent of the data subject. Such processing should be subject to suitable and specific measures so as to protect the rights and freedoms of natural persons. In that context, 'public health' should be interpreted as defined in Regulation (EC) No 1338/2008 of the European Parliament and of the Council (11), namely all elements related to health, namely health status, including morbidity and disability, the determinants having an effect on that health status, health care needs, resources allocated to health care, the provision of, and universal access to, health care as well as health care expenditure and financing, and the causes of mortality. Such processing of data concerning health for reasons of public interest should not result in personal data being processed for other purposes by third parties such as employers or insurance and banking companies.*

The Ada privacy policy also makes reference to additional legislations such as the EU Medical Devices Regulation (2017/745/EU), the German Bundesdatenschutzgesetz (BDSG), the German Medical Device Ordinance, the EU Medical Devices Directive (93/42/EC) and the German Infection Protection Act (IFSG).

### 6.3.2.5 How Long Is the User Data Kept For?

For activities numbers 1 (Website Access) and 13 (App Performance Reports) (see Table 6.2), data is kept for 14 days, except in the case of a security-related incident, in which case user data is kept until the incident has been cleared and documented. For the rest of the activities, user data can potentially be stored forever.

### 6.3.2.6 Who Has Access to the Data?

In principle anyone working at Ada Health GmbH has access to the data assets, as well as a number of third-party companies to which Ada Health GmbH might sell the data, and various contract processors (Amplitude Inc. (San Francisco), adjust GmbH (Berlin), Functional Software Inc. (San Francisco)).

### 6.3.2.7   Security Controls in Place?

Besides stating that the Ada app is certified by a number of standards (ISO/IEC 27001, CE Mark for Class I medical devices for the EEA, GDPR and BiM Badge of the German agency for quality management), the company is particularly vague about the security controls they have in place (https://ada.com/security/). However, it is only fair to assume that they have standard username/password controls for different devices and internal data resources, as well as some form of access control (AC). Their claims on controls may be assigned to various categories:

(a) *Technical controls*
Ada Health GmbH claims to follow 'security by design' whereby security is integral to the development of a product during its life cycle. Moreover, personal data is stored separate from users' health information.

(b) *Personnel controls*
Ada Health GmbH claims that each one of their employees 'fulfills their individual security responsibilities'.

(c) *Physical security controls*
Ada Health GmbH claims that they thoroughly supervise every aspect of the physical security of their offices to protect data.

(d) *Governance and legal/compliance controls:*
Ada Health GmbH claims to be regularly audited by both internal teams and external authorities to comply with the standards they adhere to. Auditing by internal teams includes penetration tests.

### 6.3.3   Privacy by Design

The *Privacy by Design* (PbD) philosophy states that security and privacy must be embedded in the design of a system from its conception, instead of these being an afterthought [259]. PbD is compulsory in Article 25 of the General Data Protection Regulation legislation (GDPR, gdpr.eu). Here we briefly discuss the *Seven principles of privacy by design* and the extent to which the design of the Ada Health app focuses on preserving users' privacy by design:

- **Principle 1. Proactive not reactive: preventive not remedial.**

  This principle forces us to consider data privacy at the outset of a project and actively avoids the 'policy of rectification' whereby security incidents are dealt with after they occur. The early identification of a system's weak points is encouraged in order to anticipate risks from known threats to privacy. Principle 1 is rather general and can be seen as the principle that sets the tone for the rest of the philosophy. In practice, Principle 1 should imply:

  (i) A top-down commitment to PbD by Ada Health GmbH and the development of the right privacy-protection culture at the company: from their privacy policy (abridged) - *'Protecting your data, privacy and personal data is very important to Ada Health GmbH. It is vitally important to us that our customers feel secure when using the Services'.* Ada Health GmbH is also GDPR-compliant and ISO 27001-certified, and holds the BiM Badge (German agency for quality management) and the CE Mark for Class I medical devices.

(ii) Assigning specific responsibilities so that every employee at Ada Health GmbH is aware of their tasks with regard to privacy: this may be identified with the following statement - *'Our Global Compliance & Ethics Department ensures every Ada employee fulfills their individual security responsibilities.'* (https://ada.com/security/).

(iii) Having controls for the early detection of processes and practices that might not be aligned with PbD: this might be inferred from their ISO 27001 certification.

- **Principle 2. Privacy as the default setting.** This principle basically states that personal data must be protected by default. There is a tension here between Ada Health GmbH's business model (selling the data to third parties) and the idea that the use of data must be minimised and its sharing restricted by default. Although opt-in and opt-out functions are enabled on the app, we can also find at least one privacy control that is deactivated by default (see below). Moreover, the principle of data minimisation is violated by design because we could run a prediction on our symptoms without having to give away a lot of other data (name, gender, DOB, email address, phone number, etc.). Thus, privacy is being sacrificed here in the name of utility.

- **Principle 3. Privacy embedded into design.** This principle argues that privacy measures are an integral part of the design instead of add-ons. In practice this means routinely using data encryption, authentication and system testing. Here, Ada Health GmbH states that *'We follow security by design, which means Ada implements security from the beginning of the product lifecycle – not afterwards and not as an add-on.'* and that penetration tests are routine (https://ada.com/security/).

- **Principle 4. Full functionality: positive sum, not zero-sum.** This principle states that privacy should not be traded for security or functionality. Since this principle describes a certain mindset, perhaps we could map this principle to the following declaration: *'Ensuring the highest levels of privacy and security for our users is absolutely fundamental to how we develop our technology, products, and manage our business. It is a core principle upon which Ada was founded'* (https://ada.com/security/).

- **Principle 5. End-to-end security: full life cycle protection.** This principle says that data privacy starts at the time of (secure) data collection, through its use, transmission and final deletion. In practice this means the implementation of specific controls which we cannot confirm without performing an inspection from the inside. However, Ada Health GmbH makes reference to key points throughout their privacy policy (https://ada.com/privacy-policy/), including data deletion, the anonymisation and pseudonymisation of data, and statements such as the following: *'Sensitive information between your browser and our Website is transferred in encrypted form using Transport Layer Security (TLS). When transmitting sensitive information, you should always make sure that your browser can validate our certificate'.*

- **Principle 6. Visibility and transparency: keep it open.** According to this principle the user should be made aware of what personal data is being collected and for what purpose. Although Ada Health GmbH declares their data processing activities and their various partners in detail (https://ada.com/privacy-policy/), as we discuss below their claims on transparency are not always real.

- **Principle 7. Respect for user privacy: keep it user-centric.** A user-centric approach means acknowledging that the data ultimately belongs to the user, and as such the user must be provided with strong privacy defaults and user-friendly options so that they can withdraw their consent regarding the use of the data. From a design perspective, the Ada app provides clear privacy controls that are easy to use.

### 6.3.4 Experimental Privacy Analysis

One problem with the *Privacy by design* principles is that they are rather vague, and given a well-written privacy policy and a small amount of goodwill, it is easy to see how the various statements from the policy map onto these principles. Another problem here is that one can only take at face value what Ada Health GmbH states in their privacy policy.

The Lumen Privacy Monitor [260] allows to experimentally determine the extent to which the Ada Health app respects user privacy. Lumen was developed at the University of California, Berkeley, under the Haystack Project (haystack.mobi) with the goal of analysing mobile phone traffic in order to identify privacy leaks inflicted by third-party apps.

Lumen was installed onto my HUAWEI P smart 2019 running Android 9, and a single medical diagnosis was carried out from made-up symptoms. Lumen did not warn about any privacy leaks and reported the outgoing traffic from my smartphone as consisting of 14 'data flows'. These flows were being sent to three subdomains from the Ada website, as well as to the api.amplitude.com subdomain. Amplitude Inc. was also classified as an *Advertising or Tracking Service* and is mentioned in Ada's privacy policy only in section 3.10 ('Provide safer services by monitoring App usage') as a data-processing company that pseudonymises usage data. However, I specifically did not give consent for this, whereas the monitoring of app usage is described in section 3.12 ('Monitor usage to ensure proper use, functioning, maintenance and improvement of the medical reasoning system and related Services'), for which I did not give consent either. Moreover, the 'Monitor app usage' policy (section 3.12) was enabled *by default* (which is really bad) and I had manually disallowed it beforehand. Most alarmingly, the Lumen Privacy Monitor identified a number of requested permissions to which I had not indirectly agreed. These include high-risk permissions such as allowing the Ada Health app to *access my precise location, write to external storage* and *read from external storage*. Medium-risk permissions included allowing the Ada Health app to *open network sockets, accessing information about networks* and *using fingerprint hardware* (Fig. 6.2).

We could do a more detailed analysis using different inputs over a longer period of time, but the above is sufficient evidence to firmly state that the Ada app does not respect the user's privacy choices or key principles such as data minimisation, and that the privacy policy is purposefully misleading and opaque. In particular, the requested permissions for reading from and writing to the external storage of my smartphone are particularly shocking, especially because this is not detailed in the privacy policy.

The authors of the Lumen Privacy Monitor previously found that over 70% of apps are intimately linked with third-party advertising and tracking services, and mapped these business relationships as part of the Haystack Project (haystack.mobi). The conclusion was that sharing private data with third party tracking companies is the norm rather than the exception [261].

In another relevant study, Grundy *et al.* used a technique called *differential traffic analysis* to investigate 24 medicines related apps. The authors found that ∼80% of these apps

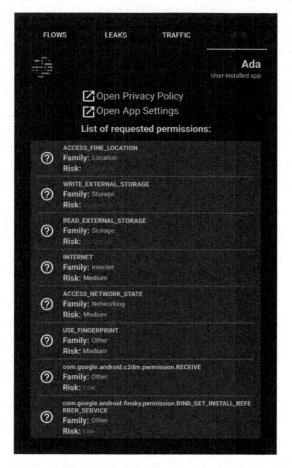

Figure 6.2 Screenshot of the output of the Lumen Privacy Monitor.

routinely share user data for commercialisation purposes to a network of 55 unique entities owned by 46 parent companies. This situation presents clear privacy risks for both clinicians and patients not only because, like we did find, the sharing of data is not done transparently, but also because very sensitive data is often shared. A patient's drug list and their location, even if provided separately, may be aggregated in such a tightly-knit ecosystem and lead to the identification of the patient and therefore the commercialisation of their data [262]. Therefore not only should data controllers be accountable when it comes to data privacy but also the entire ecosystem of data processors and how they are connected to each other.

### 6.3.5 End-to-End Security

The fifth principle of the Privacy by design philosophy [259] states that there can be no privacy without security, although it is possible to have security without privacy. For example, the information that your bank has about you may be used for (i) opening your account and keep you updated about products and services (privacy and security are maintained); (ii) selling some of your information to third parties for marketing purposes (privacy compromised, security maintained); and (iii) the bank servers are hacked and all customer data is put up for sale in the black market (both privacy and security are compromised).

On a technical level, a trade-off always exists between security and privacy. For instance, while data encryption makes transmissions resistant to eavesdropping, not knowing what is being transmitted through a network makes an organisation more vulnerable to encrypted malware attacks. This type of attacks sky-rocketed amid the pandemic and pose a serious threat to privacy [263]. Deep learning methods have recently been applied successfully in the classification of network traffic metadata for identifying (malware-containing) messages without giving up privacy [264, 265]. However, neural networks themselves are vulnerable to adversarial attacks when the training data is influenced to harm the classifier's performance (if hackers have access to the training data), or most often by probing the classifier or doing offline analysis to discover information to manipulate the predictions. However, methods are being developed to train networks with greater resistance to a wide range of adversarial attacks [266].

This section is a short introduction to computer security in the context of the Ada Health app. We outline key aspects of security, including technical and physical security, procedural and administrative controls, as well as the psychology behind data breaches. Thus, a system's security must be understood as a living entity composed of many interacting, dynamic parts. One unifying truth of computer security is described by Schneier's Law (1998) [267]:

*Anyone, from the most clueless amateur to the best cryptographer, can create an algorithm that he himself can't break. It's not even hard. What is hard is creating an algorithm that no one else can break, even after years of analysis. And the only way to prove that is to subject the algorithm to years of analysis by the best cryptographers around.*

Therefore, except for standard security solutions (covered in the next section), no company should ever attempt to design their own security. Well-known examples of Schneier's prophecy include the decryption of WhatsApp messages [268] and Adobe's 38M password disaster [269, 270].

Whenever we think about the security controls of a system, we must do so in the context of the architecture of such system. For instance, for the Ada Health app we may assume the simplified architecture depicted in Fig. 6.3 whereby users interact with the app via their phones; the app communicates with the servers in the cloud for tasks such as data processing and storage; the various offices of the company also access the cloud as the central repository of patient information; and data is made available to third party companies for processing.

The attack surface of this architecture is huge, and there are too many situations to consider here. However, the following is a high-level summary of basic controls that we should expect to be in place. Some important aspects of security such as how to generate secure passwords and their management, two-factor authentication, Virtual Private Networks (VPN) and doing regular data backups are covered in the next section.

### 6.3.5.1 Technical Controls

- **Multi-factor authentication** is a key control for protecting the confidentiality and integrity of the data in the event of compromised credentials. For employees it would suffice to implement a two-factor authentication protocol combining username/password identification and a physical, *personal* token (unexchangeable) where one-time, timestamp-bound passwords are received, for example, whenever an employee requests access to the central data repository in the cloud.

  The Ada Health app should also protect personal data in the event of phone theft. Currently, once the app is installed and we log in (via Facebook or using an email address/password combination), the app remains open. Implementing a complex form

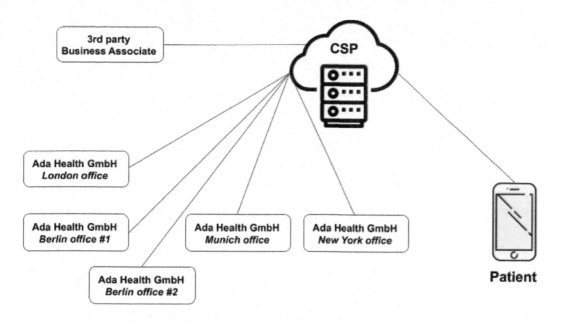

Figure 6.3 A model of the architecture of the Ada Health app.

of authentication may prevent the usability of the app, but at least the app should ask the user for some secret in order to grant access each time, which may be something as simple as a four-digit code that the user provides at the time of registration.

- **Storage of user credentials:** only *stretched, salted hashes* of (ideally) unique, strong passwords should be stored. A *hash* is the non-reversible transformation of a password into a fixed-length string (a hash code). For example, the hashed version of password 'iloveyou' using the secure SHA-256 hashing function (always) is 'e4ad93ca07acb8d908a3aa41e920ea4f4ef4f26e7f86cf8291c5db289780a5ae'. If hackers gain access to a list of hashed passwords, since most people use simplistic passwords the original passwords can often be retrieved by comparing these hashed passwords against lists of precomputed hashed passwords using the most common hashing functions for the most common passwords. This is called a *rainbow table* attack. The success rate of rainbow table attacks becomes negligible if an extra random value known as a *salt* is added to the password prior to hashing.

- **Access control (AC)** determines who has access to the data, and is the most important control following user authentication. The choice of optimal AC method should take into account the dynamic nature of the company (frequently changing roles), how fine the control must be (the who, what, when, where, why and how), as well as the diverse locations of the Ada Health GmbH offices. The finer details of an AC method can only be determined upon a detailed requirements analysis, which includes topics such as the performance level required, the ability to respond to failures, *backward security* (users with revoked privileges should not be able to access data requiring the privileges revoked), and *forward security* (a new user cannot read encrypted data even if they have proper privileges).

- **Data loss prevention software** such as intrusion-detection systems, antivirus software and firewalls are an essential monitoring control for alerting about data exfiltration and breaches that compromise the confidentiality, integrity and availability of the data. Communication over any computer network must always be encrypted using a modern protocol (e.g. TLS 1.3).

- **The secure processing and analysis of PHI** are some of the most important controls regarding data privacy. First of all, data that is both resting and in-transit, in the cloud and in any company machine, must be encrypted. Next, in our model (Fig. 6.3) patient data is sent to third party companies in anonymised form. How can we make this data available without compromising user identity?

  One option here is *pseudonymisation* (rather than *anonymisation*) because it is reversible and we could get back to the original patient IDs regarding specific treatments, research or clinical trials. Two problems with pseudonymisation are the storage of the encryption keys and that the quality of the data is reduced (and hence the value of the predictions). An alternative strategy that circumvents these problems is *homomorphic encryption* [271] where the computation can successfully be done on encrypted data [272].

- **Insider threats** are a major risk given the nature of the data and the legal and financial consequences of a data breach. Ada Health GmbH must identify their critical data assets and implement mitigation strategies, e.g. setting up highly collaborative environments (as these might decrease a *malicious insider's* sense of entitlement), having a sound AC policy with periodically reviewed access to limit the damage done by *entitled independents*, and perhaps also implement a discreet whistleblowing policy so that employees may report abnormal behaviour (e.g. to uncover *malicious leaders*). The whistleblowing policy is a double-edged sword because no matter how big the potential legal and financial consequences to the company are, employees that feel their honesty is being questioned, or their right to privacy breached, might become dissatisfied and resentful, and thus become *insider threats* [273].

  Moreover, being a data science-based company, another control Ada Health GmbH could implement is a predictive method for insider threat detection. Here careful consideration must be paid to the proper selection of sensors (system usage or network-based) and the predictive method: *Rule-based* methods can be accurate and present a low false positive rate, but they are unable to detect new types of attack. This limitation can be overcome by deep learning methods trained to detect various types of abnormal behaviour, both for static data as well as for stream (real time) data [274].

  Finally, *insider fraud* might be partially mitigated by doing background checks on applicants (credit score), as well as by monitoring access and modifications on critical data tables. *Unintentional insider threats* also represent a real risk since human fallibility is behind 60% of personal data breaches [275]—appropriate controls are discussed below in the section on Procedural and administrative controls.

- **Secure deletion of data.** Data destruction protocols must be tailored to the specific needs of Ada Health GmbH, and must be auditable and carried out by a named individual in each office. For example, whenever specific patient data must be deleted in the cloud, the data in question could be encrypted using a strong method (such as AES-256) and then the (locally stored) encryption keys deleted. This procedure is called 'cryptoshredding' [276]) and can easily be done for single files, but it is not scalable. What if the records of hundreds or thousands of patients must be deleted? Here the company should anticipate a number of alternative approaches such as file system and container-based encryption. Moreover, if Ada Health GmbH has control on how their data is deleted by the cloud servers, they must ultimately request disk destruction.

Patient data should also be deleted from smartphones following app uninstallation. However, data erasure is known to be incomplete in both Android and iOS due to Android system vulnerabilities as well as inherited security issues from the Linux kernel. Perhaps a cryptoshredding strategy would be an effective strategy for data deletion in mobile phones? [276].

### 6.3.5.2  Procedural and Administrative Controls

- **User education** is key because human error is behind 60% of personal data breaches [275]. Procedural messages should focus on *phishing attacks* as well as on how to generate and manage *secure passwords*, one per account.

  These days most malware comes in the form of small JavaScript code, server-side ASP.NET files and PHP scripts, and is undetectable by anti-virus software. Employees should understand the risks of opening unverified emails and clicking on suspicious links. Access to social media sites from the company network should be disallowed since apps like Facebook Messenger and WhatsApp are a known source of malware.

  Regarding user accounts, having many accounts per user albeit with fewer privileges is more secure than having one superaccount as this practice limits the risks associated with compromised credentials. The management of multiple passwords can be handled with a password manager (described in the next section).

- **Email:** Employee email mistakes are a frequent cause of *accidental disclosure*. One way to mitigate this is to enforce a Bcc-ing policy as well as a requirement for asymmetric encryption of the messages.

- **Bring-Your-Own-Device (BYOD)**: A clear BYOD policy must be in place to limit the risk of employees bringing into work personal laptops and smartphones that might be inadvertently infected with malware which could spread through the company's network. Laptops with limited security and authentication mechanisms are a threat too if they get stolen and contain unencrypted patient data.

- **Removable media** such as USB keys and CDs should not be allowed (or be under strict control) because they can easily introduce malware, or be used to exfiltrate data.

- **A patch management policy** whereby software is continually upgraded to the latest version is key because many patches are security patches. The failure to upgrade and secure existing software and machines is behind 57% of data breaches [277].

### 6.3.5.3  Physical Security Controls

Theft is a major cause of data breaches, and besides automatic screenlocks in laptops and vaulting doors in the building, it would be a good idea to have electronic or biometric access controls, sensor-activated alarms, CCTV and security personnel. Moreover, if the company rents space in another company's cloud, what type of physical security controls do they have in place?

### 6.3.5.4 Governance and Legal/Compliance Controls

The company needs to make sure that the cloud services provider (CSP) and third party business associates are GDPR-compliant and also respect Ada Health's legal requirements. Data breaches at third party companies will make Ada Health GmbH legally liable. The CSP must have a realistic *business continuity plan* whereby the personal data always remain available in the event of a catastrophe, and both the data and the platform itself should be readily migrated to another CSP without getting locked in.

## 6.4  A FEW SIMPLE RULES FOR OWNING YOUR PRIVACY

A number of procedures exist to counteract general privacy violations, including 'data strikes' to reduce the accuracy of recommender systems, and 'data poisoning' where a browser extension like AdNauseam (adnauseam.io) automatically clicks on every single ad to confuse advertising algorithms [278]. On the level of the individual, the following protocols can be easily implemented to enhance our level of security and privacy.

One fundamental concept is that privacy is not a binary concept, but a sort of 'volume control' that can be tuned dynamically to our advantage. For example, in the interest of their safety and autonomy a senior person might be happy to give up some of their privacy and carry around sensors that record their physical location, heart rate, temperature and when appliances are switched on and off.

1. **Passwords: Should be long and account-specific**

   - First of all, check on **Have I Been Pwned?** and **_IntelligenceX** whether your email or password have been compromised (e.g. as a result of a data breach) as they might be for sale on the dark web.

     If positive, you must change passwords immediately and report to every organisation your account and personal details are linked to. These include banks, credit agencies, healthcare providers and social media networks.

   - **Diceware** can help you generate complex passwords, but do not forget to check **How Secure Is My Password** for how long your password of choice would take to be guessed.

   - A password made up of numbers and symbols is more difficult to remember and less effective than one made up of multiple unrelated words that are nevertheless meaningful to you. For example, a password like 'papa_mama_married_ SXM_2016' is easily remembered as well as difficult to hack.

   - Using a different password for each account (email, server, etc.) is key for limiting the risk of being hacked. Most importantly, never use a private password for accessing a work account.

     Yes, we have all done it, but consider what could happen in the case of a massive data breach: any confidential data that is exposed can in turn be sold for criminals to access personal accounts on sites such as Gmail, Facebook, PayPal, Amazon Pay, Apple Pay and Samsung Pay. In 2020, Easyjet was hacked and the personal data (including full credit card details) of nine million passengers stolen [279]. In 2019 Microsoft 'lost' personal data belonging to 265 million unique users [280]. And in January 2021 we found that 533 million Facebook users had had their personal data exposed [281].

   - Change passwords regularly, e.g. every two months. Use the help of a password manager.

## 2. A password manager, the guardian of your secrets

A password manager like **1Password**, **Dashlane** or **LastPass** facilitates the secure storage of passwords while managing the automatic access to all accounts. We only need to remember the one *master password* that gives access to the password manager (such as 'papa_mama_married_SXM_2016'). A password manager by design does not necessarily require the storage of passwords in the cloud (to synchronize across multiple devices, for example).

## 3. Secure email

To keep our emails completely confidential we must use a secure (encrypted) email service such as **ProtonMail**, **Mailfence** or **Tutanota**. This is because any information that is sent using a free email provider is susceptible of being read. For example, as recently as 2018 Yahoo! was found to scan private emails in order to sell the data to advertisers [282]. I also remember how I recently started getting hotel offers in San Francisco, but could not figure out why. The reason for this is that I had received an email invitation to attend a conference in San Francisco. The invite was included in a PDF attached to the main message, which I had not yet read.

If the recipient of a ProtonMail message does not have a ProtonMail account it is still possible to send an asymmetrically encrypted message for which we must first press the padlock symbol before sending any email. We must then protect the message with a password that must be passed to the recipient via an alternative route (e.g. via a telephone call). The recipient then receives a short message that says they have an encrypted email from a specific account. The link in the message takes them to the ProtonMail website where the email can be decrypted and read following the introduction of the secret password.

Besides having an *asymmetric cryptography* protocol in place, any secure email service must also have its own servers (a private cloud) so that it does not depend on third parties. For instance, ProtonMail's data centers are in Switzerland, where any access to personal information must first be approved by a judge in the context of international law. The court must then notify us of the request for accessing our private information, to which we can appeal.

**Two-factor authentication** (2FA) is a very useful extra layer of security that can be implemented in most email services. With an 2FA protocol in place, access to our account requires not only a password but also a six-number code (with an expiration time of typically a few minutes) that we receive on our mobile phone each time we wish to access the account. Thus, if a hacker gains access to one's password (e.g. through a data breach), at least they will not be able to access our email unless they also have our smartphone (unblocked). **Google Authenticator** can be installed on mobile phones and thus have two-factor authentication set for both our Gmail and ProtonMail accounts.

Finally, if we must share an amount of data that is too large to be attached to an email, we can set up a folder in the cloud as long as we use an encryption program to protect the contents. The recipient should obtain the *encryption key* via an alternative route.

## 4. Web browsing: Brave or Firefox better than Chrome

**Chrome** stores the pages visited and sends this information to Google's servers. If it was done differently, we would not be able to access our synced history when using Chrome across devices. **Brave** and **Firefox** are open source and designed to protect our security and privacy.

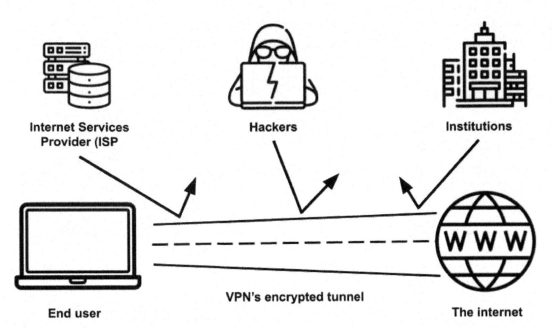

Figure 6.4 A virtual private network (VPN) allows secure communication across public networks.

- Brave is very fast and incorporates by default all the extensions that we would have to install in Firefox. Brave> Preferences allows you to select Startpage and DuckDuckGo as the default search engine, without any installation.

- In Firefox, we must install the following extensions with a single click while browsing: *Privacy Bagder* (blocks trackers), *Facebook Container* (prevents Facebook from tracking you on the Internet), *uBlock Origin* (blocks ads), *Cookie AutoDelete* (clears cookies when you close the Firefox tab), *Disable WebRTC* (disables the WebRTC protocol that comes by default in Firefox, and which could reveal your IP address even when using a VPN) and the *Startpage* or *DuckDuckGo* search engine.

5. **Web searching: Startpage or DuckDuckGo better than Google**

   Google records all our searches, even when we browse in *incognito* mode. **Startpage** and **DuckDuckGo** protect our privacy while we search as they do not store personal information. Their business model is to display the products we are searching for but they only use the words of the searches in real time. Thus these searches are neither archived nor the recommendations are the calculated result of a collaborative filtering system (Chapter 3).

6. **Virtual Private Network (VPN) on computer and smartphone**

   A VPN is a virtual network built on top of an existing physical network that allows users to send and receive encrypted data across public networks [283]. A VPN also hides your identity (IP address) from your Internet provider (including the websites you visit) and anyone else who is following you as all communication is channeled through a remote server (Fig. 6.4). Thus, a VPN allows us to be online in a manner that is both secure and anonymous.

By definition, a VPN cannot be free, but there are some very affordable VPNs. We must always choose a VPN provider that is based in a country whose laws strongly protect personal privacy, such as **NordVPN** (Panama) or **VyprVPN** and **ProtonVPN** (Switzerland). When using the ProtonMail email service we can activate ProtonVPN directly on the email dashboard.

### 7. Beware of social networks

If they are a real necessity, at least we should conceal our real name, phone number, email and physical address. We must also avoid uploading personal photos and talking to strangers, and never post comments on public sites. We must also disable any permissions that the social network does not really need. For instance, why would Twitter need to have access to your location? Snapchat does not need access to your SMS folder either.

Visiting social networks when using the work laptop is a really bad idea because a lot of malware is disseminated through applications such as Facebook Messenger and WhatsApp.

### 8. Instant messaging

We must forget about sending SMS; **iMessage** between iPhones is better. And if we cannot live without **WhatsApp**, at least the following precautions must be taken:

- Enable two-step verification (Settings> Account> Two-step verification): This is an additional layer of security in the form of a six-digit number that must be kept secret.
- Change your privacy settings (Settings> Account> Privacy) so that only our contacts (or no-one) can see our profile picture, personal information, status, or know when we were last connected.

**Signal** is a secure messaging platform where we can do exactly the same as with WhatsApp, and also schedule the destruction of messages. It was used by the Panama Papers whistleblower to communicate safely with journalists Frederik Obermaier and Bastian Obermayer [284]. Moreover, Signal is free and does not need to sell private data because it is financed through grants and donations [285].

### 9. Smartphone and phone number

- Disable location and Bluetooth.
- Delete the apps you no longer use.
- If you have to give away your phone number, use a service like **Burner** or **Hushed** to generate a disposable number that redirects calls and messages to yours without having to give it away.

### 10. Humans are the weakest link

- Our VPN must always be activated on both computer and smartphone.
- Never connect to open Wi-Fi networks that you do not know.
- Visit only secure sites. Look for the padlock in the address bar of your browser as well as for 'https' at the start of the URL. The *https* protocol is not perfectly secure but it is still much better than plain *http*.
- Online tools like **VirusTotal** and **Jotti** scan suspicious websites and files. A keylogger can easily hide inside an image and, once installed by mistake, it will relay everything you type.

TABLE 6.3 Summary of the Privacy-Enhancing Tools Discussed Here

| Tool | URL | Platform (W)eb (D)esktop (i)OS (A)ndroid | Cost (2021) |
|---|---|---|---|
| **Passwords** | | | |
| Have I Been Pwned? | haveibeenpwned.com | W | Free |
| _IntelligenceX | intelx.io | W | Free |
| Diceware | diceware.dmuth.org | W | Free |
| How Secure Is My Password | howsecureis mypassword.net | W | Free |
| 1Password | 1password.com | D/i/A | From $2.99 |
| Dashlane | dashlane.com | D/i/A | Free/1 device |
| LastPass | lastpass.com | D/i/A | Free/1 device |
| **Secure email** | | | |
| ProtonMail | protonmail.com | W/i/A | Free/500MB |
| Mailfence | mailfence.com | W/i/A | Free/500MB |
| Tutanota | tutanota.com | W/D/i/A | Free/1GB |
| Google Authenticator | bit.ly/2WCXcA7 | i/A/BlackBerry | Free |
| **Web browsing and searching** | | | |
| Brave | brave.com | D/i/A | Free |
| Firefox | mozilla.org/en-US/firefox | D/i/A | Free |
| Startpage | startpage.com | W | Free |
| DuckDuckGo | duckduckgo.com | W | Free |
| **VPN** | | | |
| NordVPN | nordvpn.com | D/i/A | From €2.80 |
| VyprVPN | vyprvpn.com | D/i/A/ router/TV | From €1.39 |
| ProtonVPN | protonvpn.com | D/i/A | Free/limited functionality |
| **Instant messaging** | | | |
| Signal | signal.org | D/i/A | Free |
| **Phone number** | | | |
| Burner | burnerapp.com | i/A | From $1.99 |
| Hushed | hushed.com | i/A | From $1.99 |
| **Malware detection** | | | |
| VirusTotal | virustotal.com | W | Free |
| Jotti | virusscan.jotti.org | W | Free |

- Do not install browser extensions that you do not know.
- Never fill in personal questions to regain access. It is not difficult to find out the name of your dog, or the school you went to.
- Never share a personal password or encryption key with anyone.

11. **Your home Wi-Fi network must be password-protected**

   We must never share our Wi-Fi network with random visitors or neighbours. Moreover, although a Wi-Fi signal is wireless, connecting the laptop to the router physically via an Ethernet cable is not only more secure but also much faster.

## 12. Update all the software you use

All software has vulnerabilities, and update patches often are security patches. The failure to update software is behind 57% of hacks and data breaches [277]. For example, the WannaCry ransomware attack of 2017 took advantage of a specific vulnerability of the Microsoft Windows operating system. As a result, over 200,000 computers that were infected with the cryptoworm across 150 different countries had their data encrypted, and ransom payments in bitcoins were demanded. The cost of this cyberattack for the National Health Service of the United Kingdom included the cancellation of 19,000 appointments, as well as 92 million pounds in damage repair costs [286].

## 13. Phishing

Work email addresses are frequent targets of phishing attempts where criminals seek to obtain information via, for instance, a link to a malicious website. Phishing was the technique behind Anthem Inc.'s devastating data breach of 2015 [233]. Malware is also often included in .doc files as few people fall for the .exe files these days.

## 14. Keep data backup copies in a safe place

This must be done regularly because if a system becomes infected by ransomware and needs to be restored from backup copies, the criminals' blackmail capacity is inversely proportional to the frequency with which the data are backed up.

For limited amounts of data we may back up our data using external hard drives which we then put away in a safe at home. However, for larger amounts of data, how could we back up regularly and efficiently?

We may do this in the cloud using a *symmetric cryptography* protocol. The encryption keys, however, must not be stored in the cloud (a potential attacker) but locally. This can be done in a physical device known as a Hardware Security Module (HSM) because it confers both logical (e.g. secure cryptography using random generators) and physical protection. HSMs incorporate hardware tamper protocols that become activated whenever they are broken into.

## 6.5 FURTHER READING

- **Websites**

  - **List of data breaches (Wikipedia)**
    URL: https://bit.ly/3BmdX1n
    *An up-to-date list of data breaches of at least 30,000 records including the method by which they were accomplished.*

  - **Privacy International**
    URL: privacyinternational.org
    *Privacy International is an independent, UK-based charity that defends citizens' right to privacy and dignity, and demands accountability from governments and corporations across the globe.*

  - **Schneier on Security**
    URL: schneier.com
    *Bruce Schneier is an original thinker and one of the world's foremost security experts. Bruce's website includes his security blog and his many books, essays, academic papers, as well as the possibility to subscribe to his popular, monthly newsletter Crypto-Gram.*

    — **The Malware Museum**
    URL: https://bit.ly/3zwbRvn
    *A museum of programs that infected home computers in the 1980s and 1990s. Very interesting because these viruses not only tell the story of contemporary security but also represent the cultural icons and fears of the time when they were engineered.*

- **Podcasts**

    — **Darknet diaries**
    URL: https://darknetdiaries.com/
    *Educational and easy-to-follow investigative reports on everyday cybersecurity topics including hacking, cybercrime and data breaches.*

    — **Smashing security**
    URL: https://www.smashingsecurity.com/
    *An accessible, light-hearted and regular discussion forum on the latest cybersecurity news with invited guests.*

    — **The social engineer podcast**
    URL: https://www.social-engineer.org/
    *This is Chris Hadnagy's podcast on the general topic of how social engineering techniques take advantage of human vulnerabilities and are used to influence people and businesses, and often compromise privacy and security. This podcast is a valuable addition to his book 'Social Engineering: The Science of Human Hacking'.*

- **Videos**

    — **Computerphile**
    URL: https://bit.ly/3sSrpHn
    *A general computer science YouTube channel by academics at the University of Nottingham that includes many outstanding videos explaining key security concepts in a practical and engaging manner.*

    — **Cybercrime Magazine**
    URL: https://bit.ly/3ynDUf1
    *Cybercrime Magazine's weekly YouTube videos offering the top security news, advice, and guests.*

    — **Security Now**
    URL: https://bit.ly/3sSb6Ku
    *The YouTube channel where pioneer Steve Gibson presents the hottest topics in cybersecurity.*

    — **Security Weekly**
    URL: https://bit.ly/3z0acxT
    *The Security Weekly YouTube channel where the latest information security news is provided and security leaders are interviewed.*

    — **What is privacy?**
    URL: https://bit.ly/3Ercut8
    *A clear 3-minute video on the definition of privacy by Privacy International.*

- Articles

  - Burgess M. What is GDPR? The summary guide to GDPR compliance in the UK (WIRED, 24 March 2020).
    URL: https://bit.ly/3EHYaMQ
    *A friendly introduction to the GDPR.*

  - Ducklin P. Anatomy of a password disaster – Adobe's giant-sized cryptographic blunder (Naked Security, 4 November 2013).
    URL: https://bit.ly/3lX9ts4
    *An accessible explanation behind the security problems of the incident whereby Adobe lost a database of 38M passwords that had basic encryption—instead of hashed and salted passwords—plus the password hints in plain text.*

  - Ellis SR. A Cryptography Primer. In Computer and Information Security Handbook. Published by Morgan-Kaufmann, Burlington (MA), United States. ISBN: 9780123943972, 2013.
    *A comprehensive yet accessible introduction to cryptographic protocols. Highly recommended reading.*

  - Greenberg A. The Confessions of Marcus Hutchins, the Hacker Who Saved the Internet (WIRED, 21 May 2020).
    URL: https://bit.ly/3h1Lqqj
    *Marcus Newman, or how to become the world's most famous ethical hacker, be invited to the most awesome parties in Las Vegas, and be arrested by the FBI. All by age 22.*

  - Handa A, Sharma A, Shukla SK. Machine learning in cybersecurity: A review. WIREs Data Mining and Knowledge Discovery 2019, e1306.
    *Signature-based methods are not able to detect even minor variants of known attacks. Therefore learning methods have taken centre stage in cybersecurity for problems such as malware analysis and intrusion detection. This is a short and accessible review on learning techniques in cybersecurity that also discusses malicious strategies for hacking the classification performance of classifiers.*

  - Hao K. How to poison the data that Big Tech uses to surveil you (MIT Technology Review, 5 March 2021).
    URL: https://bit.ly/3Eax68Q
    *How to carry out collective action to combat the tech giants' invasion of personal privacy.*

  - Honan M. How Apple and Amazon Security Flaws Led to My Epic Hacking (WIRED, 6 August 2012).
    URL: https://bit.ly/2Rcqdg5
    *A detailed account of how someone's digital life can be destroyed with a partial credit card number, an email account, and a bit of social engineering.*

  - Guccione D. What is the dark web? How to access it and what you'll find (CSO, 1 July 2021).
    URL: https://bit.ly/3ht1kKj
    *An introduction to the dark web, how to access it, what you can find and buy there, and why not all of it is bad.*

  - Kramer ADI, Guillory JE and Hancock JT. Experimental evidence of massive-scale emotional contagion through social networks. Proceedings of the National Academy of Sciences of the USA 111(24): 8788–8790, 2014.

*The paper describing Facebook's infamous experiment where 700,000 users had their News Feed manipulated to show that 'emotional contagion' of emotions could happen in the absence of direct human interaction. This study was legal, but we may want to consider whether it was also ethical, and type of powerful knowledge on human manipulation was derived.*

- **Menczer F. Facebook whistleblower Frances Haugen testified that the company's algorithms are dangerous – here's how they can manipulate you (The Conversation, 7 October 2021).**
  URL: https://bit.ly/3xPGwUd
  *The goal of social media platforms is to maximise engagement. This article is an excellent overview of the built-in biological mechanisms that social networks exploit to achieve this. The side effects of maximising engagement include a decrease in the quality of the content as well as a number of harmful consequences.*

- **Newman LH. How an accidental 'kill switch' slowed Friday's massive ransomware attack (WIRED, 13 May 2017).**
  URL: https://bit.ly/3jqBkAD
  *The story of how a simple technical trick brought the WannaCry attack to its knees.*

- **Vallina-Rodriguez N and Sundaresan S. 7 in 10 smartphone apps share your data with third-party services (The Conversation, 30 May 2017).**
  URL: https://bit.ly/3cUauNp
  *A very interesting and easy-to-read article that summarises the work of the team that developed the Lumen Privacy Monitor. The authors discuss the technology, economics and obscure legal background behind the tracking and reporting of personal data to third parties by smartphone apps.*

- **Verdegem P. Tim Berners-Lee's plan to save the Internet: give us back control of our data (The Conversation, 5 February 2021).**
  URL: https://bit.ly/3zqkhnU
  *The data-driven dominance exerted by a few large enterprises is unhealthy for society. Tim Berners-Lee has come up with the concept of 'data sovereignty' for individuals and built the technology for it.*

- **Zittrain. A World Without Privacy Will Revive the Masquerade (The Atlantic, 7 February 2020).**
  URL: https://bit.ly/2XqX07o
  *An engaging presentation of the idea that the barrel of privacy invasion has no bottom, and that the perspective of pseudonymity and living in a pseudoworld is not particularly useful either.*

- **Books**

  - Hadnagy C. *Social Engineering: The Science of Human Hacking (2nd Edition).* John Wiley & Sons, Indianapolis (IN), USA, 2018. ISBN-10: 111943338X.
    *Humans are the weakest link in the security chain because hacking the human mind tends to be easier than hacking any computer system. This book discusses the many facets of social manipulation and how to recognise it in order to protect your privacy.*

  - Mitnick KD and Vamosi R. *The Art of Invisibility: The World's Most Famous Hacker Teaches You How to Be Safe in the Age of Big Brother*

***and Big Data.*** Little, Brown and Company, Boston (MA), USA, 2017. ISBN: 0316380504.

*At one point the world's most-wanted hacker, Kevin Mitnick gives practical advice on how to protect your privacy from hackers and malicious activities, whether you use the Internet at home, work or school, either from your laptop or smartphone.*

– Schneier B. ***Schneier on Security.*** John Wiley & Sons, Indianapolis (IN), USA, 2008. ISBN: 0470395354.

*A collection of essays spanning a number of years where Bruce Schneier discusses security problems and practical solutions of varying degrees of complexity. This book is a classic and an excellent foundation to his other, more recent books.*

– Snowden E. ***Permanent record.*** Metropolitan Books, New York (NY), 2014. ISBN: 1250237238.

*This is Edward Snowden's excellent autobiography where he discusses his childhood, the development of the Internet and the progressive breakdown of personal privacy, and finally his ethical considerations for exposing the reality of mass surveillance.*

– Véliz C. ***Privacy is Power: Reclaiming Democracy in the Digital Age.*** Bantam Press, London (UK), 2020. ISBN: 1787634043.

*An entertaining account written for the layperson on how our daily habits compromise our privacy, how bad our data is being used by corporations and governments, and how this in turn takes away our power to make free choices. The book also includes controversial opinions on how the violation of privacy should be controlled.*

– Zabicki R. ***Practical security*** Pragmatic Bookshelf, Raleigh (NC), USA, 2019. ISBN-10: 168050634X.

*A short and practical guide on implementing basic security written for computing professionals who do not necessarily have any background in security.*

– Zetter K. ***Countdown to Zero Day: Stuxnet and the Launch of the World's First Digital Weapon.*** Crown, New York (NY), USA, 2014. ISBN: 077043617X.

*A detailed account of how Stuxnet, an incredibly sophisticated piece of malware that was delivered on a pen drive, sabotaged Iran's nuclear weapons program. This book offers great insight into a system's vulnerabilities, and also contains excellent advice for any programmer who wishes to write more readable and maintainable code.*

## 6.6   CHAPTER REVIEW QUESTIONS

1. Can you describe why privacy is important for individuals?

2. What did the Ada Health app case study show?

3. Sending a verification code to your mobile phone every time you try to access your email is

    (a) A form of privacy invasion.

    (b) A form of two-factor authentication.

    (c) An alternative to Google Authenticator.

    (d) A safer alternative to biometric identification.

4. What is a rainbow table attack and why must 'salt' be added to hashed passwords?

5. The availability of Open Data allows anyone to engage in almost any type of data science project. Open medical data in particular is very relevant for biomedical research. However, before releasing Personal Health Information (PHI) this must be anonymised. What are some examples of data anonymisation?

   (a) Delete the name of the patient, release the rest of the data.

   (b) Delete the name of the patient and scramble the data.

   (c) Delete and/or obscure personally identifying information as well as any other information that can lead to the identification of specific individuals.

   (d) Only let certain people have access to the information.

6. Why is updating the software that you use a key aspect of security?

7. Why is it a good idea to keep backup copies of our data in the cloud using a symmetric cryptographic protocol?

# CHAPTER 7

# What Are the Limits of Artificial Intelligence?

*Falken: Did you ever play tic-tac-toe?*
*Jennifer: Yeah, of course.*
*Falken: But you don't anymore.*
*Jennifer: No.*
*Falken: Why?*
*Jennifer: Because it's a boring game. It's always a tie.*
*Falken: Exactly. There's no way to win. The game itself is pointless! But back at the war room, they believe you can win a nuclear war. That there can be 'acceptable losses'.*

*– War Games* (1983)

Developments in machine learning, including deep learning have given rise to **narrow AI** applications that spectacularly outperform humans at very specific tasks such as beating chess and Go masters, translating across multiple languages and diagnosing rare forms of cancer that escape well-trained doctors. However, how far are we from creating a **general AI** that will be able to reason and behave like a human would across different types of problems and outside of its training?

In this chapter we explore the topic of general AI from various angles. First we discuss how machines think differently from us. For example, machine learning algorithms cannot generalise to unseen examples, can be fooled easily and are unable to learn new concepts without forgetting previously learned concepts. And once we learn to overcome these limitations, how will we decide whether a machine has achieved human-like intelligence? Even passing modern versions of the Turing test does not guarantee that a machine has essential human attributes such as (i) consciousness and intentionality and (ii) the ability to solve open-ended problems where the variable to optimise is not well defined.

Another key obstacle for the development of AI is society's acceptance of the new socio-technical relations that arise between humans and machines. Here we learn to dissect an ethical dilemma, the trolley problem, from the theoretical, practical, physiological, technological and statistical angles to conclude that it is misleading in the context of autonomous vehicles. Only by examining the various sides of an ethical problem in the light of the underlying technology will we stand a chance to change the perceptions that condition the societal acceptance of AI developments.

Finally, we cover the very important topic of human-robot relationships. Becoming emotionally attached to autonomous robots is a basic human instinct, and while we expect them

DOI: 10.1201/b23197-7

to behave in morally acceptable ways, shall we treat them likewise? Robots are a reflection of our humanity, and here we discuss whether learning to treat our machines ethically is the key that will eventually unlock the full potential of AI as well as make us reflect on our own nature in novel ways.

## 7.1 MACHINES OUTPERFORM HUMANS BUT ONLY AT VERY SPECIFIC TASKS

AI is a general term for describing the ability of a machine to think and behave like humans. AI includes many sub-fields such as robotics, vision, speech processing and evolutionary computation. And while AI and machine learning are often used interchangeably, machine learning (and deep learning) is specifically concerned with how computers can be programmed to learn, either by unsupervised learning, supervised learning, semi-supervised learning, or reinforcement learning (the ability to learn by trial and error using feedback in an interactive environment, see below). Recent developments in machine learning (especially deep learning) have provided a giant leap forward for AI.

Examples of supercomputers outperforming humans at specific tasks, include IBM's Deep Blue defeating chess champion Garry Kasparov in 1997 (although Kasparov won the first match the year before) [287, 288]. And in 2016, IBM Watson (ibm.com/watson), a supercomputer system that can answer questions asked in natural language, diagnosed a rare form of leukemia in under 10 minutes that the doctors had missed, thus saving a human life [150, 289].

Also in 2016, DeepMind's AlphaGo defeated 18-time Go world champion Lee Sedol using a combination of machine learning and tree-search techniques [290, 291]. AlphaGo was then upgraded to AlphaGo Zero [292], and then generalised as AlphaZero to also play chess and shogi [293]. AlphaZero achieved superhuman performance in chess after only four hours of learning via self-play, and in all three games in under 24 hours [294].

### 7.1.1 The Protein-Folding Problem

DeepMind's greatest breakthrough to date is the cracking of the protein-folding problem [295, 296] in 2019. Proteins are one of the major types of molecules that perform cellular functions. The functional information that our cells need to operate is encoded in our genes (DNA), but genes do not act directly. Genes need to be 'expressed' and 'translated' into amino acid sequences which, when fully translated (all parts present) adopt specific three-dimensional protein structures. In nature structure follows function, that is a given protein has a specific structure because that structure is particularly suited to performing its unique role, and both the structure and the role have been selected for through millions of years of evolution. The protein-folding problem is essentially guessing the structure of a protein from the sequence of letters in the corresponding gene or amino acid sequence [297] (Fig. 7.1, [376]). Since the number of different ways an amino acid sequence can fold into is astronomical, the protein-folding problem is one of the holy grails of molecular biology.

Traditionally the structure of a protein is determined using techniques such as X-ray crystallography or cryo-electron microscopy, but these techniques are laborious, expensive, and structures are not always solvable (such as those of cellular membrane proteins).

Although predictions are not substitutes for experiments, a reliable protein structure prediction helps accelerate our understanding of a protein's likely function and its regulation, how it may be drugged, how to fight antibiotic resistance and how to engineer enzymes that digest microplastics more efficiently. AlphaFold's predictions are virtually indistinguishable from those determined experimentally, and the set of predicted human protein structures are quickly opening new horizons in drug development [298]. Moreover, predicted structures of

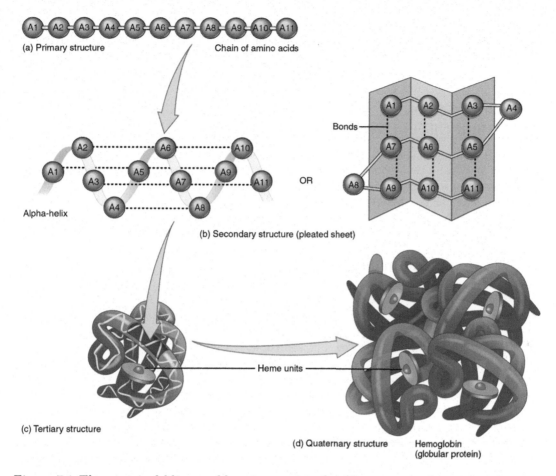

(a) Primary structure        Chain of amino acids

Alpha-helix

Bonds

OR

(b) Secondary structure (pleated sheet)

(c) Tertiary structure

Heme units

(d) Quaternary structure     Hemoglobin (globular protein)

Figure 7.1 The protein-folding problem is guessing the 3D structure of a protein from its sequence of amino acids.

viral proteins can help in pandemic response efforts to guide vaccine design [299], including SARS-CoV-2 (coronavirus) [300, 301, 302].

These impressive technological feats of narrow AI also illustrate its current limitations: computers can be programmed to outperform humans but only at very specific tasks as they lack human-like intelligence: AlphaFold makes incredibly accurate protein structure predictions, but it does not know what a protein is, or what to do with the prediction; the entire Netflix user space can be searched to make incredibly accurate film recommendations [303], but the algorithms behind these recommendations do not understand the concept of a movie. They could not even explain why they make these specific recommendations. Sophisticated DNNs may be trained with global weather information to make weather predictions, but they have no idea what weather actually is, or the difference between a sunny and a rainy day at the beach.

Besides lacking real world experience, narrow AI applications can only work within a very limited context and cannot solve problems outside of its training. For instance, Watson had to be retrained to identify genetic differences across millions of patient datasets before it could diagnose diseases. An AI that is trained to detect abnormalities in X-ray images cannot then turn around and control the temperature of your smart home. Narrow AI applications excel at processing large amounts of data efficiently and finding patterns and correlations in the data but they lack any common sense or understanding of the broader context. Still, narrow AI applications can be combined very efficiently: A self-driving car is no more (and no less!) than many different narrow AI applications working together to accomplish the single task of driving you around.

## 7.2  WHY 'TORONTO' AND OTHER EXAMPLES OF HOW MACHINES THINK DIFFERENTLY

Although computers can outperform humans at very specific tasks they also think in very different ways, and this represents a major limitation for achieving human-like intelligence. For instance, a major success of Watson was its victory at Jeopardy! in 2011, the American television game show where Watson ended up defeating long-standing Jeopardy! champions Jennings and Rutter. Watson achieved this feat using a combination of machine learning, natural language processing and information retrieval techniques [304]. Despite Watson's display of superiority over the human contestants, the most interesting part of the game was the final question in the 'US cities' category:

*Its largest airport is named for a World War II hero; its second largest, for a World War II battle*

'Chicago' is the correct answer, but somehow Watson answered 'Toronto', albeit with low confidence [305]. Whereas most people wonder how Watson could possibly think that Toronto is a US city, a more interesting question is why Watson thought that Toronto is a better answer than Chicago (which Watson did also consider right behind Toronto) [306].

Watson works by matching the words in the question to words in its own sources of information without considering what the question actually means. Thus 'Toronto' scored relatively high in this string match dimension as many documents mention 'Toronto' in connection with 'largest airport' (Toronto is the largest airport in Canada) and with 'named for a World War II hero' (not the airport but other sites in Toronto). Since the string matching algorithm does not consider the meaning of the question, Toronto scored higher than Chicago because it has been more frequently associated with the key strings in the first part of the question.

The way that Watson works behind the scenes with its string matching algorithm is part of the answer only. Also relevant to why Watson gave 'Toronto' as the final answer is how syntactically complex the question was. Watson was not able to split the question into two parts, treat each part independently and find an answer that is common to both parts. Moreover, the second question left out the word 'airport' and Watson could not possibly contextualise the second question. This is why whereas Watson's analysis of the first question yielded plausible candidates such as 'Toronto', 'Chicago' and 'New York', the second part did not produce any meaningful results, and therefore the final confidence score was low at about 30% (essentially meaning 'I don't really know').

### 7.2.1  Adversarial Examples

Watson's 'Toronto' answer is just an example of how AI systems process data and solve problems in ways that are so very different from the way that human intelligence works. Other good examples are illustrated by the application of deep learning to image recognition problems. A DNN might recognise a panda in a picture (57.7% confidence) but it is also surprisingly easy to fool: If we add a bit of input noise that is invisible to us, the same classifier now thinks it is seeing a gibbon with 99.3% confidence (Fig. 7.2, [307]). This type of image containing perturbed input is called an 'adversarial example', which were first

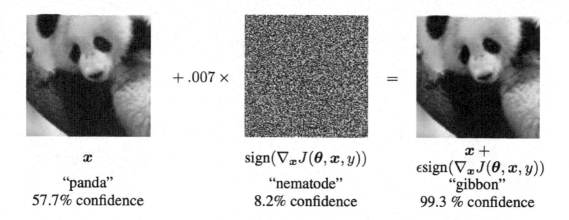

$x$

"panda"

57.7% confidence

$\text{sign}(\nabla_x J(\boldsymbol{\theta}, \boldsymbol{x}, y))$

"nematode"

8.2% confidence

$\boldsymbol{x} +$
$\epsilon \text{sign}(\nabla_x J(\boldsymbol{\theta}, \boldsymbol{x}, y))$

"gibbon"

99.3 % confidence

Figure 7.2 Learning models can misclassify adversarial examples with high confidence given the right type of perturbed input.

described in 2004 in the context of the techniques used by spammers to circumvent spam filters [308].

Most adversarial attacks are engineered by optimising specific changes to real data which, when submitted as input, make the algorithm that will process it arrive at clearly wrong conclusions. Adversarial examples have been described for every type of learning model and data type (including text, images and audio [309]), and are a very serious type of vulnerability for the development of robust AI applications: Can you imagine what would happen if a virus that introduces noise in images infects the image recognition system of an AI-driven weapon or an autonomous vehicle? In the case of the vehicle, the adversarial attack could cause the system to misclassify people in front of the car, or even make them disappear. In the healthcare industry adversarial attacks are used in the context of fraudulent reimbursements, to the point where altered images of the skin are submitted to claim treatment for skin tumours that are actually not malignant [310].

Another way to confuse DNNs is by placing a second object next to the one that is to be classified as shown in the experiment by Tom Brown and co-workers [311]. Here a banana is correctly classified as a banana, but a carefully designed patch placed next to it makes the neural network think it is a toaster (a video of the experiment is available [377]).

Algorithms can be made more resilient to adversarial attacks when trained with adversarial examples, as well as by using advanced data processing techniques that mitigate the effect of malicious input [309].

## 7.2.2 (Lack of) Common Sense

Besides adversarial examples, it is also possible to fool image classification networks by showing the same object under different lighting conditions and orientations [312]. For example, DNNs are unable to identify an object like a school bus that is flipped on its side (as in an accident) in as many as 97% of pose perturbation examples [313]. Learning algorithms are incapable of doing this trivial mental rotation because they cannot generalise to unseen (out-of-distribution) examples. This limitation in the representation of information was originally referred to as 'brittleness' by John McCarthy (1927–2011), one of the founding fathers of AI, and is a bottleneck in reaching human-level AI [314].

All types of learning algorithms present this lack of common sense, not just image classifiers. As another example, even the best trained hate speech classifiers struggle to

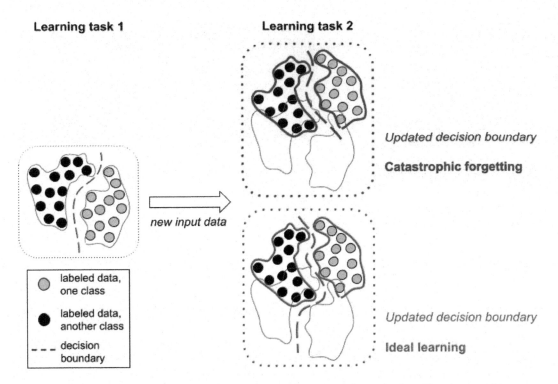

Figure 7.3 An illustration of catastrophic forgetting for a binary classification problem.

determine if words that are typically associated with hate speech are being used in a hateful way if we change the context [315]. For example, the word 'black' might not be hateful if used during the Black History Month. Speech classifiers cannot possibly be trained in every possible context and hate speech datasets are notoriously incomplete [316]. Therefore novel ways must be devised to endow them with human-like common sense.

### 7.2.3 Catastrophic Forgetting and Continual Learning

The goal of learning models is to optimise a given function, thus focusing on the end result. Halting the learning process once the end result is achieved contradicts a fundamentally human characteristic, which is that human intelligence is adaptable and can keep learning in changing environments [317]. Most importantly, however, is the fact that models cannot keep learning without forgetting previously learned training data. This phenomenon is called 'catastrophic forgetting' (Fig. 7.3) and was first described over 30 years ago [318]. Catastrophic forgetting occurs because of the **stability-plasticity dilemma** which states that a certain degree of plasticity is required for the integration of new knowledge, but also radically new knowledge (e.g. large weight changes in a DNN) disrupts the stability necessary for retaining the previously learned representations. In other words, weight stability is synonymous with knowledge retention, but it also introduces the rigidity that prevents learning new tasks [319].

A naïve way to overcome catastrophic forgetting is to build a new network for each new task, but this is neither scalable nor resource-efficient. The more ingenious approaches that have been developed for mitigating catastrophic learning can be assigned to five different classes [320]:

- *Regularisation methods*, where weights are updated under specific constraints. In particular, the technique of *elastic weight consolidation* is well-adapted to reinforcement learning problems as it focuses on the sequential preservation of the weights that contribute the most to previous tasks [321].

- *Ensemble methods* are somewhat rigid and computationally prohibitive beyond a certain point as they train and combine multiple classifiers for each predictive model.

- *Rehearsal methods* are very data-intensive since they combine data from former training sessions with the current sessions being learned.

- *Dual-memory models* emulate the mammalian brain by having one network for storing the newly learned tasks (equivalent to the hippocampus), which are progressively transferred to a more permanent network (equivalent to the neocortex), with or without rehearsal.

- *Sparse-coding methods* generate sparse representations of the learning tasks, which often limits their ability to generalise.

By applying unified metrics and benchmarks for measuring catastrophic forgetting, Kemker and colleagues showed that no single method can solve catastrophic forgetting while allowing incremental learning at the same time, and that the answer lies in finding optimal combinations of specific methods [320]. Catastrophic forgetting is therefore a major bottleneck for the development of adaptable systems that learn incrementally from the constant flow of data in the real world, such as autonomous vehicles, recommender systems, anomaly detection methods and in general any device embedded with sensors (Internet of Things, IoT).

The development of continual learning methods is key not just for machine intelligence, but also for learning scalability: By 2025 the world will be producing some 175 zettabytes annually [20], of which we will only be able to store between 3% and 12% [21]. Thus, for learning to be scalable in the future continual learning methods will need to be able to process data faster and in real time, learn on the fly and then discard the data.

### 7.2.4 Mathematical Reasoning

Machines have achieved much success in solving certain computation-intensive mathematical problems, such as the four-colour theorem [322], which states that any flat map can be coloured using only four different hues without having neighbouring countries share the same colour (Fig. 7.4, [323]).

However, there is an open debate as to how much proper mathematical reasoning computers can do. Advances in mathematics typically require a combination of intuition (inductive reasoning) and a step-by-step logical argumentation. At present computers are unable to do this type of creative thinking combined with the gap-filling work that mathematical proofs require [324]. Moreover, in a recent paper Hendrycks and coworkers showed how even the most sophisticated transformers (specific deep learning models used in natural language processing) could only solve about 5% of a set of 12,500 high school mathematics problems, and that greater computational power would not make things better but the development of new algorithms will [325].

## 7.3 HOW CAN WE TELL IF A MACHINE IS BEHAVING INTELLIGENTLY?

Narrow AI is the only type of AI that we have achieved so far. Although humans cannot process data as fast as computers, we have this unique ability to solve problems at a general level (including abstract thinking) that machines lack. We also have an understanding of the world around us and our place within it; we have our own motivations, desires and

Figure 7.4 A representation of the four-colour theorem.

emotions. In other words, humans have a fully conscious awareness of the world around them. Or did you hear Watson celebrate its victory at Jeopardy! ?

On the other hand, the goal of general AI is to actually understand, reason and behave like a human would. There are many advantages to being able to recreate human intelligence. For starters, human intelligence is much more robust than any narrow AI. When a human sees a panda, it is always a panda. Likewise, Toronto would never be a human answer. A general AI would be able to learn new skills and abilities and generalise one knowledge domain to another. For example, if you can ride a car on the road and wish to ride a motorcycle, you would not need to learn everything from scratch because there is a lot of knowledge that you can transfer from the car domain to the motorcycle domain.

The American Cold War era science-fiction movie *War Games* (1983) perfectly illustrates the aspirational goal of general AI [326]. Seattle high school student and amateur hacker David Lightman unwillingly accesses the WOPR (War Operation Plan Response), a US military supercomputer programmed to learn the best possible strategy in case of a nuclear war. Upon entering the WOPR thinking that he had accessed the server of a computer games company, David decides to play the game of Global Thermonuclear War. This action starts a nuclear war simulation between the US and Russia with potentially fatal consequences on a global scale. WOPR could engage a mass launch of nuclear US missiles given a set of 10 launch codes which the machine can crack by brute force. In the final scene of the movie and with only five codes to go for missile launch, David decides to ask WOPR to play tic-tac-toe on the side. If played optimally, a tic-tac-toe game always ends up in a draw.

**Alice**

Figure 7.5 A schematic representation of the Turing test.

However, WOPR has not yet learnt the optimal strategy for this simple game and engages in calculating all 26,830 possible games. WOPR then finds all 10 launch codes and the worldwide nuclear attack is displayed on the screens. However, WOPR never launched the missiles for real because it managed to learn just in time that, as tic-tac-toe is a game where the only winning move is not to play, so is a nuclear war. The WOPR finally understood the purpose of the game and thus acquired a level of **human consciousness**.

## 7.3.1 The Turing Test

One fundamental question is how we can assess whether a machine possesses human-like intelligence. Alan Turing (1912–1954), the father of modern computation (the Turing machine) and artificial intelligence, proposed a test in his 1950 seminal paper 'Computing machinery and intelligence' [327]. The **Turing test** states that a program can be deemed intelligent if when interacting with a human, the person cannot tell whether they are communicating with another human or with a machine (irrespective of the answers being correct). The Turing test also requires a controlled testing environment, e.g. with all interaction occurring through typed messages behind a curtain to avoid requiring that the machine has the actual appearance of a human (Fig. 7.5).

It has been argued that programs like Google Duplex have already passed the Turing test, and therefore emulate human intelligence. Google Duplex [328] is a voice agent that can be run from your smartphone and call your dentist to make an appointment with a human receptionist at the other end of the line, while throwing in all the right set of pauses and exclamations. Would you give Google Duplex a pass at the Turing test?

English mathematician Ada Lovelace (1815–1852) was the first (theoretical) computer programmer in history and devised a test where for a machine to pass for a human it had to show some degree of creativity [329]. Perhaps we should ask machines to compose music, draw, or write stories, but this would also be much more difficult to evaluate than the Turing test. But one thing that escaped Turing is that his test really is a cultural test, and endless human cultures exist on this planet. Perhaps a better version of the Turing test would be to assess some degree of cultural understanding or adaptation? Along these lines Levesque and coworkers devised a Turing test based on Winograd schemas [330]. Winograd schemas are pairs of sentences that differ by one or two words and whose difference cannot be understood without a knowledge of the world. For instance, the following sentence:

*The trophy would not fit in the suitcase because it was too **small/large***

Here, if the last word is *small*, we are talking about the suitcase, whereas if the word of choice is *large* then we mean the trophy. In another example, if we say that 'Joan made sure to thank Susan for all the help she had given', who helped who?

The key thing about the Winograd Schema Challenge (WSC) questions is that they cannot be solved using statistics because they rely on selectional preferences or word associations. Thus, a satisfactory answer requires a machine to have common sense as well as an understanding of the physical world and how it works. For this reason a Turing test based on Winograd schemas is a much better assessment of a machine's linguistic and cultural fluency than a typed conversation. After all, our ability to create and understand culture is a very unique human characteristic.

Thanks to recent progress in neural language models machines can now solve the vast majority of the questions in the WSC, but is this because machines have acquired common sense? To answer this question, Sakaguchi and colleagues developed the WinoGrande dataset of 44,000 (harder) problems in 2020, and showed that humans still outperform computers by a long way [331].

Perhaps the importance of the Turing test does not lie in a machine eventually passing it, but in that it has served as a beacon for the development of intelligent systems over the past 70 years. For example, a fundamental aspect of human intelligence is being able to tell the difference between two similar objects. This concept motivated the development of classification algorithms such as SVMs as well as the biologically-inspired ANNs, and more recently deep learning.

## 7.3.2 Computers Can Only Solve Problems That Have Clear-Cut Answers

One thing that all learning problems have in common is that the end goal always is some sort of optimisation. For example, the goal when playing chess or Go is to win; when classifying images, the goal is to maximise the percentage of images that are correctly classified. Therefore, a single scalar quantity is used to define the success of most learning problems irrespective of their intrinsic difficulty. The learning problems that are especially difficult are those where the quantity to optimise is not well defined. This situation represents the majority of problems that human intelligence has to deal with in real life. Even for a simple chatbot, what should be the scalar quantity to optimise? The engagement with the customer, being informative and supportive (and how is that measured?), or perhaps building a recurrent relationship? Dealing with this type of real-world problems where the variable to optimise is not well-defined represents a formidable obstacle for the development of learning methods whose behaviour must approximate human intelligence.

Finally, the 2014 film *Ex Machina* takes the definition of the Turing test one step further and asks whether a machine is capable of making humans doubt about themselves even when they know they are talking to an intelligent humanoid robot [332]. This film was motivated by some very interesting debates about the meaning and purpose of AI, as well as why we should treat our robots ethically.

## 7.4   IS THE TECHNOLOGICAL SINGULARITY THE REAL THREAT?

The Technological Singularity is the idea that computers will one day surpass human intelligence. The Facebook bots that created their own language in 2017, and how the media reacted to this event is just an example of how quickly people accept doomsday scenarios where we are overruled by conscious machines [333]. The science fiction literature is full of similarly catastrophic examples, including the WOPR of *War Games* [326] and Terminator's Skynet where mankind eventually becomes extinct or dominated by machines [334]. Moreover, many influential speakers like Sam Harris argue that 'if we continue to build intelligent machines, at a certain point if they don't destroy us in the meantime we'll get into the end zone where we will have built something that is super-intelligent and far better placed than we will be for designing the next iteration of itself'. This phrase is just the introduction to his TED talk that has been viewed by millions of people [335]. Harris elaborates further by stating that:

> *Machines will not become malevolent automatically, it is just that we will build machines that are so much smarter than we are that the slightest divergence between our goals and their goals will destroy us.*

Prophecy manufacturers try to capitalise on human fear towards machines by producing well-articulated speeches where dangers are described in outline only and without providing immediate evidence. In science, evidence is carefully built on top of previous evidence, and caution must be exercised when listening to speakers that fail to provide scientific proof for all these assumptions and conjectures. Big words like 'arms race' and 'Manhattan project', as well as linking super-intelligence to God, are all marketing resources exploited by doomsday visionaries. Therefore, when you hear or read stories like this you should always question the evidence that the presenter is producing to support their claims.

### 7.4.1   Consciousness and the Chinese Room Experiment

Apocalyptic theories have little scientific ground to stand on. The current state of the art in much of narrow AI is so far away from the possibility that a general AI might evolve some form of destructive consciousness that it is impossible to imagine at present. For this to happen a machine must first be aware of itself (i.e. have *consciousness*), and also possess *intentionality* [336]. Consciousness is a fundamental human trait that can be defined as the sensory awareness of internal (the self) and external (the body, the world) existence. From an anatomical point of view it is generally accepted that conscious awareness is associated with the cerebral cortex, with other parts of the vertebrate nervous system (cerebellum, spinal cord) playing key roles too [337].

Some proponents of **strong AI** support the idea that brains are effectively computers and minds are software, and therefore the very human trait of consciousness can be programmed. Of course it is a formal possibility that one day human consciousness will be encapsulated in a machine, but the main danger of claims like these is that they currently cannot stand on their own feet. At present, although we all know intuitively what consciousness is, we still do not understand how it is generated. How could we possibly achieve human-level machine intelligence if we cannot understand or replicate such a fundamental human characteristic as consciousness?

Figure 7.6 The Chinese room experiment claims that machines cannot possess human consciousness.

John Searle argues that even if a machine passes the Turing test (and thus is deemed 'intelligent'), it may not necessarily have any consciousness [338]. In his Chinese room argument a man inside a room is passed on questions in Chinese (or any other language he cannot understand). With the help of a manual that specifies how to respond to Chinese symbols and their combinations, the person is able to produce meaningful answers in Chinese, which he does not understand either (Fig. 7.6, [339]). The man is operating on a set of instructions and clearly lacks consciousness on what he does. In the same way, a machine appearing conscious to an outside observer does not necessarily mean it has any consciousness. However, the experiment cannot prove the contrary either.

The presentation of the Chinese room experiment is a bit messy and can be criticised from multiple angles [338], but it is valuable because it has sparked ardent debates among various philosophers and computer scientists. Searle's point is that it is not difficult to question the lack of consciousness of a machine and that this very unique human trait should not be taken casually. Unfortunately, Searle is unable to clearly explain what consciousness is other than saying that it is caused by the brain's 'biological causal powers' [340].

### 7.4.2 Being a Maverick Is a Very Human Trait

Another problem with the majority of claims supporting the Technological Singularity is that they take a very narrow view on human intelligence. For one thing, why should machine intelligence have to resemble human intelligence? Physicist Richard Feynman (1918–1988) argued in 1985 that we try to make things work as efficiently as we can with the materials that we have. This is why when trying to build a fast-moving machine instead of trying to replicate a cheetah, building a car with four wheels is both simpler and more effective. Likewise, airplanes do not have to flap their wings like birds to be able to fly. In the same way, any arithmetic calculation done by a machine is infinitely faster and more efficient than the same calculation done by any human, even if the processes are different [341].

Moreover, humans are so much more than logical operations and computation. Human consciousness includes a sense of self which machines will not be able to replicate anytime soon, coupled with curiosity, imagination, intuition, emotions, desires, purpose, objectives, wisdom and even humour. If we think about humour, a good sense of humour means thinking outside of the box and connecting concepts and situations in novel ways, which is something that machines are unable to do. Truly independent thinking involves so much more than being a one-trick, rule-based pony like Watson playing Jeopardy! Human intelligence is not limited to specific domains, but exists in the open to challenge currently held views. For instance, Newton and Einstein's revolutionary ideas did not follow the rules of physics established at the time. Likewise, the fine arts have no rules and also exist in the open. Therefore, thinking that a machine can achieve a level of imagination, intuition, wisdom or purpose greater than humans is, in the absence of further evidence, only discussed by those who do not fully understand the finer details of human intelligence and free will.

Narrow AI, however, will continue to evolve at a very fast pace. Perhaps there is no need to develop any general AI since narrow AI has already shown it can outperform humans in the sort of tasks we would want to employ our computer systems to do. Narrow AI will gradually replace jobs, but only those jobs that are repetitive and therefore automatable. However, it is unlikely that narrow AI will replace humans for any job that involves anything more complex than doing something well, many, many times over. The good news about this is that we humans will have more time to focus on those tasks that make us truly human as we will be able to delegate the more mundane tasks onto machines. Since computers will help us do our work better, we can say that they will make us more intelligent. In the same way, medieval universities made people more intelligent by bringing thinkers together in a specific environment. The close collaboration between humans and machines is called **augmented intelligence** and is finally within reach since it was first proposed in the 1950s [342]. Perhaps the only singularity here is that narrow AI is changing the job landscape faster than we can adapt and retrain to remain useful and productive.

## 7.5   THE TROLLEY PROBLEM

The implementation of AI developments also depends on the extent to which society accepts them. At present most AI applications work alongside people thus giving rise to a new paradigm in socio-technological relations where different ethical dilemmas frequently emerge. A well-known ethical dilemma that is always presented in the context of fully autonomous vehicles is the trolley problem, a thought experiment presented by British philosopher Philippa Foot in 1967 [343]. Here a runaway train is about to kill five bystanders that are unaware of the oncoming train. The only thing that you, the observer, can do is to pull a lever that will divert the train onto another track and kill just one person instead of five (Fig. 7.7, [344]). What would you do?

1. Do nothing—the train continues its course and all five bystanders die.

2. Pull the lever to save those five people at the expense of one human life.

Most people say they would pull the lever as killing one person appears to be better than killing five [345]. This ethical view is known as *utilitarianism*, which states that the right choice is the one that maximises happiness and well-being for all affected individuals [346].

However, moral inconsistencies started to emerge when variations of the trolley problem were introduced a few years later. For example, Judith Thomson's 'footbridge' version depicts a trolley heading towards the same five men who are standing on a track after a bridge under which the trolley must pass. A large man is standing on the bridge, and your only chance to save these five men (since there is no lever) is to push this man over the bridge and thus stop the trolley [347]. Would you push him?

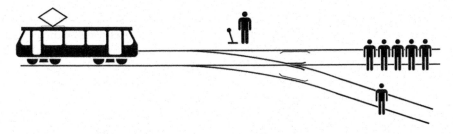

Figure 7.7 The trolley problem: Would you save the five people in danger while intentionally killing just one person?

Here most people would not push the man over the bridge even though the end result is the same (one death vs five deaths). Does this mean that our moral compass is continually shifting? If this were the case it would be a tremendous problem for enforcing ethical rules onto AI because people would continually disagree on fundamental moral choices.

Most likely the change of mindset is associated with the difference between the intention of *killing* (pushing the man over the bridge) and *letting someone die* since pulling the lever does not kill the one person directly [348]. This is a clear deviation from utilitarianism because here the moral outcome of the action does not depend on the results of the action, but on the intention. This opposing view is called *kantianism*, after German philosopher Immanuel Kant (1724–1804). Kant believed that the goodness of an action must be guided by pure reason, irrespective of the consequences [349]. Of course Kant hoped that the consequences of good actions are also good. Moreover, Kant correctly pointed out that the outcome of an action on which the moral outcome of utilitarianism rests cannot be known *a priori*, and that the idea of happiness is rather subjective and appeals to baser instincts (instead of higher intellectual powers). Therefore Kant believed that utilitarian theories are no more moral than acting out of selfishness and that by design they devalue the individuals they are meant to benefit.

Psychologist Joshua Greene sought to answer the moral contradiction of why for the same people it is acceptable to sacrifice one person to save five in the trolley dilemma but not in the footbridge dilemma [345]. To do this, Greene decided to investigate the changes in brain activity occurring in the brains of subjects interrogated for various moral-impersonal (e.g. the trolley dilemma) and moral-personal (e.g. the footbridge dilemma) questions. The technique of functional magnetic resonance imaging (fMRI) works by detecting changes in blood flow (a proxy for brain activity), and showed that moral-personal puzzles like the footbridge dilemma activate parts of the brain that are associated with emotions, which by definition prevail over logical, rational thinking. Therefore, when we decide to pull the lever we are making a (moral-impersonal) conscious choice that will result in saving a larger number of lives. However, most of us are less likely to engage in 'inappropriate' moral-personal decisions as we possess an emotional mechanism that prevents us from personally causing harm. Those subjects that selected 'inappropriate' moral-personal responses (e.g. they would push the man off the bridge) were significantly slower to respond, suggesting that they had to overcome some type of hurdle.

Since Greene found that different parts of the brain are associated with different answers to moral dilemmas, which should govern our moral actions, our emotional brain or our rational brain?

The problem actually becomes trickier because one big limitation of surveys and experiments done in nice hospital rooms is that they do not always match reality. In 2017 psychologist Michael Stevens conducted the actual trolley problem experiment by simulating a scenario where participants would have to make the choice of pulling the lever [350]. The subjects thought they were part of a focus group to provide feedback on a high speed train project. While waiting for the focus group session under the Californian sun, each subject was invited to wait inside an air-conditioned railroad switching station where an actor pretending to be an operator was friendly enough to explain what his work consisted of and eventually let each subject have a taster of pulling the lever under his supervision. Once each participant had learnt how to switch the tracks, the operator leaves the room to take a personal call and a pre-recorded video of the trolley problem with actual people on the tracks is shown on the screen as if it were a real situation. Every single participant thought they were responsible for choosing between one and five human lives.

Out of seven participants, only two actually pulled the lever. The five that did nothing justified their inaction by diffusing their responsibility ('the trains probably had sensors', 'the workers would have noticed'). The actual video of the experiment is available in [350]. In physiological terms, these five subjects simply 'froze'. The freezing response is a defensive and survival mechanism that becomes activated when we face great danger (another well-known response is the fight-or-flight reaction). For example, in the presence of a predator it may make sense to stay immobile to try to avoid detection and thus 'freeze' [351]. But can we even ask if it was wrong of them to freeze?

Freezing is an ancient, hard-wired mechanism that was developed as part of the co-evolution of prey and predator. Therefore there cannot be a right or wrong reaction to the trolley problem experiment because, like the fight-or-flight response, the freezing response is also controlled by the amygdala [351]. When we face great threat or stress, *amygdala hijack* occurs and the higher functions of the brain are temporarily shut down [352]. When you try to fight your biology, you always lose.

In summary, although there is no right or wrong answer to the trolley problem it is always presented in the context of autonomous vehicles - just think of a vehicle approaching a zebra crossing instead of a trolley on tracks. Questioning whether AI-driven vehicles will be able to make *humane* decisions limits the acceptance of AI and its incorporation into our lives. And while philosophical discussions are essential for making progress, it is equally important to be able to dissect a philosophical conundrum. In the following sections we do this by mapping the theoretical aspects of the question onto the actual underlying technology and our own human biases to show that a philosophical conundrum such as the trolley problem is, effectively, a fallacy that delays society's understanding and acceptance of AI.

## 7.5.1 Reinforcement Learning, the 4th Learning Paradigm

Reinforcement learning is a machine learning approach that is a key part of the technology that makes autonomous vehicles possible. During reinforcement learning an **agent** learns by interacting with its **environment** through the execution of sequential actions (Fig. 7.8). Each action ($A_t$) results in a positive or a negative **reward**, as well as in updated information on the agent's new **state**. The ultimate goal of reinforcement learning is that the agent learns an optimal, or nearly-optimal, policy that maximises the expected cumulative reward [353].

Recall that the traditional learning paradigms (unsupervised, supervised and semi-supervised learning) differ both in the amount of labelled input data as well as in their goals. Unsupervised learning works with unlabelled data and the goal here is to uncover the underlying structure in the data for useful insights, for instance by clustering or by association rule analysis (Chapter 2). When the data are perfectly labelled in terms of input and output values we can use a number of (supervised learning) algorithms to predict classes or continuous values. To do this, the input data must be thoughtfully separated into training and test sets, modelled and the performance of the predictive method carefully evaluated using metrics that are appropriate for the specific prediction problem (Fig. 3.4, Chapters 3 and 4). Semi-supervised learning is the intermediate situation that actually represents the majority of real-world learning problems where we wish to carry out predictions but we

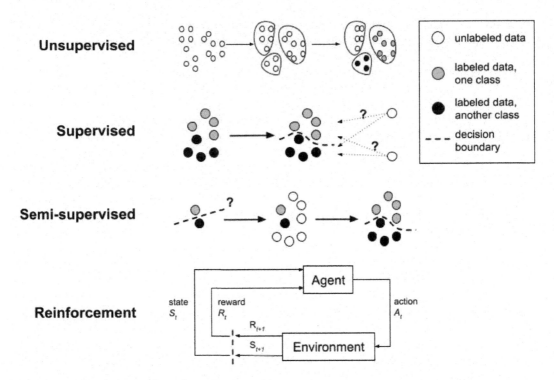

Figure 7.8 The four machine learning paradigms.

only have a small set of labelled observations. Techniques such as pseudolabelling can help label unlabelled data and thus improve the quality of the predictions iteratively (Fig. 3.5, Chapter 3).

All predictive methods involve a 'supervisor' that provides feedback on the quality of the prediction. Reinforcement learning methods, on the other hand, have no supervisor nor initial input data but they dynamically gather data and receive feedback through the interaction of the agent with its environment. The output of reinforcement learning is the action that the agent thinks will maximise its reward given its current state. Reinforcement learning is useful in any type of problem that presents a long-term vs a short-term reward trade-off, such as autonomous vehicles, games (e.g. AlphaGo), robot control, game theory, decision making and multi-agent systems.

In practice, reinforcement learning is used by autonomous vehicle companies to different extents, from start-ups like Wayve (wayve.ai) whose goal is to rely exclusive on reinforcement learning to Google's Waymo which also relies on supervised learning [354]. Supervised learning algorithms also have their place because they can address some driving situations more efficiently, such as predicting the behaviour of neighbouring vehicles (VectorNet, [355]). However, despite the ability of reinforcement learning algorithms to learn complex behaviours in high-dimensional environments, there are still many real-world challenges that must be solved before fully autonomous vehicles become a reality [356]. For example, agreeing on how to validate the performance of a reinforcement learning algorithm ('how well does it generalise?') is a very active area of research. *Sample efficiency* is another key topic: animals can learn from relatively few examples because they have prior knowledge about their environment, but more efficient reinforcement learning algorithms should be able to learn from fewer samples. Another important problem is bridging the

Figure 7.9 An autonomous vehicle learning to find the exit in a garage.

*simulation-reality gap*: Perfectly annotated simulation data is of great learning value if the knowledge could be flawlessly transferred to real-world situations.

### 7.5.1.1  A Simple Example with an Autonomous Vehicle

Reinforcement learning can be broken down into various, specific problems that are dealt with using different algorithms. As an example, let us imagine an autonomous vehicle that is parked inside a garage at position (state) (1,1) and must learn to find the exit state (5,7) (Fig. 7.9). This type of scenario is typically modelled in the form of a *Markov decision process*. Here the set of rewards for the learning exercise must be provided before the learning starts (but can be adjusted later on). A simplistic set of rewards could be as follows:

- +1 for moving into an available position

- −1 for bumping into a wall

- +25 for finding the exit position (5,7)

The set of rewards programs the agent to seek a maximum overall reward to achieve an optimal solution. An autonomous vehicle in position (1,1) that has not been exposed to any form of training thinks that all possible moves (up, down, right, left) are equally good. Once the vehicle starts interacting with its environment it soon learns that driving left or down into a wall carries a negative reward (−1), and that only by driving into the cell above or

TABLE 7.1   The Set of Updated, Predicted Rewards for
Position (1,1)

| State | (1,1) | | | |
|---|---|---|---|---|
| Action | Up | Down | Left | Right |
| Predicted reward | 0 | 0 | 0 | 0 |
| Q-value (predicted reward) | 1 | −1 | −1 | 1 |

the one to the right is associated with a positive reward. This new knowledge updates the vehicle's table of predicted rewards (Q-values) for a given position (Table 7.1).

The agent quickly learns that driving to the right has a positive reward, and thus by adopting this *greedy policy* it is likely that it will eventually find the way to the exit by following the path indicated by the black dots (Fig. 7.9). A policy simply is a strategy derived from the probability table that tells the agent the likelihood of certain actions resulting in rewards.

The path that exploits the knowledge described by the greedy policy ('driving to the right makes sense'), however, takes 14 steps from (1,1) to the exit (5,7), whereas the path indicated by the green dots takes only 10 steps and can only be discovered by challenging the initial greedy policy (Fig. 7.9). This **exploration-exploitation** trade-off is defined for each problem by adjusting penalties and rewards. If the cost of making a mistake is relatively small, then exploration is favoured because the agent learns faster, whereas if the agent operates in real time and mistakes must be kept to a minimum, then exploitation is preferable.

Many situations, however, cannot be described by (datasets of) a well-defined garage with walls and a clear exit, such as when trying to teach a drone to fly while avoiding unpredictable, dynamic obstacles like moving humans. When not enough data is available and simulations do not quite match reality, one extremely effective strategy to learn a solid navigation policy is to simply let the vehicle learn what not to do by following naïve trajectories and crashing as many as 11,500 times (often against dynamic obstacles including humans) as was done by researchers at Carnegie Mellon University [357]. Quoting Mark Twain, '*if you hold a cat by the tail, you learn things that cannot be learned in any other way*'.

Back to the garage example, once the agent has explored enough and updated its table of predicted rewards for as many positions as possible, the next problem is for the agent to devise a more global strategy. The calculation of future rewards (thanks to the Bellman equation) allows the agent to think several steps ahead. Together with additional exploration, this allows the agent to update the Q-values table detailing how desirable any given state is (Q-learning). This is similar to playing chess with an expert player who can anticipate the consequences of an action several moves ahead: Sometimes it pays off to sacrifice an immediate reward (e.g. a pawn) to gain more long-term reward (e.g. capture a bishop later). In summary, the optimisation of Q-values by Q-learning leads to the implementation of a more efficient policy that can direct the agent to finding the optimal path to the exit while maximising the overall reward.

### 7.5.1.2   Autonomous Driving in the Real World

A real driving situation is far more complex than the garage example as it is not possible to store every Q-value for every single state, for every road and for every possible situation in the world. And what about additional factors such as changing weather conditions and traffic disruptions? Here, instead of storing Q-values, the practical approach is to apply

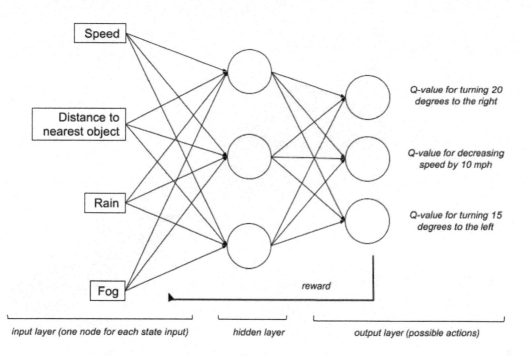

Figure 7.10 A simplified deep Q-network for a more realistic autonomous driving scenario.

deep Q-learning (neural networks) to approximate the Q-values of possible actions in real time given state inputs (Fig. 7.10).

For example, a sensor that detects another vehicle that stands still in the middle of the road will generate specific Q-values for each possible action and will probably give the order to stop (the action with the highest predicted Q-value), or otherwise the autonomous vehicle will crash, resulting in a very negative reward. Autonomous vehicles are able to perceive their environment by integrating information from many different types of sensors and other technologies (Fig. 7.11) [358]:

- **Cameras:** A combination of wide view/short range and narrow view/long range cameras provide stereo visual information on the vehicle's surroundings. Cameras operate in the visible light or the infrared range and, although inexpensive, they are unable to calculate distances accurately and do not work well in poor visibility conditions (heavy rain, fog, at night) or when the road lanes are not properly marked.

- **Radars** collect information on an object's location and speed by emitting radio waves that echo back to the sensor upon hitting an object. Unlike cameras, radars are not affected by adverse weather conditions.

- **LiDAR** (Light Detection and Ranging) sensors are similar to radars in that they emit ultra-fast laser signals that bounce back to obtain a detailed, three-dimensional picture of the vehicle's environment (cars, pedestrians and any other objects), with accurate distances. LiDAR sensors are essential in fully autonomous vehicles, but on the other hand they are costly and have important limitations [358].

- **Ultrasonic sensors** emit sonic waves below the human audible range which echo back to a sensor (like radar and LiDAR sensors), and are useful at very short distances (e.g. when parking).

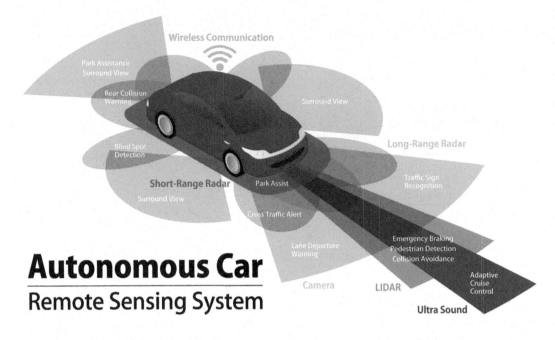

Figure 7.11 The different classes of sensors present in autonomous vehicles.

TABLE 7.2   Characteristics of the Sensor Types Found in Autonomous Vehicles

| Feature | Camera | RADAR | LiDAR | Ultrasound |
|---|---|---|---|---|
| Technology | Light | Radio wave | Laser beam | Sound wave |
| Range (m) | ~200 | ~250 | ~200 | ~5 |
| Resolution | Very good | Average | Good | Poor |
| Speed detection | Poor | Very good | Good | Poor |
| Distance detection | Poor | Very good | Good | Good |
| Interference susceptibility | Very good | Poor | Good | Good |

- **Global Positioning System (GPS)** allows finding your location anywhere on the planet by *trilateration* ('overlap') as long as the receiver can locate at least four of the 31 operational satellites that enable this technology.

All types of sensors are affected by weather conditions, but only cameras that operate in the visible light range are affected by lighting conditions. Since different sensors have specific strengths and limitations their information must be combined ('sensor fusion') to cover different ranges and conditions, speeds and vulnerabilities to changing weather, and thus ensure safe driving and collision avoidance (Table 7.2, adapted from [358]).

### 7.5.2   Is the Trolley Problem a Real Problem?

We can argue that the trolley problem is unrelated to fully autonomous vehicles for three reasons:

First, the trolley problem describes a one-off moral decision that must be taken by a person. Autonomous vehicles, on the other hand, are non-moral agents that never have to make one-off decisions like pulling a lever. Rather, each one of their sequential actions is the product of a combination of overlapping probability distributions for any one state and whose ultimate goal is to obtain the highest reward [359].

Moreover, both the trolley problem and the example of the autonomous vehicle that must learn how to exit the garage are situations where all variables and possible states are known from the start. These conditions can be conveniently modelled as Markov decision processes (Fig. 7.9). The real world, however, is not a closed system where all possible states can be known (complete knowledge), but a dynamic environment with a high degree of uncertainty that changes the original moral question. The driving of autonomous vehicles in the real world should rather be modelled as *partially observed Markov decision processes (POMDP)* [359].

Second, in an environment that can be modelled as a Markov decision process there is no more learning to do beyond a certain point. On the other hand, an agent that is placed in a dynamic and partially observable environment cannot ever learn all the possible rules or anticipate all possible situations. Thus, the continuous training and testing of autonomous vehicles in realistic settings maximises the learning and minimises the possibility of encountering unpredictable events.

Third, it is unlikely that properly designed, fully autonomous vehicles will get involved in accidents as it will be their priority to avoid them. Simply think from the legal and marketing perspectives: Would you buy an autonomous vehicle that could get you into a situation where it must choose between the lives of strangers instead of protecting its passengers in the first place?

Given a car's environment and driving conditions, the entire system is designed to integrate information and make decisions within a certain reliability range. Adverse weather conditions (e.g. fog, rain, lightning, thunder, snow) affect the performance of all types of sensors, and being able to drive safely in severe weather is one major challenge for the development of autonomous vehicles [358]. Therefore, if a system feels it is not be able to detect a hazard under the current driving conditions, it will probably increase the safety measures (e.g. distance to objects), or will directly stop. Thus, many intermediate decisions are made before an accident takes place. It would not make sense to design a system that operates in a way that cannot avoid a collision, or would be programmed to make moral choices among two negative outcomes.

### 7.5.2.1 Disentangling the Statistics also Helps with Acceptance

Understanding the details of the technology behind autonomous vehicles is key for dissipating irrational fears such as those introduced by the trolley problem.

Another key element that will lead to the acceptance of AI into our lives is having an understanding of what can be realistically expected. For example, there is this common hype that the future introduction of fully autonomous vehicles (without human driver supervision) will lead to zero fatalities. Here a simple examination of the US car accident statistics explains why this will never be possible:

In 2015 a total of 32,166 accidents involving 48,923 vehicles led to 35,092 fatalities [360]. For starters ∼21% of these accidents occurred in adverse weather conditions (mostly rain and snow) [358], which would probably have been avoided by autonomous driving systems that cannot guarantee safe driving. These figures represent an average of ∼1.5 cars per accident (since a car may also crash into a tree or a wall) and ∼1 fatality per accident. Of these 35,092 fatalities, the majority (∼68%) were occupants of the car, of which more than half were not wearing their seat belts. If the passenger of an autonomous vehicle does not wear their seat belt and dies as a result of an accident, the statistics remain the same but who will be blamed, the passenger or the autonomous vehicle on which we have put our trust?

Of the 35,092 fatalities, the remaining one third were either pedestrians (∼16%), motorcycle riders (∼14%) or cyclists (∼2%). Even the best trained autonomous vehicle will not be able to avoid a pedestrian running into the car from nowhere, or a rider suddenly taking a sharp turn without looking. In such cases we might never know who was at fault, but it is likely that the autonomous vehicle will take the lion's share of the guilt in people's minds.

Finally, drunk drivers were involved in ~15% of accidents and ~20% of deaths were attributed to fatigue (e.g. a vehicle hitting a roadside tree). Therefore, although an autonomous vehicle will never get drunk or become fatigued, it works against the acceptance of AI to irrationally believe that technologies such as autonomous vehicles must achieve absolute perfection and thus a zero fatality rate on the road. The majority of fatalities will be unavoidable because of the human element involved, be it human-driven cars, riders or pedestrians. Still, every time a prototype autonomous vehicle is involved in an accident there is massive coverage in the news despite these events being so rare compared to the deaths brought about by human drivers [360].

### 7.5.2.2 Unanswered Ethical Questions

We can assume that fully autonomous vehicles will eventually become part of our lives since they will eventually drive better than people and thus will offer many societal benefits and commercial opportunities. In fact, Google's Waymo can already drive for 8200 Km without making a single mistake [361]. However, presenting the trolley problem in the context of fully autonomous vehicles is not only meaningless but also a distraction from other ethical questions that we should be asking [359].

For example, if we assume that retailers will start using fully autonomous vehicles to provide higher levels of premium service, does this mean that those living in remote, less affluent areas will be further discriminated? If autonomous vehicles are used in public transport to reduce the mobility gap for those living in remote locations, is there a specific group of people that should be given priority to travel? How should we deal with situations of harassment and crime inside the vehicle? And what about surveillance and privacy issues?

The development of any AI-based technology presents ethical dilemmas that we must learn to discuss thoughtfully. In another example, how is your personal data processed by Siri (Apple) and Alexa (Amazon) in order to learn and improve as personal assistants? Since personal assistants improve by learning from all users, how is your right to data privacy handled while giving you access to the benefit of its processing at the same time? Over time Siri and Alexa will evolve into robots that help with household chores and interact with family members, from babies to adults. What ethical direction will we teach them when, in many cases we do not even know how to make the right ethical decisions? Robots and autonomous vehicles present examples of ethical conundrums that constitute a bottleneck for the development of many industries, and which must be solved on a level different from the one where they originated.

## 7.6  ROBOTS REFLECT OUR OWN HUMANITY

Humans have always had a love-fear relationship with machines. On the one hand they make our lives easier but on the other hand we often see them with suspicion. Biochemist and science fiction writer Isaac Asimov wrote the Three Laws of Robotics in 1950 [362, 363] (and as depicted in Will Smith's movie *I, Robot* [364]) in an effort to diminish our distrust towards machines:

- *First Law*—a robot may not injure a human being or, through inaction, allow a human being to come to harm.

- *Second Law*—a robot must obey the orders given it by human beings except where such orders would conflict with the First Law.

- *Third Law*—a robot must protect its own existence as long as such protection does not conflict with the First or Second Law.

Humans distrust those machines that perform better than us at certain tasks (a phenomenon called *algorithm aversion* [365]), but at the same time we demand a degree of perfection that we are not capable of. Despite Waymo (Google's Autonomous Vehicle) being able to safely drive for 8,200 Km [361], 56% of Americans say that they would never be driven around by a fully autonomous vehicle [366]. As discussed in the trolley problem section, having a detailed understanding of any technology and its capabilities is key for its acceptance in society.

Robots already provide tangible benefits such as relieving loneliness and facilitating communication and thus are currently used in hospitals, schools and business settings. And it will not take long before we are surrounded by home robots with significant AI capabilities. A fundamental question here is: While we expect machines to behave morally towards humans, should we also treat machines in morally acceptable ways?

The short answer is yes, because the more we interact with machines and robots, the more attached we become to them [367]. Can you remember actor Joaquin Phoenix's loving relationship with his virtual girlfriend in the movie *Her* [368, 369]?

Emotional attachment is a basic human instinct that can be both good and bad: For instance, a soldier trying to save an injured robot from a landmine field can be outright deadly, whereas autistic children therapy with robots (a field called *Social Robotics*) often yields better results than with adults [370].

Our anthropomorphism goes even further if the robot in question can move (especially if it does so autonomously) and we can also touch it: You may remember the story of hitch-BOT, a friendly robot invented by David Smith of McMaster University who could barely speak and whose only mission was to autostop [371]. hitchBOT ended up travelling throughout Europe and North America thanks to the sympathy he generated (Fig. 7.12, [372]). His murder in Philadelphia in 2015 had huge repercussions across the planet because thousands of strangers had developed *empathy* and become emotionally attached to hitchBOT [373] despite never having met him [367].

Besides solving the ethical dilemmas that developments in AI and robotics continually present (e.g. safety and privacy issues, job loss), our next frontier will be to learn to treat our machines ethically. And not because they might rebel against us but because not being ethical to them will damage us psychologically [369]. Robots are a reflection of our humanity and their development is making us question fundamental concepts in human behaviour (towards robots and towards other humans) and moral philosophy [374]. Perhaps robots' mission in disguise is to teach us how to become a better version of ourselves?

## 7.7  FURTHER READING

- **Websites**

  - **AI organisations**
    * The American Association for Artificial Intelligence (AAAI, www.aaai.org)
    * The European Coordinating Committee for Artificial Intelligence (ECCAI, www.eccai.org)
    * The Association for Computing Machinery's special interest group (www.acm.org/sigart)
  - **Continual AI**
    URL: www.continualai.org
    *Continual AI is the recently created, open and global community of continual*

Figure 7.12 hitchBOT on its way to Neuschwanstein Castle in Southern Germany.

*AI practitioners. They have a very interesting regular newsletter that keeps us informed of this essential and fast-developing field.*

- **Philosophy of Artificial Intelligence (PhilPapers, edited by Eric Dietrich)**
  URL: https://bit.ly/3F1GPxQ
  *Here is the main bibliography on the broad topic of the philosophy of artificial intelligence.*

- **The Turing archive for the history of computing**
  URL: www.alanturing.net
  *A curated archive of the life and work of Alan Turing, including declassified codebreaking documents from World War II.*

- **The Turing digital archive**
  URL: www.turingarchive.org/
  *An alternative source on the life and work of Alan Turing containing nearly 3,000*

*images scanned from the collection held at King's College, Cambridge. The images are of handwritten letters, photographs, newspaper articles, and unpublished work.*

- Podcasts

  - **Artificial Intelligence with Lex Fridman, MIT AI**
    URL: /lexfridman.com/podcast/
    *Lex Fridman is an MIT researcher working on autonomous vehicles and human-robot interaction. In his podcasts Lex interviews high-profile intellectuals and tycoons to discuss AI from multiple perspectives.*

  - **Concerning AI**
    URL: concerning.ai
    *The interviews here tend to discuss AI from a societal and philosophical perspective, but the content is accessible and entertaining.*

  - **The AI Podcast from NVIDIA**
    URL: soundcloud.com/theaipodcast
    *AI experts explain the intricacies of some cool AI applications as well as other conceptual problems in AI*

  - **This Week in Machine Learning & AI**
    URL: twimlai.com/shows/
    *Under-an-hour interviews with experts from industry and academia on a variety of cutting-edge AI topics and technologies.*

- Videos

  - **AlphaGo - The Movie**
    URL: https://bit.ly/3jbTUMl
    *The award-winning documentary behind AlphaGo, what it can teach us about us human intelligence.*

  - **Can Digital Computers Think? (Alan Turing, 1951)**
    URL: https://bit.ly/3DdT9tZ
    *This is a rerecording from Alan Turing's original script of the lecture that was broadcast by the BBC in May 1951.*

  - **Can machines think? (Richard Feynman, 1985)**
    URL: https://bit.ly/3iU5VWS
    *'Do you think there will ever be a machine that will think like human beings and be more intelligent than human beings?'—this recording is Feynman's brilliant, unprepared answer during a Q&A session after a lecture he gave in 1985. Feynman anticipated current concepts, developments and problems in AI, discusses how computational intelligence cannot possibly evolve into humanoid intelligence, and how to define the concept of intelligence—the equivalent of what we now call 'narrow AI'.*

  - **How AI can bring on a second industrial revolution (Kevin Kelly, TEDx)**
    URL: https://bit.ly/3s3c0lj
    *Kevin Kelly was for many years WIRED's Editor-At-Large and a proven visionary that is worth listening to. In this TEDx talk Dr. Kelly discussed his ideas for the future of AI. As an example of how far ahead of everyone else he typically is I recommend reading his 1999 book 'New Rules for the New Economy'.*

- **IBM Watson full Q&A session (Oxford Union, 17 July 2016)**
  URL: https://bit.ly/3Fi6sLP
  *The Oxford Union is arguably the world's most prestigious debating society, having invited the world's most prominent figures including many US presidents, the Dalai Lama, Mother Teresa, Diego Maradona and Michael Jackson. This time the guest is a robot that provides a public demonstration of IBM Watson's cognitive capabilities and discusses what the future holds for AI and augmented intelligence.*

- **Learning to fly by crashing**
  URL: https://youtu.be/u151hJaGKUo
  *This video shows the drone endowed with a self-supervised learning strategy that crashed 11,500 times in order to learn a solid navigation policy in a complex and dynamic environment.*

- **So what is a robot really? (WIRED, 23 August 2017)**
  URL: https://bit.ly/30iBzqP
  *There are many different kinds of robots and we must be careful about what we call a robot because of the many legal, contractual and ethical implications. Despite robots becoming a part of our lives, we still are unable to agree on what a robot is.*

- **The Man Vs The Machine (Frank Marshall)**
  URL: https://bit.ly/2YATdVR
  *An entertaining 17-minute documentary on Garry Kasparov's historic match against IBM's Deep Blue.*

- **The Trolley Problem in Real Life (Vsauce, 6 December 2017)**
  URL: https://bit.ly/30WFF81
  *This is Michael Stevens' documentary on the experiment he conducted on the trolley problem, including his preparation with an ethics committee.*

- **Why we have an emotional connection to robots (Kate Darling)**
  URL: https://bit.ly/2YzBez7
  *This is Kate Darling's engaging TED talk on how we are wired to develop an emotional connection with autonomous machines and what this can teach us about ourselves.*

- **Articles**

  - **AlphaFold Team. AlphaFold: a solution to a 50-year-old grand challenge in biology (DeepMind Blog Post Research, 30 November 2020).**
    URL: https://bit.ly/3lLWme7
    *An accessible account of the protein-folding problem and how AlphaFold works, written by the authors themselves.*

  - **Anderson MR. Twenty years on from Deep Blue vs Kasparov: how a chess match started the big data revolution (The Conversation, 11 May 2017).**
    URL: https://bit.ly/3DkhvSM
    *A short and entertaining account of the story behind the development of IBM's Deep Blue that beat world chess champion Garry Kasparov in 1997. This article not only discusses both hardware and software developments but also the tactical mistakes that both Kasparov and Deep Blue made. The author argues that Deep Blue's triumph was partly due to a bug in the code that made it make an unconventional move during the first game. This was interpreted by Kasparov as*

*a deeper strategy, which made him lose his composure. Was Deep Blue's victory partly due to the inherent frailty of the human mind?*

- Biggio B, Roli F. **Wild patterns: Ten years after the rise of adversarial machine learning. Pattern Recognition 84: 317–331, 2018.**
  *An excellent review of the evolution of adversarial examples and its countermeasures, detailing the main threat models and attacks, how to evaluate the security of learning algorithms and future challenges in the field of adversarial machine learning.*

- Braga A and Logan RK. **AI and the Singularity: A Fallacy or a Great Opportunity? Information 10(2): 73, 2019.**
  *This is the editorial article to a special issue on the Technological Singularity where invited experts debate from all sides. The issue can be found here: https://bit.ly/3F0v8az*

- Hadsell R, Rao D, Rusu AA and Pascanu R. **Embracing Change: Continual Learning in Deep Neural Networks. Trends in Cognitive Sciences 24(12): 1028–1040, 2020.**
  *A clearly written and insightful review on continual learning where parallels are drawn between biological mechanisms and a taxonomy of computational solutions. The authors also discuss the future and perils of continual learning.*

- Heaven D. **Why deep-learning AIs are so easy to fool. Nature 574: 163–166, 2019.**
  *An accessible and balanced overview to adversarial machine learning in the context of applications to real life, including robots, with an interesting discussion on how to make algorithms resilient to adversarial input.*

- Maxfield M. **When Genetic Algorithms Meet Artificial Intelligence (Electronic Engineering Journal, 9 July 2020).**
  URL: https://bit.ly/3vlBFJh
  *An entertaining article on the application of evolutionary algorithms to optimise the actual design of a camera system for computer vision tasks. Evolutionary algorithms are inspired by Darwin's concept of the 'survival of the fittest' to find the optimal solution across simulated generations of intermediate solutions. This is a narrow AI application in instrument design that clearly surpasses the ability of humans in the same time frame. The end result of this example is the automatic maximisation of image quality and computer vision results.*

- McCarthy J. **What is Artificial Intelligence? (Computer Science Department, Stanford University, 12 November 2007).**
  URL: https://stanford.io/3pdoMA1
  *A Q&A session with John McCarthy (1927–2011) where this pioneer who coined the term 'Artificial Intelligence' answers fundamental questions on AI in a non-technical way, including the various branches of AI and the related philosophical theories.*

- Ornes S. **How Close Are Computers to Automating Mathematical Reasoning? (Quanta Magazine, 27 August 2020).**
  URL: https://bit.ly/3DkL4Ul
  *An insightful discussion on the types of problems that computers can solve, and the ones they yet can't.*

- Strickland E. **How IBM Watson overpromised and underdelivered on AI healthcare (IEEE Spectrum, 2 April 2019).**
  URL: https://bit.ly/3FgfUiJ

*IBM Watson has enjoyed much success in specific narrow and controlled applications, but is thinking in statistical terms good enough for curing patients? What is the mismatch between how Watson thinks and the way that things work in the clinic?*

– **Turing A. Computing machinery and intelligence. Mind vol. LIX(236): 433–460, 1950.**
*This is Alan Turing's groundbreaking paper where he discusses the Turing test for the first time as an approximation to the question of whether a machine can think.*

- **Books**

  – Darling K. *The New Breed: What Our History with Animals Reveals about Our Future with Robots* Henry Holt & Company, New York (NY), USA, 2021. ISBN-10: 1250296102.
  *Kate Darling believes that robots should not be seen not as threatening replacements for humans, but more like beneficial pets or traditional working animals, and be treated ethically. Adopting this mindset will unlock the potential of robots as collaborators, and will shed light on our understanding of human-to-human and human-to-animal interactions.*

  – Hodges A. *Alan Turing: The Enigma (updated edition)* Princeton University Press, Princeton (NJ), USA, 2014. ISBN-10: 9780691164724.
  *An enlightening and meticulously researched biography of Alan Turing on which the 2014 film The imitation game [375] is based. Turing was raised by foster parents and had a life that was both fascinating and tragic. Despite working out the Nazi's encrypted messages that eventually helped to win World War II, Turing was cruelly betrayed by his own country because of his homosexuality. The mathematical parts are absorbing and discussed in sufficient detail to help us understand how Turing's knowledge of mathematics and logic was applied to solve some of the greatest challenges of his time.*

  – Lin P, Abney K, Jenkins R (editors). *Robot Ethics 2.0: From Autonomous Cars to Artificial Intelligence (1st Edition)* Oxford University Press, Oxford, UK, 2017. ISBN-10: 0190652950.
  *An interesting set of articles centered around human-robot interaction topics, including trust, legal framing, applications and ethics.*

  – Nowotny H. *In AI We Trust: Power, Illusion and Control of Predictive Algorithms.* Polity, Cambridge, UK, 2021. ISBN-10: 1509548815.
  *Helga Nowotny discusses the current, critical intersection of AI and humanity. Whereas AI is meant to make life easy and predictable, it also restricts the influence we can exert on our own future. If AI is not to limit the narrative progress of humanity we must understand its limitations and how it affects our own view of the world.*

  – Sutton RS, Barto AG. *Reinforcement Learning: An Introduction.* MIT Press, Cambridge (MA), USA, 2018. ISBN-10: 0262039249.
  *An excellent and very clearly written introduction to the key concepts in reinforcement learning and their underlying motivations.*

## 7.8   CHAPTER REVIEW QUESTIONS

1. **Watson answered 'Toronto' instead of 'Chicago' because**

    (a) The underlying algorithm failed.

    (b) Watson did not understand the question properly.

    (c) 'Toronto' being found in association with 'largest airport' more often than 'Chicago' was in its sources of information.

    (d) Toronto's airport is bigger than Chicago.

2. **A home robot that can help you cook, regulate your home temperature and order a pizza on Fridays is an example of**

    (a) A general AI application.

    (b) A narrow AI application.

3. **The goal of general AI is**

    (a) To enhance the abilities of narrow AI applications.

    (b) To replicate the way that humans understand, reason, feel and behave.

    (c) To excel at specific tasks, but with better performance.

    (d) An excuse to frighten everyone and to make cool movies.

4. **Adversarial attacks have been described for every type of learning model and data type. In the context of image recognition an adversarial attack may be engineered by**

    (a) Adding a bit of noise to the input image.

    (b) Feeding the classifier an image that is completely different from those it has been trained with.

    (c) By placing a second object next to the one being classified.

    (d) By showing the same object under different lighting conditions.

5. **Augmented intelligence is**

    (a) One of the goals of general AI, which is becoming smarter each year.

    (b) The collaboration between narrow AI applications and humans in a way that will assist us in doing our work better.

    (c) The difference between narrow AI and general AI.

    (d) A way to apply developments in AI that is more realistic than general AI.

6. **Can you define 'catastrophic forgetting' and the underlying cause for it?**

7. **When will machines outsmart humans?**

    (a) They already do, albeit for very specific tasks.

    (b) When quantum computing marries AI.

    (c) When general AI is developed.

    (d) They already have from the moment that we humans gave away our power to machines thinking that they are better than us at making any type of decisions.

# Appendix—Answers to Chapter Review Questions

*Chapter 1. A Bird's-Eye View and the Art of Asking Questions.*

1. **The prominence and success of data science today is due to:**

   (a) The exponential growth of data.

   (a) FALSE—This is one important factor, but not the only one.

   (b) The development of novel methods and algorithms.

   (b) FALSE—This is one important factor, but not the only one.

   (c) The development of faster computers and cheaper storage.

   (c) FALSE—This is one important factor, but not the only one.

   (d) All of the above.

   (d) TRUE—Larger datasets motivate the development of novel methods and technologies, and allow the training of more sophisticated algorithms that may be executed on hardware that is readily available (either a laptop or cloud services).

2. **A successful data science project or initiative rests on:**

   (a) Having as much computational power as possible.

   (a) FALSE—Think of the story about software engineer Margaret Hamilton and the design of the Apollo 11 computer.

   (b) Finding cheaper storage in the cloud so that we have access to all data available.

   (b) FALSE—While being able to store huge datasets may be important for certain projects, this is not the only important aspect.

   (c) Asking the right question.

   (c) TRUE—Asking the right question for the dataset available and in the right context is the most important aspect determining the success of a data science project.

   (d) Hiring the right people.

   (d) FALSE—Having the knowledge is essential but not if the domain is not understood or the right questions are not being asked.

3. **'Data science' means:**

   (a) It is a fancy name for statistics.

   (a) FALSE—data science and statistics share common techniques but their goals are different.

   (b) Same thing as 'Big Data'.

   (b) FALSE—'Big Data' is a term that simply refers to specific properties of the data.

   (c) It is a field whose goal is to extract actionable knowledge from data.

   (c) TRUE.

   (d) Machine learning.

   (d) FALSE—Whereas the goal of data science is to adopt a scientific approach to extract meaning and actionable insights from data, machine learning is a set of statistical learning techniques that specifically allow computers to learn from data. Machine learning techniques are nevertheless extensively used in data science projects.

4. **What sort of questions can data science answer?**

   (a) Mathematical theorems like Fermat's Last Theorem.

   (a) FALSE—Mathematical reasoning is still outside the scope of data science techniques.

   (b) Questions for which the answer is a moving target.

   (b) FALSE—unless we know which value must be optimised, data analysis is pointless.

   (c) Questions that can naturally map to existing algorithms.

   (c) TRUE—this is a start but not the full answer. Valid questions are by definition asked in the right context and are tractable—but not all of them can be answered by applying existing methods rightaway. Some questions require a bit of manipulation and reframing before the analysis step.

   (d) Only questions that require complex analytical techniques.

   (d) FALSE—the complexity of the techniques used must be appropriate for the type of question being asked. Complex techniques are not inherently superior if they are too obscure to be understood and their outcome is not much better than that of simpler but reasonably accurate methods.

5. **A basic definition of an algorithm is 'a set of steps that describe how to solve a particular problem'. Select some key characteristics of a good algorithm:**

   (a) Interpretability and legibility.

(a) FALSE—while interpretability (being able to understand how the predictions were generated) is a key aspect of a good algorithm, legibility has more to do with the implementation and the specific language.

(b) Simplicity.

(b) FALSE—while a simpler algorithm that gives a decent result is preferred over a complex one that provides a marginal gain in performance, and simplicity is a virtue in its own right, some problems require the application of algorithms that are not simple.

(c) Correctness, efficiency and interpretability.

(c) TRUE—Correctness (solving the task intended without errors), efficiency (the algorithm uses as little time and/or space as possible) and interpretability (the outcome is easily understood) are three ideal characteristics of a good algorithm.

(d) Efficiency and interpretability.

(d) While these are two key aspects of a good algorithm, they are useless if the algorithm is incapable of solving the task intended without errors (correctness).

6. **Can you name and briefly describe the six dimensions of data quality?**

Accuracy—how accurately does our data describe the real-world objects and events?

Completeness—how much of the entire dataset is available?

Consistency—if the data is distributed across multiple sites, is the data uniformly updated and quality-checked across such sites, and can this be verified?

Timeliness—whether the time of data recording is useful for the question being asked.

Uniqueness—how un-duplicated our data are.

Validity—are values syntactically valid and within a realistic range?

7. **Uber's Big Data Platform is a central piece in the evolution of Uber's data analysis requirements. Select all statements that are true.**

(a) Back in 2014 Uber was already dealing with petabytes of data stored in non-centralised relational databases.

(a) FALSE—such large amounts of data cannot be handled in such an unstructured way if a swift response is required.

(b) The Hadoop ecosystem was introduced because it was a trendy technology.

(b) FALSE—specifically when you have data in the petabyte region you cannot simply buy more database servers (horizontal scaling) and expect to have things run smoothly or fast.

(c) Kafka is a fancy name for a relational database.

(c) FALSE—the Kafka module was introduced to build real-time data processing capabilities into the Uber platform.

(d) Spark and Hive were introduced into the architecture of Uber's Big Data Platform because both are provided by the Apache Software Foundation as open source projects.

(d) FALSE—while having access to the original code is key for tuning and optimising any application, Spark and Hive were chosen for their ability to process streaming data (Spark) and for their ability to store and process (using SQL) petabyte-size datasets in integration with Hadoop (Hive).

## Chapter 2. Descriptive Analytics.

1. **You are a teacher and have been trying to implement a number of changes in your school to promote more interactive learning. If you were to analyse the posts on your school's online discussion board and split them by year, class, student gender and any other factor, would this be a descriptive or a predictive analytics exercise? For either answer, please explain your reasons.**

    (a) Descriptive—TRUE—You are using historical data to summarise the underlying patterns.

    Describing your data is always a key, first exercise that will help you decide what to do next. For example, if the students not interacting on the discussion board specifically belong in the mathematics class (but not other classes), we may think that there is a problem with that specific class instead of with the interactive learning platform.

    (b) Predictive—FALSE—You are not trying to predict who will post to the discussion board or how often, but simply trying to understand who has already done so in order to draw some conclusions from the historical data.

2. **You are an engineer in a Formula 1 team and want to find out when a particular set of tyres will burst under specific conditions of temperature and rain. For this you collect historical data first. Would this be a descriptive or a predictive analytics question? For either answer, please explain your reasons.**

    (a) Descriptive—TRUE—You may find from the descriptive analysis that there is much consistency in the data, and hence predictability. For example, if all tyres recorded burst after 100 Km and before 110 Km, then you know that all tyres should be changed before Km 95. When the data are consistent and uniform, there is limited need for further analysis.

    (b) Predictive—TRUE—This could also be a predictive analytics question. For example, if we find from the data exploration (descriptive analysis) step that there is a lot of variability as to when tyres burst, as long as all tyres have been built with the same standards we may conclude that temperature, rain, and driving style might affect all these. In a case like this we may probably want to train a neural network model that will take into account all of these factors. When the model is fed specific weather and driving style data before a race, it should be able to predict with some degree of confidence when the tyres will burst. This will help the Formula One Team design a strategy for the race that minimises the number of pit-stops.

3. **What are some descriptive statistics measures?**

(a) The optimal number of clusters in a dataset as determined by $K$-means clustering.

(a) FALSE—Clustering is part of descriptive analytics but it is not a typical descriptive statistics measure.

(b) The mode.

(b) TRUE—The mode is the most common value in a dataset.

(c) The standard deviation.

(c) TRUE—The standard deviation is a measure of how much dispersion a set of values presents around the central values.

(d) Skewness.

(d) TRUE—Skewness is a measure of how symmetrically a dataset is distributed around the mean value.

4. **What does Anscombe's quartet prove?**

It proves that four datasets can have identical numerical descriptive measures and yet be completely different, hence the importance of data visualisation as it can reveal patterns that may hide behind simple numerical analysis.

5. **Clustering is**

(a) The random grouping of data points so that at least data are a bit more organised.

(a) FALSE.

(b) The discovery of natural grouping patterns in the data which may not be apparent otherwise.

(b) TRUE.

(c) The differentiation of data into 'good' and 'bad'.

(c) FALSE.

(d) A technique for getting rid of useless data.

(d) FALSE.

6. **Can you list the sequential steps in a $K$-means clustering exercise?**

1. Calculate the distances between all observations in the dataset.
2. Use a method to decide how many ($K$) clusters the dataset shall be divided into.
3. The algorithm selects $K$ observations to serve as initial centroids.
4. Centroid update is used to recalculate the new mean value for each cluster. As a result some observations might be reassigned to different clusters.
5. Cluster evaluation and visualisation.

7. **Which of the following can be solved using association rule analysis?**

(a) Discover new symptoms associated with a particular disease.

(a) TRUE—As illustrated with the sarcopenia example, the same idea can be applied to any combination of medical symptoms.

(b) Identify the customers that spend the most so that these can be targeted in a campaign for a new, luxury product.

(b) FALSE—This problem is better approached by using $K$-means clustering.

(c) Optimise the inventory in your business.

(c) TRUE—For example, some products might only be sold rarely and in combination with other products, so you may take the leading product as a guide and calculate how much of the lagging product you have to store. This will help you optimise your cash flow and storage space.

(d) Find out the height structure of students in a school that are taller than 170 cm.

(d) FALSE—This problem is best answered by implementing a different type of clustering algorithm called hierarchical clustering. Here, students can be grouped based on their height and then set a grouping cutoff for those taller than 170 cm. This will result in a group with those taller than 170 cm, and another group with everyone else.

*Chapter 3. Predictive Analytics.*

1. **The goal of predictive analytics is**

(a) To use historical data to generate reports using descriptive statistics techniques.

(a) FALSE—This is the definition of descriptive analytics.

(b) To use animal photographs to classify new photographs intro dog breeds automatically.

(b) FALSE—This is just one example of a classification problem, but predictive analytics techniques can be used for an unlimited number of classification and regression problems.

(c) To improve upon the limitations of descriptive analytics.

(c) FALSE—Descriptive analytics has its place, and so does predictive analytics. The most important consideration is to understand the key question that should be asked with the data available as this will determine the approach and techniques to be used.

(d) To use historical data to train a learning model so that unseen values may be predicted within the same domain.

(d) TRUE—It is key to split the data into a training set and a smaller test set on which the accuracy of the predictor can be assessed. There are various ways to split a dataset into training and test sets, the most generally important of which is called cross-validation.

2. **In a decision tree, how are the top and subsequent nodes partitioned?**

(a) Randomly.

(a) FALSE—If you do anything randomly in data science you will get random answers.

(b) Using a strategy that splits the tree in the most uneven way possible.

(b) TRUE—This is called the *information gain* approach where a variable is split in a way that results in the maximum information gain downstream of a given node.

(c) By splitting the dataset on the variable with the largest values.

(c) FALSE.

(d) By splitting the dataset with the smallest values.

(d) FALSE.

3. **The goal of an SVM is to**

(a) Make labelled data from unlabelled data.

(a) FALSE—But you may use a descriptive analytics technique like clustering to try to achieve this.

(b) Separate the labelled data into their classes using a straight line.

(b) FALSE—If the data points can be separated by a straight line, then that is good. In the majority of cases, however, the function separating the data in an SVM model will require a more complex function.

(c) SVMs have no place today because DNNs will always do better.

(c) FALSE—While DNNs outperform most algorithms, they also require huge amounts of data for training and are very expensive computationally. Large amounts of training data might not always be available, and given a reasonable classification problem, SVMs might outperform DNNs.

(d) Find the hyperplane with the higher margin.

(d) TRUE—The role of an SVM is to find a hyperplane that segregates the labelled data optimally. A hyperplane with the higher margin confers robustness to the classifier.

4. **The advantage of Transfer Learning is that**

(a) You can use a pre-trained SVM for another SVM classification problem.

(a) TRUE—Although Transfer Learning has been discussed here in the context of Deep Neural Networks, the concept of Transfer Learning in computer science predates its use in the context of DNNs. As such, transfer learning has been successfully applied with SVMs in the context of image classification problems.

(b) You can re-use part of a pre-trained DNN for another classification or regression problem.

(b) TRUE—By carefully implementing a transfer learning strategy you can avoid the effort of training and optimising a large DNN model.

(c) It makes DNNs faster.

(c) FALSE—Once you have trained a DNN you can simply take the information on the weights between all neurons and run the DNN quite fast. What transfer learning makes faster is the development of new DNN models because by re-using parts of another DNN you do not have to train a complex network from scratch.

(d) It facilitates feature learning.

(d) FALSE—Feature learning is an inherent property of DNNs, whether you use transfer learning or not.

5. **Machine Learning is**

(a) The same thing as Artificial Intelligence.

(a) FALSE—Artificial intelligence is a much broader field involved with the general goal of making machines display human behaviour. As such, it involves many different fields such as robotics, natural language processing and knowledge representation. Machine Learning is just involved with how algorithms can learn from data.

(b) The ultimate goal of the Turing test.

(b) FALSE—The broad goal of the Turing test is to make a machine pass for a human being. Learning algorithms are an important part of human intelligence (but not the only part) and as such are relevant in helping a machine learn from experience.

(c) The study of how computers can learn from data.

(c) TRUE—To achieve this a number of techniques have been developed over the years and which broadly fall into the categories of unsupervised learning, supervised learning and reinforcement learning.

(d) The combination of descriptive and predictive analytics.

(d) FALSE—Predictive analytics broadly encompasses supervised learning and reinforcement learning, both of which are a part of Machine Learning. Descriptive analytics encompasses unsupervised learning (which is a part of Machine Learning) and also descriptive statistics, which is not a part of Machine Learning. Descriptive statistics, however, includes a core set of techniques that must be used before any unsupervised, supervised or reinforcement learning exercise.

6. **Briefly describe the difference between model interpretability and explainability.**

An interpretable model is one that we can inspect and understand how the predictions were calculated, such as linear regression and decision trees.

An explainable model is one that requires a second (*post hoc*) model for understanding how the predictions were generated. These algorithms are the 'black boxes' of machine learning such as random forests and deep neural networks.

7. **Explain the purpose of feature selection and briefly describe the main types of methods.**

The goal of feature selection is to reduce the number of features needed to train a model. This can be achieved using:

- Filter methods, which are very fast and choose features by their positive correlation with the response variable.

- Wrapper methods select features by their impact upon training and evaluating a model.

- Embedded methods are similar to wrapper methods but they perform feature selection as part of the process of building the learning model.

## Chapter 4. How are Predictive Models Trained and Evaluated?

1. **A supervised machine learning algorithm can be trained to predict**

(a) The future value of a stock option.

(a) TRUE—This is an example of time series forecasting, a special case of regression.

(b) The weather next week.

(b) FALSE—This answer is wrong simply because it is not specific enough. Given sufficient data a good model can forecast specific elements of the weather such as the temperature and the rainfall. It is also possible to categorise the ensemble of predictions on the various elements that make up the weather into 'Good weather', 'Bad weather', 'Rainy weather', etc. and in this case the answer would have been a bit more correct.

(c) The onset of World War III.

(c) FALSE—Although we may collect abundant data prior to the onsets of world wars I and II, the contexts in which these events occurred are very different from the geopolitical situation we have in the world today. A rare, unpredictable event that has a massive impact is also known as a 'black swan' event.

(d) Depression.

(d) TRUE—Depression, anxiety and stress levels may be predicted following the analysis of facial expression levels from videos.

2. **The goal of a supervised learning model is**

(a) To make good predictions on the training data.

(a) FALSE—The training data is used to fit a model.

(b) To fit the training data as closely as possible.

(b) FALSE—Such a model is said to be overfitted, and overfitted models cannot generalise well.

(c) To find the function that maps input values to output values most appropriately.

(c) TRUE.

(d) To build a model that has high variance and high bias.

(d) FALSE—A model with high variance is overfitted, and a model with high bias is underfitted. The goal of predictive model building is to minimise these two types of error.

3. **The poor construction of the Fukushima nuclear power plant occurred because**

   (a) The engineers did not have enough training data.

   (a) FALSE—Earthquake data was available for the preceding 400 years.

   (b) The engineers should have used a more sophisticated algorithm.

   (b) FALSE—The data they were trying to model was approximately linear, and therefore a linear function was most appropriate. More complex algorithms do not always do better.

   (c) The engineers overfitted the training data.

   (c) TRUE—A simple linear function should have been fit to the training data.

   (d) The building was not built with quality materials.

   (d) FALSE—The building was built so that it would withstand an earthquake of a magnitude smaller than what the earthquake data should have predicted.

4. **When evaluating a categorical predictor, a model with low recall and high precision**

   (a) Is better than a model with low precision and high recall.

   (a) FALSE—It depends on the context of what we are trying to predict.

   (b) Will always perform well.

   (b) FALSE—It will perform approximately as stated as long as the goal is not to classify data that is too different from the data on which it was built and tested.

   (c) Will get the predictions right most of the time, but will also fail to identify true positives.

   (c) TRUE.

   (d) Is always better than a model with very high accuracy.

   (d) FALSE—Accuracy is another metric that might be more important than precision and recall depending on the context of the prediction.

5. **When building a predictive model**

   (a) We should always start with the simplest possible model.

(a) TRUE—Models that are exceedingly complex tend to overfit and do not generalise well beyond the data they were trained on. Sometimes, even testing on a third, blind dataset is advisable. Finance professionals are very aware of the dangers of overfitting a model based on limited data that gives good classification even on the test dataset but which performs very poorly on data outside of the sample.

(b) We should always start with complex higher order polynomial functions.

(b) FALSE—Complex models tend to overfit the data. We must always start with fitting simpler functions to the data and work our way up in complexity from there.

(c) Partitioning the data properly into training and test data is the only important consideration.

(c) FALSE—While this is a very important point, fitting the right function to the training data is also an essential part of building a good predictive model.

(d) Our goal should be to minimise the bias and variance errors.

(d) TRUE—And to do this we should start using simple models first.

6. **When would you use a precision-recall curve and when would you use a Receiver Operating Characteristic (ROC) curve when comparing binary classifiers?**

ROC curves should be applied when the observations are balanced between the two classes, whereas precision-recall curves should be used with imbalance datasets.

7. **Why is using the Area Under the Curve (AUC) alone a bad idea when comparing classifiers?**

This is because by reducing the complexity of a ROC curve to a single metric ranging between [0,1] can hide a lot of the actual complexity, for example if the curves of different classifiers cross each other.

## Chapter 5. Are Our Algorithms Racist, Sexist and Discriminating?

1. **A Type I error in statistical classification is**

(a) A type of data bias in the training data.

(a) FALSE—A Type I error is a type of error that can only arise at the test stage of algorithm design.

(b) Classifying a True Negative (TN) as a Positive.

(b) TRUE—A Type I error occurs when we incorrectly reject a true null hypothesis. For example, if the null hypothesis is that a person being judged is innocent (the alternative being guilty), a Type I error here would be finding the person guilty despite actually being innocent.

(c) Accepting the null hypothesis when it should not have been accepted.

(c) FALSE—This is the definition of a Type II error.

(d) 'A shepherd thinks that there is no wolf in the village and checks this every night for five consecutive nights. Therefore, there is no wolf in the village.'

(d) FALSE—This is an example of a Type II error because the wolf actually exists and attacked on the sixth night. The null hypothesis here was that no wolf exists and the shepherd accepted the null hypothesis even though it is not true.

2. **PredPol is biased because**

(a) It is trained with historical data.

(a) FALSE—The problem is not historical data simply because it is historical; the problem is that this historical data is biased.

(b) It is trained with biased data.

(b) TRUE—The historical data with which it is trained is racially biased.

(c) It seeks to enforce the law.

(c) FALSE—There is nothing wrong with using algorithms to support those that enforce the law as long as they understand the limitations of the algorithms they are using.

(d) It is designed to search in very specific areas only.

(d) FALSE—In principle the algorithm is not designed to search anywhere specific, but the data with which it is trained because of its inherent bias tends to consider the same area over and over.

3. **Cognitive biases result from our brain's unconscious tendency to simplify the complexity of the world around us. The type of bias that tends to reinforces our previously held ideas is known as**

(a) The framing effect.

(a) FALSE—The framing effect describes the situation where our decisions are influenced by the way choices are presented, for example by making some information particularly attractive.

(b) Inattentional blindness.

(b) FALSE—Inattentional blindness is when we fail to notice certain objects because we are focusing our attention on another object or event.

(c) Confirmation bias.

(c) TRUE.

(d) Self-serving bias.

(d) FALSE—Self-serving bias is the attribution of positive outcomes to our own character and the blaming of negative outcomes to external factors (when perhaps we are responsible for them).

4. **Can you define the term 'direct discrimination'?**

   Direct discrimination is the type of discrimination that results from including *protected attributes* in the decision-making process, such as age, race, colour, nationality, religion, gender and marital status.

5. **What is 'indirect discrimination', and can you provide an example?**

   Indirect discrimination is more subtle and affects specific groups in more subtle ways. An example here would be the Pokémon GO mobile game where Pokémons could only be found in the more affluent areas of town. This bias was introduced because the developers used the geographic coordinates of an earlier game that was predominantly used by younger, male English speakers.

6. **Some good practices to reduce algorithmic bias are**

   (a) To have it thoroughly tested.

   (a) TRUE—However, testing is just the final stage. Do not forget that algorithmic bias can be introduced even in the design phase of the algorithm when things are still being discussed on paper.

   (b) To implement a bias impact statement.

   (b) TRUE—A bias impact statement is an excellent control. However, this is not the only possible answer!

   (c) To use simpler algorithms.

   (c) TRUE—Given the choice of two algorithms to solve a problem, always choose the one whose results you can rebuild manually on paper if necessary. Algorithms like DNNs are black boxes, although they are often the only way to solve certain types of problems.

   (d) To include a fair representation of society in the team.

   (d) TRUE—With the help of a good guide like a bias impact statement a socially diverse team is best equipped to identify biases and suggest solutions.

7. **In what way do equality and equity try to achieve fairness?**

   Equality tries to achieve fairness by making sure that all parties obtain the same resources, support or outcome. Equity tries to achieve fairness by giving each individual whatever they need in order to succeed.

*Chapter 6. Personal Data, Privacy and Cybersecurity.*

1. **Can you describe why privacy is important for individuals?**

   Privacy is a basic human right upon which other rights are built and which helps us define who we are in relation to the world we live in. Privacy is essential to an individual's well-being, for example to put a limit on government and corporate power, to allow one to manage one's reputation and healthy social boundaries, and to allow freedom of speech and non-discrimination on grounds of race, gender, sexual orientation and political views. Even if we have nothing to hide, the invasion of privacy has a deep psychological effect that ends up conditioning our entire behaviour.

2. **What did the Ada Health app case study show?**

The Ada Health app case study showed that privacy invasion and the selling of data to third parties can be easily disguised with a well-written yet opaque privacy policy designed to meet the GDPR as well as the 'Privacy by Design' principles. The experimental analysis carried out with the Lumen Privacy Monitor identified uses of my data for which I had not given consent and which represent clear violations of a user's privacy choices.

3. **Sending a verification code to your mobile phone every time you try to access your email is**

(a) A form of privacy invasion.

(a) FALSE—Not if you previously gave your mobile phone number to your email provider and agreed to this specific use (which can be reversed).

(b) A form of two-factor authentication.

(b) TRUE—the verification code is particularly effective if it has an expiration time. Thus, if a hacker gains access to our email password (e.g. through a data breach), at least they will not be able to access our email account unless they also have our smartphone (unblocked).

(c) An alternative to Google Authenticator.

(c) TRUE—Google Authenticator can be installed on mobile phones and set up for various email providers.

(d) A safer alternative to biometric identification.

(d) TRUE—biological traits are more permanent than time-limited verification codes, and may also be manipulated.

4. **What is a rainbow table attack and why must 'salt' be added to hashed passwords?**

Passwords are stored as hashes, i.e. they are transformed non-reversibly into fixed-length strings. A rainbow table attack is carried out with a precomputed table containing the most common passwords which have been encrypted with standard cryptographic hash functions. Thus, if hackers gain access to a list of hashed passwords in a server, since most people tend to use a number of recurrent, simplistic passwords, the original passwords can often be retrieved by comparing these hashed passwords against the list of precomputed hashed passwords. A salt is random data that is used as an additional input to the cryptographic function that hashes the password, and thus safeguards stored passwords from being guessed easily.

5. **The availability of Open Data allows anyone to engage in almost any type of data science project. Open medical data in particular is very relevant for biomedical research. However, before releasing Personal Health Information (PHI) this must be anonymised. What are some examples of data anonymisation?**

(a) Delete the name of the patient, release the rest of the data.

(a) FALSE—Even without the name, the patient might be easily identified using other data like an address or a telephone number.

(b) Delete the name of the patient and scramble the data.

(b) FALSE—This is not a solution either because the goal of data anonymisation is to not be able to identify specific persons while retaining the maximum possible value from the data. If the data are scrambled, it becomes useless by definition, and you might still be able to identify patients!

(c) Delete and/or obscure personally identifying information as well as any other information that can lead to the identification of specific individuals.

(c) TRUE—The goal of data anonymisation is to make sure that the data are transformed in a way that the identity of no-one is compromised. For example, you may delete personal data and home address, but if someone's nationality is kept and they are the only Norwegian in a small town in Spain, identifying this specific person would not be difficult.

(d) Only let certain people have access to the information.

(d) FALSE—While there should be no problem with the integrity of health professionals (e.g. nurses, doctors), they are not security experts. There are dozens of things that people do all the time that can easily compromise sensitive information. Examples of this are forgetting a USB key in a cafeteria, not logging out of your account in a shared computer at work, or unknowingly having your computer infected with malware that makes all the data in your computer available on the Internet.

6. **Why is updating the software that you use a key aspect of security?**

Because all software has vulnerabilities, and update patches often are security patches. The failure to update software is behind 57% of hacks and data breaches.

A software vulnerability that is described for the first time is known as a 'zero-day exploit'.

7. **Why is it a good idea to keep backup copies of our data in the cloud using a symmetric cryptographic protocol?**

Because if your system becomes infected by ransomware and needs to be restored from backup copies, the criminals' blackmail capacity is inversely proportional to the frequency with which the data are backed up.

Symmetric encryption is preferred for encrypting substantial amounts of data because it is much faster to run than asymmetric encryption as symmetric encryption keys are shorter and only one such key is needed.

## Chapter 7. What Are the Limits of Artificial Intelligence?

1. **Watson answered 'Toronto' instead of 'Chicago' because**

(a) The underlying algorithm failed.

(a) FALSE—Probably not; the string matching algorithm seemed to work as expected.

(b) Watson did not understand the question properly.

(b) TRUE—But this is part of the answer only; had Watson been able to decompose the question into its two sub-questions, and done the string-matching exercise on each one independently, the final answer from the aggregated results could have been different.

(c) 'Toronto' being found in association with 'largest airport' more often than 'Chicago' was in its sources of information.

(c) TRUE—This is only part of the answer, though. Watson was not able to separate the question into its constituent parts, or contextualise them.

(d) Toronto's airport is bigger than Chicago.

(d) FALSE—There is no evidence that Watson's algorithm compared the two airports by size at any stage.

2. **A home robot that can help you cook, regulate your home temperature and order a pizza on Fridays is an example of**

   (a) A general AI application.

   (a) FALSE—While the robot can do many different tasks, it lacks fundamental human traits such as consciousness, which is one aspirational aspect of general AI that computer scientists have not been able to replicate.

   (b) A narrow AI application.

   (b) TRUE—The robot has probably learned to analyse natural language. Human instructions are then matched to specific actions using maybe a rule-based algorithm.

3. **The goal of general AI is**

   (a) To enhance the abilities of narrow AI applications.

   (a) FALSE—Narrow AI applications have their own reason for existence and would not necessarily get better by becoming more intelligent in a human way.

   (b) To replicate the way that humans understand, reason, feel and behave.

   (b) TRUE—This is an ambitious goal that will teach us much about ourselves, but we will not be able to develop true general AI anytime soon.

   (c) To excel at specific tasks, but with better performance.

   (c) FALSE—Specific tasks are handled by narrow AI applications with increasing success.

   (d) An excuse to frighten everyone and to make cool movies.

   (d) FALSE—Although the idea of a machine developing humanoid intelligence and consciousness is scary, we are far from achieving this. However, there is already a lot of value in trying to replicate human intelligence because, for one thing, we learn a lot about ourselves in the process.

4. **Adversarial attacks have been described for every type of learning model and data type. In the context of image recognition an adversarial attack may be engineered by**

   (a) Adding a bit of noise to the input image.

   (a) TRUE—as exemplified by the example of the panda which, when adulterated with some noise invisible to the human eye, is taken for a gibbon.

   (b) Feeding the classifier an image that is completely different from those it has been trained with.

   (b) FALSE—The answer depends on the context, but generally an image that is not classifiable will return a very low confidence score, whereas the goal of adversarial attacks is to generate mis-classifications with high levels of confidence.

   (c) By placing a second object next to the one being classified.

   (c) TRUE—as exemplified by the carefully designed patch placed next to the banana which makes the neural network think the banana is a toaster.

   (d) By showing the same object under different lighting conditions.

   (d) TRUE—a classical example that is not mentioned in the main text is the problem of recognising tanks in combat settings: In the past they could only be identified under the same lighting conditions of the training examples (which were matched to a specific time of the day—morning vs evening, for example).

5. **Augmented intelligence is**

   (a) One of the goals of general AI, which is becoming smarter each year.

   (a) FALSE—At present general AI is more aspirational than realistic.

   (b) The collaboration between narrow AI applications and humans in a way that will assist us in doing our work better.

   (b) TRUE.

   (c) The difference between narrow AI and general AI.

   (c) FALSE—Narrow AI and general AI differ in their goals, not in their degree of intelligence.

   (d) A way to apply developments in AI that is more realistic than general AI.

   (d) TRUE—The term 'augmented intelligence' focuses on AI's role in enhancing human intelligence rather than replacing it.

6. **Can you define 'catastrophic forgetting' and the underlying cause for it?**

   'Catastrophic forgetting' refers to the fact that models cannot keep learning without forgetting previously learnt training data. This is because weight stability is required for knowledge retention, but at the same time weight stability introduces a degree of rigidity that prevents a model from learning new tasks (the stability-plasticity dilemma).

**7. When will machines outsmart humans?**

(a) They already do, albeit for very specific tasks.

(a) TRUE—It is unlikely that a human will ever beat a machine again at chess, Go or simply at doing mathematical calculations.

(b) When quantum computing marries AI.

(b) FALSE—Quantum computation will allow us to calculate more things faster. This will translate into better, specific narrow AI, but not in endowing machines with quintessentially human abilities like reasoning, having emotions and understanding one's place in the world.

(c) When general AI is developed.

(c) TRUE—The computational power available today could power general AI machines beyond our imagination, that is if general AI is ever developed.

(d) They already have from the moment that we humans gave away our power to machines thinking that they are better than us at making any type of decisions.

(d) TRUE—This is why it is so important to understand how data science works so that we can critically approach computer-based conclusions.

# Bibliography

1. Bogoch II, Watts A, Thomas-Bachli A, Huber C, Kraemer MUG, and Khan K. Pneumonia of unknown aetiology in Wuhan, China: potential for international spread via commercial air travel. *J Travel Med*, 27(2):1–3, 2020.

2. Stieg C. How this Canadian start-up spotted coronavirus before everyone else knew about it. URL: `https://cnb.cx/3s6EuuC`, 2020. [Online; accessed 1 October 2022].

3. Davenport TH and Patil DJ. Data Scientist: The Sexiest Job of the 21st Century (Harvard Business Review). URL: `https://bit.ly/30Clahe`, 2012. [Online; accessed 1 October 2022].

4. Alon U. How to choose a good scientific problem. *Molecular Cell*, 35(6):726–728, 2009.

5. Thiel P. *Zero to One: Notes on Start Ups, or How to Build the Future*. Virgin Books, London, UK, 2014. ISBN-10: 9780753555194.

6. Bernstein E, Shore J, and Lazer D. How intermittent breaks in interaction improve collective intelligence. *Proceedings of the National Academy of Sciences, USA*, 115(35):8734–8739, 2018.

7. Yanai I and Lercher M. What is the question? *Genome Biology*, 20(1):289, 2019.

8. Darwin C. *On the origin of species (5th edition)*. John Murray, London, UK, 1869.

9. Johansson F. *The Medici Effect: What Elephants and Epidemics Can Teach Us about Innovation*. Harvard Business School Press, Boston (MA), USA, London, UK, 2006. ISBN-10: 9781422102824.

10. Alvarez LW, Alvarez W, Asaro F, and Michel HV. Extraterrestrial Cause for the Cretaceous-Tertiary Extinction. *Science*, 208(4448):1095–1108, 1980.

11. Altucher J. How to make millions with idea sex. URL: `https://bit.ly/3FSRrj5`, 2021. [Online; accessed 1 October 2022].

12. Fosmoe K. The limits of Data Science. URL: `https://bit.ly/3nQFYKH`, 2017. [Online; accessed 1 October 2022].

13. Miller B. Moneyball. URL: `https://www.imdb.com/title/tt1210166/`, 2011. [Online; accessed 1 October 2022].

14. Lewis M. *Moneyball: The Art of Winning an Unfair Game*. W. W. Norton & Company, New York (NY), USA, 2004. ISBN-10: 0393324818.

15. O'Brien FJ. *The Apollo Guidance Computer: Architecture and Operation*. Springer Praxis Books, Germany, 2010. ISBN: 1441908765.

16. Puiu T. Your smartphone is millions of times more powerful than the Apollo 11 guidance computers (ZME SCIENCE). URL: `https://bit.ly/3hET5Jf`, 2020. [Online; accessed 1 October 2022].

17. Brumfiel G. High-energy physics: Down the petabyte highway. *Nature*, 469:282–283, 2011.

18. Lin W-C and Tsai C-F. Missing value imputation: a review and analysis of the literature (2006–2017). *Artificial Intelligence Review*, 53:1487–1509, 2020.

19. van Buuren S. *Flexible Imputation of Missing Data*. Chapman and Hall/CRC, Boca Raton (FL), USA, 2012. ISBN-10: 1439868247.

20. Reinsel D, Gantz J, and Rydning J. The Digitization of the World - from Edge to Core. URL: `https://bit.ly/3gQDdC4`, 2018. [Online; accessed 1 October 2022].

21. Reinsel D, Gantz J, and Rydning J. The Digitization of the World - From Edge to Core an International Data Corporation white paper. URL: `https://bit.ly/3mMxSB5`, 2018. [Online; accessed 1 October 2022].

22. Shiftehfar R. Uber's Big Data Platform: 100+ Petabytes with Minute Latency. URL: `https://ubr.to/2Z5Xi1h`, 2018. [Online; accessed 1 October 2022].

23. Rudin C. Stop explaining black box machine learning models for high stakes decisions and use interpretable models instead. *Nature Machine Intelligence*, 1:206–215, 2019.

24. Anscombe FJ. Graphs in Statistical Analysis. *The American Statistician*, 27(1):17–21, 1973.

25. McGill R, Tukey JW, and Larsen WA. Variations of Box Plots. *The American Statistician*, 32(1):12–16, 1978.

26. Ghosh D and Vogt A. Outliers: An evaluation of methodologies (Proceedings of the Survey Research Methods Section, American Statistical Association). URL: `https://bit.ly/3GO2FFS`, 2012. [Online; accessed 1 October 2022].

27. Aggarwal CC. *Outlier analysis (2nd Edition)*. Springer, Cham, Switzerland, 2017. ISBN: 9783319475776.

28. Ross SM. Peirce's criterion for the elimination of suspect experimental data. *Journal of Engineering Technology (Fall 2003)*, 20(2), 2003.

29. Chauvenet W. *A Manual of Spherical and Practical Astronomy V. II.* Dover, New York (NY), USA, 1891. ISBN: 9783319475776.

30. Dean RN and Dixon WJ. Simplified Statistics for Small Numbers of Observations. *Anal. Chem.*, 23(4):636–638, 1951.

31. Grubbs F. Procedures for Detecting Outlying Observations in Samples. *Technometrics*, 11(1):1–21, 1969.

32. Snow J. *On the Mode of Communication of Cholera*. John Churchill, London, England, 1855.

33. Nightingale F. *Notes on Nursing: What It Is, and What It Is Not.* Dover Publications, USA, 1969. ISBN-13: 9780486223407.

34. Vinten-Johansen P, Brody H, Paneth N, Rachman S, and Rip MR. *Cholera, Chloroform, and the Science of Medicine: A Life of John Snow*. Oxford University Press, UK, 2003. ISBN-13: 9780195135442.

35. de Ségur P-P. *Defeat: Napoleon's Russian Campaign*. NYRB Classics, New York (NY), USA, 2008. ISBN-10: 1590172825.

36. Sutherland NS. Outlines of a theory of visual pattern recognition in animals and man. *Proceedings of the Royal Society B (Biological Sciences)*, 171:297–317, 1968.

37. Kaas JH and Balaram P. Current research on the organization and function of the visual system in primates. *Eye Brain*, 6(1):1–4, 2014.

38. Midway SR. Principles of effective data visualization. *Patterns*, 1(9):1–7, 2020.

39. Nussbaumer Knaflic C. *Storytelling with Data: A Data Visualization Guide for Business Professionals*. John Wiley & Sons, Hoboken (NJ), USA, 2015. ISBN-10: 1119002257.

40. Telea AC. *Data Visualization: Principles and Practice (2nd Edition)*. CRC Press, Boca Raton (FL), USA, 2015. ISBN-10: 9781466585263.

41. Healy K. *Data Visualization: A Practical Introduction*. Princeton University Press, Princeton (NJ), USA, 2018. ISBN-10: 0691181624.

42. Borkin MA, Vo AA, Bylinskii Z, Isola P, Sunkavalli S, Oliva A, and Pfister H. What makes a visualization memorable? *IEEE Transactions on Visualization and Computer Graphics*, 19:2306–2315, 2013.

43. Harrower M and Brewer CA. Colorbrewer.org: an online tool for selecting colour schemes for maps. *The Cartographic Journal*, 40(1):27–37, 2003.

44. Waskom M. seaborn: statistical data visualization. URL: `https://seaborn.pydata.org/index.html`.

45. Neuwirth E. Rcolorbrewer: Colorbrewer palettes. URL: `https://cran.r-project.org/web/packages/RColorBrewer/index.html`.

46. Dilla WN and Raschke RL. Data visualization for fraud detection: Practice implications and a call for future research. *International Journal of Accounting Information Systems*, 16, 2015.

47. Singh K and Best P. Anti-Money Laundering: Using data visualization to identify suspicious activity. *International Journal of Accounting Information Systems*, 34, 2019.

48. Xu D and Tian Y. A Comprehensive Survey of Clustering Algorithms. *Annals of Data Science*, 2:165–193, 2015.

49. von Luxburg U, Williamson RC, and Guyon I. *Clustering: Science or Art? In Proceedings of ICML Workshop on Unsupervised and Transfer Learning (PMLR), 27:65–79, 2012*. Proceedings of Machine Learning Research, Bellevue (WA), USA, 2012. URL: https://bit.ly/3J2AeWt.

50. Nugent R and Meila M. An overview of clustering applied to molecular biology. *Methods Mol Biol*, 620:369–404, 2010.

51. Celebi ME, Kingravi HA, and Vela PA. A Comparative Study of Efficient Initialization Methods for the $K$-Means Clustering Algorithm. *Expert Systems with Applications*, 40(1):200–210, 2013.

52. von Luxburg U. A tutorial on spectral clustering. *Statistics and Computing*, 17:395–416, 2007.

53. James G, Witten D, Hastie T, and Tibshirani R. *An Introduction to Statistical Learning: with Applications in R*. Springer, New York (NY), USA, 2021. ISBN-10: 1071614177.

54. Agrawal R, Imieliński T, and Swami A. *Mining association rules between sets of items in large databases. Proceedings of the 1993 ACM SIGMOD international conference on Management of data - SIGMOD '93*. Association for Computing Machinery, New York (NY), USA, 1993. ISBN: 0897915925.

55. Daniel J. Power. Ask dan! - what is the "true story" about data mining, beer and diapers? (DSSResources.com). URL: `https://bit.ly/3EnpOND`, 2002. [Online; accessed 1 October 2022].

56. Kim YS and Yum B-J. Recommender system based on click stream data using association rule mining. *Expert Systems with Applications*, 38(10):13320–13327, 2011.

57. Sánchez D, Vila MA, Cerda L, and Serrano JM. Association rules applied to credit card fraud detection. *Expert Systems with Applications*, 36(2):3630–3640, 2009.

58. Soni J, Ansari U, Sharma D, and Soni S. Predictive data mining for medical diagnosis: an overview of heart disease prediction. *International Journal of Computer Applications (0975 – 8887)*, 17(8):43–48, 2011.

59. Fürnkranz J and Kliegr T. *A Brief Overview of Rule Learning. In In: Bassiliades N., Gottlob G., Sadri F., Paschke A., Roman D. (eds) Rule Technologies: Foundations, Tools, and Applications. RuleML 2015. Lecture Notes in Computer Science, vol 9202*. Springer, Cham, Switzerland, 2015. ISBN: 9783319215419.

60. Molnar C. Interpretable Machine Learning - A Guide for Making Black Box Models Explainable. URL: `https://bit.ly/2NCvrmR`, 2021. [Online; accessed 1 October 2022].

61. Hanser T, Barber C, Marchaland JF, and Werner S. Applicability domain: towards a more formal definition. *SAR and QSAR in Environmental Research*, 27(11):865–881, 2016.

62. Miranda-Saavedra D and Barton GJ. Classification and functional annotation of eukaryotic protein kinases. *Proteins: Structure, Function, and Bioinformatics*, 68(4):893–914, 2007.

63. Guillaumin M, Verbeek J, and Schmid C. *Multimodal semi-supervised learning for image classification. In CVPR 2010 - 23rd IEEE Conference on Computer Vision & Pattern Recognition, June 2010, San Francisco. pp. 902–909*. IEEE Computer Society, Washington (DC), USA, 2010. ISBN: 9781424469840.

64. Alvari H, Shakarian P, and Snyder JEK. Semi-supervised learning for detecting human trafficking. *Security Informatics*, 6(1), 2017.

65. Grandvalet Y and Bengio Y. *Semi-supervised Learning by Entropy Minimization.* In *Advances in Neural Information Processing Systems 17 [Neural Information Processing Systems, NIPS 2004, December 13–18, 2004, Vancouver, British Columbia, Canada.* MIT Press, Cambridge (MA), USA, 2005. ISBN: 9780262195348.

66. Lee D-H. *Pseudo-Label : The Simple and Efficient Semi-Supervised Learning Method for Deep Neural Networks.* In *ICML 2013 Workshop : Challenges in Representation Learning (WREPL), June 2013, Atlanta, USA.* URL: `https://bit.ly/3So5gfm`.

67. Oliver A, Odena A, Raffel C, Cubuk ED, and Goodfellow IJ. *Realistic evaluation of deep semi-supervised learning algorithms.* In *NIPS'18: Proceedings of the 32nd International Conference on Neural Information Processing Systems, December 2018, Montreal, Canada. pp. 3239–3250.* Curran Associates Inc., New York (NY), USA, 2018. URL: https://dblp.org/db/conf/nips/nips2018.html.

68. LeCun Y, Bengio Y, and Hinton G. Deep learning. *Nature*, 521(7553):436–444, 2015.

69. Engelstad PE, Hammer H, Kongsgård KW, Yazidi A, Nordbotten NA, and Bai A. *Automatic Security Classification with Lasso.* In *16th International Workshop on Information Security Applications (WISA 2015), Jeju Island, Korea, 20–22 August, 2015.* Springer, Cham, Switzerland, 2015. ISBN: 9783319318745.

70. Kaggle. TV, Radio and Newspaper advertising dataset. URL: `https://www.kaggle.com/thorgodofthunder/tvradionewspaperadvertising`, 2020. [Online; accessed 1 October 2022].

71. Legendre AM. *Nouvelles méthodes pour la détermination des orbites des comètes.* Firmin Didot, Paris, France, 1805.

72. Angrist JD and Pischke JS. *Mostly Harmless Econometrics: An Empiricist's Companion.* Princeton University Press, Princeton (NJ), USA, 2009. ISBN-10: 0691120358.

73. Galton F. Typical Laws of Heredity. *Nature*, 15:492–495, 1877.

74. Boyd CR, Tolson MA, and Copes WS. Evaluating trauma care: The TRISS method. Trauma Score and the Injury Severity Score. *The Journal of Trauma*, 27(4):370–378, 1987.

75. Steyerberg EW. *Clinical Prediction Models. A Practical Approach to Development, Validation, and Updating.* Springer, New York (NY), USA, 2019. ISBN: 9783030163983.

76. Cramer JS. The origins of logistic regression. *Tinbergen Institute Working Paper*, 119(4):1–15, 2002.

77. University of California Los Angeles. Graduate Admissions Statistics Dataset. URL: `https://stats.idre.ucla.edu/r/dae/logit-regression/`. [Online; accessed 1 October 2022].

78. Russell JA. Management of sepsis. *New England Journal of Medicine*, 355:1699–1713, 2006.

79. Drewry AM and Hotchkiss RS. Sepsis: Revising definitions of sepsis. *Nature Reviews Nephrology*, 11(6):326–328, 2015.

80. Klappenbach A. Most spoken languages in the world 2020. URL: `https://bit.ly/3oCAMbi`, 2022. [Online; accessed 1 October 2022].

81. Universe Today. How many atoms are there in the universe. URL: `https://bit.ly/3i3Ak35`. [Online; accessed 1 October 2022].

82. Kaggle. The Titanic passengers dataset. URL: `https://www.kaggle.com/c/titanic`. [Online; accessed 1 October 2022].

83. Breiman L, Friedman J, Stone CJ, and Olshen RA. *Classification and Regression Trees*. Chapman and Hall/CRC, London, UK, 1984. ISBN-13: 9780412048418.

84. The Comprehensive R Archive Network (CRAN). Package 'rpart'. URL: `https://cran.r-project.org/web/packages/rpart/rpart.pdf`, 2020. [Online; accessed 1 October 2022].

85. Koren Y. The BellKor Solution to the Netflix Grand Prize. URL: `https://www.netflixprize.com/assets/GrandPrize2009_BPC_BellKor.pdf`, 2009. [Online; accessed 1 October 2022].

86. Bonab H and Can F. Less Is More: A Comprehensive Framework for the Number of Components of Ensemble Classifiers. *IEEE Transactions on Neural Networks and Learning Systems*, 30(9):2735–2745, 2019.

87. Breiman L. Bagging Predictors. *Machine Learning*, 24:123–140, 1996.

88. Ho TK. Random Decision Forests. *Proceedings of the 3rd International Conference on Document Analysis and Recognition, Montreal (QC), 14–16 August 1995*, 278–282, 1995. Institute of Electrical and Electronic Engineers (IEEE), Pistacaway (NJ), USA, 1995. ISBN: 0818671289..

89. Breiman L. Random Forests. *Machine Learning*, 45(1):5–32, 2001.

90. Galton F. Vox Populi. *Nature*, 75:450–451, 1907.

91. Fernandez-Delgado M, Cernadas E, Barro S, and Amorim D. Do we Need Hundreds of Classifiers to Solve Real World Classification Problems? *Journal of Machine Learning Research*, 15(2014):3133–3181, 2014.

92. Freund Y and Schapire RE. *A decision-theoretic generalization of on-line learning and an application to boosting. In: Vitányi P. (eds) Computational Learning Theory. EuroCOLT 1995. Lecture Notes in Computer Science (Lecture Notes in Artificial Intelligence)*, 904:33–37. Springer, Berlin, Heidelberg, 1995. ISBN: 0818671289.

93. Vapnik V and Lerner A. Pattern recognition using generalized portrait method. *Automation and Remote Control*, 24:774–780, 1963.

94. Boser BE, Guyon IM, and Vapnik VN. *A training algorithm for optimal margin classifiers. In COLT '92: Proceedings of the Fifth Annual Workshop on Computational Learning Theory (pp. 144–152)*. ACM Press, New York (NY), USA, 1992. ISBN: 9780897914970.

95. Vapnik VN. *The Nature of Statistical Learning Theory*. Springer-Verlag, New York (NY), USA, 1995. ISBN: 9781475732641.

96. Drucker H, Burges C, Kaufman L, Smola A, and Varnik VN. *Support Vector Regression Machines. In Advances in Neural Information Processing Systems 9, NIPS 1996, 155–161*. MIT Press, Cambridge (MA), USA, 1997. ISBN: 9780262100656.

97. Cortes C and Vapnik V. Support-vector networks. *Machine Learning*, 20(3):273–297, 1995.

98. Ben-Hur A, Horn D, Siegelmann HT, and Vapnik V. Support Vector Clustering. *Journal of Machine Learning Research*, 2:125–137, 2001.

99. Haykin SO. *Neural Networks and Learning Machines (3rd ed.)*. Pearson, 2009. ISBN-10: 0131471392.

100. McCulloch W and Pitts W. A Logical Calculus of Ideas Immanent in Nervous Activity. *Bulletin of Mathematical Biophysics*, 5(4):115–133, 1943.

101. Turing AM. *Intelligent Machinery. In: Ince DC, editor. Collected works of AM Turing — Mechanical Intelligence*. Elsevier Science Publishers, Amsterdam, The Netherlands, 1992. ISBN-13: 9780444880581.

102. Rosenblatt F. The Perceptron: A Probalistic Model For Information Storage And Organization In The Brain. *Psychological Review*, 65(6):386–408, 1958.

103. Chrislb. Artificial neuron model. URL: `https://commons.wikimedia.org/wiki/File:ArtificialNeuronModel_english.png`.

104. Freund Y and Schapire RE. Large margin classification using the perceptron algorithm. *Machine Learning*, 37(3):277–296, 1999.

105. Hopfield JJ. Neurons with graded response have collective computational properties like those of two-state neurons. *Proceedings of the National Academy of Sciences, USA*, 81(10):3088–3092, 1984.

106. Leijnen S and van Veen F. The Neural Network Zoo. *Proceedings*, 47(1):9, 2020.

107. The Asimov Institute. The neural network zoo project. URL: `https://www.asimov institute.org/overview-neural-network-zoo/`.

108. Cox T. Inverness caledonian thistle don't employ a cameraman as their camera is programmed to follow the ball throughout the match (Twitter). URL: `https://twitter.com/seagull81/status/1320132156774023168?lang=en`, 2020. [Online; accessed 1 October 2022].

109. Vincent J. AI camera operator repeatedly confuses bald head for soccer ball during live stream (The Verge). URL: `https://bit.ly/35P3Ghb`, 2020. [Online; accessed 1 October 2022].

110. Minsky M. *Perceptrons: an introduction to computational geometry (Expanded Edition)*. The MIT Press, Cambridge (MA), USA, 1987. ISBN-10: 0262631113.

111. Hinton GE, Osindero S, and Teh Y-W. A fast-learning algorithm for deep belief nets. *Neural Comput.*, 18(7):1524–1554, 2006.

112. Bengio Y, Lamblin P, Popovici D, and Larochelle H. *Greedy layer-wise training of deep networks. In: Schölkopf, Platt and Hoffman (eds). Advances in Neural Information Processing Systems, vol. 19: 153–160*. The MIT Press, Cambridge (MA), USA, 2007. ISBN: 9780262256919.

113. Ranzato MA, Poultney C, Chopra S, and LeCun Y. *Efficient learning of sparse representations with an energy-based model. In: Schölkopf, Platt and Hoffman (eds). Advances in Neural Information Processing Systems: 1137–1144*. The MIT Press, Cambridge (MA), USA, 2007. ISBN: 9780262256919.

114. Schmidhuber J. Deep learning in neural networks: An overview. *Neural Networks*, 61:85–117, 2015.

115. Deng J, Dong W, Socher R, Li L, Li K, and Fei-Fei L. *ImageNet: A large-scale hierarchical image database. 2009 IEEE Conference on Computer Vision and Pattern Recognition (CVPR 2009), pp. 248–255.* Institute of Electrical and Electronics Engineers (IEEE), Pistacaway (NJ), USA, 2009. ISBN: 9781424439928.

116. Szegedy C, Ioffe S, Vanhoucke V, and Alemi A. Inception-v4, Inception-ResNet and the Impact of Residual Connections on Learning. URL: `https://arxiv.org/abs/1602.07261`, 2016.

117. Krizhevsky A, Sutskever I, and Hinton GE. Imagenet classification with deep convolutional neural networks. *Communications of the ACM*, 60(6):84–90, 2017.

118. Yosinski J, Clune J, Bengio Y, and Lipson H. How transferable are features in deep neural networks? *Advances in Neural Information Processing Systems*, 27:3320–3328, 2014.

119. Zhuang F, Qi Z, Duan K, Xi D, Zhu Y, Zhu H, Xiong H, and He Q. A Comprehensive Survey on Transfer Learning. *Proceedings of the IEEE*, pages 1–34, 2020.

120. Wolpert DH. The Lack of A Priori Distinctions Between Learning Algorithms. *Neural Computation*, 8(7):1341–1390, 1996.

121. Wolpert DH and Macready WG. No Free Lunch Theorems for Optimization. *IEEE Transactions on Evolutionary Computation*, 1(1):67–82, 1997.

122. Scheirer W, Rocha A, Micheals R, and Boult T. *Robust Fusion: Extreme Value Theory for Recognition Score Normalization. In European Conference on Computer Vision: Computer Vision – ECCV 2010, 481–495.* Springer, Berlin, Heidelberg, Berlin, Germany, 2010. ISBN: 9783642155574.

123. Domingos P. A Few Useful Things to Know About Machine Learning. *Communications of the ACM*, 55(10):78–87, 2012.

124. Bellman RE. *Curse of dimensionality. In Adaptive Control Processes: a guided tour.* Princeton University Press, Princeton (NJ), USA, 1961. ISBN-10: 0691079013.

125. Koutroumbas K and Theodoridis S. *Pattern Recognition (4th ed.).* Burlington Books, Athens, Greece, 2008. ISBN: 9781597492720.

126. Trunk GV. A Problem of Dimensionality: A Simple Example. *IEEE Transactions on Pattern Analysis and Machine Intelligence*, 3:306–307, 1979.

127. Fernandez M and Miranda-Saavedra D. Genome-wide enhancer prediction from epigenetic signatures using genetic algorithm-optimized support vector machines. *Nucleic Acids Research*, 40(10):e77, 2012.

128. Street WN, Wolberg WH, and Mangasarian OL. *Nuclear feature extraction for breast tumor diagnosis. Proc. SPIE 1905, Biomedical Image Processing and Biomedical Visualization, (29 July 1993).* San Jose (CA), USA, 1993. URL: `https://bit.ly/3R2YgDB`.

129. Mangasarian OL, Street WN, and Wolberg WH. Breast cancer diagnosis and prognosis via linear programming. *Operations Research*, 43(4):570–577, 1995.

130. UCI Machine Learning Repository. Breast cancer wisconsin (diagnostic) data set. URL: `https://bit.ly/3cEWRRx`.

131. Welcsh PL and King M-C. BRCA1 and BRCA2 and the genetics of breast and ovarian cancer. *Human Molecular Genetics*, 10(7):705–713, 2001.

132. Yu HF et al. Feature Engineering and Classifier Ensemble for KDD Cup 2010. *IEEE Transactions on Neural Networks and Learning Systems*, 30(9):2735–2745, 2010.

133. Adomavicius G and Tuzhilin A. Toward the Next Generation of Recommender Systems: A Survey of the State-of-the-Art and Possible Extensions. *IEEE Transactions on Knowledge and Data Engineering*, 17(6):734–749, 2005.

134. Linden G, Smith B, and York J. Amazon.com Recommendations. Item-to-Item Collaborative Filtering. *IEEE Internet Computing*, 1(1):76–80, 2003.

135. Smith B and Linden G. Two Decades of Recommender Systems at Amazon.com. *IEEE Internet Computing*, 21(3):12–18, 2017.

136. Jahrer M, Toscher M, and Legenstein RA. Combining predictions for accurate recommender systems. *KDD '10: Proceedings of the 16th ACM SIGKDD international conference on Knowledge discovery and data mining*, pages 693–702, 2010. ISBN: 9781450300551.

137. Mackenzie D. Fukushima radioactive fallout nears Chernobyl levels (New Scientist). URL: `https://bit.ly/2PGWspX`, 2011. [Online; accessed 1 October 2022].

138. Zhan Z. Gutenberg–Richter law for deep earthquakes revisited: A dual-mechanism hypothesis. *Earth and Planetary Science Letters*, 461:1–7, 2017.

139. Silver N. *The Signal and the Noise: Why So Many Predictions Fail—But Some Don't*. Penguin Books, London, UK, 2012. ISBN-13: 9780143125082.

140. Kohavi R. *A study of cross-validation and bootstrap for accuracy estimation and model selection. In IJCAI'95: Proceedings of the 14th international joint conference on Artificial intelligence, vol.2, pp. 1137–1143 (2 August 1995)*. Morgan Kaufmann Publishers Inc., San Francisco (CA), USA, 1995. ISBN: 9781558603639.

141. Harter HL. The Method of Least Squares and Some Alternatives: Part I. *International Statistical Review*, 42(2):147–174, 1974.

142. Hand DJ. Measuring classifier performance: a coherent alternative to the area under the ROC curve. *Machine Learning*, 77:103–123, 2009.

143. Wikipedia. Face ID. URL: `https://en.wikipedia.org/wiki/Face_ID`. [Online; accessed 1 October 2022].

144. Faggella D. Facebook artificial intelligence and the challenge of personalization. URL: `https://bit.ly/3dMCO3e`, 2019. [Online; accessed 1 October 2022].

145. Abdulkader A, Lakshmiratan A and Zhang J. Introducing DeepText: Facebook's text understanding engine. URL: `https://bit.ly/3t6mAcP`, 2016. [Online; accessed 1 October 2022].

146. Falcon R. Google maps adds dish-covery to the menu. URL: `https://bit.ly/3s6w5HF`, 2019. [Online; accessed 1 October 2022].

147. Miklós B. Computer, respond to this email: Introducing smart reply in inbox by Gmail. URL: `https://bit.ly/3d1IQPf`,2015. [Online; accessed 1 October 2022].

148. Ometov A, Bezzateev S, Mäkitalo N, Andreev S, Mikkonen T, and Koucheryavy Y. Multi-Factor Authentication: A Survey. *Cryptography*, 2(1):1, 2018.

149. Allrecipes. Introducing the AllRecipes Skill for Amazon Alexa! | Cooking Skills | Allrecipes.com. URL: `https://bit.ly/3sakmYq`, 2016. [Online; accessed 1 October 2022].

150. Williams O. IBM's Watson AI Saves Woman's Life By Diagnosing Rare Form of Leukaemia (HuffPost). URL: `https://bit.ly/321KaeH`, 2016. [Online; accessed 1 October 2022].

151. Kelly K. How AI can bring on a second industrial revolution. TEDSummit. URL: `https://bit.ly/3s3cO1j`, 2016. [Online; accessed 1 October 2022].

152. Brennan T, Dieterich W, and Ehret B. Evaluating the predictive validity of the COMPAS risk and needs assessment system. *Criminal Justice and Behaviour*, 36: 21–40, 2009.

153. Larson J, Mattu S, Kirchner L and Angwin L. How We Analyzed the COMPAS Recidivism Algorithm (PROPUBLICA). URL: `https://bit.ly/3dS7GAd`, 2016. [Online; accessed 1 October 2022].

154. Dressel J and Farid H. The accuracy, fairness, and limits of predicting recidivism. *Science Advances*, 4(1):eaao5580, 2018.

155. Angelino E, Larus-Stone N, Alabi D, Seltzer M, and Rudin C. Learning certifiably optimal rule lists for categorical data. *The Journal of Machine Learning Research*, 19:1–79, 2018.

156. BBC Science Focus Magazine. Can an algorithm deliver justice? URL: `https://bit.ly/3uDMF35`, 2018. [Online; accessed 1 October 2022].

157. Kay M, Matuszek C, and Munson SA. *Unequal Representation and Gender Stereotypes in Image Search Results for Occupations. In CHI '15: Proceedings of the 33rd Annual ACM Conference on Human Factors in Computing Systems, April 2015, Pages 3819–3828.* Association for Computer Machinery, New York (NY), USA, 2015. ISBN: 9781450331456.

158. Wikipedia. List of highest paid film actors. URL: `https://bit.ly/39ZNYkY`. [Online; accessed 1 October 2022].

159. Russo A and Russo J. Avengers: Endgame. URL: `https://www.imdb.com/title/tt4154796/`, 2019. [Online; accessed 1 October 2022].

160. Russo A and Russo J. Avengers: Infinity War. URL: `https://www.imdb.com/title/tt4154756/`, 2018. [Online; accessed 1 October 2022].

161. Whedon J. The Avengers. URL: `https://www.imdb.com/title/tt0848228/`, 2012. [Online; accessed 1 October 2022].

162. Favreau J. Iron Man 2. URL: `https://www.imdb.com/title/tt1228705/`, 2010. [Online; accessed 1 October 2022].

163. Nickerson RS. Confirmation bias: A ubiquitous phenomenon in many guises. *Review of General Psychology*, 2(2):175–220, 1998.

164. Adams R, Weale S and Barr C. A-level results: almost 40% of teacher assessments in England downgraded (The Guardian). URL: `https://bit.ly/39XFBGC`,2020. [Online; accessed 1 October 2022].

165. Harkness T. How Ofqual failed the algorithm test. the embarrassing truth is that their mathematical model was a prejudice machine. URL: `https://bit.ly/3wIXe6W`,2020. [Online; accessed 1 October 2022].

166. Witherspoon S. RSS alerts Ofqual to the statistical issues relating to exam grading and assessment in 2020 (Royal Statistical Society). `https://bit.ly/3fX7GSn`, 2020. [Online; accessed 1 October 2022].

167. Lum K and Isaac W. To predict and serve? *Significance*, 13(5):14–19, 2016.

168. Demetis D and Lee AS. When Humans Using the IT Artifact Becomes IT Using the Human Artifact. *Journal of the Association for Information Systems*, 19(10):5, 2018.

169. Haselton MG, Nettle D, and Murray DR. *The Evolution of Cognitive Bias. In The Handbook of Evolutionary Psychology, pp. 968–987.* John Wiley & Sons, Inc., Hoboken (NJ), USA, 2015. ISBN: 9781118763995.

170. Mehrabi N, Morstatter F, Saxena N, Lerman K, and Galstyan A. A survey on bias and fairness in machine learning. URL: `https://arxiv.org/abs/1908.09635`, 2019.

171. Tigwell GW and Flatla DR. *Oh that's what you meant!: reducing emoji misunderstanding. In MobileHCI '16: Proceedings of the 18th International Conference on Human-Computer Interaction with Mobile Devices and Services Adjunct, September 2016, Pages 859–866.* Association for Computer Machinery, New York (NY), USA, 2016. ISBN: 9781450344135.

172. Hardesty L. Study finds gender and skin-type bias in commercial artificial-intelligence systems (MIT News). URL: `https://bit.ly/3uIcEX1`, 2018. [Online; accessed 1 October 2022].

173. Wilson B, Hoffman J, and Morgenstern J. Predictive Inequity in Object Detection. URL: `https://arxiv.org/abs/1902.11097`, 2019.

174. Casas-Roma J and Conesa J. *Towards the Design of Ethically-Aware Pedagogical Conversational Agents. In Proceedings of the 15th International Conference on P2P, Parallel, Grid, Cloud and Internet Computing (3PGCIC-2020), Pages 188–198.* Springer, Berlin, Germany, 2020. ISBN: 9783030611057.

175. Kruger J and Dunning D. Unskilled and unaware of it: how difficulties in recognizing one's own incompetence lead to inflated self-assessments. *Journal of personality and social psychology*, 77(6):1121–1134, 1999.

176. Wagner CH. Simpson's Paradox in Real Life. *The American Statistician*, 36(1):46–48, 1982.

177. Bickel PJ, Hammel EA, and O'Connell JW. Sex Bias in Graduate Admissions: Data From Berkeley. *Science*, 187(4175):398–404, 1975.

178. Baeza-Yates R. Bias on the Web. *Communications of the ACM*, 61(6):54–61, 2018.

179. Wu S, Hofman JM, Mason WA, and Watts DJ. Who says what to whom on Twitter. *Big Data*, 2(4):196–204, 2014.

180. Broido AD and Clauset A. Scale-free networks are rare. *Nature Communications*, 10(1017), 2019.

181. Lazer DMJ. The science of fake news. *Science*, 359(6380):1094–1096, 2018.

182. Fetterly D, Manasse M, and Najork M. On the evolution of clusters of near-duplicate webpages. *Journal of Web Engineering*, 2(4):228–246, 2003.

183. Agarwal D, Chen B-C, and Elango P. *Explore/exploit schemes for Web content optimization. In Proceedings of the Ninth IEEE International Conference on Data Mining, Miami, Florida.* IEEE Computer Society, Washington (DC), USA, 2009. ISBN: 9780769538952.

184. Baeza-Yates R. *Bias in Search and Recommender Systems. In RecSys '20: Fourteenth ACM Conference on Recommender Systems Virtual Event (Brazil).* Association for Computing Machinery, New York, USA, 2020. ISBN: 9781450375832.

185. Olteanu A, Castillo C, Diaz F, and Kiciman E. Social Data: Biases, Methodological Pitfalls, and Ethical Boundaries. *Front. Big Data (11 July 2019)*, 2019.

186. Wang T and Wang D. Why Amazon's ratings might mislead you: The story of herding effects. *Big Data*, 2(4):196–204, 2014.

187. Saxena NA. *Perceptions of fairness. In Proceedings of the 2019 AAAI/ACM Conference on AI, Ethics, and Society (AIES '19), Honolulu, Hawaii.* Association for Computing Machinery, New York (NY), USA, 2009. ISBN: 9781450363242.

188. Nisbett RE. *The Geography of Thought: How Asians and Westerners Think Differently.* Nicholas Brealey Publishing, Boston (MA), USA, 2019. ISBN: 1529309417.

189. Simonite T. When It Comes to Gorillas, Google Photos Remains Blind (WIRED). URL: `https://bit.ly/3CliItd`, 2018. [Online; accessed 1 October 2022].

190. Snow J. Amazon's Face Recognition Falsely Matched 28 Members of Congress With Mugshots (ACLU). URL: `https://bit.ly/3s7YvCL`, 2018. [Online; accessed 1 October 2022].

191. Kooragayala S and Srini T. Pokémon GO is changing how cities use public space, but could it be more inclusive? (Urban Institute Report). URL: `https://urbn.is/3hS3UKq`, 2016. [Online; accessed 1 October 2022].

192. Lippert-Rasmussen K. *Born free and equal? A philosophical enquiry into the nature of discrimination.* Oxford University Press, New York (NY), USA, 2013. ISBN-10: 0199796114.

193. Binns R. Fairness in Machine Learning: Lessons from Political Philosophy. *Proceedings of Machine Learning Research*, 81:1–11, 2018.

194. Kleinberg J, Mullainathan S, and Raghavan M. Inherent Trade-Offs in the Fair Determination of Risk Scores. URL: `https://arxiv.org/pdf/1609.05807v1.pdf`, 2016.

195. Rice C. How blind auditions help orchestras to eliminate gender bias (The Guardian). URL: `https://bit.ly/3iUeSzL`, 2013. [Online; accessed 1 October 2022].

196. Weinberger D. How machine learning pushes us to define fairness (Harvard Business Review). URL: `https://bit.ly/3BR4VLK`, 2019. [Online; accessed 1 October 2022].

197. Hao K. This is how AI bias really happens—and why it's so hard to fix (MIT Technology Review). URL: `https://bit.ly/3xpFXil`, 2019. [Online; accessed 1 October 2022].

198. Selbst AD, Boyd D, Friedler SA, Venkatasubramanian S, and Vertesi J. *Fairness and Abstraction in Sociotechnical Systems. In FAT\* '19: Proceedings of the Conference on Fairness, Accountability, and Transparency, pp. 59–68.* Association for Computing Machinery (ACM), New York (NY), USA, 2019. ISBN: 9781450361255.

199. Buolamwini J and Gebru T. Gender Shades: Intersectional Accuracy Disparities in Commercial Gender Classification. *Proceedings of Machine Learning Research*, 81: 1–15, 2018.

200. Chouldechova A. Fair prediction with disparate impact: A study of bias in recidivism prediction instruments. *Big data*, 5(2):153–163, 2017.

201. Resnick P Lee NT and Barton G. Algorithmic bias detection and mitigation: Best practices and policies to reduce consumer harms (Brookings Institution). URL: `https://brook.gs/3d5JWtl`, 2019. [Online; accessed 1 October 2022].

202. FAT/ML. Principles for Accountable Algorithms and a Social Impact Statement for Algorithms. URL: `https://bit.ly/3xKLtMC`, 2021. [Online; accessed 1 October 2022].

203. Content Directorate-General for Communications Networks and Technology. Ethics guidelines for trustworthy AI. URL: `https://bit.ly/2QdTs4N`, 2019. [Online; accessed 1 October 2022].

204. Thomas R. Artificial intelligence needs all of us (TEDx). URL: `https://bit.ly/3s46hvK`, 2018. [Online; accessed 1 October 2022].

205. Fisher D and Heymann D. Q&A: The novel coronavirus outbreak causing COVID-19. *BMC Medicine*, 18:57, 2020.

206. Worldometer. Reported cases and deaths by country or territory. URL: `https://www.worldometers.info/coronavirus/#countries`.

207. Scommegna P. Which country has the oldest population? it depends on how you define 'old.' URL: `https://bit.ly/3t7DVSA`, 2019. [Online; accessed 1 October 2022].

208. Onder G, Rezza G, and Brusaferro S. Case-Fatality Rate and Characteristics of Patients Dying in Relation to COVID-19 in Italy. *JAMA*, 323(18):1775–1776, 2020.

209. Zhao S, Lin Q, Ran J, Musa SS, Yang G, Wang W, Lou Y, Gao D, Yang L, He D, and Wang MH. Preliminary estimation of the basic reproduction number of novel coronavirus (2019-nCoV) in China, from 2019 to 2020: A data-driven analysis in the early phase of the outbreak. *Int J Infect Dis*, 92:214–217, 2020.

210. Wikipedia. Basic reproduction number. URL: `https://en.wikipedia.org/wiki/Basic_reproduction_number`. [Online; accessed 1 October 2022].

211. Sanche S, Lin YT, Xu C, Romero-Severson E, Hengartner N, and Ke R. High Contagiousness and Rapid Spread of Severe Acute Respiratory Syndrome Coronavirus 2. *Emerg Infect Dis*, 26(7):1470–1477, 2020.

212. Associated Press. Iran says official who played down coronavirus fears is infected. URL: `https://bit.ly/39V8Iuj`, 2020. [Online; accessed 1 October 2022].

213. BBC News. Coronavirus: Iran's deaths at least 210, hospital sources say. URL: `https://bbc.in/323ROAk`, 2020. [Online; accessed 1 October 2022].

214. Howell E. Satellite Images show Iran's mass graves for coronavirus victims. URL: `https://bit.ly/2QbabWr`, 2020. [Online; accessed 1 October 2022].

215. Payne A. Iran has released 85,000 prisoners in an emergency bid to stop the spread of the coronavirus. URL: `https://bit.ly/3uEdyuV`, 2020. [Online; accessed 1 October 2022].

216. Wikipedia. Tourism in Iran. URL: `https://en.wikipedia.org/wiki/Tourism_in_Iran`. [Online; accessed 1 October 2022].

217. @Nyscalo. Twitter thread. URL: `https://bit.ly/3dXpzxU`, 2020. [Online; accessed 1 October 2022].

218. Giglio M. Would you sacrifice your privacy to get out of quarantine? (The Atlantic). URL: `https://bit.ly/38qg9Zh`, 2020. [Online; accessed 1 October 2022].

219. Bellamy RKE, Dey K, Hind M, Hoffman SC, Houde S, Kannan K, Lohia P, Martino J, Mehta S, Mojsilovic A, Nagar S, Ramamurthy KN, Richards J, Saha D, Sattigeri P, Singh M, Varshney KR, and Zhang Y. AI Fairness 360: An Extensible Toolkit for Detecting, Understanding, and Mitigating Unwanted Algorithmic Bias. URL: `https://arxiv.org/abs/1810.01943`, 2018.

220. Wexler J, Pushkarna M, Bolukbasi T, Wattenberg M, Viégas F, and Wilson J. The What-If Tool: Interactive Probing of Machine Learning Models. *IEEE Transactions on Visualization and Computer Graphics*, 26(1):56–65, 2019.

221. Bender EM, Gebru T, McMillan-Major A, and Shmitchell S. *On the Dangers of Stochastic Parrots: Can Language Models Be Too Big? In FAccT '21: Proceedings of the 2021 ACM Conference on Fairness, Accountability, and Transparency, Virtual Event Canada, 3–10 March, 2021.* Association for Computing Machinery, New York (NY), USA, 2021. ISBN: 9781450383097.

222. Collins V and Lanz J. Managing Data as an Asset. *The CPA Journal*, 89(6):22–27, 2019.

223. Garcia Martinez A. No, data is not the new oil (WIRED). URL: `https://bit.ly/3kOBEXc`, 2019. [Online; accessed 1 October 2022].

224. Ignoffo Z. Dark Web Price Index 2021. URL: `https://bit.ly/3yjnOmJ`, 2021. [Online; accessed 1 October 2022].

225. Gomez M. Dark Web Price Index 2020. URL: `https://bit.ly/2YOXBwM`, 2021. [Online; accessed 1 October 2022].

226. Sen R. Here's how much your personal information is worth to cybercriminals – and what they do with it (The Conversation). URL: `https://bit.ly/3941mGi`, 2021. [Online; accessed 1 October 2022].

227. Wikipedia. List of data breaches. URL: `https://bit.ly/2YUIcyw`. [Online; accessed 1 October 2022].

228. Risk Based Security. 2020 q3 report. URL: https://bit.ly/3UKxVgQ, 2020. [Online; accessed 1 October 2022].

229. IBM. Cost of a Data Breach Report 2021. URL: https://ibm.co/3ktFXsV, 2021. [Online; accessed 1 October 2022].

230. HIPAA Journal. Healthcare industry has highest number of reported data breaches in 2021. URL: https://bit.ly/3Cifwhf, 2021. [Online; accessed 1 October 2022].

231. Anthem. Statement regarding cyber attack against Anthem. URL: https://bit.ly/38QswOJ, 2015. [Online; accessed 1 October 2022].

232. California Department of Insurance. Anthem Data Breach. URL: https://bit.ly/3n3UgHK, 2015. [Online; accessed 1 October 2022].

233. Zetter K. Health Insurer Anthem Is Hacked, Exposing Millions of Patients' Data (WIRED). URL: https://bit.ly/3jfnYHn, 2015. [Online; accessed 1 October 2022].

234. Tabbaa B. Take out - how Anthem was breached (Medium, 17 February 2019). URL: https://bit.ly/3h9wOoy, 2019. [Online; accessed 1 October 2022].

235. Experian. The potential damages and consequences of medical identity theft and healthcare data breaches. URL: https://bit.ly/3kRBsc0, 2010. [Online; accessed 1 October 2022].

236. Eddy N. Healthcare data at big risk as hackers innovate and hone their techniques (Healthcare IT News). URL: https://bit.ly/3tjdQAJ, 2019. [Online; accessed 1 October 2022].

237. Ferenstein G. The age of optimists: A quantitative glimpse of how Silicon Valley will transform political power and everyday life. URL: https://bit.ly/3znQrj2, 2015. [Online; accessed 1 October 2022].

238. McCreary L. The right to privacy. *Harvard Law Review*, 4(5):193–220, 1890.

239. Westin AF. *Privacy and freedom*. Ig Publishing, Great Bookham, Surrey, UK, 1967. ISBN-10: 1935439979.

240. Kang J. Information Privacy in Cyberspace Transactions. *Stanford Law Review*, 50(4):1193–1294, 1998.

241. Burt A. Privacy and cybersecurity are converging. here's why that matters for people and for companies (Harvard Business Review). URL: https://bit.ly/2BVxfO0, 2019. [Online; accessed 1 October 2022].

242. Sprenger P. Sun on privacy: 'get over it' (WIRED). URL: https://bit.ly/3zbfiq8, 1999. [Online; accessed 1 October 2022].

243. Kirkpatrick M. Facebook's Zuckerberg says the age of privacy is over (New York Times). URL: https://nyti.ms/3k7J1fl, 2010. [Online; accessed 1 October 2022].

244. Wong JC. Former Facebook executive: social media is ripping society apart (The Guardian). URL: https://bit.ly/3kaPRkh, 2017. [Online; accessed 1 October 2022].

245. Wall Street Journal staff. The Facebook files. A Wall Street Journal investigation (WSJ, September-November 2021). URL: https://on.wsj.com/3diHXkN, 2021. [Online; accessed 1 October 2022].

246. Haugen F. Highlights From Facebook Whistleblower Testifying At Senate Hearing (NBC News, 5 October 2021). URL: `https://bit.ly/3rtddpv`, 2021. [Online; accessed 1 October 2022].

247. Greenwald G. NSA collecting phone records of millions of Verizon customers daily (The Guardian). URL: `https://bit.ly/3nwODUt`, 2013. [Online; accessed 1 October 2022].

248. Snowden E. *Permanent record*. Metropolitan Books, New York (NY), USA, 2014. ISBN: 1250237238.

249. Collins K. Google collects Android users' locations even when location services are disabled. URL: `https://bit.ly/3EhTKff`, 2017. [Online; accessed 1 October 2022].

250. Fussell S. The microphones that may be hidden in your home (The Atlantic). URL: `https://bit.ly/3AdWxnh`, 2019. [Online; accessed 1 October 2022].

251. Dalton J. Airlines admit having cameras installed on back of passengers' seats (The Independent). URL: `https://bit.ly/3fpntv0`, 2019. [Online; accessed 1 October 2022].

252. Buttarelli G. Privacy matters: updating human rights for the digital society. *Health and Technology*, 7:325–328, 2017.

253. Friman. Presidio modelo 2. URL: `https://commons.wikimedia.org/wiki/File:Presidio-modelo2.JPG`.

254. Berg B. Flexible working: the future of work or oppressive panopticon? (Erasmus Magazine), URL: `https://bit.ly/2VSPgur`, 2018. [Online; accessed 1 October 2022].

255. Kandias M, Mitrou L, Stavrou V, and Gritzalis D. *Which side are you on? A new Panopticon vs. privacy. In 2013 International Conference on Security and Cryptography (SECRYPT), 2013, pp. 1–13*. IEEE, Pistacaway, (NJ), USA, 2013. ISBN: 1479946389.

256. Office for Civil Rights. The HIPAA privacy rule United States Department of Health and Human Services. URL: `https://bit.ly/2XF1hUy`, 2020. [Online; accessed 1 October 2022].

257. Woodward M. 16 countries with GDPR-like data privacy laws Security Scorecard. URL: `https://bit.ly/3hZ5J81`, 2021. [Online; accessed 1 October 2022].

258. Nikolova S. Is AI already good enough to transform healthcare? – interview with Daniel Nathrath, founder and CEO at Ada Health (Research 2 Guidance). URL: `https://bit.ly/3ndeOxt`, 2020. [Online; accessed 1 October 2022]

259. Cavoukian A. Privacy by design: the definitive workshop. A foreword by Ann Cavoukian, Ph.D. *Identity in the Information Society*, 3:247–251, 2010.

260. UC Berkeley International Computer Science Institute. The Lumen privacy monitor at the Google Play store. `https://bit.ly/391JEvE`.

261. Razaghpanah A, Nithyanand R, Vallina-Rodriguez N, Sundaresan S, Allman M, Kreibich C, and Gill P. *Apps, Trackers, Privacy, and Regulators: A Global Study of the Mobile Tracking Ecosystem. In Network and Distributed Systems Security (NDSS) Symposium 2018, 18–21 February 2018, San Diego, (CA), USA*. The Internet Society, Reston (VA), USA, 2018. ISBN: 11891562495.

262. Grundy Q, Chiu K, Held F, Continella A, Bero L, and Holz R. Data sharing practices of medicines related apps and the mobile ecosystem: traffic, content, and network analysis. *British Medical Journal*, 364(1920):1–11, 2019.

263. Vijayan J. Malware hidden in encrypted traffic surges amid pandemic (Dark Reading). URL: `https://bit.ly/39gOHxy`, 2020. [Online; accessed 1 October 2022].

264. Rezaei S and Liu X. Deep Learning for Encrypted Traffic Classification: An Overview. *IEEE Communications Magazine*, 57(5):76–81, 2019.

265. Prasse P, Machlica L, Pevny T, Havel J, and Scheffer T. *Malware Detection by Analysing Encrypted Network Traffic with Neural Networks. In Joint European Conference on Machine Learning and Knowledge Discovery in Databases (ECML PKDD), 2017, pp. 73–88.* Springer, New York (NY), USA, 2017. ISBN: 9783319712451.

266. Madry A, Makelov A, Schmidt L, Tsipras D, and Vladu A. Towards Deep Learning Models Resistant to Adversarial Attacks. URL: `https://arxiv.org/abs/1706.06083`, 2019.

267. Schneier B. Schneier's law (Schneier on Security). URL: `https://bit.ly/2XSSHSZ`, 2011. [Online; accessed 1 October 2022].

268. Ibrahim M. How to decrypt WhatsApp crypt5 database messages (StackPointer.io). URL: `https://bit.ly/3kJx2VU`, 2014. [Online; accessed 1 October 2022].

269. Ducklin P. Adobe customer data breached – login and credit card data probably stolen, all passwords reset (Naked Security). URL: `https://bit.ly/2Zsi52D`, 2013. [Online; accessed 1 October 2022].

270. Ducklin P. Anatomy of a password disaster – Adobe's giant-sized cryptographic blunder (Naked Security). URL: `https://bit.ly/32BImN8`, 2013. [Online; accessed 1 October 2022].

271. Compagnucci MC, Meszaros J, Minssen T, Arasilango A, Ous T, and Rajarajan M. Homomorphic Encryption: The 'Holy Grail' for Big Data Analytics & Legal Compliance in the Pharmaceutical and Healthcare Sector? *European Pharmaceutical Law Review*, 3(4):144–155, 2019.

272. Vizitiu A, Nita CI, Puiu A, Suciu C, and Itu LM. Applying Deep Neural Networks over Homomorphic Encrypted Medical Data. *Computational and Mathematical Methods in Medicine*, 4:1–26, 2020.

273. Mehan JE. *Insider Threat: A Guide to Understanding, Detecting, and Defending Against the Enemy from Within: chapter 2 (Insider threat models and indicators).* IT Governance Publishing Ltd., Ely, United Kingdom, 2016. ISBN: 9781849288415.

274. Kim A, Oh J, Ryu J, Lee J, Kwon K, and Lee K. SoK: A Systematic Review of Insider Threat Detection. *Journal of Wireless Mobile Networks, Ubiquitous Computing, and Dependable Applications (JoWUA)*, 10(4):46–67, 2019.

275. Egress. Alarming statistics show human error remains primary cause of data breaches. URL: `https://bit.ly/3kycHm5`, 2019. [Online; accessed 1 October 2022].

276. Shu J, Zhang Y, Li J, Li B, and Gu D. Why Data Deletion Fails? A Study on Deletion Flaws and Data Remanence in Android Systems. *ACM Transactions on Embedded Computing Systems*, 16(2):1–22, 2017.

277. Ponemon Institute. The 2018 state of endpoint security risk. URL: `https://bit.ly/2WWZfz2`, 2018. [Online; accessed 1 October 2022].

278. Hao K. How to poison the data that Big Tech uses to surveil you (MIT Technology Review). URL: `https://bit.ly/3Eax68Q`, 2021. [Online; accessed 1 October 2022].

279. Wakefield J. Easyjet admits data of nine million hacked (BBC News). URL: `https://bbc.in/3D1SVln`, 2020. [Online; accessed 1 October 2022].

280. Bonifacic I. Microsoft accidently exposed 250 million customer service records (engadget). URL: `https://engt.co/3Ds0Y04`, 2020. [Online; accessed 1 October 2022].

281. Fingas J. Personal data for 533 million facebook users leaks on the web (engadget). URL: `https://engt.co/3sUNWDj`, 2021. [Online; accessed 1 October 2022].

282. MacMillan D, Krouse S and Hagey K. Yahoo, bucking industry, scans emails for data to sell advertisers (Wall Street Journal). URL: `https://on.wsj.com/3mGANfU`, 2018. [Online; accessed 1 October 2022].

283. Harmening JT. *Virtual Private Networks. In Computer and Information Security Handbook (Third Edition), pp. 843–856.* Morgan Kaufmann, Burlington, (MA), USA, 2017. ISBN: 9780128038437.

284. Obermayer B and Obermaier F. *The Panama Papers: Breaking the Story of How the Rich and Powerful Hide Their Money.* Oneworld Publications, London, UK, 2016. ISBN: 1786070472.

285. Open Whisper Systems. Signal. URL: `https://bit.ly/3yqMNEJ`. [Online; accessed 1 October 2022].

286. Field M. Wannacry cyber attack cost the NHS £92m as 19,000 appointments cancelled (The Telegraph). URL: `https://bit.ly/3yPVjgu`, 2018. [Online; accessed 1 October 2022].

287. Anderson MR. Twenty years on from Deep Blue vs Kasparov: how a chess match started the big data revolution (The Conversation). URL: `https://bit.ly/3DkhvSM`, 2017. [Online; accessed 1 October 2022].

288. Newborn M. *Deep Blue: An Artificial Intelligence Milestone.* Springer, New York (NY), USA, 2012. ISBN-10: 1468495674.

289. Strickland E. How IBM Watson overpromised and underdelivered on AI healthcare (IEEE Spectrum). URL: `https://bit.ly/3FgfUiJ`, 2019. [Online; accessed 1 October 2022].

290. BBC News. Artificial intelligence: Go master Lee Se-dol wins against AlphaGo program. URL: `https://bbc.in/3j3Wl3y`, 2016. [Online; accessed 1 October 2022].

291. DeepMind. AlphaGo. URL: `https://bit.ly/3DhEbD4`, 2017. [Online; accessed 1 October 2022].

292. Silver D, Schrittwieser J, Simonyan K, Antonoglou I, Huang A, Guez A, Hubert T, Baker L, Lai M, Bolton A, Chen Y, Lillicrap T, Fan H, Sifre L, Driessche G, Graepel T, and Hassabis D. Mastering the game of Go without human knowledge. *Nature*, 550(7676):354–359, 2017.

293. Silver D, Hubert T, Schrittwieser J, Antonoglou I, Lai M, Guez A, Lanctot M, Sifre L, Kumaran D, Graepel T, Lillicrap T, Simonyan K, and Hassabis D. A general reinforcement learning algorithm that masters chess, shogi, and go through self-play. *Science*, 362(6419):1140–1144, 2018.

294. Knapton S. Entire human chess knowledge learned and surpassed by DeepMind's AlphaZero in four hours (The Telegraph). URL: `https://bit.ly/3aPZ4ZK`, 2017. [Online; accessed 1 October 2022].

295. Senior AW, Evans R, Jumper J, Kirkpatrick J, Sifre L, Green T, Qin C, Žídek A, Nelson AWR, Bridgland A, Penedones H, Petersen S, Simonyan K, Crossan S, Kohli P, Jones DT, Silver D, Kavukcuoglu K, and Hassabis D. Protein structure prediction using multiple deep neural networks in the 13th Critical Assessment of Protein Structure Prediction (CASP13). *Proteins: Structure, Function and Bioinformatics*, 87(12):1141–1148, 2019.

296. Senior AW, Evans R, Jumper J, Kirkpatrick J, Sifre L, Green T, Qin C, Žídek A, Nelson AWR, Bridgland A, Penedones H, Petersen S, Simonyan K, Crossan S, Kohli P, Jones DT, Silver D, Kavukcuoglu K, and Hassabis D. Improved protein structure prediction using potentials from deep learning. *Nature*, 577:706–710, 2020.

297. The AlphaFold Team. AlphaFold: Using AI for scientific discovery (DeepMind Blog Post Research). URL: `https://bit.ly/3FRunlj`, 2020. [Online; accessed 1 October 2022].

298. The AlphaFold Team. AlphaFold Protein Structure Database. URL: `https://alphafold.ebi.ac.uk/`, 2021. [Online; accessed 1 October 2022].

299. Higgins MK. Can We AlphaFold Our Way Out of the Next Pandemic? *Journal of Molecular Biology*, 433(20):1–7, 2021.

300. Hassabis D. Putting the power of AlphaFold into the world's hands. URL: `https://bit.ly/3G4GSub`, 2021. [Online; accessed 1 October 2022].

301. Gupta M et al. CryoEM and AI reveal a structure of SARS-CoV-2 Nsp2, a multifunctional protein involved in key host processes. URL: `https://bit.ly/3lLkQEw`, 2021. [Online; accessed 1 October 2022].

302. AlphaFold Team. Computational predictions of protein structures associated with COVID-19. URL: `https://bit.ly/2ZOmCZO`, 2020. [Online; accessed 1 October 2022].

303. Gomez-Uribe CA and Hunt N. The Netflix Recommender System: Algorithms, Business Value, and Innovation. *ACM Transactions on Management Information Systems*, 61(4):1–19, 2016.

304. Markoff J. Computer wins on 'Jeopardy!': Trivial, it's not (New York Times). URL: `https://nyti.ms/2YWBjMX`, 2011. [Online; accessed 1 October 2022].

305. Jeopardy IBM Challenge. Jeopardy Watson's final Jeopardy answer fail. `https://bit.ly/3l8ZQHD`, 2011. [Online; accessed 1 October 2022].

306. McIlraith S. Why Toronto? URL: `https://bit.ly/3A9gRFS`. [Online; accessed 1 October 2022].

307. Goodfellow IJ, Shlens J, and Szegedy C. Explaining and Harnessing Adversarial Examples. URL: `https://arxiv.org/abs/1412.6572`, 2015.

308. Dalvi N, Domingos P, Mausam, Sanghai S, and Verma D. *Adversarial classification. In KDD '04: Proceedings of the tenth ACM SIGKDD international conference on Knowledge discovery and data mining, Seattle (WA), USA August 22–25, 2004, pp. 99–108.* ACM, New York (NY), USA, Ely, United Kingdom, 2004. ISBN: 9781581138887.

309. Biggio B and Roli F. Wild patterns: Ten years after the rise of adversarial machine learning. *Pattern Recognition*, 84:317–331, 2018.

310. Finlayson SG, Bowers JD, Ito J, Zittrain JL, Beam AL, and Kohane IS. Adversarial attacks on medical machine learning. *Science*, 363(6433):1287–1289, 2019.

311. Brown TB, Mané D, Roy A, Abadi M, and Gilmer J. Adversarial Patch. URL: https://arxiv.org/abs/1712.09665, 2018.

312. Kurakin A, Goodfellow I, and Bengio S. Adversarial examples in the physical world. URL: https://arxiv.org/abs/1607.02533, 2017.

313. Alcorn MA, Li Q, Gong Z, Wang C, Mai L, Ku W-S, and Nguyen A. Strike (with) a Pose: Neural Networks Are Easily Fooled by Strange Poses of Familiar Objects. URL: https://arxiv.org/abs/1811.11553, 2019.

314. McCarthy J. From here to human-level AI. *Artificial Intelligence*, 171(18):1174–1182, 2007.

315. Kennedy B, Jin X, Davani AM, Dehghani M, and Ren X. Contextualizing Hate Speech Classifiers with Post-hoc Explanation. URL: https://arxiv.org/abs/2005.02439, 2020.

316. Röttger P, Vidgen B, Nguyen D, Waseem Z, Margetts H, and Pierrehumbert JB. HateCheck: Functional Tests for Hate Speech Detection Models. URL: https://arxiv.org/abs/2012.15606, 2021.

317. Hadsell R, Rao D, Rusu AA, and Pascanu R. Embracing change: continual learning in deep neural networks. *Trends in Cognitive Sciences*, 24(12):1028–1040, 2020.

318. McCloskey M and Cohen NJ. Catastrophic interference in connectionist networks: The sequential learning problem. *Psychology of learning and motivation*, 24:109–165, 1989.

319. Abraham WC and Robins A. Memory retention - the synaptic stability versus plasticity dilemma. *Trends in Neurosciences*, 28(2):73–78, 2005.

320. Kemker R, McClure M, Abitino A, Hayes T, and Kanan C. *Measuring Catastrophic Forgetting in Neural Networks. In Proceedings of the AAAI Conference on Artificial Intelligence, 32(1).* AAAI Press, Palo Alto (CA), USA, 2018. ISBN: 9781577358008.

321. Kirkpatrick J, Pascanu R, Rabinowitz N, Veness J, Desjardins G, Rusu AA, Milan K, Quan J, Ramalho T, Grabska-Barwinska A, Hassabis D, Clopath C, Kumaran D, and Hadsell R. Overcoming catastrophic forgetting in neural networks. *Proceedings of the National Academy of Sciences, USA*, 114(13):3521–3526, 2017.

322. Robertson N, Sanders D, Seymour P, and Thomas R. The Four-Colour Theorem. *Journal of Combinatorial Theory, Series B*, 70(1):2–44, 1997.

323. Rillke. Four colour map example. URL: https://commons.wikimedia.org/wiki/File:Four_Colour_Map_Example.svg.

324. Ornes S. How Close Are Computers to Automating Mathematical Reasoning? Quanta Magazine. URL: `https://bit.ly/3DkL4U1`, 2020. [Online; accessed 1 October 2022].

325. Hendrycks D, Burns C, Kadavath S, Arora A, Basart S, Tang E, Song D, and Steinhardt J. Measuring Mathematical Problem Solving With the MATH Dataset. URL: `https://arxiv.org/abs/2103.03874`, 2021.

326. Badham J. War Games. URL: `https://www.imdb.com/title/tt0086567/`, 1983. [Online; accessed 1 October 2022].

327. Turing A. Computing machinery and intelligence. *Mind*, LIX(236):433–460, 1950.

328. Gewirtz D. Google Duplex beat the Turing test: Are we doomed? (ZDNet). URL: `https://zd.net/3AKpG9p`, 2018. [Online; accessed 1 October 2022].

329. Gewirtz D. The Turing Test of Computer Intelligence Is Too Easy (Smithsonian Magazine). URL: `https://bit.ly/3DK1QyU`, 2014. [Online; accessed 1 October 2022].

330. Levesque HJ, Davis E, and Morgenstern L. *The Winograd Schema Challenge. In KR'12: Proceedings of the Thirteenth International Conference on Principles of Knowledge Representation and Reasoning, June 2012, Rome, Italy.* AIII Press, Palo Alto (CA), USA, 2012. ISBN: 9781577355601.

331. Sakaguchi K, Le Bras R, Bhagavatula C, and Choi Y. *WinoGrande: An Adversarial Winograd Schema Challenge at Scale. In Proceedings of the Thirty-Fourth AAAI Conference on Artificial Intelligence, 34(05), 8732–8740. February 2020, New York (NY), USA.* AIII Press, Palo Alto (CA), USA, 2020. ISSN: 2159–5399.

332. Garland A. Ex machina. URL: `https://www.imdb.com/title/tt0470752/`, 2014. [Online; accessed 1 October 2022].

333. Bradley T. Facebook AI creates its own language in creepy preview of our potential future (Forbes). URL: `https://bit.ly/2Z4wTE4` [Online; accessed 1 October 2022].

334. Mostow J. Terminator 3: Rise of the Machines. URL: `https://www.imdb.com/title/tt0181852/`, 2003. [Online; accessed 1 October 2022].

335. Harris S. Can we build AI without losing control over it? | Sam Harris (TED Talks). URL: `https://bit.ly/3DeQQHO`, 2016. [Online; accessed 1 October 2022].

336. Kriegel U. Is intentionality dependent upon consciousness? *Philosophical Studies*, 116:271–307, 2003.

337. Koch C. What Is Consciousness? *Nature*, 557:S8–S12, 2018.

338. Cole D. The Chinese room argument (The Stanford Encyclopedia of Philosophy, Winter 2020 Edition). URL: `https://stanford.io/3jiaTg9`, 2020. [Online; accessed 1 October 2022].

339. Tan A. A Chinese speaker's take on the chinese room (Towards Data Science, 2019). URL: `https://bit.ly/3Q8EcAA`, 2019. [Online; accessed 1 October 2022].

340. Warfield TA. Searle's Causal Powers. *Analysis*, 59(1):29–32, 1999.

341. Feynman RP. Can machines think? URL: `https://bit.ly/3iU5VWS`, 1985. [Online; accessed 1 October 2022].

342. Zheng NN, Liu ZY, Ren PJ, Ma YQ, Chen ST, Yu SY, Xue JR, Chen BD, and Wang FY. Hybrid-augmented intelligence: collaboration and cognition. *Frontiers of Information Technology & Electronic Engineering*, 18:153–179, 2017.

343. Foot P. The Problem of Abortion and the Doctrine of Double Effect. *Oxford Review*, 5:5–15, 1967.

344. Zapyon. Trolley problem. URL: `https://commons.wikimedia.org/wiki/File:Trolley_Problem.svg`.

345. Greene JD, Sommerville RB, Nystrom LE, Darley JM, and Cohen JD. An fMRI investigation of emotional engagement in moral judgment. *Science*, 293(5337):2105–2108, 2001.

346. Driver J. The history of utilitarianism (The Stanford Encyclopedia of Philosophy, Winter 2014 Edition). URL: `https://stanford.io/3vMIh3B`, 2014. [Online; accessed 1 October 2022].

347. Thomson JJ. Killing, Letting Die, and the Trolley Problem. *The Monist*, 59(2):204–217, 1976.

348. D'Olimpio L. The trolley dilemma: would you kill one person to save five? (The Conversation). URL: `https://bit.ly/3OOfTmb`, 2016. [Online; accessed 1 October 2022].

349. Johnson R and Cureton A. Kant's moral philosophy (The Stanford Encyclopedia of Philosophy, Spring 2021 Edition). URL: `https://stanford.io/3GdWXhb`, 2021. [Online; accessed 1 October 2022].

350. Stevens M. The trolley problem in real life (Vsauce). URL: `https://bit.ly/3OWFF81`, 2017. [Online; accessed 1 October 2022].

351. Roelofs K. Freeze for action: neurobiological mechanisms in animal and human freezing. *Philosophical Transactions of the Royal Society B: Biological Sciences*, 372(1718):20160206, 2017.

352. Goleman D. *Emotional Intelligence: Why it Can Matter More Than IQ*. Bloomsbury Publishing PLC, London, UK, 1996. ISBN-10: 0747528306.

353. Sutton RS and Barto AG. *Reinforcement Learning: An Introduction*. MIT Press, Cambridge (MA), USA, 2018. ISBN-10: 0262039249.

354. Bansal M, Krizhevsky A, and Ogale A. ChauffeurNet: learning to drive by imitating the best and synthesizing the worst. URL: `https://arxiv.org/abs/1812.03079`, 2018.

355. Gao J, Sun C, Zhao H, Shen Y, Anguelov D, Li C, and Schmid C. *VectorNet: Encoding HD Maps and Agent Dynamics From Vectorized Representation*. In Proceedings of the IEEE/CVF Conference on Computer Vision and Pattern Recognition (CVPR), 2020, 11525–11533. June 13–19, Seattle (WA), USA. IEEE (Curran Associates, Inc.), Red Hook (NY), USA, 2020. ISBN: 9781728171692.

356. Kiran BR, Sobh I, Talpaert V, Mannion P, Al Sallab AA, Yogamani S, and Perez P. Deep Reinforcement Learning for Autonomous Driving: A Survey. URL: `https://arxiv.org/abs/2002.00444`, 2020.

357. Gandhi D, Pinto L, and Gupta A. Learning to Fly by Crashing. URL: `https://arxiv.org/pdf/1704.05588.pdf`, 2017.

358. Vargas J, Alsweiss S, Toker O, Razdan R, and Santos J. An overview of autonomous vehicles sensors and their vulnerability to weather conditions. *Sensors*, 21:5397, 2021.

359. Roff HM. The folly of trolleys: Ethical challenges and autonomous vehicles (Brookings Institution). URL: `https://brook.gs/31nfeZb`, 2018. [Online; accessed 1 October 2022].

360. Eliot L. Self-driving cars: Zero fatalities, zero chance (AI Trends). URL: `https://bit.ly/3GDYlcY`, 2017. [Online; accessed 1 October 2022].

361. Waymo. Waymo's fully autonomous driving technology is here. URL: `https://bit.ly/2YyQ716`, 2017. [Online; accessed 1 October 2022].

362. Asimov I. *Runaround*. Doubleday, New York (NY), USA, 1950. ISBN: 9780385423045.

363. Wikipedia. Three laws of robotics. URL: `https://bit.ly/3llojJJ`. [Online; accessed 1 October 2022].

364. Proyas A. I, Robot. URL: `https://www.imdb.com/title/tt0343818/`, 2004. [Online; accessed 1 October 2022].

365. Dietvorst BJ, Simmons JP, and Massey C. Algorithm Aversion: People Erroneously Avoid Algorithms after Seeing Them Err. *Journal of Experimental Psychology: General*, 144(1):114–126, 2015.

366. Smith A and Anderson M. Americans' attitudes toward driverless vehicles (Pew Research Center). URL: `https://pewrsr.ch/3uUkApE`, 2017. [Online; accessed 1 October 2022].

367. Darling K, Nandy P, and Breazeal C. *Empathic concern and the effect of stories in human-robot interaction. In 24th IEEE International Symposium on Robot and Human Interactive Communication (RO-MAN) 2015, Kobe, Japan, August 31 - September 4, pp. 770-775*. IEEE, Washington (DC), USA, 2015. ISBN: 9781467367042.

368. Jonze J. Her. URL: `https://www.imdb.com/title/tt1798709/`, 2013. [Online; accessed 1 October 2022].

369. Darling K. *'Who's Johnny?' Anthropomorphic Framing in Human-Robot Interaction, Integration, and Policy. In Robot Ethics 2.0: From Autonomous Cars to Artificial Intelligence (1st Edition), 2017, 173*. Oxford University Press, Oxford, UK, 2017. ISBN-10: 0190652950.

370. Pennisi P, Tonacci A, Tartarisco G, Billeci L, Ruta L, Gangemi S, and Pioggia G. Autism and social robotics: A systematic review. *Autism Research*, 9(2):165–183, 2016.

371. Smith DH and Zeller F. hitchBOT's Twitter page. URL: `https://twitter.com/hitchbot`, 2015. [Online; accessed 1 October 2022].

372. hitchBOT. Meine Freunde haben es möglich gemacht: Ich komme gerade von Neuschwanstein. Genau der richtige Ort für Valentinstag! URL: `https://twitter.com/hitchBOT/status/566608366063988738`, 2015. [Online; accessed 1 October 2022].

373. Skipper C. Cruel Americans Murder Friendly Canadian Hitchhiking Robot (GQ). URL: `https://bit.ly/3DkTzPa`, 2015. [Online; accessed 1 October 2022].

374. Broadbent E. Interactions With Robots: The Truths We Reveal About Ourselves. *Annual Review of Psychology*, 68:627–652, 2017.

375. Tyldum M. The imitation game. URL: `https://www.imdb.com/title/tt2084970/`, 2014. [Online; accessed 1 October 2022].

376. OpenStax (Rice University). The shape of proteins. URL: `https://bit.ly/3Cb0dK4`, 2013. [Online; accessed 1 October 2022].

377. Brown T. Adversarial Patch. URL: `https://bit.ly/3BNz9iI`, 2018. [Online; accessed 1 October 2022].

# Index

**A**

Accuracy, 130–132
Ada Health app study, 175–188
    experimental privacy analysis, 182–183
    security controls, 183–188
AdaBoost, 85
Adversarial examples, attacks, 184, 202–203
AlexNet, 95–97
Algorithm aversion, 221
Algorithm definition of, 12
Algorithms, machine learning, *See* Machine
    learning algorithms
Alternative hypothesis, 2
Anscombe, Francis (statistician), 26
Anscombe's quartet, 26–27
Anthem, Inc., 169–171, 193
Apollo Guidance Computer, 7–8
Apriori algorithm, 48
Area under the curve (AUC), 134–135
Aristotle, 80, 84, 172
Artificial intelligence
    general, 199, 206, 209, 211
    limits of, 199–222
    narrow, 199, 201–202, 205–206, 209,
        211
    technological singularity, 209–210
    Turing test, 207–208
Artificial neural networks, 89–94
    Asimov, Isaac (biochemist and science
        fiction writer), 220; *See also* Laws
        of robotics
Association rule mining, 42–49
    limitations of, 48
    support, confidence and lift, 45–48
Autonomous vehicles, 216–220

**B**

Backpropagation, 64, 91, 95, 97
Bagging (bootstrap aggregating), 82–83
Basic rate of reproduction ($R_0$), 160
Bengio, Yoshua (computer scientist), 95
Bentham, Jeremy (philosopher), 174; *See
    also* Utilitarianism
Bias, types of

activity, 151–152
    algorithmic, 152
    behavioural, 148, 152
    confirmation, 143, 148
    historical, 148
    incomplete data, 149
    interaction, 152
    online learning, 149
    self-selection, 149, 152
    Simpson's paradox, 149–151
    surrogate objectives, 151
    Web data, 152
Bias impact statement, 157–158
Bias-variance dilemma, 124–125
Binarisation, 108
BlueDot Inc., 2, 142
Boosting machines, 85
Bootstrap aggregation, 82–83
Box plot, 26–30
    comparing distributions, 29
Breiman, Leo (statistician), 82, 84
Buolamwini, Joy (computer scientist), 157

**C**

Catastrophic forgetting, 204–205
Categorical data, *See* Variable types
Chinese room experiment, 209–210
Classification and regression trees (CART),
    79–81
Classifier performance, evaluation of,
    129–134
Clustering, 36–43
    distance functions, 38
    heatmaps, 39
    hierarchical, 43
    *K*-means, *See* Machine learning
        algorithms
    USarrests dataset, of, 37–41
ColorBrewer, 35
Colour blind friendly palette, *See*
    ColorBrewer
COMPAS algorithm, 102, 142–143, 148,
    157–158
Confusion matrix, 130–131

Continuous data, *See* Variable types
Continuous data predictions, evaluation of, 134–136
Convolutional neural networks, 95–97
CORELS algorithm, 143
COVID-19, 2, 92, 142, 145
    biased data and, 160–161
    global map dashboard, 22–23
Cross-validation, 126–127
    *K*-fold cross-validation, 127
Cryptography, 189, 193
Curse of dimensionality, 103

**D**
Dashboard, 3, 12, 22–23
Data analysis, types of
    descriptive, 21–22, 56–58, 100
    predictive, 21–23, 29–30, 55–59
Data collection, 60, 148, 175, 181; *See also* Data life cycle
    incomplete or biased data, of, 157
Data generation; *See also* Data life cycle
    annual rate in the world, 175
    CERN's Large Hadron Collider and, 10
Data life cycle, 8–12
Data processing, 7, 10–14, 96, 142, 159, 175, 178–179, 182, 184, 186, 201, 203; *See also* Data life cycle
Data storage, 13, 60, 169, 175, 177, 182, 184–186; *See also* Data life cycle
Data visualisation
    choosing the most appropriate chart, 34–36
    comparing distributions, 29
    famous examples, 30–34
    importance of, 26
    knowing your audience, 34–35
    methods by data type, 36
    use of colour, 35
Datasets
    breast cancer, 106–107
    ImageNet, 95–97, 153, 159
    Japan earthquakes, 125–126
    mtcars, 71–72
    Titanic, 78–81
    TV advertising expenditure, 65–69, 90–91
    two moons, 61–62
    UCLA graduate admissions, 72–75
    USarrests, 37–41
    WinoGrande, 208
Deep learning, 94–97
DeepMind, 200–201, 214
Dendrogram, 42–43
Dimensionality reduction, 4, 64, 106–108
Direct discrimination, 153

**E**
Ensembles, 82–85
Equality vs equity, 155–157
Error rate, 130–132
Explainability, *See* Model interpretability vs explainability
Exploratory data analysis, *See* Data life cycle

**F**
$F_1$-score, 132–133
Fairness, 152–160
    machine learning methods and, 158–159
False positive rate (FPR), 130, 133
Feature engineering, 108
Feature learning, 108
Feature scaling, 100
Feature selection, 102–106
    embedded methods, 106
    filter-based methods, 103–105
    wrapper methods, 105
Feynman, Richard (physicist), 210
Fight-or-flight response, 33, 213
Final testing set, 127–128
Foot, Philippa (philosopher), 211
Freund, Yoav, 85
Fukushima nuclear plant disaster, 125–126

**G**
Galton, Sir Francis (polymath), 71, 84
Gauss, Carl Friedrich (mathematician), 65, 70–71
Gebru, Timnit (computer scientist), 157
Gender Shades project, 149, 158
General Data Protection Regulation (GDPR), 169, 175–178, 180–181, 188
Goldman, Jonathan (physicist and data scientist), 2–5
Greene, Joshua (psychologist), 212

**H**

Haystack project, 182
Heatmaps, 39
Hierarchical clustering, 42–43
Hinton, Geoffrey (computer scientist), 95
hitchBOT, 221–222
Ho, Tin Kam (computer scientist), 84
Hopfield, John (computer scientist), 94–95

**I**

IBM Deep Blue, 200
IBM Watson, 142, 200–202, 206, 211
ImageNet Large Scale Visual Recognition
 Challenge (ILSVRC), 95–97, 153,
 159
Imbalanced datasets, 41, 131, 133, 149
Inception-ResNet-v2, 95, 102
Indirect discrimination, 153–155
Interpretability, *See* Model interpretability
 vs explainability
Interquartile range (IQR), 25, 28

**J**

Jeopardy!, 202, 206, 211

**K**

*K*-fold cross-validation, 127
*K*-means clustering, 37–42
*K*-nearest neighbours (KNN) algorithm, 75,
 101, 114
Kant, Immanuel (philosopher), 212; *See
 also* Kantianism
Kantianism, 212
Khan, Kanram (physician and
 epidemiologist), 2, 4
Kurtosis, 26

**L**

Law of large numbers, 149
Laws of robotics, 220–221
Le-Cun, Yann (computer scientist), 95
Legendre, Adrien-Marie (mathematician),
 65, 70–71
Linear regression, 65–71
LinkedIn, 2–3, 5, 109, 171
Logistic regression
 multiple, 73–75
 simple, 71–73
Lovelace, Ada (mathematician and
 theoretical computer scientist),
 208

**M**

Macready, William (computer scientist),
 98
Machine learning algorithms
 artificial neural networks, 89–94
 association rule mining, 42–49
 bagging (bootstrap aggregating), 82–83
 boosting machines, 85
 classes of (overview), 63–65
 classification and regression trees
  (CART), 79–81
 convolutional neural networks, 95–97
 curse of dimensionality, 103
 decision trees, 78–82
 ensembles, 82–85
 *K*-means clustering, 37–42
 linear regression, 65–71
 logistic regression, simple, 71–73
 logistic regression, multiple, 73–75
 naïve Bayes, 75–78
 random forests, 83–85
 support vector machines, 85–89
Machine learning paradigms, 58–63, 214
Margaret Hamilton (computer scientist and
 systems engineer), 7–8
McCarthy, John (computer scientist), 203
Mean absolute error (MAE), 135
Mean squared error (MSE), 135
Measures of central tendency, 25
Measures of dispersion, 25
Median absolute deviation (MAD), 100
Medici effect, 5
Minard, Charles (civil engineer and
 statistician), 32–33
Minsky, Marvin (computer scientist), 94
Modality, 25
Model interpretability vs explainability,
 101–102
Model Zoo, 97
*Moneyball*, 6

**N**

Naïve Bayes, 75–78
National Security Agency (NSA), 173
Natural language processing, 63, 95, 97,
 140–142, 200, 202, 205
NetflixGrand Prize winning strategy, 114
Nightingale, Florence (nurse and
 statistician), 30–32
No free lunch theorem, 55, 98–100
Null hypothesis, 2–3

**O**

Ofqual algorithm, 145, 148
Outliers, 29–30
    boxplots and, 27–29
    choice of distance metric and, 38
    clustering and, 36, 58
    dendrograms and, 42
    feature scaling and, 100
    *K*-means and, 41
    Kurtosis and, 26
    linear regression and, 68
    logistic regression and, 75
    mean squared error (MSE) and, 135
    median and, 25
    support vector machines and, 86
    trees and, 85
Overfitting, 123–126

**P**

Panopticon, 174
Perceptron, 89–91
Personal identifiable information (PII), 170
Personal health information (PHI), 172, 175
    HIPPA privacy rule, 175
Precision, 130–132
Precision-recall curve, 132–133
PredPol algorithm, 6, 146–148, 157
Principal component analysis (PCA), 42,
    64, 106–108
Privacy, controls for the individual, 188–193
Privacy, importance of, 172–175
Privacy by design (PbD), 169, 175,
    180–183, 242
Protein-folding problem, 200–201
Pseudolabelling, *See* Semi-supervised
    learning

**Q**

Quartiles, 25, 27–28
Questions
    characteristics of good, 3–5
    that cannot be answered by data
        science, 5–6

**R**

Random forests, 83–85
Recall, *See* true positive rate
Recommender systems, 109–115
    cold start problem, 109
    collaborative filtering methods,
        109–110

    collaborative filtering, manual building
        of recommender, 112–114
    content-based filtering methods,
        109–110
    data strikes, 188
    hybrid methods, 110
    item-to-item collaborative filtering
        methods, 111
    Netflix Grand Prize, 114–115
Receiver operating characteristic (ROC)
    curve, 133–134
Reinforcement learning, 213–218
    exploration-explotation tradeoff, 216
Root mean squared error (RMSE), 135
Rosenblatt, Frank (psychologist and
    computer scientist), 89

**S**

Schapire, Robert (computer scientist), 85
Schmidhuber, Jürgen (computer scientist),
    95
Scientific method, 2–3
Searle, John (philosopher), 210, *See also*
    Chinese room experiment
Semi-supervised learning, 60–63
    human trafficking and, 61
    pseudolabelling strategy, 61–63
    two moons dataset, 62
Sensitivity, *See* True positive rate
Severe acute respiratory syndrome (SARS),
    2, 160, 201
Simpson's paradox, 149–151
Skewness, 26, 29
Snow, John (physician and epidemiologist),
    31–32
Snowden, Edward (computer intelligence
    consultant), 173
Spanish flu, 160, 162
Standard deviation, 25, 100
Standarisation, *See* feature scaling
Stevens, Michael (psychologist), 212
Supervised learning, 56–60
    algorithms, *See* Machine learning
        algorithms
    algorithms, how to choose, 100–101
    feature selection methods, in, 103–106
    general training strategy, 122
    model evaluation, *See* Supervised
        learning model evaluation
    model interpretability vs explainability,
        101–102